Reconfiguring Chinese Nationalism

Reconfiguring Chinese Nationalism

How the Qing Frontier and its Indigenes Became Chinese

James Leibold

palgrave
macmillan

RECONFIGURING CHINESE NATIONALISM

First published in 2007 by
PALGRAVE MACMILLAN™
175 Fifth Avenue, New York, N.Y. 10010 and
Houndmills, Basingstoke, Hampshire, England RG21 6XS.
Companies and representatives throughout the world.
PALGRAVE MACMILLAN is the global academic imprint of the Palgrave Macmillan division of St. Martin's Press, LLC and of Palgrave Macmillan Ltd. Macmillan® is a registered trademark in the United States, United Kingdom and other countries. Palgrave is a registered trademark in the European Union and other countries.

ISBN-13: 978-1-4039-7479-2

Library of Congress Cataloging-in-Publication Data is available from the Library of Congress.

A catalogue record of the book is available from the British Library.

Design by Scribe, Inc.

First edition: December 2007

10 9 8 7 6 5 4 3 2 1

Printed in the United States of America.

Transferred to Digital Printing in 2009

To my parents, Frank and Danielle Leibold

Contents

Acknowledgments

This book is the culmination of a long and often circuitous process—one that would not have been possible without the assistance and support of many. It began some ten years ago as a doctoral dissertation at the University of Southern California under the mentorship and steady guidance of Charlotte Furth. I would like to thank Charlotte and the other members of my committee, John Wills Jr., Eugene Cooper, and Michael Robinson, for their thoughtful suggestions, comments, and encouragement throughout my time in Los Angeles.

The current manuscript evolved during my time at the University of Melbourne and La Trobe University in Australia. I would like to thank all my colleagues at both universities for their support, stimulation, and words of reassurance. I consider myself lucky to have landed in Melbourne, where its pleasant environs and active, internationally-engaged Chinese studies community have provided an ideal setting in which to live, work, and raise a family. I would like to especially thank John Fitzgerald and Antonia Finnane for their assistance, friendship, and encouragement since arriving in Australia in 2000.

Chen Zhihong, Alice Falk, John Fitzgerald, Hon Tze-ki, and Laurence Schneider read the entire manuscript while another anonymous reviewer read several chapters in draft form. Tom Mullaney, Brian Moloughney, and Jeff Kyong-McClain read and offered their comments on several final chapters. Together they provided thoughtful and constructive comments that significantly improved the final version.

Numerous others have either commented on previous versions of my work or offered helpful suggestions, citations, resources, or critical insights along the way: Joseph Allen, Dennis Altman, Stefan Auer, Thomas Bartlett, Alan Baumler, David Bello, Gordon Berger, Kathryn Bernhardt, Anya Bernstein, David Bradley, Judith Brett, Clayton D. Brown, Rob Culp, Thomas DuBois, Arianne Gaetano, Hua Tao, Gerhard Hoffstaedter, Huang Jianli, James Huffman, Bruce Jacobs, Robin Jeffrey, Joel Kahn, William Kirby, P. T. Lee, Li Liangyu, Jonathan Lipman, Liu Xiaoyuan, Raymond Lum, Colin Mackerras, Robert Manne, Angus McIntyre, Jenny McGregor, Anne McLaren, Stanley Mickel, Charlie Musgrove, Kaori Okano, Raj Pandey, Qin Can, Merle Ricklefs, Eugene Swanger, Justin Tighe, Saul Thomas, Isenbike Togan, Paul Van Dyke, Geoff Wade, Wang Dong,

Wang Gungwu, Wang Xi, Trevor Wilson, and Yang Zhenya. Collectively these individuals have helped to save me from numerous embarrassing mistakes and have helped to shape many of the ideas developed here. Needless to say, any remaining mistakes (and I am sure there are some) and final conclusions remain my own.

Librarians are often the unsung heroes of historical research, especially those involving such a rich literary tradition like China's. I would like to thank the librarians and staff at the following institutions for their assistance and infinite patience in tracking down many of the primary and secondary sources on which this book rests: the Doheny Library at the University of Southern California; Richard C. Rudolph East Asian Library, University of California, Los Angeles; C. V. Starr East Asian Library at the University of California, Berkeley; Harvard-Yenching Library at Harvard University; Nanjing University Library; Shanghai Municipal Library; the Nanjing Municipal Library; the Fu Ping Shan Library at Hong Kong University; the National Library of Australia; Menzies Library at the Australian National University; the East Asian Collection at Melbourne University; and finally the amazing interlibrary loan staff at Borchardt Library, La Trobe University, who helped me search the world for obscure Chinese books and journal articles during the final stages of this project.

A number of funding bodies have provided financial support for this project, including the Social Science Research Council's Abe Fellowship Program, the U.S. Department of Education's Foreign Language and Area Studies Fellowship Program, the U.S. State Department's NSEP David Boren Graduate Fellowship Program, Harvard-Yenching Library, the University of Southern California and La Trobe University. I would also like to acknowledge the helpful people at Palgrave Macmillan who guided me through the publication process, especially Alessandra Bastagli, Chris Chappell, Brigitte Shull, Emily Leithauser, Katie Fahey, and Daniel Constantino at Scribe.

Some of the material presented here was published in an earlier form. I am grateful to the publishers for allowing me to reuse portions of the following works: "Positioning 'Minzu' within Sun Yat-sen's Discourse of Minzuzhuyi," *Journal of Asian History* 38.2: 163-213, copyright 2004 by Harrassowitz Verlag; "Rethinking Kuomintang National Minority Policy: The National Question and Regional Warlordism on the Early 20th Century Chinese Frontier," in Cindy Yik-Yi Chu and Ricardo K.S. Mak, eds. *China Reconstructs* (Lanham: University Press of America), copyright 2003 by Rowman & Littlefield Publishing Group; "Un-mapping Republican China's Tibetan Frontier: Politics, Militarism and Ethnicity along the Kham/Xikang Borderland," *The Chinese Historical Review* 12.2 (Fall): 167-201, copyright 2005 by The Chinese Historians in the United States, Inc.; "Competing Narratives of Racial and Unity in Republican China: From the Yellow Emperor to Peking Man," *Modern China* 32.2 (April): 181-220, copyright 2006 by Sage Publications.

Finally, this project would have never been conceived, sustained, or completed without the loving support, patience, and encouragement of my families on both sides of the Pacific: Frank and Danielle Leibold, Liz and John Lonergan, Debbie and Darryl Czuchra, and Lori and Phil Wentworth in the United States; and Don and Adrienne Axup and David and Stella Axup in Australia. And finally my own family, Kate, Bridget, and Harry, helped nurture and sustain this project through the countless hours of research, reading, writing, and rewriting. Kate Axup, in particular, got perhaps more than she bargained for when we first met in Nanjing in 1996. Footnote after footnote, library after library, and rewrite after rewrite, she has served "quietly" and confidently as my financial supporter, editor in chief, intellectual sounding board, emotional consoler, and now proud mother of three—Bridget, Harry, and *Reconfiguring Chinese Nationalism.*

James Leibold
Melbourne, August 2007

Introduction

To most observers, China appears to be a uniquely bounded and indivisible entity with a long and unbroken history as a single, unified civilization. The eminent English historian Eric Hobsbawm is not alone in claiming that China (like Korea and Japan) is "indeed among the extremely rare examples of historic states composed of a population that is ethnically almost or entirely homogeneous."[1] Recent archaeological discoveries have revealed the highly advanced nature of the civilization that took root in the Yellow River valley more than five thousand years ago. With its stratified social order, plant and animal domestication, and sophisticated bronze tools, this civilization, in the words of the best-selling author and evolutionary biologists Jared Diamond, had a "disproportionate" influence on its neighboring peoples, drawing them into an "ancient melting pot" and creating today's political, cultural, and linguistic monolith.[2] It was the "civilizing superiority" of this culture that led the doyen of American sinology, John Fairbank, to conclude that by the beginning of their written history "the Chinese people had already achieved a degree of cultural homogeneity and isolated continuity hard to match elsewhere in the world."[3] Chinese scholars share a similar confidence in the unified and primordial nature of the Chinese people. While admitting that consciousness of a distinct *Zhonghua minzu* (Chinese race/nation) developed only in the course of the country's resistance to Western imperialism, China's most famous ethnographer Fei Xiaotong has argued that the Zhonghua minzu has a long history rooted in more than five thousand years of racial and cultural melding (*minzu ronghe*).[4] For the Chinese party-state, the term Zhonghua minzu refers not only to the political unity of the fifty-six officially recognized *minzus* (usually glossed in English as "nationalities") living within the People's Republic of China (PRC) today, but also to the cultural and racial imbrication of countless ethnonyms recorded throughout the written annals of a temporally ancient but spatially finite "China." Asserting that it is slightly absurd to ask how China became

Chinese, Jared Diamond states that "China has *been* Chinese, almost from the beginnings of its recorded history."[5]

Yet, the very concepts of nation, race, nationality and ethnic minority are modern political constructs. While they reflect social processes that are both ancient and universal, these idioms (as they are currently understood) are deeply embedded within the epistemology of modernity, and in the case of China, its mediated form that arose during the transition from a premodern empire to a modern nation-state. In early twentieth-century China, these discursive categories (and the norms, practices, and policies associated with them) were crucial to the process of imagining "China" as a contiguous and homogeneous nation-state. This study seeks to explore the efforts of Chinese male elites to fold the fluid ethnic diversity of the empire into the homogeneity of a new national imaginary. More specifically, it aims to place the frontier and its indigenous inhabitants at the center of the state and nation-building process in modern China, shedding new light on the important role of the periphery in shaping the modern sense of "Chineseness."

Following the collapse of the multiethnic Qing dynasty (1644–1911), the empire's massive territory unraveled along its ethnic and provincial seams. Over the course of their long rule, the empire's Manchu rulers had fashioned a loose nomadic-style confederation of five ethnic constituencies (today codified as the Manchu, Han, Mongol, Tibetan, and Hui nationalities), doubling the size of the previous Ming dynasty's territory and boosting its population to 420 million from 130 million.[6] Yet, this phenomenal growth was not balanced. The empire's population ballooned at the geographic and political center among its sedentary, densely populated Sinic communities (today reimagined as a homogeneous Han nationality), while its territorial advances occurred along the empire's rugged nomadic and seminomadic periphery.[7] It should come as no surprise that once this rather bloated and deformed "geo-body" started to decay in the nineteenth century, it was set upon by predators from both within and without.[8] By late 1911, the core provinces of Ming China had broken away from the Qing court while many of its impoverished peasants sought out new land and opportunities in the remote and formerly sequestered frontier regions. At the same time, the dependencies (*fanshu* or *shudi*) of Mongolia, Tibet, and Xinjiang sought their political independence from "China" while England, Russia, Japan, and other imperialist powers carved deeper zones of influence on the rotting Qing geo-body. Attempting to stem this tide of disunity, Chinese revolutionaries quickly announced the establishment of a new Republic of China (1912–1949) and declared their intention to assert sovereignty over all the former subjects and territories of the Qing empire, which was reconstituted as a free and equal "republic of five races" (*wuzu gonghe*).

One can read the story of twentieth-century China as the attempt by an inherently weak Republican state to, in the words of Benedict Anderson, stretch "the short, tight skin of the nation over the gigantic body of the empire,"[9] fashioning a bounded and homogeneous Chinese nation from among the fluid and polyethnic boundaries of the Qing empire, while replacing the Manchu court with a Han-dominated autocratic state. This state- and nation-building project engendered new political strategies and discursive narratives aimed at domesticating the ethnic Other and its territory, while recasting a more inclusive yet doggedly unitary "Chinese nation" as the autonomous subject of linear, progressive history. This drama—with its tales of imperialist intrigue, backward minorities, bloodthirsty warlords, and heroic Chinese patriots—took place on a dramatically altered stage, as the new global discourse of competing nation-states and its accompanying assumptions, categories, and political norms transformed the landscape of Chinese identity. The empire, with its geographic and ethnic variegation, Peter Purdue reminds us, became "the spectre that haunts the modern nation."[10] For Chinese policymakers and intellectuals, the long shadow of the Qing geo-body posed two significant and interrelated challenges for the new Republic: the "frontier question" (*bianjiang wenti*)—namely the challenge of mapping, colonizing, and politically incorporating the thousands of square miles of remote and desolate frontier that now formed the frontline in the struggle to defend the nation's territorial sovereignty—and the "national question" (*minzu wenti*), namely the task of identifying, classifying, and assimilating the twenty to forty million frontier indigenes into a single national identity.

One of the central focuses of this book is the key role these two problems, or at least the perception of these problems, played in reconstituting the Qing geo-body as a Sinic-centered, multiethnic Zhonghua minzu. Indeed, these two questions overlapped in significant ways to produce a shared discourse of "national unity" (*minzu tuanjie*) among the Republic's two most bitter ideological rivals, the Nationalist Party or Guomindang (GMD) and the Chinese Communist Party (CCP). Both political parties were quick to realize the strategic importance of the frontier—with less than 6 percent of the new Republic's population but upwards of 60 percent of its territory, much of it rich in natural resources—for modernizing the economy and protecting national sovereignty.[11] Their shared goal was not only to win the political allegiance of the Tibetans, Mongolians, and other frontier peoples toward the political center, but also to construct a new myth of national belonging deeply rooted in the perception of a common history, soil, and blood.

De-centering the Nation

In China today, the nation-state is routinely presented as a "unitary, multiethnic state" (*tongyi de duo minzu guojia*) with a long and glorious past. "China is not only one of the world's largest countries but also one of its most populous and ancient," begins a recent Central Party School textbook. "Our mighty fatherland is a state composed of many different nationalities united together; besides the Han there are also fifty-five minority nationals, who collectively are known as the

Zhonghua minzu."[12] China is not unique in depicting itself as bounded and ancient. In order to naturalize its political power and construct a myth of national belonging, state elites employ idioms of space and time—dividing the global into discrete geographic entities (China, Australia, America) and distinct "time zones" of progress (the "new" and "immature" nationalism of East Timor compared to the "mature" and "sophisticated" democracy of America). Space (geography) and time (history) serve as the two primordial axials that order human variation in the modern nation-state—powerful technologies for marking the boundary between national Self and Other. Along one axis, individuals are placed in finite, and in theory homogeneous, nation-space according to their blood/race, language/ethnicity, or tradition/culture. The other axis measures linear progress, or the path and current location of a given people along the continuum from saveragy to civilization. This nexus of national space and time presents China and other nation-states as rooted and eternal *places* rather than dynamic and political *processes*. For scholars, these "natural nations" present an analytical hurdle that can easily distract us from exploring the complex interactions among discrete, yet fuzzy and imbricated, cultural traditions over space and time, and from discovering how these traditions are mediated by the globally circulating discourses and practices of modernity.[13] We must seek to unbound the nation-state, breaking down the teleology of national time and the confines of national space, to reveal the various historical and social contingencies that contributed to the existing national entities and their cultural traditions.

The last couple of decades have witnessed an upsurge of interest in issues of ethnicity and nationalism in contemporary Chinese society, greatly contributing to our understanding of the politics of representation in this rather unusual polyethnic mosaic. Yet, this burgeoning new literature has paid little attention to the complex ways in which the nation has been socially constituted and historically mediated over space and time. In China, unlike Europe and America, the history of nationalism, modernity, and imperialism are closely intertwined.[14] Modernity authenticates the nation-state system as the only legitimate expression of sovereignty, with nations replacing gods and empires as the subject of history and linear progression superseding cyclical transcendence. At the same time, modernity and its political form, nationalism, were the driving forces behind imperialism in Asia, with the rhetoric of nationalism employed to legitimate the territorial imperative driving the modern state's pursuit of global capital and perceived racial survival. In the process, once remote frontier regions were transformed into important sites of ideological and material struggle. In contrast to previous studies, my treatment of Chinese nation and state building de-centers linear teleology by demonstrating how the frontier and its indigenous inhabitants were central rather than peripheral to the process of revolution in modern China.

Like other empires, the Qing tended to tread lightly on its frontier after conquest, adopting a *jimi* (loose rein) policy that allowed most regions to maintain their own political, legal, and institutional structures as long as they remained loyal to the Manchu court. But the rise of modern imperialism and nationalism in Asia made this laissez-faire approach to state building on the margins increasingly untenable. The state could no longer afford to wait for the "barbarians" to *laihua* (come and be transformed); instead the newly conceptualized *shaoshu minzu* (national minorities or literally, *minority* nationals) needed to be integrated into centralized state structures and narratives of national unfolding through an active process of *hanhua* (sinification or literally, the act of "becoming Chinese"), lest their territory be lost to competing nation-states. This national project was one of the central concerns of politicians and intellectuals associated with the new Chinese state. As both the GMD and the CCP struggled to extend its political authority over state territory, the frontier became an important site of contention, with numerous actors (autonomous warlords, party cadres, minority elites, and imperialist agents) vying for control while professing competing claims of sovereignty.

The significance of the frontier as a liminal zone of cultural hybridity was first noted by the American historian Frederick Jackson Turner, who in 1920 defined the frontier as "the meeting point between savagery and civilization."[15] Turner's successors (including Owen Lattimore, writing on China) expanded the frontier concept to explore the role of these contested borderlands in the imperial rivalries that marked the death of empires and the birth of the nation-states system and its new international legal framework. Interimperial tensions shaped not only "the peculiar and contingent character of foreign relations,"[16] but also, as I will demonstrate, the language, domestic politics, and cultural boundaries of a nation's identity. In certain circumstance, the periphery can play a decisive role in the discourse of emerging nation-states, becoming "the *mythomoteur* for an entire society."[17] The rapid growth of professional organizations, academic journals, and government bodies focused on the frontier and national questions in Republican China reflected the centrality of the frontier to China's new national imaginary. Because the Chinese state was weak and divided, and sovereignty over its more than thirteen thousand miles of national borders was contested, the significance of these borderlands to the revolutionary strategies of both the CCP and the GMD increased dramatically.

It has become axiomatic within the academic literature that the struggle against foreign imperialism helped define both China and its identity. In other words, what it means to be Chinese in a modern context has been formed through an unequal dialogic process in which the Chinese Self is continually redefined in opposition to the Western Other—a process that John Fitzgerald refers to as a "reversed colonial racism."[18] In a desperate attempt to replace the backward ethnography of "old John Chinaman" perpetuated in treaty port literature with a more authentic identity, Chinese nationalists paradoxically created a "mirror image of John Chinaman." As Fitzgerald explains, "nationalist ethnography came to bear an uncanny resemblance to essentialist, racist European writings on the curious habits, customs, and morals of the Chinaman of the European imagination," which nationalists had to confront to "begin to reclaim the Chinese people for themselves."[19] For Tsu Jing, the very language of "failure" becomes an important "modality of cultural identity" in turn-of-the-century China, as the anxiety, humiliation, and injury of colonial victimization shaped the contours of Chinese national identity while also holding out the alluring promise of future self-regeneration.[20] This awkward and ambivalent engagement with the West lies behind what R. Bin Wong has termed the "schizophrenic" nature of early twentieth-century Chinese nationalism, as the state attempted to root its national identity simultaneously in a common Confucian cultural essence and in an ethnically based identity premised on resistance to foreign exploitation.[21] The former approach was intensely criticized as backward and outmoded, while the latter left unresolved the place of the non-Sinic peoples and their vast territory in the modern world.

What these scholars have identified here is the active boundary-making process involved in "awakening" modern Chinese subjectivity and its "derivative" relationship with foreign imperialism.[22] Yet, we must also remember that China's external boundaries with "John Bull" and other foreign powers overlapped and interacted with its internal borders with the *siyi*, or the so-called barbarians of the four directions. The alien Other had only recently sailed across the seas from the West. This more familiar Other, in contrast, had long helped define Chinese identity and now seemed to provide the basis for a morally affirmative and culturally dynamic subjectivity—one that promised to strengthen China in its struggle against foreign imperialism. Having experienced the humiliation of Western material (and some believed cultural) supremacy, the Chinese saw, in their long history of moral stewardship over the frontier barbarians, a brighter past that foretold a more confident national future. During a time when a racial and moral hierarchy set the terms of the world order, Chinese identity was forged in conversation with both a "superior" alien Other and an "inferior" familiar Other. To put it another way, the Chinese may have been treated like dogs in the treaty ports of Shanghai and Canton, but on the Mongolian and Tibetan steppe, they came to see themselves as sages of modernity and revolutionary liberators. As anthropologists have demonstrated, contemporary China's representation of the ethnic minorities as backward, exotic, and even erotic has more to do with the construction of Han majority subjectivity than the minorities themselves.[23] I take this insight a bit further to explore the complex negotiation between Western narratives of race/nation (minzu and *zhongzu*) and the rich imperial tradition of distinguishing *xia* (Chinese) from *yi* (barbarian), demonstrating how this dialectic produced a more encompassing (yet equally hegemonic) multiethnic Chinese national identity—a truly *national* identity that sits (often uncomfortably) above these majority/minority and modern/primitive alterities. It specifically includes both the Han majority and the fifty-five officially recognized minority nationals set within a single bounded and homogeneous Zhonghua national/racial identity, or what Fei Xiaotong has termed "the plurality and organic unity of the Zhonghua minzu."[24]

The arrival of foreign imperialists on China's shores dramatically jolted the meaning of "being Chinese" in late imperial and early Republican society and precipitated a new national project aimed at scrutinizing, redefining, and in some cases abandoning traditional cultural values in the search for a new, more robust identity.[25] For many of the Republic's new citizens, this identity took the form of modern practices and symbols, such as unbound feet and felt hats or a series of "invented traditions" such as the Sun Yat-sen suit or the cheongsam. It has been argued that these distinctly modern practices proved more important than traditional birth, death, and marriage rituals in shaping the contours of China's "imagined community."[26] In other words, the arrival of the West rendered traditional Chinese identity largely meaningless and contributed to a "major crisis in self-identification."[27] In contrast, I hope to demonstrate how China's familiar Other (and the problems it posed for the new state) contributed to the recasting of Chinese national identity in the form of a territorially defined, Sinic-dominated multinationality—one that took as its model the rich tradition of Confucian universalism. China's national project is ongoing, requiring agents of the state to daily construct and sustain a "symbolic regime of authenticity" aimed at reinforcing Chinese identity,[28] yet its origins can be traced to a unique convergence of nationalism, imperialism, and modernity in the late nineteenth and early twentieth centuries and the way it mediated, altered, and reconstituted imperial Chinese identity.

As should be clear now, this is not a book about nation and state building in modern China per se; nor is it a history of the transition from premodern notions of ethnic diversity to the nation's modern classificatory technologies. Rather it is a partial, and perhaps overly ambitious, history of how the vast Qing empire became "Chinese," and more particularly, the role played by the new categories of frontier and minority nationals in constructing political and cultural narratives of Chinese nationhood. As such, this study has a number of important limitations, chiefly its emphasis on state and elite discourse as represented by the Republican Period's two leading political parties, the CCP and the GMD and their affiliated intellectuals. This narrow focus reduces the voices of the ethnic subaltern to a mere murmur and leaves largely unexamined important sites of resistance to the dominant discourse of a centralizing and unifying nation-state. Unlike the excellent regional histories of the Republican frontier or the recent proliferation of ethnographic research on individual minority groups in contemporary China,[29] the book concentrates on elite Chinese narratives of the nation as they relate to the geographic and ethnic variation of the new Republican state. My interest is not the dynamics of minority agency and the complex negotiation of state identity categories or the actuality of control/resistance, but rather the nature of the Chinese state's *claims* over the frontier and its people. And though I reject the existence of a primordial or unchanging nation, I attempt to demonstrate how historical narratives of "Chineseness" were appropriated, repositioned, and institutionalized as a part of modern state building. My aim is to complement the growing body of literature on regional and ethnic cultures in China and shed some new light on the strategies and practices adopted by the political center in confronting the problem of diversity in early twentieth-century China.

The Nation's New Discursive Terrain

Before beginning, it is crucial that I pause briefly to discuss several of the key Chinese terms that will reappear (often untranslated) throughout this book. Together they reflect the discursive terrain on which modern Chinese identity was fashioned. Lydia Liu has urged us to pay careful attention to how loanwords and neologisms circulated between East and West, introducing new norms, categories, and modes of representation in what she terms a unique form of "translated modernity."[30] Intense social and political upheaval in late nineteenth- and early twentieth-century China was accompanied by radical linguistic transformation. In addition to the development of a new vernacular written language, literally hundreds of new words (one study has identified 1,266 new terms) emerged as Chinese elites tried to make sense of the novel ideas pouring into the country. Many of these terms were filtered through Japanese writings, which in turn had distilled major Western intellectual trends. Through this dynamic process, meanings were "not so much 'transformed' when concepts pass[ed] from the guest language to the host language as invented within the local environment of the latter."[31] This "translingual practice," as Liu has called it, helped shape a distinctly Chinese version of modernity and its associated practices and assumptions.

Minzu, arguably the single most important of these new concepts, provides the discursive parameters for defining national, ethnic and cultural identity in China today. When it first entered the Chinese lexicon during the late 1890s, minzu referred to the peoples of foreign countries. The term is thought to be the Chinese equivalent of the Japanese neologism *minzoku*, which itself was coined to translate the German term *Volk*. Not until the first decade of the 1900s did the idiom become commonplace within Chinese writings when it began to refer to the people(s) of China.[32] Much like minzoku in Japan, minzu proved a linguistic "chameleon" in China, coming to index a "surplus of meanings" related to group identity.[33] In early twentieth-century China (and arguably today), minzu connoted a cluster of meanings and associations similar to those captured in English by race, nation, people, ethnic group, and nationality. Some Chinese authors went to great lengths to define the term, listing any number of objective criteria necessary for minzu formation. Others took a loose and even inconsistent approach, often using it interchangeably with other (equally ambiguous) neologisms such as *zhongzu* (race), *guojia* (state), *guomin* (citizen), and *renmin* (people).

Although most believed that the term expressed a specific objective and scientific reality, such uncertainty heightened its polemical value. As Partha Chatterjee has pointed out, "'politics' necessarily operates in an ideological world in which words rarely have unambiguous meanings; where notions are inexact, and have political value precisely because they are inexact and hence capable of suggesting a range of possible interpretations."[34] The fluidity of minzu and other Chinese neologisms related to group identity requires that we avoid a priori definitions (when possible) and instead base our interpretations on the specific context in which the neologisms are employed. In fact, the precise boundaries of minzu—who was included and excluded, where and on what basis the line was to be drawn, and even how many existed—was a central topic of debate among late nineteenth- and early twentieth-century Chinese intellectuals (and one of the key focuses of this book). Despite considerable disagreement over the scope of China's minzu(s), nearly all Chinese commentators agreed that when it came to minzu, size did matter. The term, as Charlotte Furth has suggested, was always meant to designate large, territorially based peoples, not small, disparate minority groups.[35] The challenge for Chinese state officials and intellectuals was finding room within this new minzu construct for the smaller non-Sinic peoples living on the fringes of the Manchu empire.

By the late Qing period (if not much earlier), most subjects of the empire (both Sinic and non-Sinic) accepted the existence of a distinct, albeit fuzzy, "Chinese" identity, even if that community seemed to lack a single, precise autonym for itself. To avoid confusion with the modern, invented category of the "Han nationality" (*Han minzu*), I refer to this more fluid yet recurrent identity as Sinic or Chinese. Historically speaking, the boundaries of the Sinic community were culturally dynamic and situationally contingent, with considerable movement in and out of the community along its margins. Yet during the late nineteenth century, its boundaries hardened as the Qing empire came into contact with foreign imperialism and global capital. Prior to its ossification, the Sinic community had a number of different exonyms and autonyms, with *Hanren* (literally, "people of the Han dynasty") used interchangeably and intermittently with *Huaren*, *Xiaren*, *Huaxia*, *Zhonghua*, *Zhongguoren*, and other idioms. These terms reflected the mercurial ecological boundary between the largely sedentary inhabitants of the *neidi* (interior), *fudi* (hinterland, literally, "belly-land"), or *zhongyuan* (central plains) and the nomadic or swidden communities of the *waifang* (exterior), *xiyu* (western regions), or *bianqu* (borderlands).[36] The Western discourse of social Darwinism (with its related concepts of race and nation) caused the membrane around the Sinic community to become less permeable until it was eventually reimagined as a patrilineal descent group, or what Zhang Binglin first called the *Hanzu* (Han lineage-race).[37] Thus while the concept of a unified, homogeneous Han ethnic majority is a modern construct,[38] its authenticity rests on a much older spatial distinction between the Sinic realm of civilization (*wen*) and the barbarism (*ye*) of the periphery—what the Chinese literary canon referred to as *yixia zhibie*, or "distinguishing between the Chinese and the barbarians."

Over time, the various ethnonyms for the Sinic community became closely intertwined with a distinct toponym that Lydia Liu has labeled, the *Zhongguo/China* "super-sign." The term *Zhongguo* (central state[s]), which dates back as far as the tenth century BCE, was originally a geographic and political term used in reference to the sedentary and technologically sophisticated polities of the Yellow River valley region. Throughout the first and second millennium, both indigenous and conquest regimes employed the term when referring to their rule over the zhongyuan (the central lands or central plains of the Yellow, and over time, Yangtze, and Pearl river valleys)—the distinct topography that the West came to know as "China." While dynastic titles—*Da Ming Guo* (Great Ming state) or *Da Qing Guo* (Great Qing state)—were regularly used domestically, Zhongguo was often employed in dealings with foreign counties and peoples and eventually became coupled (apparently via the Sanskrit term *cīna*) with the English signifier "China" and its European-language variants.[39] The Qing followed the Ming in consciously referring to its empire as Zhongguo/China in its foreign affairs, but it also creatively expanded the super-sign's meaning to include by 1911 the Mongols, Tibetans, and other non-Sinic peoples that traditionally had lain outside of geopolitical boundaries of Zhongguo. Similarly, as early as the 1650s, the Manchu court began referring to its subjects, both Sinic and non-Sinic, as "Chinese" (*Zhongguo zhi min*, *Zhongguo zhi ren*, and during the late Qing, *Zhongguoren* or *Zhonghuaren*), laying the basis for a more inclusive and multicultural ethnonym.[40]

For Liang Qichao and other turn-of-the-century Chinese nationalists, the lack of a single, consistent name for the Sinic community was a source of deep embarrassment. "The names that people ordinarily think of, such as Zhuxia, Han or Tang, are titles of bygone dynasties," wrote Liang in 1901. "Foreigners call our country *cīna* or China, but that is not how we view ourselves."[41] In addressing this concern, some proposed using Huaxia, others *Zhina*, but Liang seemed to prefer first, *Zhongguo minzu* and then by 1907, Zhonghua minzu as the most appropriate autonym for the Chinese nation-state and its people. Unlike the more exclusionary Hanzu or *Hanzhong* (Han race), championed by Zhang Binglin and other racial nationalists who sought to overthrow the Manchu dynasty, Zhonghua minzu was broad and ambiguous enough to incorporate both the Sinic and non-Sinic peoples of the Qing empire.[42] The political exigencies of nation building and the idiom's convenient imprecision (at once singular and plural) combined to make the term widely popular among Chinese intellectuals and officials throughout the twentieth century.[43] Indeed, its centrality challenges the assertion that "the political leaders of the Republic until 1949 and the People's Republic after 1949 have reinvented subject peoples in border areas as mere subbranches of the Han,"[44] and behooves us to pay careful attention to the ways in which the term has been employed in modern Chinese political discourse.

In China, as in Europe and America, with the rise of modern nationalism came two additional concepts that helped shape the public discourse on national identity: bianjiang (frontier) and shaoshu minzu (minority nationals). The transition from premodern empires to modern nation-states reconfigured the world's political geography into finite and bounded entities. A system in which authority radiated outward from the center, with borders elastic and imprecise, was replaced by one in which "state sovereignty [was] fully, flatly, and evenly operative over each square centimeter of a legally demarcated territory."[45] This shift had important implications along the margins of empires, transforming them from peripheral borderlands—where sovereignties overlapped because sovereigns were remote—into valuable and vulnerable *bordered lands* where territory needed to be patrolled and guarded day and night.[46] The very concept of Zhongguo presupposes the existence of other, peripheral states or civilizations, and thus it is not surprising that the Chinese term bianjiang can be traced back as far as the fourth century BCE, where the *Zuo zhuan* describes it as an intermediary zone between two sovereign states. But only during the Qing period did the term become common in state discourse with its modern connotation of a linear and exclusionary boundary (*bianjie*) represented on Qing and European maps.[47] Unlike the indistinct waifang (exterior) of old, the bianjiang was in peril under the new global nation-state system unless the state fully exercised its authority over the frontier. In twentieth-century China, the state constructed thousands of miles of roads, telegraph lines, and, most important, railway lines, gradually projecting state power—in the form of its military, political, educational, and economic institutions—into the furthest corners of the nation.

This new spatial concept of bianjiang helped engender the ethnic and political category of shaoshu minzu. In the concentric and hierarchical model of premodern Chinese space, there was no "minority": everyone, barbarian and Chinese alike, was assigned an appropriate place within the social order.[48] It was distance from the center rather than size that determined one's place in the moral hierarchy. In the modern episteme of social Darwinism, however, states were recast as organisms; and population size became a key determinant of space, with the German notion of *Lebensraum* (living space) employed to justify the territorial imperative of what Liang Qichao termed the "race-state" (*guozu*).[49] A distinction was now made between populous, historically viable nations (what Hegel called "world-historical peoples" and Liang Qichao "historical races") and small, ahistoric "ruins of peoples" (Liang's "ahistorical races" and Karl Kautsky's "old family furniture"), who were now seen as having no independent future outside of the confines of the world's great race-states.[50] Liang Qichao appeared to have coined the term guozu in 1903 to refer to the most advanced stage of human evolution, the struggle between large, territorially distinct (yet expansionist) peoples for biological survival and political and economic domination.[51] In a quest to secure its boundaries, the race-state drew a ring of sovereignty around its vulnerable frontiers, nationalized its minorities, and set about homogenizing its national space. In China, the barbarians (yi) were reclassified as minority nationals (shaoshu minzu) and subordinated to the Han majority; and this new demographic hierarchy came to underpin the discourse of national identity in China. In contrast to bianjiang, shaoshu minzu is a distinctly modern neologism. Its earliest usage has been traced to the 1924 manifesto of the first CCP/GMD United Front,[52] in which members of both parties were grappling with different methods of incorporating the frontier and its peoples into the new nation-state.

The Scope and Plan of the Book

The political transition from a monarchic dynasty to a republican nation-state is predicated on a radical shift in ideology and policy, as centralizing and universalizing impulses replace a decentralized emperorship. The nation's transformative agenda—with its emphasis on popular mobilization, conformity, and discipline—renders the cultural mosaic of the empire problematic and creates an immediate tension between the exclusivist logic of nationalism ("us" versus "them") and the universalizing rhetoric of national integration ("we are all one").[53] These competing loyalties drive and threaten to undermine China's state- and nation-building projects. Yet, although some Republican elites were initially drawn to exclusionary racial nationalism, there emerged a remarkable consensus on the urgent need to suture together a new national fabric that would firmly fit around the vast political boundaries of the old Qing empire. This need explains, in part, the rich intellectual foment of Republican China and its various experiments with anarchism, socialism, Marxism, federalism, liberalism, conservatism, and other transformative isms associated with modernity. My main interest lies in exploring the complex nexus between these transformative ideologies and the shared desire of GMD and CCP elites to reimagine China as a unified yet inclusive Zhonghua nation-state. Thus, I focus on the maneuvers, narratives, and practices intended to fold the diversity of the frontier into the homogeneity of the center, examining how this political and cultural imperative mediated the transformative ideologies of modernity.

The opening chapter lays out the conceptual and historical framework for the more empirical chapters that follow. Chapter 1 traces China's tumultuous shift from empire to nation-state and explores the impact of its imperial past on the ways in which identity is formulated today. Problematizing the sinocentric narrative of *tianxia* (all-under-heaven), the chapter highlights the tension running throughout China's long imperial history between creating an exclusivist community of difference and an inclusivist community of sameness, showing how it helped to shape the boundaries of modern Chinese identity. The chapter also traces the origins of the modern frontier and national questions to the policies and ideologies of the Qing dynasty, arguing that the Manchu empire provided the imprimatur for a multinational, Sinic-centered Zhonghua identity set firmly within the territorial boundaries of the Qing dynasty. In addition, I discuss how the modern discourse of race and nation altered and then reformulated the imperial alterity of Chinese/barbarian, firmly binding the new scientific categories of frontier, minority nationals, and Han nationality to a hierarchy of competing race-states striving to protect their territorial sovereignty.

The remainder of the book is divided into two parts that mix politics with culture in exploring the narrative strategies and political policies of GMD and CPP elites as they undertook state- and nation-building projects on the frontier. Geoff Eley and Ronald Suny have argued that the creative processes of "political intervention" and "cultural innovation" lie at the heart of modern nationalism;

the former aims to combine disparate cultural communities into a single political collective while the later seeks to authenticate that union through the construction of an ideological regime of national belonging. "Thus," they write, "if politics is the ground upon which the category of the nation was first proposed, culture was the terrain where it was elaborated, and in this sense nationality is best conceived as a complex, uneven, and unpredictable process, forged from an interaction of cultural coalescence and specific political interventions, which cannot be reduced to static criteria of language, territory, ethnicity, or culture."[54] Building on this insight, I have chosen to divide the two parties' tactics into the analytical and organizational categories of political intervention and cultural innovation, and structure my chapters accordingly.

Part I, which centers on strategies of political intervention, investigates the efforts of the GMD and CCP to incorporate the Qing frontier and its peoples into the new Republican state. The imposition of state authority over the hinterland was hampered by logistical limitations and its jumbled ethnic geography. In dealing with the frontier minorities, the Chinese state essentially had three policy options: assimilation, autonomy, or self-determination. Though Sun Yat-sen, Chiang Kai-shek, and Mao Zedong each used the term national self-determination (*minzu zijue*), Chinese political leaders never seriously considered granting the Mongols, Tibetans, and other frontier peoples the right to permanently secede from the Republic of China. Because Chinese elites viewed the problem of "backward," "weak," and "numerically insignificant" minorities through a social evolutionary framework, the principle of self-determination applied only to the evolutionarily fit and historically dynamic Han majority. "The Tibetans, Mongols, Hui and Manchus lack the ability of self-defense," Sun declared in 1921; "thus, the task of fostering a glorious and large *minzuzhuyi* (nationalism/racialism)—that is assimilating the Tibetans, Mongols, Hui and Manchus into our Hanzu and constructing the biggest possible race-state—rests solely with the self-determination of the Han people."[55] Assimilation was the more Darwinian of the two remaining options and was the ultimate goal of both the CCP and the GMD. But forced to accept the reality of their own political weakness, both parties tended to view national integration as a long-term evolutionary and organic process, which in turn rendered limited regional autonomy an expedient strategy for exercising (at least partial) national sovereignty over the recalcitrant frontier while buying additional time for the natural processes of evolution to work.

Chapter 2 focuses on the Guomindang's handling of the frontier question and in the process seeks to challenge the scholarly consensus. Whereas others, claiming that the GMD denied the very existence of non-Han identity, have compared its policies to the fascist racism of Nazi Germany, I make use of recently declassified documents from the party's Commission on Mongolian and Tibetan Affairs to argue that the GMD adopted a pragmatic yet inherently conservative frontier policy that was rooted in the language and administrative precedents of the Qing court. In its approach to the Mongolian and Tibetan frontiers, the party consistently advocated political and cultural autonomy as it lacked the political resolve (and, more important, military might) to impose its will over the objections of the frontiersmen who were streaming into the areas. Here the GMD had to contend with a competing notion of sovereignty, one that favored Chinese settlers over the frontier minorities and profits over the lofty goals of national unity. The chapter emphasizes that in exercising its authority over the "middle ground" of the borderlands, the Republican state had to contend with a number of independent actors.

Chapter 3 turns the focus to the CCP and its handling of the national question. It critically reexamines the influence of Marxist theory on CCP policymakers, charting their creative adaptation of Marxist nationality discourse to suit their state-building agenda. Despite the inclusion (at the insistence of the Comintern) of an explicit policy of national self-determination within the CCP's political program, the party's leaders first circumscribed and then abandoned this key Leninist plank in favor of limited regional autonomy set firmly within a fully bounded Chinese nation-state. Like the GMD, the CCP viewed the frontier minorities as potential allies in their struggle for national power; and on the frontier, it stressed the importance of national unity over class antagonism. Here Lenin's united front tactic, which called for the party to work closely with the "upper stratum" of the frontier minorities, proved more influential than his strategy of national self-determination. Through its sinification of Marxism, I argue that the CCP transformed the national question from a problem of fostering transnational class consciousness into a purely domestic issue of national integration.

At the same time as the state's political leaders were proffering autonomy to the frontier minorities, its intellectuals were attempting to construct a myth of historical belonging that would refashion the disparate polities of the Republic as a primordial and eternal guozu (race-state). Part II shifts the focus from space to time, exploring various narratives of cultural innovation. As Stevan Harrell has pointed out,

> Any government that wishes to gain the loyalty of its citizens must convince them that they are citizens by virtue of their historical and cultural attachment to the nation and that this attachment is a long, glorious, and immutable one. A government must not simply ignore, it must also actively attempt to hide, the fluid, multivalent nature of ethnic identity. It does this, ordinarily, by constructing narratives of national unfolding, what Homi Bhabha calls "the attempt by nationalist discourse persistently to produce the idea of the nation as a continuous narrative of national progress" or what Benedict Anderson characterizes as "the process of reading nationalism *genealogically*—as the expression of an historical tradition of serial continuity."[56]

By reconfiguring narratives of the past, Chinese intellectuals hoped to demonstrate the organic unity and antiquity of a single Zhonghua people that included all the inhabitants of the Republic's territory. "Getting its history wrong," Ernest Renan declared in his famous 1882 Sorbonne lecture, "is part of being a nation."[57] Yet, in the modern era of science, history needed to be grounded in "facts." And the art of cultural innovation came to rely on empirically verifiable "proof" produced by the new scientific disciplines that were established during the twentieth century and became closely intertwined with the nation-building project in China. As such, this section of the book highlights the centrality of modern science in reformulating and naturalizing the imperial distinction between a civilized Chinese center and a backward, barbarian periphery, while simultaneously placing both communities firmly within a single, overarching minzu identity. In writing its "biography" for the nation,[58] the Chinese state turned to a new generation of professional scientists who eagerly descended on the frontier with their calipers and notebooks.

Chapter 4 examines several competing narratives of nationhood offered by Guomindang-affiliated scholars and academics. Following the Japanese invasion of Manchuria in 1931, Chinese intellectuals seeking to fashion a new, more inclusive national imaginary looked backward into their own history for scientific evidence to counter the claims of Japanese scientists that the Manchus and other former frontier subjects were actually independent national peoples. This chapter focuses in particular on the tension between, on the one hand, a racial formulation that placed the source of Chinese unity in the common origin (*tongyuan*) of its people and, on the other hand, a cultural formulation that located this unity in the gradual, evolutionary melding (*ronghe*) of several distinct peoples into a new composite culture. In the process, it highlights the role played by the newly emerging scientific disciplines of history, archaeology, and ethnology in the construction of a myth of Chinese national identity. Finally, I suggest that these two formulations uncomfortably converged with the publication of Chiang Kai-shek's 1943 political tract, *China's Destiny*, which increased pressure on Chinese academics to contribute to this mythmaking project while curtailing any research on the ethnic and cultural diversity of the Republic.

Chapter 5 looks at the CCP's narratives of cultural innovation. Initially, Communist historians adopted a discursive strategy closely resembling that of Guomindang intellectuals. In their early histories, Communist scholars highlighted the significance of the Yellow Emperor and Peking Man in binding the heterogeneous peoples of the former Qing empire into a single, organic minzu, which, following Sun Yat-sen and Chiang Kai-shek, they termed the Zhonghua minzu. Yet, the heightened ideological struggle that accompanied the collapse of the Second United Front and the publication of *China's Destiny* forced CCP historians to adopt an alternative myth of national unfolding. In particular, Communist intellectuals pointed to the recent discovery of a racially distinct South Pacific hominid to counter the "fascist racism" of the Guomindang and assert the multiracial origins of the Chinese people. At the same time, faced (as were GMD scientists) with Japan's manipulation of ethnic aspirations along the Qing frontier, CCP historians also manufactured intricate ethnogenealogies that placed the minorities at the very origin of Chinese history and linked the multivalent "Chinese" minzus together into a single organic, Han-centered whole. In doing so, the Communists (like the Nationalists) projected Sun Yat-sen's desire for a future state of national unity backward in time, using history, ethnology, and archaeology to demonstrate the fundamental consanguinity and antiquity of the Zhonghua minzu.

CHAPTER 1

From Empire to Nation: The Bounding of the Chinese Geo-body

This opening chapter explores China's tumultuous transition from empire to nation, examining the role of historical memory and political revolution in the construction of modern Chinese identity. It asks how China's past traditions came to mediate globally diffused practices of modernity and produce the shared assumptions and categories through which the state and its elites chose to situate the diversity of the frontier within the narratives and policies of Chinese nationhood. The chapter thus sets the scene for a more detailed treatment of the frontier and national questions among Republican-era elites by exploring how the problem of the frontier and its inhabitants came to play such a central role in the process of revolution in twentieth-century China.

A long and rich tradition of scholarly analysis on the origins, meaning, and mechanics of nationalism has developed into a growing academic specialization following the end of the cold war and the apparent revival of nationalist sentiments in a new regressive reaction to the thickening forces of globalization.[1] Yet most of this literature approaches the issue from a distinctly Eurocentric position; leading theorists such as Ernest Gellner, Anthony Smith, Eric Hobsbawm, and Liah Greenfeld have either ignored or provided only superficial coverage of the origins and development of nationalism in Asia.[2]

Among these analysts, Asia—and in particular East Asia—is frequently dismissed as either an unproblematic exception or a derivative discourse of a purer, more fully developed European and American model of nationalism. Hobsbawm and others view East Asia as an anomaly. Because China and other East Asian countries are "ethnically almost or entirely homogeneous,"[3] they have avoided the problem of ethnic secessionism that plagued other countries in the transition from empires to nation-states. China's treatment as a rare example of a "historic nation" that exists "more or less, within [its] historic frontiers" suggests that

China lacked the internal dynamism that was central to the development of modernity in the West.[4] Thus Gellner sees China as "untypical" in that its elite high culture overlapped with the state bureaucracy, creating the type of cultural homogeneity that was anathema to European nationalism.[5] China and other East Asian countries appear to be at a theoretical dead end; for them, nationalism and modernity require an external shock.

In his highly influential book, *Imagined Communities*, Benedict Anderson suggests a way out for Asia, proposing one of the first systematic theories about the spread of nationalism from Paris and Washington to Jakarta and Beijing. Referring to "colonial nationalism" as "the last wave," Anderson postulates that the nation is "modularly imagined" in Asia and Africa from political and cultural idioms that originated in the West.[6] Ironically, though Anderson is rare among major theorists of nationalism for his deep knowledge of the rich historical and cultural traditions of Asia, he cannot explain colonial nationalism without looking to the "complex historical experiences" of the Americas and Europe. At stake here is not the existence of "a distinctively Asian form of nationalism," which Anderson denies, but rather the role of premodern traditions and categories of identity in its formation and development.[7] The past is dismissed as unimportant by modernists who argue that Asian nationalists uncomplicatedly drew on European/American models and where something was missing, invented traditions and filled in the gaps thereby ensuring, in the words of Partha Chatterjee, that Asians were "perpetual consumers of modernity" whose very imaginations remained fully colonized.[8]

The result, as Peter Perdue has astutely pointed out, is "a dual erasure of East Asia from the analysis of nationalism: if the nationalists essence is seen as deriving smoothly from the imperial heritage, then it is unproblematic; or if it is seen as a derivative late developer, the earlier European experience becomes the focal point of analysis."[9] As a result, nationalism in East Asia, and particularly in China, has been undertheorized. Much of this neglect is directly related to the way that "sinology," as an Orientalist discourse, has tended to erase ethnic and cultural difference from the story of China's past.[10] For the sinologist, imperial China operated within a universal cosmology of Confucian "culturalism" in which ethnic identity was malleable and largely irrelevant—an oversight recently identified by one scholar as the "main shortcoming" of previous literature on Chinese nationalism.[11]

This chapter argues that China's cultural past is crucial for understanding its national present. By exploring some of the premodern cultural and historical roots of the modern Chinese nation, I highlight the process by which the state incorporated the empire's fluid borderlands into the fixed borders that came to precisely delineate the sovereignty of the Republic of China. Knowledge of the continuities and cultural resources that spanned China's transition from empire to nation-state puts us in a better position to appreciate how new categories of horizontal social identity (chiefly, for my analysis, nation and race) entered

China during the twentieth century and the complex ways they interacted with indigenous grammars in bounding the Chinese geo-body.

Arguably the three most important imperial contributions to modern Chinese identity were (1) the formation of an ethnocentric or Sinic political and cultural community around which the new Chinese nation-state would be imagined; (2) the massive expansion of state territory during the Manchu Qing dynasty that established the geopolitical framework and international boundaries of the modern Chinese nation-state; and (3) the Qing construction (building on the Mongol Yuan dynasty) of a multiethnic empire of the Han, Manchu, Mongol, Tibetan, and Sino-Muslim peoples that provided the foundation for reconstituting the new Chinese nation as a unitary yet multiethnic state. The first of these provided the basis for the invention of the Han race or nationality (*Hanzu*), the ethnic majority around which the nation was to be built and imagined. The second engendered the modern concept of the frontier and what the Chinese nationalists would term the "frontier question"—namely, the challenge of exerting full state sovereignty and control over a remote zone of untamed wilderness while protecting it from foreign encroachment. And the third spawned a new category of citizens, the minority nationals or the marginalized and backward peoples living along the frontiers of the nation, thereby creating for the state the problem of classifying and assimilating these marginalized citizens into the geo-body of the nation—what the Chinese Communists called the "national question." As we will see, it was the tension between the first of these historical legacies, the Sinic cultural and political core, and the desire to maintain the second, the Qing territorial boundaries, that made the third necessary and sparked a groundswell of public discussion on the frontier and national questions among contemporary Chinese intellectuals and state officials following the collapse of the Qing dynasty in 1911.

Rethinking the Chinese World Order: The Sinic Self and the Barbarian Other

From the start of its recorded history, Chinese scholar-officials have struggled to come to terms with the diversity of peoples and cultures inhabiting the Yellow River valley and its surroundings. Not surprisingly, they put forward a variety of political strategies for unifying these communities into a single polity while bring their heterogeneity into an overarching imperial cosmology. But though this imperial discourse on *yixia zhibie* (distinguishing Chinese and barbarians) is rich, modern historiography has tended to focus rather narrowly on one representation of political community in premodern China: the *tianxia* (all-under-heaven) ideal that subsumed all diversity under the single universal rulership of the "Son of Heaven" (*Huangdi*).

In the West, this orthodoxy was most clearly articulated in John Fairbank's landmark 1968 edited volume, *The Chinese World Order*.[12] Fairbank and other contributors outlined the normative set of ideas and practices that were said to govern China's relations with their non-Chinese neighbors. In this sinocentric worldview, the closeness of one's relationship to the Son of Heaven was determined by both physical proximity to the capital and cultural affinity with China proper and was governed by a set of rituals formalized in the tribute system. One of the central cultural assumptions of this cosmology was that non-Chinese barbarians could be transformed through increased contact with Confucian rituals and norms. Through this process of "sinicization," the Mongols, Manchus, and others could assume the "Mandate of Heaven" and establish their own "Chinese" dynasties such as the Yuan and the Qing. According to Fairbank, the Chinese world order was based on an assumption of Chinese cultural superiority that was markedly dissimilar from Western notions of competing sovereign states, bounded national territories, and diplomatic equality.

For Joseph Levenson, this distinct form of Chinese culturalism helped explain China's failure to respond to the West and meet the challenge of Western modernity.[13] Levenson argued that the sinocentric worldview outlined by Fairbank and others was incompatible with modern nationalism and yielded only under the assault of Western imperialism and the emergent nation-state system. Fairbank's Chinese world order paradigm and Levenson's culturalism-to-nationalism thesis dominated Western scholarship on China during the 1970s and 1980s, and academics in Taiwan and the Chinese mainland similarly emphasized the strength and durability of Chinese culture. For example, Hsiao Kung-chuan, a leading authority on Chinese political thought, calls the traditional sinocentric worldview found in the Chinese expressions tianxia and *datongzhuyi* (doctrine of the great community) a type of "political solipsism." Within this "authoritarian" notion of political community, Hsiao argues, "little attention was given to ethnic distinctions but there was great emphasis on cultural identity or variance."[14] Anyone could become Chinese who mastered Chinese culture, which in turn signified political submission: "The result of this, throughout the whole two-thousand-year period during which China's power remained great . . . nationalism [*min-tsu ssu-hsiang*; this term can be also translated 'ethnic consciousness' or 'racism' in some other contexts] was underdeveloped."[15] In other words, "the concept of the modern nation-state was lacking."[16]

Some, however, have chosen to view China from its margins. As early as the 1930s, Owen Lattimore introduced the concept of a "reservoir zone"—a multi-ethnic, multicultural zone on China's Inner Asian frontiers that served as a bridge between the nomadic steppe and the sedentary central plains and a potential source of administrators familiar with both cultural systems.[17] Wolfram Eberhard, Joseph Fletcher, Denis Twitchett, Herbert Franke, Morris Rossabi, and Thomas Barfield are among those who have depicted a more fluid and "symbiotic relationship" between China and its border regions. This was a relationship in which "transfrontiersmen" crossed a constantly moving frontier zone carrying back and forth not only economic goods (e.g., horses, tea, and medicine) but also culture and ideas (e.g., the legalist notion of "rule by law" and the Mongol concept of "rule by joint deliberation," *khuriltai*).[18] Leading Chinese scholars on both sides of the Taiwan Straits, including Chen Yinke and Xiang Da, have contended that frontier rulers intentionally exploited Chinese institutions for their own gain and in the end, affected Sui, Tang, and Song society more than China affected them.[19] Here the sinocentric worldview is displaced by a focus on a dynamic "polyethnic" or "multistate" system whose cultural and political core was in a constant state of flux. The excellent collection of essays put together by Stevan Harrell in 1995 marked the arrival of this new approach to the mainstream of Chinese studies, sparking calls for a "new frontier history" that would bring the complex frontier *processes* back into the center of our discussions about national identity, economic development, and state formation in China.[20]

This new research agenda contributed to a major rethinking of ethnic identity in imperial China. The cultural dynamics of the steppe/sown, or nomadic/sedentary, relationship have forced scholars to reexamine the role of identity in the Mongol Yuan and Manchu Qing dynasties, two of the most successful "conquest dynasties" that, according to sinicization theory, could govern China only by adopting Chinese cultural and political practices. The fine collection of essays in *China under Mongol Rule* convincingly demonstrates the persistence of a distinctly Mongolian identity as well as the cultural interpenetration of the Chinese and Mongolian peoples.[21] And Western analysts working in the field of Qing studies have complicated our understanding of Manchu identity, demonstrating the persistence of a distinct Manchu "ethnic sovereignty" and showing how Manchu identity was central both to the expansion and consolidation of the Qing empire and its ultimate downfall.[22]

On a theoretical level, Pamela Crossley has argued that the circularity of the sinicization concept undermines its analytical usefulness: "To be 'sinicized' was to become 'like the Chinese,' who were only those who have been previously sinicized."[23] In other words, sinicization is premised on a static, unidirectional, and ahistorical understanding of ethnogenesis. Ethnic identity is viewed as a set of objective cultural traits that can be adopted by anyone; yet once eroded, no sense of "genuine" ethnic sentiment can ever return, nor can multiple sources of identity be authentic. Yet as the dramatic rise of ethnic sentiment among the formerly "sinicized" Manchus or the re-emergence of Jewish (*youtai*) identity in China today clearly demonstrates, self-ascribed ethnic identity is highly subjective, resilient, and situationally constructed. When viewed as a dynamic *process* of boundary creation, ethnicity emerges as a powerful heuristic device for understanding social change in a historical context.[24]

The concept of sinicization was central to the culturalism-to-nationalism thesis, which describes the Manchus as "champions of the Chinese way of life" and thus "impervious to attack on a culturalistic basis."[25] Instead, the unprecedented identity crisis caused by Western imperialism forced Chinese nationalists like Liang Qichao to ultimately reject Chinese tradition and embark on the path of modernity. Here nationalism is viewed as a radically novel form of identity, one that breaks down and subdivides the Confucian world order into distinct national entities. Yet, it is important to remember that modern nationalism is not "a unique and unprecedented mode or form of consciousness"; its newness lies in the global system of territory-based nation-states and its insistence that the nation is the only legitimate form of sovereignty.[26] Underlying both the culturalism-to-nationalism and the sinicization thesis is the assumption that imperial China lacked a tradition of ethnocentrism—that Confucian culturalism rendered ethnic difference anathema and any attack on Manchu or other non-Sinic forms of identity was an iconoclastic repudiation of the past. "In order for it to exist as a pure expression of cultural superiority," Prasenjit Duara reminds, "culturalism would have to feel no threat from an Other seeking to obliterate these values. In fact, this threat arose historically on several occasions and produced several reactions from the Chinese literati and populace."[27]

Unburdened of these powerful assumptions, we can discern at least two distinct, yet complementary narratives of political community in imperial China: an inclusive and largely descriptive identity based on culture and an exclusive and ascriptive identity based on ethnic difference.[28] The former served to legitimate the territorial expansionism of the Chinese state under the Han, Yuan, and Qing dynasties and, ultimately, the boundaries of the PRC; the latter contributed to the recurrence and continuity of a distinct Sinic identity throughout the long course of Chinese history. The exclusivist or ethnocentric representation, in the pursuit of social order, stressed the fundamental and unbridgeable gap between *xia* (Chinese) and *yi* (barbarian), while the inclusivist representation, in the pursuit of social totality, emphasized the similarity of all practitioners of Confucian culture regardless of innate physical and environmental differences. In the former narrative, differences in *xing* (nature/essence/disposition) or *qi* (psycho-physical energies) required a strict policy of ethnic segregation; in the latter narrative, the adoption of Chinese ritual behavior (*li*), morality (*de*), and surnames (*xing*) had a transformative effect, breaking down the barriers between barbarism and civility and validating the universalism of the emperor's rule.

One can find textual support for both of these positions in the Chinese philosophical and historical canon, most clearly articulated in the New Text Gongyang (*Gongyang zhuan*) and Old Text Zuo (*Zuo zhuan*) commentaries on the *Spring and Autumn Annals* (*Chunqiu*). Following Mencius' transformative interpretation of Confucianism, the Gongyang asserted that the culturally superior Chinese could absorb the barbarians through a process of *laihua* (come and be transformed) or *hanhua* (becoming Chinese). The Gongyang likewise stressed inclusiveness under the tianxia ideal of *wangzhe wuwai*, or "the King leaves nothing and nobody outside his realm."[29] The Zuo commentary, in contrast, tended to emphasize the unbridgeable chasm between barbarian and Chinese nature and being, stating in one famous line, "If he be not of our kin, he is sure to have a different mind" (*fei wo zulei qi xin bi yi*).[30]

These two competing ideologies fostered a series of different policy options for dealing with the barbarian Other. The inclusivists spoke of "cherishing" (*huairou*) and "assimilating" (hanhua) the barbarians through education and moral leadership, while the exclusivists preferred a *jimi* (loose rein) policy of accommodation and bribery—euphemistically referred to as *longluo* (to win over by all means) or *yinsu erzhi* (to rule by customs)—to maintain the boundary between xia and yi. Both at times advocated military expeditions (*zhenfa*), whether to forcibly bring recalcitrant barbarians into the Chinese cultural and political orb (the inclusivists) or to prevent the barbarians from breeching the Great Wall and raiding the central plains (the exclusivists).

These policy options were first intensely debated during the Han dynasty in relation to the powerful Xiongnu tribal confederation on the Mongolian steppe. After the failure of a military campaign launched by its first emperor, Han Gaozu, the court adopted what it called a *heqin* (peace and kinship) policy toward the Xiongnu. It agreed to grant the Xiongnu fixed annual payments of silk, wine, and grain and to formally recognize the equal status of the Xiongnu *chanyu* (chieftain) through a series of intercourt marriages. Han officials, such as Dong Zhongshu, argued that the Xiongnu could be controlled only by appeasement with the "five baits" (clothing, food, music, buildings, and gifts): their barbarian nature "cannot be converted by humanity and justice, but can only be appeased with huge profit, and tied down with an appeal to Heaven."[31] Others, such as Jia Yi, argued that this policy of bribery violated the tianxia principle, creating a demeaning situation where "the feet are placed above the head,"[32] and insisted that "there is no one in the world that cannot be transformed into the Emperor's subject."[33]

The relationship between these two formulations was complex and firmly rooted in the institutions, literary canon, and historical memory of imperial China. Depending on the specific political and historical context, social actors could draw on either, or a contradictory combination of both, to reify or redraw the boundaries for inclusion or exclusion within the Chinese political community. In other words, both exclusivist ethnocentrism and inclusivist universalism were actively involved in the process of shaping what it meant to be Chinese, ironically giving the periphery a key role in shaping the center and transforming Chinese identity into a "residual category comprised of all those who were not barbarians."[34] In spite of its rhetoric of cultural universalism, imperial China could not and did not exist in isolation. Surrounded by different ethnic and cultural communities, it came to rely on the barbarian Other to constitute and legitimize its own cultural and ethnic identity.[35]

The creation of cultural boundaries between subject and object positions, which possess the potential to harden into exclusive communities of difference, is a key theme running throughout the sociology of identity.[36] Group identity, much like personal identity, is formed through a complex, ongoing negotiation between "us" and "them"—or in the case of imperial China, between the xia and yi. Chinese sensitivities to this "relational alterity" can be traced back as far as

Chuang Tzu who reportedly stated, "If there is no 'other' then we do not have a 'self,' if there is no 'self,' then we do not have anything to grasp."[37] In imperial China, this boundary-marking process helped form a fluid yet distinct premodern Chinese identity. This Sinic political community—loosely bound together by a shared myth of patrilineal descent, sedentary lifestyle, centralized bureaucracy and educational system, standard written language, and common set of ritual practices associated with Confucianism—shifted between a soft position, which allowed passage in and out in accordance with the principle of Confucian universalism, and a hard position, which reified the distinction between xia and yi and accentuated what it meant to be "Chinese."[38]

Over the last couple of decades, the degree of cultural cohesiveness exhibited by premodern Chinese society has been intensively debated. Some have argued that China exhibited a higher degree of cultural uniformity than premodern Europe, explaining at least partially the unique durability of the Chinese state and its socio-political institutions.[39] Others have claimed that below the level of elite state discourse there existed a rich range of cultural practices, or "heteropraxies," that on closer examination seemed to call into question the usefulness of "Chinese culture" as a unitary and objective analytical category.[40] Thus far, however, most of this discussion has focused on the degree of orthopraxy in late imperial Chinese society or its vertical standardization, missing the important role the cultural Other played in demarcating a set of shared values, practices, and norms that were shaped in contrast to the nomadic or swidden lifestyles of those living on the periphery of Chinese society.[41] Over the *longue durée*, this horizontal alterity helped to define the boundaries of a distinct yet mercurial Chinese identity. Furthermore, the structuring of this subject position in the cultural traditions, bureaucratic institutions, and the historical memory of the late imperial state served to underpin, define, and authenticate modern Chinese national identity, both in its more exclusive Han formulation and its more inclusive Zhonghua minzu expression.

The Qing Empire: Imprimatur for the Zhonghua minzu

Recent scholarship on the Manchu Qing dynasty, which some have labeled "new Qing history" or a "Manchu-centered perspective,"[42] has shed new light on the interplay between Confucian universalism and a more narrowly defined Chinese political community. This new research has also helped demonstrate the role of the Qing multiethnic empire in fashioning many of the cultural and linguistic idioms and political institutions and policies available to modern Chinese elites in confronting the national and frontier questions following the collapse of the Qing in 1911. In sharp contrast to previous historiography, these scholars have stressed the centrality of ethnic difference in the formation and operation of the Manchu empire and the important legacy it left twentieth-century intellectuals and policymakers. By placing the Qing empire in the broader context of Asian and world history, they have made clear that the Qing deployed many of the same policies, ideologies, and technologies long associated with European "early modernity," including the ethnic-linguistic cleavage that has been identified as a central factor in the rise of nationalist in Europe and America.[43]

The growing power of the Jurchen tribal confederation in Manchuria produced a shift in late Ming rhetoric on Chinese civilization and identity. Increasingly concerned about the loyalty of the Chinese-speaking inhabitants of the culturally mixed Liaodong reservoir located northeast of the Shanhai Pass in the Great Wall, the Ming state adopted a more exclusivist definition of Chinese identity. It began using genealogical records to distinguish between friend and foe on the frontier, with lineage transformed into proof of identity and loyalty toward the Ming state. The rising Jurchen state, on the other hand, initially downplayed ethnic identity, satisfied to incorporate anyone who would pledge allegiance to the Nurgaci khanate.[44]

After the newly named "Manchu" (*manju*) people toppled the Ming dynasty in 1644, a group of Ming loyalists redeployed the idiom of kinship to challenge the legitimacy of the new Qing dynasty. Wang Fuzhi, perhaps posthumously the most influential of these thinkers on modern Chinese nationalists, transformed the Zuo commentary's dictum on the importance of distinguishing lineages (*zulei*) into a systematic theory of human variation. Wang began his most famous work, *Yellow Book* (*Huang shu*), by denying the existence of any physical or emotional differences between the barbarians and Chinese: "The Chinese are like the barbarians insofar as their general physical characteristics are similar and they are both subject to assemblies and divisions, but the Chinese cannot be put in the same category as the barbarians. Why is this?"[45] Wang looked to nature rather than culture for his answer.

He argued that the barbarians and the Chinese were of fundamentally different xing (nature) and *zhi* (substance), as man was from horse and snow was from jade, which was passed from one generation to the next and resulted in different moralities and cultural customs. Like the Tang scholar Du You and the Song thinker Chen Liang before him, Wang Fuzhi believed that one's xing and zhi were environmentally determined. "The Chinese and the barbarians are born in different lands," Wang wrote in 1656, "and these different lands have dissimilar qi which produces separate customs, and finally different customs result in discrepancies in understanding and behavior."[46] Wang contended that the Chinese inhabitants of the central plains were composed of "heavenly qi" (*tianqi*) while the frontier barbarians were fashioned of "impure qi" (*jianqi*). Furthermore, the "purity of categories" (*qinglei*) could be maintained only through the creation of firm territorial boundaries between these dissimilar natures.

Wang did not completely deny the possibility of transformation. He believed that different lineages were at different levels of human development; and while progress moved all societies upward, they retained their respective places on this "escalator" of human development—with the immoral barbarians and the cultivated Chinese divided by an unbridgeable gap of historical time.[47] Moreover, all species, from humans to insects, aim to protect and perpetuate their own kind: "It is because if man does not draw lines of demarcation in order to set himself apart from other creatures, the order of Heaven is violated." As Wang explained in the *Yellow Book*, "if the Chinese do not draw lines of demarcation in order to set themselves apart from the barbarians, terrestrial order is violated."[48] In other words, if separation was not maintained between the Chinese and the Manchus, conflict was inevitable; for different lineages would naturally endeavor to destroy each other in order to preserve their own position of power. Because of the drive toward self-preservation, Wang concluded that when the natural divide had been breeched (as was the case under Manchu rule), "it was not inhumane to exterminate them [the barbarians]; it was not unrighteous to rise in force against them; and it was not unfaithful to beguile them."[49]

Members of the Manchu court attempted to discredit Wang Fuzhi and other Ming loyalists by demonstrating their own Confucian credentials. Early in its rule over China proper, the court decided to retain the Ming civil administration and its examination system and began to actively patronize the Chinese arts and literature. Under the Kangxi emperor, Confucian ethics and cultural practices were normalized and institutionalized at a local level in the former Ming territories. With the distribution of thirty million copies of the moral maxims contained in the emperor's *Sacred Edict* in 1670 and the staging of bimonthly public lectures on its significance, the Manchus attempted to bridge the gap between elite and popular culture in China proper. In so doing, they greatly strengthened the sense of common Sinic identity among the sedentary inhabitants of the empire.[50] As a result, by the end of the sixteenth century the literati establishment came to accept Manchu rule as legitimate. With the precedent of Mongol rule in the not so distant past, they adopted the rhetoric of universalism, stressing that culture rather than ethnicity defined the boundaries of Chinese rulership over the central plains.[51]

On the steppe and desert lands of Central Asia, the Manchus looked to the Mongols for a model of state formation and rulership, one that enabled them to amass an empire rivaled only by that of the Great Khubilai Khan.[52] By 1780, the Qing had more than doubled the size of Ming territory and established (with a few exceptions) the current boundaries of the PRC. Qing innovation was one of the keys to the success of this colonial project—for example, the banner system (*baqi zhidu*) enabled fewer than two million "conquest elites" to establish and control this massive empire of over four hundred million subjects for nearly four hundred years.[53] And the Manchus were at their most creative in the realm of ideology. As Pamela Crossley has demonstrated, the Qing emperors were master impersonators, adopting different "personas" to legitimize their rule over multiple imperial constituencies. Following successful military campaigns in southern China (1683), Mongolia (1690), Tibet (1720), Kokonor (1723), and Turkestan (1757), the Qianlong emperor drew together five major constituencies—today reified as the Han, Manchu, Mongol, Hui, and Tibetan nationalities—into a single, multicultural empire.[54] While members of the Manchu court adopted the name *Da Qing* (Great Qing) for their empire, they also consciously identified themselves with the historically potent concept of Zhongguo/China, using the terms interchangeably and thereby encouraging both Western and Chinese elites to view Qing boundaries as markers of "Chinese territory" and its subjects as "Chinese subjects."[55] The Qing, as Laura Hostetler and others have shown, were aware not only of the rich diversity within their empire but also of "their own kingdom's position as one country located on a finite globe," and they set about engraving the boundaries of their rule on stone tablets as well as canvas maps.[56]

What distinguished Qing universalism from earlier Chinese notions of culturalism and from the multiculturalism of twentieth-century China was the court's insistence on maintaining the ethnic and political boundaries between its imperial constituencies. In the normative ideal, the cultural superiority of Zhongguo draws non-Chinese peoples toward the center and transforms them in the image of the emperor. Yet under the Qing, especially its great Qianlong emperor, different cultures and languages were not only preserved but actively promoted by the imperial court. In other words, the Qing empire was not sinocentric, as represented by the map of concentric rings found in the tenth-century BCE *Tribute of Yu* (*Yugong*), but rather emperor-centric, as symbolized by a five-spoke Buddhist spinning wheel (*Dhamachakra*) with the emperor at the center and his moral authority radiating outward. In sharp contrasted to the "melting-pot" style of multinationality on display in China today, the Qing attempted to fix and naturalize these ethnic boundaries by imposing different legal and governance structures, collecting and maintaining genealogical records, and promoting different cultural practices.[57] Somewhat paradoxically, the exclusivist loose rein (jimi) and rule by customs (yinsu erzhi) policies helped maintain the internal boundaries of Qing culturalism and contributed to its overall stability.

The Manchu court was quick to learn and adopt the Chinese language in its rule over China proper. Yet the written and spoken languages of the other four constituencies were also cultivated and used to administer their territories and peoples. The emperor, as the hub of this multiethnic empire, made an effort to master the five main languages (Chinese, Manchu, Mongolian, Tibetan, and Uyghur) of his realm, and had their scripts etched on important markers of the empire, such as the main gate at the imperial palace at Chengde. In fact, this imperial retreat and the imperial hunting ground at Mulan served as "a practical and symbolic command center" for Manchu rule over their Central Asian domains.[58] In replicating the key cultural monuments and landscapes of China, Tibet, and Central Asia, Chengde provided a microcosm of the empire where subjects could feel at home while appreciating the grandeur of the Qing emperor and presenting their "tribute." To regulate the visits of Central Asian leaders and ensure the preservation of their cultural traditions, the Qing created a unique administrative organ, the Lifanyuan (Court of Colonial Affairs). Staffed purely by banner officials, the Lifanyuan was responsible for managing all the court's relations with Central Asia, from appointments to religious and cultural affairs.[59]

The Qing also cultivated different forms of rulership to legitimate their hegemony over their imperial constituencies: a Confucian monarch among the Chinese; a "divine lord" among the Manchus; a "great khan" among the Mongols; and Manjusri, the Bodhisattva of Wisdom, among the Tibetans. Only the prohibition against nonbelievers acting as patrons in Islam prevented the Muslims of Central Asia from being fully incorporated under the Qing system of cosmological universalism.[60] Such cultivation of Islam, Confucianism, and, perhaps most important, Buddhism played a pivotal role in the consolidation and naturalization of the Qing empire. With the authority to appoint and dismiss banner officials in Mongolia, begs in Central Asia, and reincarnated lamas in Tibet, the Qing count exercised direct administrative control over its vast empire while its system of banner garrisons dealt harshly with any acts of disloyalty. These institutions were crucial to transforming the Manchu confederation into a stable empire, redirecting loyalties toward a central Qing subjecthood and away from shifting regional and ethnic ones.[61] With the non-Chinese peoples of the south, the Qing instead encouraged assimilation and the establishment of Chinese institutions, though not with total success. As such, they denied its "motley throng" the legitimacy of an imperial constituency worthy of preservation.[62]

Vastly outnumbered by their Chinese subjects, the Manchus found it increasingly difficult to preserve their cultural identity. The largely sedentary life of occupation gradually eroded the "Manchu way" (*Manjusai doro*) of archery, horse riding, frugality, and Manchu language use, leading the court to regularly chastise bannermen for forgetting the customs of their ancestors. At the same time, the fluid nature of banner identity and the material rewards of membership (which included a monthly silver and grain stipend) encouraged an increasing number of "false Manchus" to attach themselves to the system during the seventeenth century, creating a major financial crisis for the Qing state. In response, the court took a page out of Wang Fuzhi's *Yellow Book* and began emphasizing genealogical descent as the ultimate marker of banner identity. In 1727 the Yongzheng emperor launched a major reorganization of the banner registry, using genealogical records to weed out impersonators.[63] The Qianlong emperor took this cleanup a step further in 1742, expelling all members of the Eight Chinese Banners (*baqi hanjun*), a group of transfrontiersmen who had participated in the Manchu conquest but were now declared to be "Chinese in origin" and hence unworthy of banner membership. Lineage had long served as a marker of identity in China, but these reforms marked an important turning point in the use of genealogies to create more rigidly fixed "racial typologies."[64] Tianxia universalism legitimized the external boundaries of the empire over the lands of the five constituencies, while narratives of descent increasingly marked the internal boundaries between the Manchu, Han, Mongol, Tibet, and Hui peoples.

By institutionalizing genealogy as the primary marker of identity, the Qing court provided "both a literature of descent and a political imprimatur for racial thinking."[65] This new discourse of race flourished during the late nineteenth century and ultimately contributed to the downfall of the Qing empire. As the court grappled with internal decay and foreign imperialism, its opponents mapped this new language of kinship onto the rich tradition of ethnocentrism to label the Manchus an alien, barbarian race. The Taiping rebels were perhaps the first group of modern Chinese nationalists to refer to the Manchus as a "race of demons," with Manchu emperor Xianfeng tagged a "Tartar dog" of "barbarian origins."[66] Even more serious was the challenge posed by the biological metaphor of "blood" and the Darwinian "law of natural selection," when the new idiom of minzu entered China around the turn of the century.

Racial Revolution: Whither the Minzu?

The increased threat of Western imperialism following the Opium War and the ineffectiveness of the Manchu court in stemming the decline of the empire following the Taiping Rebellion created a crisis of political authority in Qing China. A new generation of intellectuals responded to it in different ways. Some identified Western imperialism (*fandi*) as the major challenge; others focused on the incompetent nature of Manchu rule (*paiman*), arguing that reform was impossible without first removing the Manchu court.

This political crisis was accompanied by an epistemological shift in how difference was conceptualized in China. While the inclusivist and exclusivist formulations were revived and reformulated by Chinese nationalists, the ideological structures and accompanying discursive terrain altered. The introduction of the originally Western concept of biologically constituted "races" (minzu, renzhong, or zhongzu) set within a global system of territorial-bounded and naturally competitive race-states (guozu) significantly altered Chinese thinking on ethnic difference. Western forms of classification did not replace or supplant indigenous belief systems per say; but rather reaffirmed traditional sinocentrism while reconfiguring and reifying the boundaries of ethnic identity in modern China: first, they reinforced age-old stereotypes and biases against the non-sedentary peoples of the bianjiang (frontier); second, they transformed Han racial identity (Hanzu)—which itself was codified from the empire's Sinic cultural community—into the demographic and political core of a newly bounded guozu (race-state); and finally, they recast the non-Sinic constituencies of the Qing empire as evolutionarily unfit shaoshu minzu (minority nationals) set firmly within the territorial confines of a fully sovereign Zhonghua minzu (Chinese race/nation).

The globally circulating discourse of race served as the "knowledge system" through which modern Chinese intellectuals viewed the dual challenge of dynastic decay and foreign imperialism.[67] Guided by social Darwinism, Chinese elites came to see the world as divided into immutable, biologically based racial groups who were locked in a fierce struggle for physical survival as they competed for limited resources. And unlike the more speculative cosmologies of difference in imperial China, these new technologies of classification were supported by "empirical" data supplied by modern "scientific" disciplines: biology, sociology, history, geography, ethnology, archaeology and others. In the episteme of modern science, the heterodoxy of environmental qi (psycho-physical energies) gave way to the orthodoxy of consanguineous *xue* (blood) as the boundary between civility (xia) and barbarism (yi) hardened.

The science of race was predicated on a new notion of human history—a linear story of racial evolution undergone by different races at different rates. Indeed, Darwin's theory of evolution seemed to prove that some races were ill-suited to or even incapable of advancing history. Some argued that only the world's "historical nations," those with a clearly defined territory, dynamic economy, and large population, could evolve independently toward progress and civilization. Thus the large territorial state—what became known as the "nation-state" in the West and the guozu or minzu in China—became the only authentic expression of sovereignty; and its imperialist oppression of the hapless and backward "ahistorical races"—what Engels once termed "ethnic trash" (*Völkerabfall*) destine for the dustbin of history—was legitimated.[68] The once dark and remote frontiers became the new laboratory and battleground of human progress.

In China, Darwin's message underscored the importance of an impending "racial war" (*zhongzhan*) among the world's historical populations. In his highly influential 1895 essay, "Whence Strength?" (*Yuan qiang*), the eminent translator Yan Fu introduced the key ideas behind Herbert Spencer's multivolume *Principles of Sociology* in the wake of China's humiliating defeat at the hands of its former vassal state Japan. Yan Fu explained how Spencer used Darwin's biological organism as a paradigm for society: "When a *qun* (group or society) is formed, it is in body, function, and capability no different from the body of a living thing. . . . If we know what keeps our own bodies alive, we will know what makes a qun secure."[69] Yan Fu was convinced that both group and biological survival hinged on what he called "group solidarity" (*qunzhuyi*, literally, "groupism"): unity, he stressed to his readers, was the key to progress, evolutionary survival, and the acquisition of wealth and power. Early twentieth-century Chinese intellectuals therefore asked themselves, What qun shall we unite: the Han or the Manchu, the Hunanese or the Cantonese, the Chinese or the entire yellow race? In other words, where should the boundaries of the minzu be drawn? Naturally, this key question elicited a variety of responses as Chinese nationalists tried to come to terms with the potential "death of the state and extinction of the race" (*wangguo miezhong*).

Sun Yat-sen, who is today honored as the "father of the nation" (*guofu*) on both sides of the Taiwan Straits, was one of the first to identify the Sinic population of the former Ming dynasty—the Huaren (Hua people) in his initial terminology—as the group that mattered most in this evolutionary struggle. Sun established his first revolutionary organization, the *Xingzhonghui* (Revive China Society), in 1894 and called on its members to swear a secret oath to "drive out the Tartar caitiffs and restore China" (*quchu dalu huifu Zhongguo*). This represented a slight revision of the slogan, "expel the northern barbarians and restore China" (*quzhu hulu fuxing Zhonghua*) that was used by the founder of the Ming dynasty, Zhu Yuanzhang, as he sought to overthrow the Mongol Yuan dynasty. The Xingzhonghui's charter stressed the incompetence and corruption of Qing rule while echoing Wang Fuzhi in identifying the Manchus as a "different lineage" (*yizu*) from the majority of the Chinese people (Huaren). Initially, at least, Sun's rationale for overthrowing the Qing rested chiefly on the belief that the Manchu court had lost the "mandate of heaven" (*tianming*) by abandoning the Confucian rites and morality of the Han, Tang, and Ming dynasties.[70]

The new discourse of race was applied to Sun's call for revolution by another group of Chinese nationalists, active in the Yangtze River delta cities of Shanghai and Hangzhou. They attacked the Manchus as belonging to a fundamentally and immutably different race than the vast majority of the Chinese people. In his 1900 *Qiushu* (*Book of Persecution*), Zhang Binglin merged the Qing discourse of "distinguishing lineages" (*bian zulei*) with the social evolutionist metaphor of blood (xue) to contend that the Chinese subjects of the Qing empire, whom he called the Hanzu (Han race), shared a common biological lineage. The sacred consanguinity of the Hanzu was rooted in their unbroken descent from the Yellow Emperor (Huangdi), the first ancestor of the Chinese people. Zhang also claimed that the "Manchu race" (*Manzhouzu*), an uncivilized race descended from the *Donghu* (eastern barbarians) of the Jin dynasty, was attempting to usurp the "heirship" (*zongzi*) of the Hanzu by systematically destroying its racial consciousness through the institutionalization of alien customs and practices like the queue hairstyle.[71] In 1903, the publication of "Gemingjun" ("Revolutionary Army") in the popular Shanghai newspaper *Subao* by the eighteen-year-old radical Zou Rong helped to simplify and popularize Zhang's message among the increasingly nationalistic Chinese youth. Zou Rong's subsequent imprisonment by the Manchu authorities and tragic death in prison quickly fueled increasingly violent calls for "racial revolution" (*minzu geming*) in Qing China.[72]

This battle cry did not go unchallenged. Manchu reformers and their supporters stressed the fundamental unity of the five constituencies of the empire, pointing out that they were a "single family," "different branches of a single tree," or even equal "citizens."[73] These reformers were the first to urge that the Qianlong emperor's multiconstituency empire be transformed into a modern, multiethnic nation-state, what they termed a *wuzu gonghe* (republic of five races).[74] But the most vocal advocate was Liang Qichao, the young Cantonese intellectual who was also the principal disciple of Darwin in China. Liang believed that Zhang Binglin and other racial nationalists were focusing on the wrong group. The differences between the Manchus and the Han paled in significance next to those between the imperialist West and China. Through his prolific journalism, Liang attempted to redirect public attention to what he believed was the crux of evolutionary struggle—the impending battle between the yellow and white races and in particular, its two strongest racial cores: the Chinese and the Teutons.

In his 1903 call for a "new historiography" (*xinshixue*), Liang Qichao coined the term guozu to describe what he saw as the highest stage of human evolutionary struggle: the conflict between large, territorially distinct race-states that have already made their mark on history by engulfing inferior, "ahistorical races" (*feilishi de renzhong*).[75] China's guozu, though at the center of this current contest, suffered from the lack of a single name, with Liang noting that in the past China was identified by various dynastic designations—Zhuxia, Han, and Tang—rather than by a consistent national designation. To correct this shortcoming, Liang began employing the terms Zhongguo minzu (Chinese race/nation), Zhongguo zhongzu (Chinese race), and eventually Zhonghua minzu to refer to this new subject of a linear national history in China.[76]

In his own systematic inquiry into Chinese history,[77] Liang identified six races (renzhong)—the Miao, Han, Tibetans, Mongols, Xiongnu (Sino-Muslim inhabitants of Xinjiang), and Tungus (Manchus)—as active subjects throughout the spatiotemporal scope of the Chinese geo-body. Here he notably expanded the Qing taxonomy to include the Miao, a catchall for the numerous southern indigenes left out of the Qing fivefold classificatory system. Liang rejected the notion of racial purity and argued that each of these races shared a long history of intermarriage, and their mixed blood created a single Chinese minzu. Yet the destiny of these races clearly rested with the four-hundred-million-strong Hanzu—what Liang would later call the "backbone" (*gugan*) of the Zhonghua minzu—the largest and most culturally advanced of them.[78] Despite their backwardness, the other five racial elements helped forge the spatial boundaries of the Chinese minzu, which Liang argued included five distinct yet geographically interlinked sections: China proper, Xinjiang, Qinghai and Tibet, Mongolia and Manchuria.[79] The introduction of Western geography and the proliferation of Western-style maps helped to appropriate and naturalize the boundaries of the multiethnic Qing empire into the historic typography of China. If races were the actors in the modernist drama of world history, national territory served as its stage, resulting in a definition of China that was as much spatial as it was racial.[80]

As early as 1898, Liang stressed the importance of racial mixing to China's evolutionary survival, noting that "racial improvement arises from the amalgamation of many different races."[81] The future of the Chinese minzu could be guaranteed only by the continued melding of inferior races, such as the Manchus, into its superior Han core. Liang was one of the first Chinese intellectuals to urge the Qing court to "tear down the boundaries between Manchu and Han" (*ping Man-Han zhijie*). And the court's reform efforts—in particular the February 1902 edict lifting the ban on Han-Manchu intermarriage—led him to assert that the Manchus were "completely assimilated" (*yijin tonghua*), thus invalidating the revolutionaries' claims about the alien nature of the Manchu court.[82] As Peter Zarrow points out, Liang subverted the Western notion of racial purity by insisting on their fundamental mutability, putting the concept minzu to work in justifying his vision of an inclusive, multiethnic Chinese state.[83]

Liang found another source of support for the unity of the Chinese minzu in the work of the Swiss legalist Johann Bluntschli. In 1903, Liang pointed to the important distinction between the legal concept of *guomin* (citizenry) and the ethnological term minzu in Bluntschli's *Theory of the Modern State* (*Lehre vom modernen Staat*, 1875–76) and particularly embraced Bluntschli's observation that a guomin need not contain only a single minzu. Liang used this notion to criticize the "petty minzuzhuyi" (*xiao minzuzhuyi*) contained within Zhang Binglin's racist anti-Manchuism and to call instead for a "broad minzuzhuyi" (*da minzuzhuyi*). China's very survival, Liang wrote, "requires us to adopt imperialist tactics to unite the Han, Manchu, Mongol, Hui, Miao and Tibetan peoples in constituting a single large minzu with the Han at its core."[84] Liang's ultimate goal, according to Pamela Crossley, "was not a Chinese republic, but a Chinese national empire"[85]—what he viewed as a liberal and progressive type of "national imperialism" (*minzu diguozhuyi*) that would see the mighty Han people dominate and eventually assimilate the weaker, ahistorical races on the environmental margins of the Chinese geo-body. Thus, at the center of what many have termed Liang's civic or state nationalism, there remained an essentialized racial core, complicating (in the case of China, at least) the popular analytical distinction between civic and ethnic nationalism.

Though scholars have generally viewed Liang and Sun Yat-sen as leading figures in opposing camps, dividing late Qing intellectuals into "reformers" and "revolutionaries,"[86] their essays and speeches on nationalism are in fact uncannily similar in their language and conclusions. Both men feared the destructive potential of Zhang Binglin's "racial revengism" (*zhongzu fuchou zhuyi*) and saw the struggle against Western imperialism as China's key battle for racial survival. Liang's "broad minzuzhuyi" clearly resonated with Sun's vision for the future; yet Sun could not accept Liang's assessment that the Manchus had already been assimilated by the Han majority. To do so would obviate the need for revolution—the Xingzhonghui's stated goal.[87]

Whereas Zhang defined the nation narrowly, Sun seemed to favor a more inclusive, spatial representation of China, and like Liang Qichao, he placed the Sinic community at its racial, cultural, and geographic core. Unlike Liang, Sun envisioned a Chinese-dominated state in the form of a republic rather than a constitutional monarchy. Yet its boundaries would be the same as those of the monarchy, as spatially imagined by Sun in a 1899 map of "contemporary China" that he drew up while in exile in Japan.[88] Only a couple of years after pledging to "drive out the Tartar caitiffs and restore China,"[89] Sun proposed a massive system of railway lines that would physically bind Qing territory together into a new "Chinese" geo-body. This vast network of railways—what he once termed "the arteries (*mingmai*) of the nation"[90]—intricately wove "central China" (*Zhina benbu*) together with the Manchu, Mongol, Uyghur, Tibetan, and East Turkestan "dependencies" (*dishu*), creating a series of red lines that spread out on the map like the veins of a new, fully bounded national body. Sun continued to develop his infrastructure plan for China after the 1911 Revolution, eventually calling for one hundred thousand miles of railway tracks, one million miles of bitumen roads, and an equally immense telephone and telegraph network that would facilitate a massive "cultivation and colonization" (*fuzhi zhimin*) scheme aimed at bringing thousands of landless Chinese peasants and decommissioned soldiers onto the frontier in the name of "national development."[91] In other words, the emperor had to go, but the empire, or at least its territory, was to remain.

The revolutionary movement to overthrow the Qing dynasty coalesced in 1905 with the formation of a new "revolutionary alliance," the Tongmenghui. Though Sun Yat-sen was its nominal leader, it drew together a variety of provincial-based revolutionary groups with radically different ideas about the composition and future direction of the Chinese minzu. Attempting to seize early control of its direction, Sun proposed "three great isms" (*sandazhuyi*) as the guiding ideology of the new organization: *minzuzhuyi* (literally, "the doctrine of the people's lineage"), *minquanzhuyi* ("the doctrine of the people's sovereignty"), and *minshengzhuyi* ("the doctrine of the people's livelihood").[92] They established a set of concrete yet vaguely defined goals: the elimination of the Manchus and the restoration of China, the establishment of a republic, and the equalization of land.[93] The task of expanding these sweeping goals into a systematic ideology was left to Sun's trusted Cantonese lieutenants, Wang Jingwei, Hu Hanmin, Zhu Zhixin, and Feng Ziyou, in their capacity as editors of the Tongmenghui's mouthpiece, *Minbao*. During the first year of *Minbao*'s existence, overseen by Sun, these men crafted what came to be known as the Three Principles of the People (*sanminzhuyi*). In several ways the task of theorizing minzuzhuyi proved most difficult. The entire Tongmenghui agreed on the need to overthrow the Manchu Qing dynasty, yet there was little consensus on the significance and future of the various non-Han peoples within the new republic.

On one end of the spectrum, Zhang Binglin and Zou Rong were among those apparently advocating a racially homogeneous Han republic, arguing that "it is impossible for two minzus to stand side-by-side under a single government."[94] In *Revolutionary Army*, Zou Rong urged the Han to forcibly expel the Manchus from China (or even better, exterminate their entire race), while Zhang Binglin declared in 1907 that "if the Muslim chiefs' hatred for the Manchus has so penetrated them to the bone that they extend their grudge to us, and fiercely desire independence to restore the domains of their Turkic ancestors, then we should give in to their desires, knowing they but look on us as we look on the Manchus."[95] There is, in fact, reason to suspect that Zhang and other extremists were ambivalent at best about the breakup of the empire; nevertheless, their rhetoric suggested to many that Qing territory should be divided up into a series of small race-states with the core provinces of the Ming dynasty reserved for the Han.[96]

At the opposite extreme, some were drawn to Liang Qichao's call for the fusion of all China's races into a single Zhonghua minzu pastiche. Liang argued that Western and Eastern scholars alike recognize the historical strength of China's "assimilationist powers" (*tonghuali*). The Manchus, like the Jurchen and Mongols before them, had already been drawn into Chinese civilization and transformed. In order for China's remaining races—the Han, Mongols, Tibetans, Hui, and Miao—to construct a strong, democratic state, it was necessary for all of them to be "smelted together in the same furnace" (*rong er ru yu yilu*) as the Han majority continued to serve as the cultural and racial core of the new Zhonghua minzu. During his visit to the United States in 1903, Liang had been struck by America's efforts to assimilate its immigrant population into a single national melting pot. Now back in China, he became convinced that China's evolutionary survival required the creation of a similarly mixed guozu.[97]

Sun Yat-sen's own position on this question seems unclear, if not contradictory. The Chinese academic Yu Xintun has argued that Sun contemplated trading Manchuria and Mongolia to the Japanese in exchange for material assistance for his revolutionary movement. In 1906, Sun's close friend Tōyama Mitsuru, who was one of the leaders of the ultranationalist Black Dragon Society (*kokuryū -kai*), claimed that Sun had offered Manchuria and Mongolia as a bargaining chip for Japanese support in establishing a Chinese republic south of the Great Wall. This offer, it is suggested, eventually resulted in a concrete proposal by Japanese officials to buy these two dependencies for between ten to twenty million yen in 1912.[98] Yet nothing in Sun's voluminous collected works suggests that he ever seriously considered directing the breakup of the Qing empire; if he did, it was likely only a short-term political strategy for removing the Manchus. Certainly by 1913, as will be discussed, Sun and other Chinese nationalists were actively fighting to preserve the empire's territory.

Unlike the extremists, Sun Yat-sen appeared to envision an inclusive nationalism, one that would bind the Chinese people together in their struggle against white imperialism. In a Tokyo speech before six thousand Chinese expatriates in 1906, Sun cautioned against violent and destructive racial vengeance: "I have heard claims among our brothers that the minzu revolution aims to exterminate the Manchus as a minzu. This is utterly mistaken." Sun continued, "We do not hate the Manchus per se, but only those Manchus who are harming the Han. If, when we achieve the aims of our revolution, the Manchus do not oppose us or do us harm, there will be no reason for us to fight against them."[99] He stressed instead that "minzuzhuyi certainly does not mean that whenever people meet a person of a different minzu they exclude them, but rather that they do not permit a person of a different minzu to steal their minzu's sovereignty."[100] Returning political authority to the hands of the Han majority did not preclude a republic that contained the Manchus and other frontier indigenes.

But while Sun Yat-sen and other moderates within the Tongmenghui had no problem with Liang Qichao's call for the assimilation of the evolutionarily unfit minorities, accepting his entire formula would nullify the very foundation of revolutionary activism: the need to overthrow the Manchu dynasty. Sun's predicament hinged on the need to exclude the Manchus from political power in order to legitimate the establishment of a Han-dominated republic while still inheriting the territorial boundaries and by extension the various ethnic polities of the Qing empire.[101]

The difficult task of squeezing Sun's minzuzhuyi between the racial exclusionism of Zhang Binglin and the spatial inclusionism of Liang Qichao fell to Sun's most trusted polemist, Wang Jingwei. In a long two-part article, "A Minzu of Citizens," Wang tackled the meaning of Sun's minzuzhuyi. He began his discussion by accepting Bluntschli's distinction between the legal concept of guomin and the ethnological term minzu and then asking whether it was necessary for a single minzu to constitute a single guomin.[102] Wang answered this question by arguing that the world's most evolutionarily fit states were those composed of only a single, pure minzu. Only a racially homogeneous state, Wang contended, could completely ensure equality and freedom. Members of the same minzu shared innate feelings of fraternity toward one another. Wang called this "natural equality" (*tianran zhi pingdeng*), inverting the classic Zuo commentary dictum, "If he be not of our kin, he is sure to have a different mind " to contend that those of the same minzu were of a single mind and thus naturally inclined to protect their freedom. It was this natural inclination, Wang told his readers, that served as the basis for Sun Yat-sen's principle of minzuzhuyi. Natural equality could be suppressed but never eliminated.

At this point, Sun's minzuzhuyi differed little in its goals from a racially homogeneous state mapped out by Zhang Binglin. Yet Wang went on to explicitly criticize the narrow racial revengism of Zhang while echoing Liang Qichao's call for the assimilation of all Chinese minzus into a single "minzu of citizens" (*minzu de guomin*). Where Wang disagreed with Liang was not on the need to assimilate China's frontier minorities, but rather on the current state of this evolutionary process. The bulk of his long essay is devoted to examples demonstrating that the Manchus not only have preserved their own language, customs, and bloodline, but also have attempted to assimilate the Han by destroying their minzu consciousness. The process of natural selection was gradual, and it still had not run its course in China. Because they were inhibiting the natural process of assimilation, the Manchu rulers needed to be removed from power.

This more inclusivist discourse of racial amalgamation (*minzu tonghua* or *minzu ronghe*), as institutionalized in Sun Yat-sen's principle of minzuzhuyi, provided the ideological structure that shaped how both the Chinese Nationalist Party and the Communist Party approached the problem of ethnic diversity following the collapse of the Qing empire. The formulation's unique authority lies in its apparent scientific empiricism and its ability to, first, reinforce and authenticate the old ethnocentric distinction between a civilized Sinic Self and a barbarian Other to, second, reimagine the Chinese world order as a natural and evolutionary process whereby the Self and the Other are organically fused into a new spatially delineated form of *Chinese* universalism.

For most, if not all twentieth-century Chinese intellectuals, social Darwinism provided not only a scientific framework for analyzing social diversity and change but also a new constitutive discourse to replace the crumbling imperial cosmology. Just as Confucius had once argued that the frontier barbarians needed to adopt "Chinese ways" to become human and participate in the universal cosmology (tianxia), Darwin now seemed to be telling Chinese intellectuals that the small, weak, and environmentally disadvantaged races of the margins of the Qing empire needed an infusion of Han blood to survive and remain part of world historical progress. It was blood, Sun Yat-sen concluded in 1924, that was the most powerful force in minzu formation and the key to evolutionary survival. "Since the blood of one's ancestors is always transmitted by heredity down through the minzu," Sun asserted, "bloodline (*xuetong*) is the greatest force."[103]

For Chinese nationalists such as Sun Yat-sen and Liang Qichao, the significance of blood was closely related to population size. Passing one's blood, and by extension culture, to future generations was a decisive factor in determining the difference between those that perish and those that survive. It was precisely because their populations were small and comparatively insignificant that the Mongol, Tibetan, and other peoples on the fringes of the Qing empire had no choice but to physically meld together with the numerically and culturally superior Han Chinese. When Sun noticed the relative decline of the Han population in comparison to the other leading race-states, he was quick to stress that "just like the Miao, Yao and other indigenous Chinese people, whose ancestral sacrifices of blood and food have long ago been severed, if we [Han] do not broaden our horizons and use the strength of all our lineages (*zongzu*) to form a single guozu in resisting the foreigners, our ancestors might some day find themselves without sacrifices."[104] Among turn-of-the-century Chinese nationalists, social Darwinism (with its interrelated discourses of race, nation, and history) served to reconstitute imperial China's Sinic cultural core into a consanguineous Han race and through its inevitable absorption of the Qing ethnic penumbra, they believed it would create a new composite and evolutionarily superior race-state.

The Republic of Five Races: Emergence of the Frontier and National Questions

The latent tension between the spatial boundaries of the empire and the homogeneous requirements of the minzu became obvious following the collapse of the Qing. The nearly fifty years of anti-Manchu rhetoric since the Taiping Rebellion ensured that once full-fledged revolution broke out in October 1911, a significant amount of bloodshed was inevitable. As armed conflict spread, tens of thousands of Manchu bannermen and officials became the target of angry revolutionaries seeking racial revenge, and in several cities this racial bigotry extended to other non-Han peoples. But within a couple of months, more conservative forces associated with the New Army and the provincial gentry joined forces with the revolutionaries in calling for an end to the violence.[105]

Surrounded by hostile imperial powers intent on carving out spheres of influence on the decaying Chinese geo-body, nationalist leaders of nearly all political persuasions in China concluded that the minzu's survival depended on retaining the territorial boundaries of the Qing empire. When representatives of the various revolutionary factions gathered in Shanghai on December 4, there was a marked shift in their rhetoric as they began working toward a more encompassing, multiethnic coalition that would peacefully inherit the territorial boundaries and peoples of the Qing empire. Revolutionary leaders started to echo those reformers within the Manchu court who had called for the creation of a republic of five races, and they proposed to symbolize this union with a new five-color flag that included red, yellow, blue, white, and black stripes to represent the Han, Manchu, Mongol, Hui, and Tibetan peoples respectively. The presence of Zhang Binglin and other leading anti-Manchuists among the diverse group of delegates that attended the Shanghai meeting reflected the near universal acceptance of this new, more inclusive language.[106]

After establishing a provisional government at Nanjing on January 1, 1912, the leaders of the new Zhonghua Republic (*Zhonghua minguo*) were quick to stress the territorial integrity of the new state. In his inaugural address as provisional president, Sun Yat-sen emphasized the importance of racial and territorial unity:

> The foundation of the state lies in the people's ability to unite the Han, Manchu, Mongol, Hui and Tibetan territories into a single country (*yiguo*) and to unite the Han, Manchu, Mongol, Hui, Tibetan races into a single people (*yiren*). This is called minzu unity. Since the Wuhan Uprising ten provinces have successively declared their independence; yet, this so-called independence represents only a breaking away from the Qing court through alliance with other provinces. The desire of Mongolia and Tibet is the same. The entire movement represents not a divergence, but rather a movement toward the center, and a consolidation of the four corners of China. This is territorial unity.[107]

To help shore up this fragile unity, the provisional Senate acted quickly to approve the five-color banner as the new national flag, which remained in use until the Guomindang Central Government was established by Chiang Kai-shek in 1928. In February, the Foreign Ministry issued a promulgation to all foreign ambassadors in China declaring that Manchuria, Xinjiang, Tibet, and Mongolia were integral parts of the territory of the new Chinese state, a stipulation written into Article 3 of the republic's provisional constitution in March.[108]

In a deal to secure the peaceful abdication of the last Manchu emperor, the revolutionaries agreed that the former Qing prime minister, Yuan Shikai, should be appointed the first president of the Republic and consented to a series of laws protecting the property, livelihood, and political equality of the Manchus and other ethnic minorities.[109] The abdication edict, which was drafted by the republicans and revised by Yuan, transferred Qing sovereignty to the entire minzu and stressed the desire of the Qing emperor that the "territories of the five racial groups—Manchu, Mongol, Han, Muslim, and Tibetan—would unite to form one great Republic of China."[110] President Yuan followed the edict up with his own proclamation, stating that "the Republic is composed of five racial groups—all of Mongol, Tibet and the Hui areas are the territory of the Republic, and the Mongol, Tibetan, and Hui people of Xinjiang are all citizens of the Republic."[111]

The president's elaborate inauguration ceremony in March 1912 served as a highly visual representation of this new union, with delegates of each of the five minzus bowing before Yuan Shikai and the five-color national flag while foreign representatives looked on in a carefully staged display of the Republic's inheritance of the former Qing empire's territory and subjects. In sharp contrast, the Wuhan revolutionaries had made more traditional sacrificial offerings to the Yellow Emperor as they recited a military anthem calling on the Han to seek racial vengeance on the Manchus.[112] Rather than exterminate the Manchus and other non-Han peoples, the Republican state now called for their betrothal, with a new presidential proclamation overturning the Qing ban on racial intermarriage and actively encouraging the five minzus to meld together into a single minzu.[113]

In the end, all these lofty pronouncements could not smooth over the deep regional fissures that were opening up beneath the fragile surface of the Qing geo-body. The sudden shift in revolutionary rhetoric did not fool the frontier peoples as they sought to free themselves from Chinese hegemony. With Russian support, the Khalkha princes of Outer Mongolia formally declared their independence from China in December 1911, arguing that the collapse of the Qing dynasty ended Manchu suzerainty and thus enabled the Mongols and the Han Chinese to establish their own independent states. With the assistance of Russian troops, the princes escorted the imperial regent to the new "border" between Mongolia and China. In Lhasa, the thirteenth Dalai Lama ordered the expulsion of all Chinese and Manchu officials from Tibet during the early months of 1912 and signaled his desire to remain independent of the new Chinese Republic. The political independence of these two frontier regions was mutually recognized when their governments signed the Tibetan-Mongolian Treaty of Independence on December 24, 1912.[114]

The government of Yuan Shikai initially attempted to use a carrot-and-stick policy to lure the "rebellious" Mongolian and Tibetan peoples back into the national fold. Yuan issued a presidential proclamation apologizing for the excesses of Chinese troops in Tibet and formally restoring the Dalai Lama's title and rank. The new Mongolian and Tibetan Office within the Ministry of Internal Affairs also issued its "Outline of Regulations for the Treatment of Tibet," which restored nearly all the feudal titles and powers enjoyed by the Tibetan religious and secular nobility under the Qing dynasty.[115] Yuan's government issued similar orders for the restoration of the titles, enfeoffments, and stipends of the Mongol princes. Yet, when the princes of Inner Mongolia began expelling Chinese merchants and settlers and declared their intention to join the Outer Mongolian state, Yuan dispatched troops to unmercifully crush the rebellion and reestablish Chinese control over Inner Mongolia. At the same time, he began mobilizing a one-hundred-thousand-man-strong expeditionary force in Sichuan with the objective of reasserting Chinese control over Tibet. But because he was afraid of provoking war with England and Russian, Yuan took no direct military action against Tibet and the Outer Mongol princes. His fragile new government was dependent on continued foreign recognition and financial assistance for its survival.[116] Unable to accept that these backward and remote frontier peoples might themselves establish viable independent states, Chinese nationalists blamed the imperialist powers for actively encouraging and supporting their efforts to break away from the Republic. This remote frontier became the battleground on which Chinese nationalist leaders began to reimagine the shape and composition of the new nation-state.

During the winter of 1912–13, the issue of foreign encroachment exploded onto the stage of public opinion in China when news broke that Mongolia and Czarist Russia had signed a secret agreement that committed Russia to protect Mongolia from Chinese invasion in exchange for special trading privileges.[117] For the first time, new communication technologies enabled Sinic elites in the distant corners of the Republic and even overseas to begin to imagine themselves as members of a single community—a "deep, horizontal comradeship" worth both fighting and dying for.[118] Telegrams from every major city in China flooded into the Beijing government's offices demanding that war be declared on the Mongols immediately and a military expedition dispatched to regain China's "lost sovereignty" over this distant frontier, even at the risk of provoking war with Russia. The Guangdong provincial government, under Hu Hanmin, established a special bureau to solicit contributions to the war effort and equip a division of the region's men to fight in Mongolia. The Hunan provincial government offered to grant Beijing nearly one million yuan as soon as it declared war on the Mongolian separatists, while overseas Chinese in Singapore remitted twenty thousand yuan in support of the war cause. Throughout the winter, massive public demonstrations were held in major cities from Sichuan to Hubei, with patriotic subscription campaigns launched to raise money for the war effort. Anti-Russian boycotts were also launched in Beijing and Qingdao, while numerous Societies for Saving Mongolia (*shou Menghui*) were established throughout the provinces.[119] The chief political strategist for the newly formed Guomindang, Song Jiaoren, personally assisted in founding the Hunan branch in January 1913, declaring in his speech at the organization's opening ceremony that it was the responsibility of all members to encourage the use of force to "regain our territory and awe the Russian's with our [military] might."[120]

Many of the future leaders of the GMD and CCP were at the forefront of the call to arms. In a December 3, 1912, circular telegram addressed to President Yuan Shikai, the state council, provincial governors, and the offices of all national newspapers, Sun Yat-sen declared that "extraordinary events require extraordinary measures." The very existence of the Chinese minzu, Sun asserted, hung in the balance: "Rather than bow our heads and accept partition, why not choose the wiser course of rousing ourselves to defeat the powerful Russians in a single battle and thus consolidate for future generations the foundation of our state? Our national morale is now high, and the body politic is new. There is a road by which we can fight and win. To not fight will bring us certain extinction. We do not need the wisdom of a sage to know which is the better course."[121] Sun's twenty-one-year-old private secretary, Dai Jitao, wrote a series of essays for a popular Shanghai magazine denouncing Russian, Japanese, and English encroachment on the new Republic's frontier, declaring in one that war was "the only course of action for consolidating the Zhonghua Republic and crucial to the future survival of the Han minzu."[122] To prevent future instability, Dai Jitao and other nationalists proposed a federalist model along the lines of the United States, arguing that a voluntary union was the most expedient method for fostering the natural, evolutionary melding of different elements of the Chinese minzu.[123]

In response to a question from an American reporter about the apparent contradiction between the new Republic's imperialist attitude toward Mongolia and the vilification of foreign encroachment in China, Dr. C. C. Wu, the future GMD foreign minister, pointed out that other great republics had acted similarly during their infancy: "France at the beginning of her existence as a republic crushed the revolt in Vendée and the United States fought a bloody civil war in order that the number of stars in their flag might not be diminished."[124] Chiang Kai-shek, then a twenty-four-year-old regimental commander in Chen Qimei's Shanghai army, wrote a number of articles calling for a "blood and iron policy" (*tiexuezhuyi*) to deal with Russian and British intrusion on China's frontier. "Now is the time to urgently rouse ourselves," Chiang wrote, "wielding an adroit hand by adopting a plan for a thunderbolt of activity aimed at suppressing these rebellions. If we are not able to successfully put down this frontier trouble and restore order, it will spread and consolidate, leading to the ruin of Tibet and Mongolia at the hands of the rebels and a disastrous carving up of China."[125]

Foreign encroachment on the Qing frontier elicited an equally strong reaction from the future leaders of the CCP. When in 1915 Yuan Shikai appeared to give into Japan's Twenty-One Demands for control over Germany's lease holdings in Shandong province and the right to exploit and colonize Mongolia and Manchuria, a young but fiery Mao Zedong complained to a friend that "[China] is ten thousand *li* [Chinese miles] in length and breadth but has submitted herself to the three [Japanese] islands; [China] has four hundred million people but has allowed them to be enslaved by the thirty million [Japanese]. Should Manchuria and Mongolia be lost, the northern frontiers would be shaken and the barbarians' cavalries (*hu qi*) would pour into the Central Plains. . . . Within twenty years [China's] survival will have to be settled by war [with Japan]."[126] Li Dazhao, one of the cofounders of the CCP, blamed China's current weakness and division on the misguided notion of a republic of five races. Echoing Sun Yat-sen, he called in 1917 for a "new Zhonghua nationalism" rooted in the country's past: "In the distant recesses of our country's history, the various minzus of Asia smelted together in forming a single Zhonghua minzu that eliminated all previous boundaries and blood lineages and forged our minzu's lofty and effervescent spirit."[127] With the establishment of a free and equal republican system, Li believed that "residual historical names" such as Manchu, Han, Mongol, Hui, and Tibetan would gradually disappear, leaving a single Zhonghua Republic composed of a homogeneous and united Zhonghua minzu.

Foreign advances on the Qing frontier and the inherent weakness of the new Republican state together fashioned a new spatial and temporal definition of the minzu, one in which the frontier and its minority nationals were seen as vital to the health and future progress of the entire minzu. For Chinese nationalists, geographical boundaries rather than cultural or racial traits became the defining marker of their imagined community. The fuzzy, concentric, and constantly shifting demarcation between the Sinic cultural core of the sedentary *neidi* (interior) and the barbarian Other of the nomadic or swidden *waifang* (exterior) was no longer tenable in the new global system of competing nation-states, in which national boundaries were fixed with linear and unequivocal precision and all those on one side or the other were *nationalized.*

The speed with which the Mongolian crisis of 1912–13 spread among the Republic's elite also marked a dramatic compression of time and thereby signaled the opening of new political spaces for the articulation of Chinese identity. Frontier affairs shifted from the private domain of government officials to the realm of public opinion. Sovereignty was now rooted in an awakening citizenry (guomin or *gongmin*) and in the active participation in the life of the minzu. Yet the price of this participation was unprecedented conformity to a common set of political, cultural, and ethnic assumptions.[128] The minzu's well-being and territorial integrity became an important concern for each and every citizen—particularly the Sinic intelligentsia who made use of the state's growing commercial press, telegraph, and railway systems to forge an imaginary fraternity across the vast spaces of the Republic. The minzu was now the physical embodiment of its people and territory, and the duty of shepherding the barbarian periphery forward into history was transferred from the emperor and his court to the Chinese state and its elites.

These changing notions of space and time created new and unanticipated problems for the state. The old periphery was now central to the minzu's health, as the once geographically distant barbarians became underdeveloped minority nationals who had to be fused into the modernity of the majority.[129] As they lifted the veil on the frontier, state officials began calling for specialized academic research to facilitate the minzu's development and integration. And the resulting discourse of minzu unity (*minzu zhi tongyi* or minzu tuanjie) placed the "frontier question"—namely, the challenge of exercising complete sovereignty over the remote boundaries of the nation-state—and the "national question"—the task of physically incorporating the frontier minorities into the nation-state—at the center of policymaking.

For Sun Yat-sen and other Chinese nationalists, the solution was to construct a new national imaginary, one that would fold all the peoples and territories of the former Qing empire into a unitary Zhonghua minzu. As Liang Qichao had first done in 1901, Republican-era elites began speaking in unison about a single multiethnic, yet Sinic-centered Chinese race-state; and they called for the assimilation of the frontier minorities into a more evolutionarily robust guozu. When the GMD was founded in 1912, the goal of racial amalgamation became a central component of Sun's principle of minzuzhuyi, with the "strict implementation of racial assimilation" (*zhongzu tonghua*) now listed among the party's five political goals.[130] As the core of this new race-state, the "Han majority" had an important role to play in fashioning a more positive or constructive nationalism, sacrificing itself to merge with the other races "in a single furnace to create the new order of the Zhonghua minzu" and thereby enabling China to "quickly surpass America and Europe and become first in the world."[131] Uncomfortable from an early stage with the tenuous republic of five races,[132] Sun envisioned a composite "melting pot" with the superior Han race at its core. "When we speak of China," he stated in 1921, "no matter what minzu may be added to our country in the future, they must be assimilated into our Hanzu."[133]

Yet the reality of China's weak international position prevented successive Chinese administrations from fully exercising state control over the frontier regions and implementing Sun's vision for the future. During the early decades of the twentieth century, a succession of warlord regimes dominated the political scene and spent most of their time and energy vying for control over the Chinese heartland. Such turmoil left China's frontier regions exposed and invited continued foreign involvement in the affairs of Tibet, Xinjiang, Mongolia, and Manchuria. At the same time, the popular sentiments expressed during the 1912–13 Mongolian crisis ensured that no Chinese government could maintain its political legitimacy without at least appearing to uphold the sovereignty of the minzu. The Chinese state was assisted by a new global system of spatially constituted sovereign polities that eliminated the fuzzy borderlands of the age of empires. *National* borders were now defined not only by military power but also by diplomacy, international treaties, and their resulting map protocols. An emerging system of mutually recognized and legally binding diplomatic agreements helped clearly demarcate international boundaries and nationalized all political space.

Through the tactic of nonrecognition and some clever negotiating, the Chinese state refused to relinquish its legal sovereignty over the territory of the former Qing empire. Meanwhile, the imperialist powers keep one another in check, preventing any single power from occupying parts of the former empire without protest from both the Chinese government and others within the international community. Despite continued British involvement in the affairs of Tibet, the tripartite Simla Conference held between Britain, China, and Tibet in

1913 recognized Chinese "suzerainty" over Tibet in exchange for a commitment to extensive Tibetan autonomy.[134] Two years later, a similar conference in Kyakhta between Russia, Mongolia, and China recognized Chinese suzerainty over Outer Mongolia and that it was "part of Chinese territory."[135] Although the Red Army occupied Outer Mongolia in 1921, the Sino-Soviet Accord signed by the new USSR and the Beijing government of Cao Kun in 1924 stated that: "The Government of the Union of Soviet Socialist Republics recognizes that Outer Mongolia is an integral part of the Republic of China and respects China's sovereignty therein."[136] Finally, Japan's unprecedented land grab in 1931 was unequivocally condemned by the international community's new representative body, the League of Nations, which declared Japan's occupation of Manchuria an unlawful violation of Chinese sovereignty.[137]

Throughout the Republican period, the Chinese state lacked both the military muscle and often the political will to fully garrison its vast frontier. Yet by carefully guarding over its legal sovereignty in the voluminous paperwork of international diplomacy, the Republican state provided the framework for the PRC to assume control over nearly all Qing territories after 1949. William Kirby has called this dogged refusal to relinquish any claim of sovereignty over the massive Qing empire "the greatest accomplishment of Republican diplomacy."[138] Yet, as later chapters will detail, the task of physically and culturally incorporating the frontier and its minorities into the Chinese nation-state would prove much more difficult.

The Territorial Nation

The transition from empire and nation bequeathed a number of unresolved problems for the nascent Chinese Republic. Chief among these were two radically different conceptions of nationhood: one that saw the nation as an inclusive civic community and the other as an exclusive racial community. While nationalist and revolutionary leaders alike demised small and marginalized cultural communities as historically irrelevant in nineteenth-century Europe, state elites in China found themselves awkwardly trapped between the political alternatives of national self-determination and forced assimilation. They feared the former and were unsure how to proceed with the latter, while stuck with the reality of their own political impotence as the Qing empire swiftly unraveled. The birth of the Chinese Republic occurred during the apex of what Charles Maier has identified as the epoch of "territoriality," where state elites around the world drew on new technologies of steam, rail, post, telegraph, electricity, and bureaucracy to "saturate," "enclose," and "energize" national space.[139] The "filling in" of space in China required the increased mobilization, homogenization, and control of its populace, as "identity space" was brought in line with "decision space," and allegiance to a bounded geographic community replaced premodern social hierarchies and vertical forms of group identity.

Despite their small numbers compared to the four-hundred-million-strong Sinic majority, the Republic's frontier minorities inhabited nearly 60 percent of the country's territory, much of which was rich in the natural resources required for economic development and political modernization. Chinese elites were quick to recognize that while these small minorities might lack a long-term future as independent minzus either inside or outside the Chinese state, they were crucial to the short-term territorial integrity of a Chinese geo-body beset on all sides by stronger foreign powers. No longer the distant concern of the imperial court; the frontier minorities were now both an asset (in that their territory was now national territory) and a liability (in their challenge to the nation's putative homogeneity and unity). Nation and state building in early twentieth-century China involved not only the transformation of imperial subjects into national citizens, but also the identification and classification of the barbarian Other as *minority* nationals set within a unitary and enclosed Zhonghua minzu.

China's shift from empire to nation-state differed from the common pattern in Europe. Unlike other large agrarian states, including the Ottoman, Habsburg, and Czarist empires, Qing China did not permanently fissure along its ethnic and sociocultural cracks following the empire's collapse.[140] To explain this rather unique turn of events, some have suggested that China remains "an empire without an emperor" or the "last remaining major multicultural empire."[141] Yet the modern Chinese state makes no pretension of empire, putting itself forward as a fully bounded and sovereign nation-state just like other members of the so-called international community. Furthermore, the Republic was predicated on a novel form of group identity, as the "one-as-all" model of Qing subjecthood gave way to the "all-as-one" melting pot formula of Republican citizenhood.[142] Others have argued that competing claims over the scope and nature of China's national culture—a reformulated cultural universalism versus a more narrowly conceived ethnic particularism—helps explain the continuity of its territorial boundaries.[143] In a similar vain, John Fitzgerald has coined the term "nationless state" to signify the lack of consensus on the political and ethnic composition of the modern Chinese state. He identifies four different formulations of the "nation" (as civilization, citizen, race, and social class) before concluding, "The state which *is* China has no given nation."[144] I believe that there is another formulation—a common spatial imaginary—that was shared by nearly all twentieth-century Chinese intellectuals and helped to contribute to the unique durability of its political community during China's tumultuous transition to modernity.

During the late Qing and early Republican periods, Chinese intellectuals experimented with a number of different spatial representations of the nation—ranging from provincial self-rule or temporary independence to an ethnocentric Han republic comprising the core Ming provinces and even a pan-Asianism rooted in a common East Asian civilization.[145] But ultimately—and certainly by the 1930s—they accepted that the boundaries of the new Zhonghua minzu should ultimately assume the same geographical space as the Manchu empire. This differed sharply from the Qing conception of its boundaries, which were seen as fluid and completely dependant (like other premodern empires) on ever changing economic and security concerns.[146] The enclosure of national space in China reflected widespread acceptance of the new global system of spatially constituted nation-states, as Chinese elites discovered the world and other national and anticolonial movements and began to define their own place within these global structures.[147] The dramatic increase in the usage of the term national sovereignty (*guojia zhuquan*) among late Qing elites was coupled by the repeated recognition of China's territorial boundaries in the numerous international treaties the Qing and Republican states signed with the foreign powers.[148] While many of these treaties granted the imperialist powers significant economic and political concessions deep within China, they also tended to reinforce and naturalize the territorial boundaries of the Chinese geo-body. Isolated coastal islands like Hong Kong, Ryūkyū, and Taiwan were partitioned off, and the independence of the former tributary states of Annam and Korea was recognized; but sovereignty, or at the very least suzerainty, was maintained over Xinjiang, Mongolia, Manchuria, and Tibet. Yet this only partially explains why Chinese elites doggedly refused to relinquish sovereignty over the remote and backward frontier regions of the Qing empire.

Here I would also like to suggest that the appropriation of a spatially defined history and the long tradition of a bounded and eternal "China" in the imagination of both Western and Chinese elites lent the new Chinese Republic a remarkable geographic cohesion as it entered the twentieth century. Tang Xiaobing has highlighted "the nationalist unity of history and territory" in Liang Qichao's voluminous and highly influential writings.[149] In his pioneering essays on history and geography, Liang was perhaps the first modern Chinese intellectual to lay claim to a long linear and unbroken history with "China" as its subject and Qing imperial space as its stage—what everyone from Sun Yat-sen to Mao Zedong and Chiang Kai-shek referred to as "the four thousand years of Chinese history." In Liang's spatiotemporal definition of the nation, everything within the confines of Qing territory and stretching back to the time of the mythical Yellow Emperor was *nationalized* as part of the Chinese geo-body. While the appropriation and reification of this history as a part of "China" (first Zhongguo and then Zhonghua) and as belonging to the "Chinese" (first Zhongguoren, then Zhongguo minzu, and eventually Zhonghua minzu) coalesced only during the late Qing, the West had long referred to this bounded yet fluid topography as "China" (*cīna* in Sanskrit; *chīnī*, Persian; *la Chine*, French; and *Shina*, Japanese). When the toponym reentered Qing China via Western missionaries, the Manchu court strategically appropriated it for their growing empire, expanding its scope and meaning to cover the steppes and deserts of Central Asia and stretching its meaning well beyond the historical boundaries of previous dynasties.[150] For most in China and the West, the toponym Zhongguo/China served to authenticate the Republic's inheritance of the vast majority of Qing territory.

The "Manchu-centered perspective" of the new Qing historians has helped rebalance our previous interpretations of the dynasty, highlighting the significance of a distinct Manchu identity and ideology to Qing rule. At the same time, it is important to remember that the outside world came to view the dynasty as a "Chinese empire" in no small part because the Manchu court projected this image of itself both domestically and to an even greater extent internationally. Whereas Zhongguo had traditionally been defined in opposition to the barbarian Other, Western and Japanese imperialism required a new, more hardened boundary be drawn around Zhongguo/China, causing the Qing borderlands to be swallowed whole by the Republican state and thereby increasing the importance of the frontier and national questions in twentieth-century China.

PART I

Strategies of Political Intervention

CHAPTER 2

Borderlands of State Power: The Nationalists and the Frontier Question

In the PRC historians generally depict the Guomindang's national minority policy in starkly negative terms. They contend that Chiang Kai-shek's central government denied the very existence of minority nationalities and attempted by force to assimilate all ethnic diversity into a single Chinese race/nation. This "fascist" or "chauvinistic" approach is frequently contrasted with Sun Yat-sen's policy of minority self-determination and self-rule, which was said to be formulated during the last years of his life and implemented under the rule of the CCP. A recent textbook published by the Central Party School of the CCP, for example, described Guomindang policy as one of "discrimination, oppression, and assimilation" and contended that it represented a complete reversal of Sun Yat-sen's principle of minzuzhuyi.[1]

Historians writing outside China have uncritically perpetuated this characterization.[2] Some have suggested that the Guomindang (in sharp contrast to the Communists) "had no answer" to the problem of integrating the Republic's political culture with the diverse geocultural boundaries of the Qing empire, asserting that its "exclusivist nationalism" precluded the type of "universalizing rhetoric" necessary for national integration.[3] Others have argued that Chiang Kai-shek's emphasis on national unity led him to strongly oppose any form of political or cultural autonomy for the frontier minorities.[4] It is common within the existing literature to paint a sharp contrast between the Guomindang's idealist "policy of *Hanhua* (Hanification or Sinification)" and the CCP's "instrumental strategy" that accepted (at least initially) the ethnic self-determination of Chinese minorities.[5] Here, the father of the nation, Sun Yat-sen, has been put forward as both an early champion of Han racism and then later in life a leading architecture of Chinese multiculturalism. Claiming that he turned his back on the virulent anti-Manchu racism of the 1911 revolution, Western and Chinese scholars alike speak of a "remarkable ideological shift" in Sun's thinking under Comintern influence, causing Sun to begin advocating equality, self-determination, and self-rule for China's ethnic minorities in the waning years of his life.[6] It is this latter policy that is said to have continued under the Communists, albeit in a more limited, unstable, and coercive fashion according to outside observers.

This chapter and the next call into question these highly polemical depictions of GMD and CCP policy toward the Republic's frontier minorities. I show instead the underlying similarities in the two parties' approaches to the problem of diversity within the new nation-state and how the contingencies of revolution shaped this common response. This chapter begins by clarifying Sun Yat-sen's understanding of the principle of self-determination and qualifying his support for limited self-rule in the fragile nation-state's frontier regions. Next, it draws on recently declassified documents from the Commission on Mongolian and Tibetan Affairs (CMTA) to explore the development of what the Guomindang Central Government of Chiang Kai-shek came to call the "frontier question." In discussing Guomindang national minority policy, Chinese and Western scholars alike frequently refer to the party's famous 1943 political tract *China's Destiny* (*Zhongguo zhi mingyun*), which asserts that all "Chinese" citizens, including the Manchu, Mongol, Tibetan, Hui, and other frontier minorities, were interrelated "lineage branches" (*zongzhi*) of a single, consanguineous Zhonghua minzu.[7] The book, which was published in Chiang Kai-shek's name but actually ghostwritten by the Guomindang historian Tao Xisheng, represented the party's ideal discursive imagining of the Chinese nation-state as ancient, unified, and homogeneous (see Chapter 4). In reality, a weak Guomindang state was forced to adopt a more pragmatic and inherently conservative approach to the frontier question. Here, the linguistic and administrative precedents of the Qing dynasty's Lifanyuan proved more useful for dealing with the Republic's ethnic penumbra. By adopting the laissez-faire frontier policies of the late Qing empire, the Guomindang state hoped to consolidate its political base and control over central China in preparation for a future drive toward national unity and economic revitalization.

To demonstrate the flexibility with which Guomindang policymakers approached the frontier, I focus on the party's policy toward Tibet and Inner Mongolia during the Nanjing Decade (1927–37). In exchange for its acknowledgment of Chinese sovereignty, the Guomindang Central Government was willing (at least temporarily) to extend a high degree of political and cultural autonomy to the Tibetans, Mongols, and other frontier minorities. In a trailblazing study of the CCP's "ethnopolitical strategy," Liu Xiaoyuan has asserted that the Guomindang Central Government "never had an ethnic policy as such. The government pushed for assimilating the non-Han peoples of the borderlands but viewed the process as merely part of its 'frontier administration' (*bian zheng*)."[8] This chapter demonstrates to the contrary that the Guomindang developed a frontier policy that was every bit as sophisticated as the CCP's and likewise aimed at securing the allegiance of the frontier minorities in the hope of extending their rule over the vast territory of the new Republic. By acknowledging minority grievances, the Guomindang sought not only to bolster its nationalist credentials, but also to prevent the frontier from being used as a base for imperialist intrigue, warlord militarism, and, most importantly, Communist infiltration. I do not mean to suggest that the Guomindang was any less paternalistic or deeply committed to national unity than the Communists; but rather I would like to cast a more critical light on the relationship between state and nation building in Republican China, revealing the complex and multilayered nature of the Chinese state's attempts to deal with the frontier question in a fluid political environment.

Throughout the Republican period, policymakers from both the GMD and the CCP made repeated overtures to the Republic's new ethnic minorities, hoping to eliminate foreign interference and secure Chinese sovereignty over the Qing geo-body. In these contacts, both parties had to negotiate with not only imperialist agents but also the autonomous power of a number of Chinese warlords who viewed the frontier as their personal colony and, together with the predatory "transfrontiersmen," fiercely resisted any outside encroachment.[9] Here Guomindang and Communist officials had to contend with a completely different notion of sovereignty, one that gave priority to regional and provincial autonomy and the "civilizing" and "opening up" of frontier "wasteland" in the name of economic development and, most importantly, profit. Stevan Harrell has employed the term "civilizing project" to describe the hegemonic dialogue of inequality where the center attempts to improve the cultural, economic, and political standing of the periphery in the name of progress and modernity. Yet, the three distinct projects he identifies for China—Confucian, Christian, and Communist—do not help us understand the complexities of ethnic relations on the Republican frontier; for in each he emphasizes the moral, political, and military dominance of the center.[10] In Republican China, in contrast, neither the GMD nor the CCP had a monopoly on political power or the state apparatuses of coercion and violence. Instead, the "center" had to compete with a variety of independent actors—foreign imperialists, regional warlords, frontier minorities, political factions, and third parties—each with different conceptions of the nation-state and its composition. In studying this period, we must guard against the temptation to read the PRC's current civilizing project backwards (as much of PRC historiography does) into the more protean and volatile environment of pre-1949 China.

Self-determination: Sun Yat-sen and Outer Mongolia

On January 20, 1924, nearly two hundred members of the newly formed CCP and recently reorganized GMD converged on the grand auditorium of the Guangzhou National Teachers College for the Chinese Nationalist Party's First National Congress. This so-called Reorganization Congress formally marked the commencement of a political alliance between China's two largest revolutionary parties. In exchange for military and political assistance from the Bolshevik-controlled Third Communist International (Comintern), Sun Yat-sen had agreed, over the objections of many veteran members of his party, to admit individual members of the CCP into the GMD so that they could create a revolutionary united front against their common enemy—domestic warlordism and international imperialism.

The Comintern's influence, through its charismatic Russian advisor Mikhail Borodin, made an immediate impact on the Guomindang. Borodin oversaw the inclusion of Lenin's *Theses on the National and Colonial Question*, with its call for a revolutionary alliance between the proletariat of the "advanced countries" and the various movements for national liberation in the "backward colonies" of Asia and Africa, into the language and policies of the party.[11] The final manifesto of the Reorganization Congress also set forth a new strategy for dealing with the problem of small nationalities living on the margins of large states like China. Sun Yat-sen and other Chinese nationalists had sought the incorporation of the frontier peoples of the former Qing dynasty into the new Republic, but Lenin contended that frontier minorities needed to be granted national self-determination, including the right of political secession, before their eventual reunion with other members of the proletariat in a borderless world free from national and class oppression. Borodin attempted to incorporate Lenin's tactic of national self-determination into the congress's manifesto with the following pledge:

> The Guomindang's principle of minzuzhuyi contains two meanings: (1) the self-seeking liberation of the Chinese minzu and (2) the equality of all the minzus living within Chinese territory. In support of the first aim, the GMD proposes to secure the recognition of the freedom and independence of China among the nations of the world. . . . When imperialism has been beaten down, the people can then enlarge their activities and unify themselves to accomplish the other aims of the revolution. . . . In support of the second aim . . . the GMD will work for alliances and organize discussion of problems that concern us all. The GMD hereby formally guarantees the right of self-determination for all domestic minzus; and as soon as the revolution achieves victory over the imperialists and the warlords, we will do our best to organize (upon the voluntary agreement of all minzus) a free and united Zhonghua Republic.[12]

On its face, this promise appears to depart radically from Sun's strong commitment to national unity; but the manifesto's silence on the exact meaning and implication of self-determination in China complicates its interpretation.

What Sun Yat-sen meant by the term *minzu zijue* (national self-determination) continues to be debated. Many Western scholars refer uncritically to Sun's usage of the term in describing a fundamental shift in his discourse of minzuzhuyi, signaling support for the minority people to determine their own political form free from Chinese interference;[13] but few have analyzed it in any detail. The political scientist Walker Connor claims that Sun never took the concept seriously—failing to envision an actual desire among the minorities for secession from their fatherland—and allowed it to be inserted into the manifesto only under intense pressure from his Comintern advisers. The Taiwanese scholar Hong Quanhu, on the other hand, believes that Sun's interpretation of the concept contained two complementary meanings: the self-seeking liberation and independence of the entire Chinese nation and the implementation of self-rule (not secession) and equality among the national minorities of China.[14] Both arguments contain a kernel of truth; yet, to fully appreciate what Sun meant by minzu zijue, it must be placed within the context of the Guomindang-Comintern alliance.

Late in his life, Sun Yat-sen admitted being greatly inspired by the "current trend toward national self-determination" championed by President Woodrow Wilson at the end of World War I in his Fourteen Points.[15] China—like Poland, Turkey, Czechoslovakia, and other oppressed European nations—should also have the right to rid itself of foreign imperialism and carry out its own national liberation. Sun first used the term minzu zijue in a March 6, 1921, speech in Canton, stating that Wilson's principle of national self-determination was "essentially the same as our party's principle of minzuzhuyi."[16] Initially, Sun applied the principle only to the evolutionary development of the Chinese minzu as a whole, making no mention of its relevance to what he began to refer to as the "domestic minzus" (*guonei zhu minzu*) or the "various minzus within Chinese territory" (*Zhongguo jingnei ge minzu*).[17] But the manifesto of the Guomindang's Reorganization Congress clearly promised to "formally guarantee the right of self-determination for all domestic minzus," showing the clear influence of Lenin's application of the principle to more marginalized national minorities like the Turkmens and the Mongols.[18]

Recently declassified Russian documents reveal the contested and conditional entrance of the Bolshevik policy of national self-determination into GMD party policy. Sun Yat-sen and other GMD leaders played only a minor role in the actual drafting of the Reorganization Congress's manifesto. Rather, Sun asked Borodin to draft an English copy, which was then translated into Chinese by Liao Zhongkai and checked personally by him.[19] But Sun and other GMD leaders did not know that Borodin was strictly following a November 28, 1923, Comintern Central Executive Committee directive that outlined a new interpretation of Sun's Three Principles of the People. Among other things, the directive called for the explicit inclusion in Sun's minzuzhuyi of the "principle of national self-determination for all nationalities within China."[20]

Yet when Borodin's draft was read out loud before the delegates of the Reorganization Congress on January 20, 1923, it was fiercely opposed by several party veterans who felt Borodin's broad-ranging reinterpretation of the sanminzhuyi betrayed the original meaning. In particular, Wang Jingwei, Hu Hanmin, and others objected to Borodin's insistence that the GMD grant its frontier minorities the right of political self-determination prior to the triumph of the Chinese revolution.[21] In a private meeting with Borodin several days later, Sun Yat-sen suggested replacing the disputed text with a more innocuous document, *Jianguo Dagang* (*Outline for National Reconstruction*), recently drafted by Sun.[22] In the *Outline*, all explicit mention of minority independence was removed—its place taken by a more paternalistic and vaguely worded statement of the national government's responsibility to "cultivate" (*fuzhi*) the ability of all China's "domestic, small, and weak minzus" (*guonei zhi ruoxiao minzu*) to "self-determination and self-rule" (*zijue zizhi*).[23] In order to save his manifesto, Borodin agreed to revise and in some places water down its language (particularly on the national and land questions) and to have Sun's *Outline for National Reconstruction* published alongside it.

The precise language of the manifesto, finally approved by the Reorganization Congress on January 23, reveals the extent of Borodin's compromise. First, the Guomindang promised to recognize only "the right of self-determination for all minzus within China (*Zhongguo yinei ge minzu zhi zijuequan*)," refusing to accept the Comintern's demand that national self-determination explicitly include the right of political secession. Here in the final manifesto, for the first time, the term shaoshu minzu (minority nationals) is used to identify the various non-Han minzus living "within Chinese territory," which is set in contrast to a unitary Zhongguo minzu (Chinese race/nation).[24] For both the Guomindang and the CCP, "minority" (*shaoshu*) became an important qualifier of minzu, allowing a subtle but important distinction between the struggle of the entire Chinese minzu for its national self-determination and the inclusion and possible equality of the minority nationals within a Han-dominated state. Second, the carefully worded promise of self-determination was immediately followed by a contradictory pledge that the party would "organize (upon the voluntary agreement of all minzus) a free and united Zhonghua Republic."[25] Finally, the manifesto stated that the implementation of domestic minzu self-determination could occur only "after the revolution achieves victory over the imperialists and the warlords." In a report before the CCP, Borodin admitted his disappointment with the vague and contradictory nature of the Guomindang's policy of minority self-determination and called on the CCP to publicize these inconsistencies and work for a revision of its wording.[26]

Bruce Elleman has used Sun Yat-sen's apparent ambivalence toward the Soviet Union's 1921 occupation of Outer Mongolia to argue for a dramatic "metamorphosis" in his principle of minzuzhuyi: from "Wilsonian nationalism to Leninist nationalism."[27] Though Sun accepted the status quo in Outer Mongolia as a part of the 1923 Sun-Joffe Accord that formalized Comintern support for the Guomindang, he continued to voraciously insist on the inclusion of Outer Mongolia in a unitary Zhonghua nation-state and was repeatedly reassured of this fact by his Comintern advisors.[28] In late 1923, he rejected out of hand a personal plea by CCP chairman Chen Duxiu for the Guomindang to apply the principle of national self-determination and formally recognize the political independence of Outer Mongolia.[29] Sun also used the presence of Soliyn Danzan, the chairman of the USSR-backed Mongolian People's Revolutionary Government, at the Guomindang's Reorganization Congress to highlight the common historical destiny of the Chinese and Mongolian peoples. Even though Danzan was under strict orders from Moscow not to discuss Outer Mongolia's political relationship with China, Sun put his interpretation on Danzan's attendance during a welcoming ceremony for the delegates: "The reason for Mr. Danzan's visit to Canton was to call for Mongolia to again unite with China in creating a single, large Zhonghua Republic."[30] In one of his lectures on minzuzhuyi after Danzan's departure, Sun even claimed that when the Mongolian representative saw "the fostering of small and weak minzus and lack of imperialist thought within our congress's political program, he enthusiastically advocated the uniting of everyone together in creating one of the Orient's largest countries."[31]

In the minds of Sun Yat-sen and other Chinese elites, national self-determination was a principle that could apply only to the majority Han minzu. This fact was confirmed not only by the evolutionary backwardness of China's minority peoples, but also by their inability to stop the gradual transformation of their frontier territories into imperialist spheres of influence. Because "Manchuria was surrounded by the Japanese, Mongolia by the Russians and Tibet by the English," Sun Yat-sen stated during a 1921 speech, China's minority peoples "no longer possess the ability to defend themselves" and must now "depend on the help of the Hanzu."[32] Thus, he declared later that year that "the task of fostering a glorious and large minzuzhuyi and assimilating the Tibetans, Mongols, Hui, and Manchus into our Hanzu in constructing of the biggest possible race-state rests solely with the self-determination of the Han people."[33] Yet because the Guomindang was weak, the party and its leaders had to be both flexible and realistic when it came to its frontier policy. In the case of Outer Mongolia, Sun was willing to accept the status quo of Soviet occupation in exchange for material assistance in building an army that would one day be capable of reuniting the country and reestablishing direct Chinese control over the frontier regions.

Self-Rule: Chiang Kai-shek and Inner Mongolia

The violent collapse of the GMD-CCP united front following the death of Sun Yat-sen in 1925 and the establishment of a new "national government" did little to alter the view of Guomindang party leaders. Initially, the new government headed by Chiang Kai-shek controlled little outside of its capital in Nanjing. But by 1929 it had convinced most regional powers in China proper and Manchuria to join Chiang's regime in the name of national unity, thereby securing international recognition. Real power, however, remained in the hands of the provincial armies headed by such career militarists as Feng Yuxiang, Zhang Xueliang, Yan Xishan, and Liu Wenhui.[34]

Despite the decision to jettison the five-color flag as the national emblem, the Guomindang Central Government continued to stringently uphold Chinese sovereignty over the former frontier regions of the Qing empire. Calling for the "uniting of our 400,000 million people into a single, large guozu (race-state)," the party's Third National Congress in 1929 rewrote Sun Yat-sen's ideological legacy by formally removing the Reorganization Congress's manifesto and its controversial pledge of national self-determination from the list of Sun's core political texts.[35] However, it kept Sun's *Outline for National Reconstruction* with its promise to nurture the ability of the frontier minorities to carry out limited self-rule. In a bid to consolidate state control over the Tibetan and Mongolian frontiers, the government had announced in August 1928 the establishment of three new Inner Mongolian provinces—Suiyuan, Chahar, and Jehol—and its intention to create another province called Xikang along the Sichuan frontier with Tibet. Chiang also accepted in late 1929 the proposal of one of the party's few non-Han members, the Mongolian Bai Yunti (Serengdongrob), for the creation of a special commission to formulate central government policy toward Mongolia and Tibet and help promote domestic and international awareness of the imperialist plot to break apart the Zhonghua minzu under the bogus banner of national self-determination. The new CMTA, with its large staff and ministerial rank, was given broad authority to draft legislation and implement central government policy toward the frontier regions.[36]

For its language and administrative precedents, the new commission drew heavily on Qing frontier policy as developed by the Lifanyuan. Initially, Qing frontier policy was guided by the dual principles of "combining the use of force with imperial grace" (*enwei bingshi*) and "ruling by customs" (*yinsu erzhi*). But when its political power started to wane in the late 1700s, the Qing court began emphasizing the "grace" side of the enwei bingshi balance more than "force," providing the frontier regions with great latitude as long as they did not openly rebel.[37] From the beginning, the Qing used the traditional ruling classes to govern the frontier in accordance with local customs. In exchange for a high degree of autonomy, frontier princes and lamas were required to pledge their loyalty to the Qing court through the highly symbolic tribute system. It was these "loose rein" (*jimi*) or "winning over by all means" (*longluo*) policies that appealed most to CMTA administrators as they began to formulate their own approach to the frontier question, aiming above all else to hold the fragile Chinese Republic together against the corrupting forces of domestic warlordism and foreign imperialism.[38]

One of the first policy challenges the CMTA faced was the rapidly expanding encroachment of Chinese settlers on Inner Mongolian pastureland. For more than two thousand years, the Chinese state had been attempting to settle the loess steppe of Inner Mongolia. During times of imperial strength, Chinese farmers and merchants would establish their authority over the region, only to be driven back by the Mongol nomads during periods of dynastic decline. Yet, as Owen Lattimore astutely noted, the invention of the gun and the railway forever altered the balance of power in favor of the Chinese, causing the Sinic population of Inner Mongolia to swell from a few thousand merchants to nearly two million settlers by 1927 as thousands of acres of land were brought under cultivation.[39] Finding it increasingly difficult to locate suitable pastureland for their herds, Mongol princes began petitioning the new Guomindang Central Government for assistance in restoring the cultural and political autonomy they had enjoyed under the Qing.

Given the Guomindang's political weakness and Sun Yat-sen's own pledge to "cultivate" the frontier minorities, the CMTA moved quickly to address the concerns of the Mongol princes. In late November 1928, CMTA standing committee member Zhang Ji recommended to Chiang Kai-shek that the Guomindang express its sympathy for the plight of the Mongol princes and tentatively support the establishment of the Autonomous Mongolian Banner Council (*Mengqi zizhi weiyuanhui*) to check further Chinese encroachment onto Mongolian bannerland.[40] The CMTA also employed Wu Heling (Unenbayan), a young Mongolian noble living in Beiping, as an adviser and asked him to draw up a detailed plan for Inner Mongolian autonomy. But Chinese civil and military officials in the frontier provinces shared little of the central government's paternalism, viewing Mongolian autonomy instead as a direct threat to their authority over the frontier. This concern was the principal thrust of a letter of protest sent by a group of Jehol provincial officials to the Executive Yuan in late 1928. They expressed astonishment at the proposal drafted by Wu Heling, arguing that "there no longer exists an Inner Mongolia beyond the scope of Suiyuan, Jehol, and Chahar provinces."[41]

Attempting to diffuse the growing tension between the Mongol princes and the transfrontiersmen, the Guomindang government convened a special "Mongolian Conference" in Nanjing during the summer of 1930. The heated debates ultimately failed to forge a consensus on the future of the banner system, the colonization of Mongolian pastureland, and other contentious issues.[42] Despite strong CMTA support for Inner Mongolian autonomy, Chiang Kai-shek's fragile regime was not in a position to politically override the strong resistance from its powerful allies in the frontier provinces. Fearful of provoking a revolt among the northern warlords Yan Xishan, Feng Yuxiang, and Zhang Xueliang, the Guomindang proposed a compromise solution. The Organizational Law of Mongolian Leagues, Banners, and Tribes (*Menggu meng-bu-qi xuzhifa*), which was passed by the Legislative Yuan in October of 1931, called for the preservation of the Mongolian banner system in all those regions occupied by Mongolian people *and not currently under Chinese county administration*; and the Mongolian banners were placed directly under the jurisdiction of the Executive Yuan in Nanjing. While the central government would assume control of military, diplomatic, and other issues of national concern, the banners would be granted autonomy to govern their people according to local tradition and custom. The resolution also called on the Mongols and local administrators to consult one another on all issues of mutual concern, including Chinese colonization of Mongolian pastureland.[43]

During the early Republican period, Chinese militarists looked increasingly to the frontier in their effort to create a zone free from the central government's control. These remote frontier regions offered an excellent source of both military recruits and the natural resources needed to keep Nanjing at bay. A symbiotic relationship gradually developed between the transfrontiersmen and the regional militarists as both attempted to safeguard their political and economic self-interests from the Nationalist Party government. These warlord regimes struck a far different tone than the paternalism voiced by the CMTA, as they stressed the importance of developing the frontier and civilizing its backward nomads in the name of progress.

In the popular propaganda of these regional administrations, "virgin" frontier land was frequently referred to as a "gold vault" (*jinjiao*) or "treasure trove" (*baoku*), as border officials urged the "opening up of wasteland" (*kaiken*), "excavating of mines" (*kaikuang*), and "clearing of forests" (*kailin*) in the name of the Han man's "heavenly mission" (*tianzhi*) to "civilize" (*kaihua*) the barren frontier and its inhabitants. Frontier administrators writing in the journal *Mongolian Banner Biweekly* (*Mengqi xunkan*), published by the General Affairs Office of Zhang Xueling's Manchurian regime, argued that "military colonization" (*tunken*) was the most effective way to systematically exploit the frontier's untapped riches while deterring foreign invasion. One Chinese official called the task of "cutting down the thicket and opening up the wilderness" one of humanity's most noble and important pursuits, pleading with Han soldiers to build their houses among the "barren desert and wild grasses" of Mongolia in order to seek their personal fortunes while enriching the glory of the Zhonghua minzu.[44] But the real prize for the militarists and their supporters came from the sale and taxation of opium. Owen Lattimore has compared the role of opium in China to that of gold in America and Australia, providing the economic incentives necessary to draw Chinese settlers onto the rugged frontier and bring thousands of acres of land under cultivation and Chinese-style administration.[45]

De Wang and the Bailingmiao Autonomous Movement

Following the consolidation of his power in the Northwest, Yan Xishan launched an aggressive new plan to colonize the remaining grassland of the Inner Mongolian steppe in 1931. The newly created province of Suiyuan, under the control of Yan's trusted deputy Fu Zuoyi, became an important frontier zone in this struggle between hoe and bridle. The division of Inner Mongolia into forty-nine separate banner administrations and now five new Chinese provinces made collective resistance among the Mongols difficult. Yet, the charismatic and canny

Prince Demchugdongrob, the thirty-one-year-old leader of the West Sunid Banner who was better known by his Chinese name, De Wang, successfully galvanized this growing anti-Chinese sentiment into a cohesive and highly public movement for Inner Mongolian autonomy during the 1930s.[46]

During the winter of 1932, De Wang led a delegation of Mongol princes from the Shilingol and Ulanchab Leagues to Nanjing. They warned Chiang Kai-shek and other Guomindang officials about the growing Japanese threat and protested Yan Xishan's efforts to colonize Mongolian grassland. Though Nanjing officials offered to appoint De Wang to a position within the CMTA, they were largely powerless to address his real concerns. Frustrated and feeling slighted, he returned to Inner Mongolia where he convened a congress of Inner Mongolian banner delegates at the Bailingmiao temple (*Beile-yin sume*, in Mongolian) located deep within the Yinshan highlands of northern Suiyuan province. When the congress opened on July 26, 1933, opinion was divided, but De Wang persuaded the Ulanchab League chieftain, Prince Yon (Yondonwangchug), and Shilingol League chieftain, Prince So (Sodnamrabdan), to formally petition Nanjing for a "high degree of autonomy" (*gaodu zizhi*). The masterfully worded petition, drafted by De Wang and cabled to the central government on July 27, tapped into the anxious national mood following the Japanese annexation of Jehol province and the humiliating Tanggu Truce of May 31. After admitting that Sun Yat-sen's *Outline for National Reconstruction* called for the central government to "cultivate" the frontier minorities through a period of political tutelage in preparation for a future state of "self-determination and self-rule" (*zizhi zijue*), the petition went on to claim that extraordinary times called for extraordinary measures. The imminent threat of foreign invasion required that the period of tutelage be cut short and a single, unified Inner Mongolian Autonomous Government immediately be created.[47]

De Wang's Bailingmiao movement won the support of Wu Heling, Bai Yunti, and other Mongols closely associated with the Guomindang, and the petition's publication in the domestic and foreign press garnered national attention. The government bureaucracy was slow to react, however. After waiting several months for a reply, De Wang decided to convene a second Bailingmiao Congress in October. Taking matters into their own hands, the nearly 150 delegates voted to form an Inner Mongolian Autonomous Government (*Neimenggu zizhi zhengfu* or IMAG) that claimed authority over all Mongols living within the *original territory* of the Inner Mongolian leagues, banners, and tribes, as well as the right, with the exception of military and diplomatic affairs, to regulate all affairs within its territory.[48] In a cable to Nanjing, De Wang announced the creation of the IMAG and called for an immediate halt to the establishment of county (*xian*) administrations and further Chinese colonization on its territory. The new government requested Nanjing's active assistance in building an autonomous Inner Mongolia free from Chinese exploitation and foreign encroachment.[49]

Predictably, Yan Xishan's administration reacted strongly. Following the first meeting at Bailingmiao, Fu Zuoyi attempted to block any further gatherings, using violence and threats to prevent Ikhchao and Ulanchab League officials from attending the second congress.[50] He also dispatched Mongolian spies to infiltrate the Bailingmiao movement, and in regular cables sent back to Nanjing stressed De Wang's evil intentions.[51] At the same time, leading Suiyuan provincial officials sent their own petitions to Nanjing expressing their intense opposition to Mongolian autonomy. They contended that the Bailingmiao movement was driven solely by the selfish desire of the feudal princes to expand their personal authority and had little or no support among the Mongolian people. An October 1933 petition argued that the Mongols lacked the basic economic, political, and educational requirements for self-rule and needed a lengthy period of Han tutelage before being able to manage autonomous political activity. They also stressed that according to Sun Yat-sen's Three Principles of the People, only the county could serve as the basic unit of self-rule in China. Thus any future form of autonomy in Inner Mongolia must be located at the level of individual banners and counties rather than the entire Inner Mongolian region, as De Wang suggested.[52] In a second petition, the officials insisted that they would accept no form of Mongolian self-rule without strict conditions restricting it to the banner level, limiting its extent, ensuring a period of tutelage to prepare the Mongols, minimizing the cost to settlers, and guaranteeing their rights.[53]

The Guomindang's initial response to the Bailingmiao movement was divided. First, the CMTA proposed a two-stage solution. In the short term, it called on Fu Zuoyi to dispatch officials to dissuade Mongol princes from attending any future gatherings at Bailingmiao. And more substantively, it asked Wu Heling to draft another report, this time with the assistance of two Chinese CMTA officials, examining whether Inner Mongolian autonomy was warranted.[54] That report argued that the right of minority self-rule was contained within the Guomindang's party program and thus should be permitted as long as it was directly supervised by the central government and did not interfere with national unity, foreign policy, or national defense. Wu's report called for the immediate creation of a Preparatory Committee for Mongolian Autonomy to pave the way for a unified and autonomous Inner Mongolian government.[55] Top Guomindang officials, however, rejected the CMTA's proposal out of hand.

The party leadership clearly valued its relationship with Yan Xishan more than it did a handful of discontented Mongol princes. Though Nanjing had defeated the anti-Chiang northern coalition in the civil war of 1930, its control over external provinces remained weak. The central government continued to face the direct threat of rebellion from the powerful southern militarists of Guangdong and Guangxi who formalized their autonomy from Nanjing at the end of 1931 with the creation of the Southwest Political Council (SWPC) and the Southwest Headquarters of the Guomindang Central Executive Committee. In this precarious position, Nanjing deemed the support of Yan Xishan's northern regime to be crucial, or at least wanted to prevent him from joining forces with the SWPC in a move that would likely topple Chiang's government.[56] Therefore, it was not surprising that Nanjing's initial response to De Wang's autonomous movement closely mirrored the opinions and policy suggestions of Yan Xishan's frontier officials.

On October 7, 1933, Wang Jingwei, chairman of the Executive Yuan, forwarded Fu Zuoyi's policy recommendation on the crisis to CMTA chairman Shi Qingyang, recommending that the central government adopt a traditional "threaten and console" (*weilen*) approach to "snuff out De Wang's deceitful scheme."[57] Like Fu, Wang Jingwei contended that most Mongol princes opposed De Wang's movement, and the central government should stop at nothing to win them over in order to isolate and then exterminate De Wang's movement. Three days later the Executive Yuan approved the Draft Revision of Mongolian Administration,[58] which aimed at placating De Wang even as it brought the Mongols more firmly under provincial control. The plan called for the creation of several local autonomous councils that would deal directly with banner affairs and prepare the Mongols for an undisclosed future state of unified self-rule; in the meantime, however, they were to be placed directly under the jurisdiction of Chinese provincial officials. Banner and provincial officials were to staff these autonomous councils, which would be chaired by a top provincial official.

In order to convey the central government's new plan to De Wang and the Mongols, the Executive Yuan dispatched to Bailingmiao a delegation of top government and party officials led by Minister of the Interior General Huang Shaoxiong and CMTA vice chairman Zhao Pilian.[59] General Huang's mission arrived in Bailingmiao on November 10, 1933, under military escort from the Seventeenth Army Group, ensuring their safety and setting the tone for the talks. The general met with top IMAG officials and presented the Executive Yuan's plan to De Wang. He also issued a public proclamation to the Mongolian people that had been written by Wang Jingwei on behalf of the Central Government. "Presently," it declared, "the Inner Mongolian people wish to carry out self-rule, but the Central Government in all generosity cannot allow this; instead it desires to cultivate and guide [the Mongolian people] so that they might fully mature." The proclamation cautioned against "skipping over normal stages" and called for an extensive but fixed period of central government tutelage aimed at raising the level of education, culture, and economic well-being of the Mongolian people. It also warned against any damage to the existing system of provincial rule, referring to the local autonomous councils as a "preliminary trial in self-rule."[60] Realizing that central government support was crucial to any genuine future Mongolian autonomy, De Wang expressed his willingness to consider the proposal and called on General Huang to negotiate the details in Bailingmiao.

During an extended period of talks, Huang Shaoxiong agreed to present De Wang's eleven-point counterproposal to the central government if he would approve the creation of two separate autonomous political councils (divided along the lines of Chahar and Suiyuan provinces) that, as the general insisted, would be placed under *Executive Yuan jurisdiction* while working closely with the authorities of the two frontier provinces. De Wang reluctantly assented, and on November 19, General Huang departed Bailingmiao with a promise to personally deliver De Wang's new proposal to Premier Wang Jingwei.[61] But rather than returning directly to the capital, General Huang traveled secretly to Taiyuan to meet with Yan Xishan, whose endorsement he realized was necessary if any compromise was to succeed.

As General Huang arrived in Taiyuan, events were unfolding in southern China that would ensure that, for the time being at least, Yan Xishan and not De Wang or even the central government would have the final word on the political shape of Inner Mongolia. On November 20, 1933, a coalition of Fujian-based anti-Nanjing rebels—led by the immensely popular Chen Mingshu and his Nineteenth Route Army, the "national heroes" who defended Shanghai against Japanese attack in January 1932—declared Fujian province's independence from the Nanjing government. Claiming that Chiang Kai-shek's regime was slowly destroying the nation, the rebels called on other provinces to break with Nanjing. The Fujian rebellion momentarily shook the balance of power in China, setting off a race for allies that, according to Lloyd Eastman, "forced all elements in the Chinese political world to shift, or threaten to shift, their positions in order to maintain themselves in the new political equilibrium."[62] Initially, it appeared that the powerful SWPC would support their neighbors in Fujian, while the position of Yan Xishan's northwestern regime was less clear. Yan declared his support for Nanjing but simultaneously dispatched representatives to meet with the Fujian rebels. He also approached other northern warlords such as Feng Yuxiang and Han Fuqu about a possible anti-Chiang coalition.

With the Mongolian autonomous movement a prickly thorn in the side of Yan's regime, General Huang moved quickly to solve the problem and maintain his neutrality in the Fujian revolt. In their Taiyuan talks, the two men agreed on a secret alternative plan calling for a largely symbolic and virtually meaningless form of Inner Mongolian autonomy, which in reality placed the Mongolian banners firmly under the control of Yan Xishan's frontier officials.[63] On the surface, the Taiyuan plan looked similar to De Wang's compromise proposal. For example, it called for the creation of two autonomous Inner Mongolian political councils under the authority of the Executive Yuan; but it gave sweeping economic and political authority to provincial officials in regulating the affairs of the two councils.[64] When he returned to the capital in December, General Huang presented the secret Taiyuan proposal to the Executive Yuan, claiming that the plan was De Wang's own. Following a round of discussions by the Central Political Bureau of the Guomindang, the central government officially endorsed the Eleven Methods for Inner Mongolian Autonomy on January 17, 1934.[65]

Nanjing's Reversal and the Emergence of Chiang Kai-shek's Frontier Policy

Only eleven days after the passage of the Taiyuan plan, Premier Wang Jingwei held a closed-door meeting with top Mongolian officials in Nanjing. In attendance were more than one hundred Mongolian leaders and top Guomindang officials, including Dai Jitao, Zhang Ji, Huang Shaoxiong, and Zhao Pilian. Led by Wu Heling, the Mongols aggressively pressed Wang Jingwei to reverse the government's January 17, 1934, decision and provide a greatly expanded and genuine form of Mongolian autonomy. After the meeting, Wang Jingwei asked Wu Heling to draft an alternative plan more acceptable to the Mongols; and on February 28, 1934, in an unprecedented reversal, the Guomindang's Central Political Bureau approved Wu Heting's eight-point plan to create a single, unified Mongolian Local Autonomous Political Affairs Council (*Menggu difang zizhi zhengwu weiyuanhui* or *Mengzhenghui*, the Mongolian Political Council, MPC). Several weeks later, in an astonishing turn of events, the Executive Yuan issued an order calling for the implementation of this plan, which closely resembled De Wang's original eleven-point proposal handed to General Huang back in November.[66]

At least three factors seemed to lie behind this sudden reversal. First, the central government was no longer worried that Yan Xishan would revolt. As Yan and other provincial militarists were contemplating whether to join the Fujian rebels, Chiang's army launched a massive military offensive in late January; many rebels defected, and the rebellion was easily crushed.[67] The event marked the last direct threat to the authority of the Guomindang Central Government. The speed and ease with which Chiang's increasingly powerful military triumphed persuaded Yan Xishan and his fellow warlords to choose self-preservation within a loosely centralized Nationalist Party government over outright resistance.

Second, De Wang's representatives in Nanjing brought enormous pressure to bear on the Nanjing government. After General Huang left Bailingmiao, De Wang dispatched a delegation of Mongolian dignitaries, led by the politically savvy Wu Heling, to keep the pressure on the central government. In Nanjing, Wu rallied the expatriate Mongolian community. Through a series of carefully orchestrated press conferences and symbolic outings to Sun Yat-sen's tomb and other places of historical and political significance, the Mongols manipulated public opinion to highlight that their struggle for autonomy was faithful to Sun Yat-sen's Three Principles of the People. In nearly daily reports, the Nanjing and Shanghai newspapers sympathetically chronicled the activities of the Mongolian representatives. Following the public disclosure of General Huang's secret meetings with Yan Xishan, the Mongols presented a detailed and passionate petition to Lin Sen, the Chairman of the Nationalist Party government, claiming that the general had negotiated in bad faith at Bailingmiao and had failed to keep his promise to submit the proposal to the Executive Yuan. Around the same time, the chieftain and vice chieftain of the Ikhchao League cabled the central government claiming that Fu Zuoyi had coerced them into declaring their opposition to the Bailingmiao congresses.[68]

Third, and perhaps most importantly, Chiang Kai-shek decided to personally throw his support behind De Wang's autonomous government.[69] Chiang was busy directing the fifth and final encirclement campaign against the CCP's Jiangxi Soviet from his military field headquarters in Nanchang and had no involvement in the Executive Yuan's day-to-day handling of the Mongolian situation as events were unfolding. By late January 1934, however, the Mongolian autonomous movement had become front-page news throughout China. Chiang would have feared any shift in public attention away from his government's efforts to destroy the Communist bandits and consolidate control over the provinces. Or, in an equally dangerous shift, the plight of the Mongols might redirect public attention toward the growing threat of Japanese encroachment in northern China. In contrast to the transfrontiersmen, Chiang seemed to have believed that establishing a pro-Nanjing regime in Inner Mongolia would provide a useful buffer zone against Japanese imperialism and a counterbalance to Yan Xishan's regionalism.

In his first public speech on the GMD government's frontier policy in March 1934, Chiang expressed his support for Mongolian autonomy. He began by asserting that the so-called frontier question was actually a question of diplomacy. A country that is powerful enough can rely on brute force to solve the frontier problem and secure its borders against foreign encroachment; but if, like China, a country is weak and faced with both internal and external enemies, it must rely instead on a careful and well-crafted strategy. At its current stage, Chiang argued, a conciliatory (*rouxing)* policy was the most effective means for dealing with the frontier question. Since the Chinese state currently lacked the strength to directly control the frontier, it was better to create a balance of power aimed at maintaining long-term stability, while strengthening itself domestically and preparing for the day when it would be able to consolidate its frontier. "If we let them go and rule themselves," Chiang stressed, "the border people will enjoy their freedom. Yet amongst their traditional customs there still exists a good deal of room for loose rein (jimi) and enticement (longluo). If we put up a bold front, they will become alienated and divided. This is the only way that we can hope to rule them."[70] Moreover, if their requests for self-rule were denied, the Inner Mongols and other frontier peoples would turn to the imperialists for help and invite further foreign interference in China's internal affairs. Thus, only a tolerant and magnanimous policy of self-rule could solve China's frontier problem. Somewhat ironically, Chiang put forward the USSR as a model worth emulating, concluding that:

> We must seek the road of preservation in the intense conflict with the various imperialist powers—strengthening our national power while quietly waiting for the opportunity to recover our lost territories, stabilize the frontier and revive our country. Now all we can do is stand and wait. Yet, the current situation

> requires a plan and the establishment of a clear policy. I believe that the most appropriate policy is to follow the example of the Soviet Union's voluntary federation (*lianbang ziyou*) and in the spirit of a republic of five races (wuzu gonghe) call for the establishment of a federation of five races (*wuzu lianbang*).[71]

As this important, yet previously overlooked speech demonstrates, Chiang's pragmatic approach to the frontier question was rooted in what he viewed as the proven historical precedents of imperial Chinese and Soviet Russian frontier policy. Like Sun Tzu wrote some 2,500 years ago, "He who is prudent and lies in wait for an enemy who is not, will be victorious."[72]

But in the end, even Chiang's public support was not enough to overcome the spirited opposition of the transfrontiersmen to Inner Mongolian autonomy, as they fought nearly as hard over taxes as land. Both the Mongols and the provincial warlords realized that an autonomous Mongolian government was toothless without the ability to collect its own revenue. In his final negotiations with Guomindang officials, Wu Heling won a modest monthly subsidy from the central government to cover the administrative cost of the MPC and a promise that the Inner Mongolian government could collect its own taxes from within banner territory. When the monies from Nanjing arrived late and below the levels pledged, De Wang decided to test the wording and spirit of the new agreement by taxing Yan Xishan's extremely profitable opium caravans as they passed through Mongolian territory. The predictable result was a tense standoff between the MPC and the Suiyuan and Shanxi provincial authorities, who quickly dispatched heavily armed troops to secure the opium route. In an effort to force the MPC into submission, Fu Zuoyi's Suiyuan government also imposed a grain embargo on the Mongolian banners and bribed some of their princes into publicly criticizing the MPC. De Wang's repeated protests to Nanjing brought no response.[73]

In early summer, De Wang dispatched one of his top officials, Togtakhu, to Lushan to request assistance directly from Chiang Kai-shek while he also began to explore other options, including the possibility of Japanese support for Inner Mongolian autonomy. Togtakhu complained to Chiang about provincial interference in the MPC's affairs and warned him of Japanese attempts to court Mongolian officials. Chiang agreed to provide the MPC an increased monthly stipend of 300,000 yuan, a construction grant of 120,000 yuan, and the weapons and equipment needed to strengthen its fledgling administration. Yet, once again, the money and equipment failed to arrive in full; most was confiscated by provincial authorities before it reached Bailingmiao. In one last-ditch effort to secure help, Prince Yon and De Wang traveled to Guihua in September 1934 to meet with Chiang during his tour of the northwest frontier. De Wang pressed Chiang for the promised funding and weapons to protect the Mongolians and the entire nation against the growing threat of Japanese invasion. But this time, Chiang showed very little interest in their plight.[74] It appears that sometime during the summer of 1934, the Guomindang leader wrote off De Wang and his Mongols, turning his attention and all his resources to his efforts to exterminate the Chinese Communists. Frustrated, De Wang began open negotiations with the Japanese, eventually flying to Changchun to sign a formal agreement of cooperation between the MPC and the puppet state of Manchukuo. As Owen Lattimore concluded, De Wang did not "go over" to Japan, as Chiang and others claimed; instead, he was "tied hand and foot and thrown to the Japanese."[75]

Liu Wenhui and the Xikang/Kham Borderland

In the southwest, Chiang's Nanjing government adopted a similar policy aimed at coaxing Tibet firmly back into the Chinese political orb. Yet, like Inner Mongolia, the Nationalist Party government had to contend with the autonomous power and competing interests of the transfrontiersmen and their warlord patrons. Following the collapse of the Qing dynasty, Sichuan split into several competing militarist regimes, each vying to control the fertile Sichuan basin and win greater independence from the central government. The success of the Northern Expedition and the establishment of the new Guomindang national government made little difference. After declaring their allegiance to the Guomindang and adopting the necessary revolutionary rhetoric, each of the Sichuan militarists and their armies were symbolically incorporated into the new National Revolutionary Army. However, as Robert Kapp has pointed out, the early Republic marked one of the high marks of Sichuanese autonomy and independence from outside influences.[76] When the Nationalist Party government picked what it believed was the best of the lot to head its new government in the province—a government that existed in name only—General Liu Wenhui, the charismatic thirty-two-year-old commander of the two-hundred-thousand-strong Twenty-fourth Army, became its chairman.[77] The real prize for General Liu was his appointment as commander in chief of the Sichuan-Xikang Border Defense Force (*Chuan-kang bianfangjun*) following the retirement of Liu Chengxun in 1927. Along the Xikang frontier zone between Sichuan and Tibet, General Liu saw the untapped resources he hoped would permanently tip the balance of power in Sichuan in his favor.

Liu Wenhui's relationship with the Guomindang Central Government in Nanjing was tense from the beginning. When Nanjing established the Inner Mongolian provinces of Suiyuan, Chahar, and Jehol in 1928, it also announced plans to create a new province of Xikang from the territory of the former Sichuan border region with Tibet. General Liu immediately sent a letter of protest to Nanjing, claiming that the size and resources of the proposed province were insufficient; more than half of the thirty-three counties would be controlled by the Tibetan military. He asked Nanjing to increase the number of revenue-producing counties to forty-five by adding eight counties from neighboring

Sichuan, Yunnan, and Qinghai provinces. He also requested thousands of dollars from the government treasury in order to develop Xikang and restore Chinese sovereignty over Tibet.[78] Nanjing ignored Liu's plea and dispatched its own team of officials, led by the Tibetan CMTA official Kesang Tsering,[79] to "assist" him in preparing for the establishment of the new province. Refusing to cooperate with Kesang, Liu Wenhui set up his own Xikang Special Administrative Committee (*Xikang tequ zhengwu weiyuanhui*) without Nanjing's approval.[80] When Kesang attempted to establish a rival Xikang Provincial Defense Force and Commission for the Establishment of Xikang Province (*Xikang jiansheng weiyuanhui*) in Batang, Liu started executing members of Kesang's staff. Nanjing quickly backed down and ordered Kesang to leave the region, recognizing the authority of Liu's administrative committee.[81] Given its tenuous hold over most of China at the time, Nanjing could ill afford to alienate those frontier warlords who were willing to pay lip service to its authority. Chiang Kai-shek had little hope of consolidating his rule over China without the support of powerful regional allies.

Over the next two and a half decades, Liu Wenhui ruled Xikang as his personal fiefdom and potential springboard for eventual rule over all of Sichuan. Working from their offices in Kangding, members of the Xikang Special Administrative Committee drew up detailed plans to build new roads, railway lines, factories, mines, and agricultural research centers that they hoped would open the region's vast forests, grasslands, and mineral resources to exploitation. But to undertake such development while also increasing the size of his army, Liu Wenhui needed to attract colonists and administrators to the underpopulated region.[82] While millions did not flock to Xikang, the relative stability of Liu's regime and profits from opium—which reportedly Liu called the "lifeline" of the Twenty-fourth Army—together with the lucrative tea trade with Tibet,[83] did produce a sharp rise in the Chinese population of Xikang. For example, the population of Kangding county grew from 2,900 to 8,234 families between 1930 and 1934. In 1936, it was estimated that the Chinese constituted 16 percent or 600,000 of Xikang's 3.8 million people.[84]

To cultivate the expertise necessary for the development of Xikang, in September 1929 the offices of the Twenty-fourth Army launched the first Chinese journal dedicated specifically to frontier administration, *Bianzheng* (*Frontier Administration*). The journal employed the new language of "revolution"—national unity, political representation, and economic development, as couched in Sun Yat-sen's Three Principles of the People—to promote the interest of the region and its people. By describing Xikang as a "gold vault" and "treasure trove" rich in gold, silver, copper, timber, medicinal herbs, and other natural resources, the journal's editors hoped to lure additional Chinese colonists to the region. They also warned, however, that this untapped wealth was attracting the greedy eyes of foreign imperialists and called on the central government to allocate special funds to develop this strategic "buffer zone."[85] Like other militarist regimes on the fringes of Republican China, Liu Wenhui's Twenty-fourth Army was quick to adopt the modern discourse of revolution to advance its control and domination over local resources and garner the support of the political center—or, at the very least, keep it at arm's length and out of local affairs.[86]

Unique insight into Liu Wenhui's modernist, revolutionary discourse is offered by a propaganda play serialized in *Bianzheng* during the fall of 1929. Titled *To the Frontier* (*Dao biandi qu*), the play tells the story of a Chengdu youth's decision to forsake his elderly parents and childless wife for the hardships of the Xikang frontier.[87] The story's protagonist, Kong Zhenyuan (or Kong the Pacifier of Distant Lands), learns of the importance of the Xikang frontier after returning from studying geology in England. One of his friends tells him that England has recently sent troops into Tibet and is cunningly inciting the Tibetans to raise an army and attack the interior, threatening not only Xikang and Sichuan but all of China. Another laments that the abundant natural resources of Xikang remain untapped because of the shortage of experts and colonists. Patriotism stirs Kong into action. Arguing that "family-ism" (*jiazuzhuyi*) needs to be replaced with "race-state-ism" (*guozuzhuyi*), Kong ignores the emotional pleas of his family and departs for the frontier.

During his journey of several months on foot to the Yangtze border town of Batang, Kong and his trusted servant Old Wang endure numerous hardships—a diet of *tsampa* (barley paste gruel), dirty inns, freezing weather, and harsh travel conditions—before finally being stripped of all their outer garments and money by ruthless bandits. Aided by one of Liu Wenhui's officers, Kong at last reaches Batang, where he is treated like a messiah-king by a mob of childlike Tibetan barbarians (*yizhong*) who sing and dance in wild excitement when they learn of Kong's intention to "bridge the boundary between the Han and barbarians, abolish their suffering, and foil the secret plans of the English imperialists to invade China."[88]

During one of the final scenes titled "A Glimpse at the Accomplishments," the audience learns of the rewards reaped by Kong's numerous sacrifices and by extension other Chinese youths willing to head out into the frontier. When a couple of old friends from Chengdu pay a visit to the offices of his Xikang Construction Department in Chamdo, Kong explains the recent accomplishments of his office. Detailed survey maps have enabled the Twenty-fourth Army to advance within sixty miles of Lhasa. Kong's development plans have led to the opening of numerous mines, factories, tanneries, and dairies, while more than one hundred thousand *mu* of wasteland have been brought under cultivation. The comments of his friends made clear that Kong has benefited financially from his selfless contribution to his country. The play ends with Kong's triumphant return home over the New Year holiday to discover that his wife has given birth to their first child—a son, of course! General Liu hoped that performances of this play and others would attract the talent and resources he needed to develop the Xikang frontier region and maintain his independent fiefdom.[89]

Mapping the Disputed Sino-Tibetan Border

As the tale of Kong Zhenyuan illustrates, the Xikang border with Tibet was a locus of intense conflict between Lhasa and Liu Wenhui's autonomous regime. Throughout the late Qing and the early twentieth century, control over the rugged Sino-Tibetan borderland seesawed back and forth between the Tibetan army and the Sichuan warlords. During the waning years of the Qing dynasty, the Sichuan General Zhao Erfeng led an expeditionary force to within sixty miles of Lhasa, only to be pushed back across the upper reaches of the Yangtze River after the Manchu dynasty collapsed.[90] The Tibetans, under the leadership of the thirteenth Dalai Lama, drove out the Manchu/Chinese officials from Lhasa and declared Tibet proper—together with the ethnically Tibetan, although largely autonomous, regions of Amdo (Qinghai) and Kham (Xikang)—part of an independent Tibetan state. Hoping to mediate the conflict along the disputed border and secure a zone of influence in Tibet, the British government pressured the Chinese into attending a three-party conference at Simla in 1913. Following several months of intense negotiations, the parties agreed to recognize Chinese suzerainty over Tibet in exchange for extensive Tibetan autonomy and the recognition of England's special interests in the region.[91]

Determining Tibet's border with China proved much more difficult, however. Although an 821 peace treaty signed between Tibet and Tang China marked the border between the two powers in perpetuity, the line between Chinese and Tibetan civilization remained in flux throughout the premodern period.[92] The aristocratic and monastic rulers of Kham and Amdo looked, at different times and with differing degrees of emphasis, to both Tibet and China as sources of political patronage and trade. The new nation-state that established a clear link between sovereignty and territoriality had changed the stakes. The three powers that met at Simla intended to map a fixed boundary that would secure their maximum national benefit.[93]

The Chinese insisted on using the line of Zhao Erfeng's furthest conquest and drew the boundary through Giamda, sixty miles east of Lhasa. The Tibetans wanted the Buddhist monasteries of Amdo and Kham included within their territory and proposed a Tibetan frontier stretching northeast into modern-day Qinghai and southeast through Kangding, the capital of Xikang. Attempting to ensure England's continued influence in Lhasa, Sir Henry McMahon proposed his compromise border (the so-called McMahon line) running along the upper reaches of the Yangtze River and dividing Tibet into "Inner" and "Outer" halves. The towns of Outer Tibet, west of the Yangtze, were to be placed directly under the administration of Lhasa, while those within Inner Tibet, east of the Yangtze, would be jointly administered, with the Tibetans retaining full control over all religious affairs. Under intense public pressure to stand firm on the frontier question following the revelation of open Russian interference in Outer Mongolia, the Beijing government of Yuan Shikai refused to sign the final agreement.[94]

Liu Wenhui's rise to power in Xikang only exacerbated this border dispute. During the late 1920s, the Twenty-fourth Army pushed the Tibetan forces west of the Yangtze, gradually garrisoning a number of settlements on the river's eastern shores. In the summer of 1930, the Tibetan militia in Kham counterattacked Liu's positions in Xikang on the pretext of assisting the Tibetan monks of the Targye Monastery in their long-running dispute with the Twenty-fourth-Army-backed Pehru tribal chieftain (*tusi*). Thanks to its new weaponry and training received from the British, the Tibetan army quickly pushed the overextended forces of Liu Wenhui back to within one hundred miles of Kangding.[95] At the request of the thirteenth Dalai Lama, the central government redispatched CMTA official Kesang Tsering to mediate the conflict. Liu Wenhui again refused to cooperate with Nanjing, preferring to solve the problem militarily rather than politically. Attempting to override Liu Wenhui's authority, Kesang dispatched his own officials to Kanze with orders to negotiate an immediate armistice. The draft accord reached on November 7, 1931, recognized the Tibetans as the victors in the conflict, agreeing to their demands that a demilitarized zone be established in western Xikang and that Liu Wenhui's Xikang regime pay an indemnity of twenty thousand yuan. Yet, when word of the agreement slipped out, it not only sent Liu Wenhui's administration into an uproar, but also captured the attention and ire of the national media in China. At a time of rising nationalist sentiment—Japan had invaded Manchuria only two months earlier—the Chinese media blamed the British imperialists for instigating the incident and criticized the government for appeasing rather than fighting China's enemies. This public pressure forced the central government to cable Kesang with instructions not to sign the accord, and CMTA chairman Shi Qingyang stepped down in embarrassment.[96]

Nanjing had little choice but to cable Liu Wenhui with complete authority to solve the matter on his own. Within weeks the Twenty-fourth Army launched a massive counteroffensive against the Tibetan forces. Assisted by the Qinghai warlord Ma Bufang, Liu hoped to put an end to the border conflict once and for all by marching all the way to Lhasa. Liu's forces quickly drove the Kham militia west of the Yangtze River and in the summer of 1932, began preparing for an attack on Chamdo. The Dalai Lama cabled Nanjing for assistance, and again the central government called on both sides to put down their arms and resolve the border problem peacefully. Liu Wenhui simply ignored the central government, forcing Nanjing to admit to the Dalai Lama that it was helpless to prevent the "self-defense activities of local officials."[97] The Twenty-fourth Army might have succeeded in marching to Lhasa had not an outside party intervened. Sensing that Liu Wenhui had overextended the resources of his Twenty-fourth Army, his uncle and fellow Sichuan warlord Liu Xiang launched an offensive against Liu Wenhui's position in Sichuan. Liu Wenhui quickly sought a truce with the Tibetans so that his Xikang forces could join the raging civil war in Sichuan. The October 8, 1932, cease-fire called for the Tibetans to remain west of the Yangtze

River and the Chinese to the east, temporarily returning an uneasy state of peace to the Sino-Tibetan border.[98]

Tensions flared up again in the fall of 1933 when the thirteenth Dalai Lama issued an ultimatum to Liu Wenhui's troops to withdraw further east or face yet another attack from the Tibetan army.[99] But when the Dalai Lama died suddenly on December 17, 1933, the balance of power shifted back to the Chinese. Hoping to take advantage of the political instability that followed the Dalai Lama's death, Liu Wenhui cabled Chiang Kai-shek asking for the central government's assistance in sending a massive expeditionary force against Tibet. Liu Wenhui argued that the Tibetan "barbarians" understood only force, or as one of his border officials once declared, "I advocate the use of force first and grace second. . . . to give a barbarian a bit of respect is not as good as beating him a bit."[100] In Nanjing, however, Dai Jitao and other close advisers to Chiang Kai-shek called for a conciliatory policy toward the Tibetans. Dai also saw the death of the Dalai Lama as providing an excellent opportunity for the Nanjing government to demonstrate its respect for Buddhism and reestablish its position as the external protector of Tibetan Buddhism. He stressed that Buddhism, which had historically linked all five of the Republic's minzus, created the foundations for a natural bond between the Chinese and Tibetan peoples.[101] On December 23, 1933, the central government urged Liu Wenhui to show restraint, claiming that dispatching troops would only invite more trouble.[102] Paying his usual attention to Nanjing's orders, Liu would have probably marched on Lhasa himself had his Twenty-fourth Army not suffered a big defeat at the hands of his uncle's forces and had to retreat to Xikang to rebuild its strength.

Huang Musong's Mission and the Failure of Sino-Tibetan Rapprochement

The death of the thirteenth Dalai Lama and the defeat of Liu Wenhui's troops presented the central government with its first real chance to seize the initiative in Sino-Tibetan relations. In recent years, the Dalai Lama and the religious elite had become disenchanted with the aggressive, pro-British military officers of the Tibetan army. The almost constant state of conflict with Liu Wenhui's Twenty-fourth Army was draining precious resources from the monasteries and threatening to destabilize Tibet internally. Furthermore, these tensions had greatly reduced Tibetan exports to China and caused the price of Chinese tea to rise tenfold in Lhasa, placing an even further strain on the Tibetan economy.[103] The religious establishment in Lhasa viewed Sino-Tibetan rapprochement as a potential counterbalance to Liu Wenhui's military adventurism on the Xikang frontier. As the Dalai Lama told CMTA official Liu Manqing in 1929, he hoped that the new Chinese government would remove the "corrupt and adventurous [Chinese] civil and military officers" in Kham and replace them with honest men who would work for the mutual interests of the Tibetan and Chinese people.[104]

The prospects for better relations increased with the selection of a pro-Chinese Kashag, or cabinet (led by the twenty-four-year-old regent, Reting Rinpoche), to serve as the interim government until the next Dalai Lama was discovered and grew to maturity. Attempting to seize the initiative in this new political environment, the Guomindang proposed in late 1934 to send a delegation to Lhasa to offer the nation's condolences on the death of the Dalai Lama and discuss Sino-Tibetan relations. Chiang Kai-shek selected General Huang Musong—one of his most trusted and skilled frontier diplomats and a devout Buddhist—to lead more than eighty specially selected CMTA officials and staff members. Besides representing the central government at a special memorial service for the thirteenth Dalai Lama, Nanjing also authorized General Huang to carry out high-level negotiations with the Tibetan government. In exchange for pledging their loyalty to the Guomindang government and acknowledging that Tibet was part of a single, unified Zhonghua Republic, the central government was willing to grant the Tibetans the same degree of political, cultural, and religious autonomy they had enjoyed under the Qing dynasty. When the Kashag agreed to the delegation, Nanjing seemed on the verge of a historic solution to the Tibetan problem.[105]

But the hopes of the Guomindang government were quickly shattered. On his way to Lhasa, General Huang stopped in Chengdu to consult with General Liu Wenhui, whose support seemed crucial for success, but he received little encouragement or assistance. Fearing, perhaps, that Nanjing was willing to sacrifice Xikang for the sake of resuming relations with Lhasa, Liu Wenhui stressed the importance of maintaining, at the very least, the Yangtze River border between Tibet and Xikang. He also expressed his desire that the Chinese quickly regain control over Chamdo before a new, permanent border was created along the Taniantaweng Mountains east of the Salween River.[106] Quickly realizing that the border question was beyond his control, General Huang hoped to restrict talks with the Tibetans to the more general issue of Sino-Tibetan relations. Yet after he arrived in Lhasa on August 28, 1934, Reting Rinpoche made very clear to him that the Tibetan government's first priority was to solve the border issue. General Huang replied that the minor issue of the border could be quickly resolved once relations had been resumed and emphasized that the central government was willing to be "highly flexible" over the exact nature of those relations. In the following weeks, Huang's staff repeatedly pressed the Kashag to specify in writing the exact nature of the relationship it desired with Nanjing. The Kashag ignored these requests, insisting on discussing the border issue first.[107]

With negotiations deadlocked before they even began, General Huang announced that the Chinese government had magnanimously agreed to a major concession: it would discuss the border issue and the resumption of Sino-Tibetan relations simultaneously.[108] Again, the general asked the Kashag for a written list of conditions that the Tibetans felt had to be met before good relations could be established with Nanjing. The Tibetans finally acquiesced, and on October 5, 1935, they handed the Chinese a document that disappointed if not shocked them. The Kashag's letter stated that to improve relations with Tibet, the central government should first "return all land and peoples where the Han and Tibetan cultures and languages exist side-by-side to the control of the Tibetan government."[109] The Kashag made it clear that a precondition was returning to Tibetan control the entire region of Kham (Xikang) and Amdo (Qinghai), which had been under direct Chinese administration since the Qing dynasty. General Huang was clearly frustrated as he was under direct orders from Chiang Kai-shek to avoid the border issue at all costs.[110]

Premier Wang Jingwei, on the other hand, saw room for optimism in Huang Musong's cables back to Nanjing. In particular, Wang was encouraged by the details of the general's informal discussions with Reting Rinpoche during which the regent expressed his willingness, in exchange for "complete Tibetan autonomy" (*Xizang wanquan zizhi*), to cooperate with the other four minzus in the creation of a single Zhonghua minzu. In a cable to Huang, Wang Jingwei stressed that "Sino-Tibetan relations have already amassed an importance that is difficult to back away from; since negotiations are difficult, we need to loosen our desires."[111] Wang told Huang to offer Tibet a level of autonomy similar to that recently granted to Inner Mongolia and promised that the Nanjing government would take concrete steps to diffuse the border issue. The Kashag agreed to bring Nanjing's proposal to the Tibetan National Assembly. Once again, however, the Tibetan response fell short of Chinese expectations. The National Assembly claimed that the Chinese system of a republic of five races did not suit Tibet's special theocratic system of government and would violate Tibetan sovereignty. Instead, it once again called for an immediate return of Amdo and Kham to Tibetan administration. By mid-October the negotiations had reached an impasse, and General Huang was ordered to pack his bags and return to Nanjing.[112]

Huang Musong's decision to leave Lhasa appeared to set off a wave of panic throughout the Tibetan administration. Realizing that nothing had been achieved that could lower tensions along its borders, the Kashag urged him to remain a few more days in order to discuss their new thirteen-point oral proposal for the resumption of Sino-Tibetan relations. General Huang immediately cabled a summary of the Kashag's new proposal back to Nanjing. Despite recommending that the central government tactfully reject the Tibetan proposal, owing to its insistence that Tibet be permitted to handle its own foreign affairs, General Huang was optimistic that much of its language could serve as a basis for a future agreement restoring Sino-Tibetan relations. Once again, however, the Xikang border issue was the sticking point.[113] The central government was willing to grant Tibet a high degree of political and cultural autonomy within the framework of the traditional priest-patron relationship; but it was not willing—or, more to the point, able—to accept the Tibetan government's repeated requests for the return of all land in Kham and Amdo to Tibetan administration. On November 10, Wang Jingwei stressed to General Huang that "there is no possibility to negotiate the Xikang-Tibetan dispute yourself."[114] Huang Musong was again told to pack his bags for Nanjing.

Wang Jingwei did, however, authorize General Huang to draft one final counterproposal before leaving Lhasa, but warned that it should be a personal letter rather than an official submission on behalf of the Chinese government.[115] The exact nature of the general's final offer is unclear, and the Chinese archives appear to hold no official record of it. According to one of the delegation's political advisers, General Huang's letter did not raise the contentious border issue but rather focused on the need to alter the language of the Tibetan proposal to ensure central government control over foreign policy and other national issues.[116] Norbhu Döndup, the British-Indian officer in Lhasa, claims that Huang presented the Kashag with a detailed fourteen-point counterproposal. According to Döndup, the general's plan agreed to recognize "the boundary existing at the time of the Emperor Guangxu"—namely, the Yangtze River boundary agreed on in the 1932 armistice with Liu Wenhui.[117] In their otherwise positive reply, the Kashag demonstrated some flexibility on the border issue but again rejected Huang Musong's proposed solution to the Xikang problem. The Tibetans were willing to concede control over much of Amdo/Qinghai but not Kham/Xikang, where Liu Wenhui's Twenty-fourth Army continued to pose a direct threat to their government's future stability. They replied, "In order to improve Sino-Tibet relations while avoiding future disputes and stabilizing the border region, the northeastern boundary between Qinghai and Tibet should be maintained as proposed the year before last [1932], with Golok, which has long been under Tibet, to be included on the Tibetan side. As for the boundary between Tibet and Sichuan, the territory and people of Dege, Nyarong, Kanze, and the Targye monastery [east of the Yangtze River] should be turned over to the Tibetan government at the earliest possible date."[118] This final response made it clear that the Kashag's overriding concern was the creation of a buffer zone in western Xikang to protect Tibet from any future aggression by General Liu Wenhui and his Twenty-fourth Army.

A recent reevaluation of General Huang's mission to Lhasa and GMD policy toward Tibet has argued that the party adopted a "vague, ad hoc attitude toward Tibetan affairs," querying whether its leadership was ever "genuinely anxious about losing Tibet, or even other outlying ethnic borderlands."[119] Misreading the GMD's policy pragmatism as a lack of desire and intension to exercise complete sovereignty over the frontier, the author seems to underestimate the constraints on Guomindang authority outside the capital. The strategic choice not to further alienate Liu Wenhui does not necessarily reflect a "reluctance to substantiate China's imagined and fictitious sovereignty over Tibet in the early 1930s."[120] Rather it seems to suggest that Chiang Kai-shek desired to first consolidate his party's control over the interior before attempting to exercise direct authority (both military and political) over the frontier.

While Huang Musong was in Lhasa negotiating with the Tibetan authorities, Chiang Kai-shek's troops had the Chinese Communists on the ropes and were chasing a tired Red Army north through Yunnan toward the Yangtze River. With the Communists set to cross the border into Xikang, Chiang Kai-shek had no hope of dealing Mao's Communists a final blow without the support of Liu Wenhui's Twenty-fourth Army—and Liu would never agree to Tibetan control over western Xikang. Furthermore, an unstable or Tibetan-controlled Kham might well provide safe haven for the Communists. In the struggle against the Communists, General Liu Wenhui appeared to be a more important ally than the Tibetans. Chiang Kai-shek therefore tried to draw him closer to the central government, declaring the government's intention to finance the creation of a new province in Xikang and naming General Liu chairman of the preparatory committee. Yet it is hardly surprising that the Red Army slipped through Xikang on their way north without General Liu's troops firing a single shot.[121] Trust was in short supply throughout the southwest.

Autonomous Borderlands: The Limits of GMD State Authority

Unlike Europe, state and nation building occurred alongside one another in China, laying the foundation for a hegemonic ideology that stressed "the sovereignty of the 'national whole' and a strong state as the representative of the nation."[122] Yet, as this chapter has demonstrated, the messy and mercurial nature of political power on the Republican frontier forces us to rethink the relationship between regionalism and national sovereignty in early twentieth-century China. In recent years, the postcolonial critique of nationalism has set its sights on deconstructing the nation-state as the grand narrative of linear, progressive history—"rescuing," it is hoped, repressed and subaltern narratives of subjecthood.[123] A number of leading historians have highlighted the positive role regional militarists played in promoting an alternative and more progressive vision of Chinese sovereignty built around regional autonomy and often set within a federalist framework.[124] In the failed provincial self-rule movements of Tan Yankai in Hunan or Chen Jiongming in Guangdong, they see a "cultural and political process whereby the hegemonic, centralist national ideology delegitimated and destroyed an alternative, federalist one."[125]

Yet, in the case of the ethnic frontiers of Republican China, the discourse of ethnic autonomy added another layer of complexity to the process of constructing the Chinese nation-state, producing both "centripetal" and "centrifugal" forms of nationalism and complicating the moral position of these regionalist strategies.[126] While at times ethnic self-interest intersected with the movement for regional autonomy, as in the case of the Sino-Muslim warlords of Gansu,[127] other frontier areas operated in a more fluid environment. Along the Inner Mongolian and Tibetan frontiers, the local versus center power dialogue between the militarists and the Guomindang Central Government was obscured by competing and often overlapping aspirations and identities—national self-determination, regional autonomy, irredentist nationalism, centralizing modernity, transnational class solidarity, and anti-Chinese imperialism—that pushed and pulled political actors in different directions depending on the specific situation.

This political web of interaction points up the limitations of any static center-periphery or state-local model of social change. Liminal borderlands, such as the Tibetan highlands and the Inner Mongolian steppe, present complex and multi-layered environments with multiple centers of authority. Here, independent structures and institutions operate outside a statist center-periphery model with some autonomous regimes, like those of Liu Wenhui and Fu Zuoyi, functioning as "parasitic" or "predatory" polities within the seams of large states and empires.[128] Their rule over and exploitation of frontier resources—opium and tea in Xikang and opium and wool in Inner Mongolia—clearly disrupted and frustrated the centralizing ambitions of Nanjing. At the same time, the highly decentralized and concentric system of political and cultural authority radiating throughout Tibetan and Mongolian society recalls the nested and unstable "galactic polities" that predated the modern system of territory-based nation-states.[129] Many current models of state building inadequately describe semi-colonial and developing countries like China, which until quite recently lacked the coercive authority and centralizing capacities of Western nation-states. In his classic study on the Great Lakes region of North America, Richard White describes a cultural and political "middle ground" where Native Americans and Europeans interacted as equals in the fluid spatial matrix that existed prior to the development and use of superior firepower by the English after the War of 1812.[130] Similarly, neither the GMD nor the CCP possessed the administrative, financial, and military resources necessary to impose their will along China's massive frontier region during the Republican period, rendering them contested ethnic and political spaces within a newly bounded yet fragile Chinese geo-body.

It is hardly unexpected that the Guomindang Central Government, operating within the confines of these contested and shifting notions of sovereignty and space in Republican China, adopted a cautious and conservative approach to the frontier question. What is perhaps more interesting is the language they chose to employ in rationalizing their policy. It merged elements of Sun Yat-sen's revolutionary discourse of minzuzhuyi with the historical and administrative precedents of Qing empire building. Stability and peace along the frontier were viewed as crucial to the consolidation of Guomindang power. During times of military weakness, such as the late Qing and Republican periods, the Chinese state adopted a compromising and loose-rein strategy aimed at drawing the frontier and its elites toward the political center. For centuries, Chinese dynasties had been toppled by rebellions that originated and festered along the frontier before threatening the Chinese heartland. Much like its Qing predecessors, the Guomindang state was quick to realize the truth in the traditional saying, "turmoil on the frontier brings rebellion to the interior."[131] Ability to maintain peace along the frontier was the ultimate signifier of a government's strength, authority, and majesty. And during times of weakness, the state sought to secure "tribute" or symbolic recognition from the "external vassals" in order to create the illusion of cosmic unity and moral superiority. Yet unlike the Chinese militarists or even the frontier administrations of the Dalai Lama and De Wang, state elites (working for both the GMD and CCP) were masters of international relationships. They were quick to realize the importance of diplomacy in mapping and clearly demarcating the boundaries of the nation's geo-body in the new global system of competing nation-states. Throughout the twentieth century, the Chinese state consistently asserted its sovereignty over the threatened frontier regions of the former Qing empire and resisted attempts by the British (in Tibet), Russians (in Xinjiang and Mongolia), and Japanese (in Manchuria, Mongolia, and then all of China) to invade and dismember the Chinese nation-state.

It is slightly ironic, yet far from surprising, that the Communist party-state co-opted the civilizing discourse of the Chinese warlords after their victory in 1949. Those frontier militarists who were peacefully incorporated into the Communist regime, such as Liu Wenhui in Xikang and Fu Zuoyi in Inner Mongolia, were praised by the party-state for their Herculean efforts to "develop the frontier," "resist foreign imperialism," and "assist the frontier minorities." By heaping the past history of exploitation onto the Guomindang Central Government, Communist scholars downplay the involvement of these so-called champions of national unity in the forced colonization and exploitation of frontier peoples and resources. Instead, their assimilationist policies are heaped on Chiang Kai-shek and his "reactionary regime," which, it is claimed, never seriously contemplated frontier autonomy.[132] This highlights the importance of reading Chinese secondary sources with caution, counteracting the trend in PRC historiography to project a unitary and bounded Chinese nation-state into earlier and much more dynamic periods. This tendency to read national history backwards not only distorts the historical record, but also plays into the hands of state-sponsored nationalism and its attempts to consolidate and reinforce its political power and erase alternative formulations.

CHAPTER 3

Domesticating Minzu: The Communists and the National Question

In his 1984 study *The National Question in Marxist-Leninist Theory and Strategy*, Walker Connor analyzed the role of Marxist nationality theory in the development of the CCP.[1] Contending that Communists around the world "manipulate nationalism into the service of Marxism,"[2] Connor attempted to show how Bolshevik parties in the Soviet Union, China, Vietnam, and Yugoslavia strategically employed the promise of national self-determination to gain power within a multiethnic environment. According to Connor, during its struggle with the Guomindang, the CCP proffered the Mongol, Hui, Tibetan, and other strategically important ethnic minorities' political independence from Chinese hegemony in order to secure their support, or at least a promise of neutrality toward its bid for national power. Yet after its triumph over the GMD in 1949, the Communists abruptly broke their promise and incorporated the minorities by force into a unitary state structure under central party rule. Though his work was pioneering, Connor had limited access to primary source materials (and all those in translation); the result is a misleading depiction of the CCP's engagement with the "national question" (*minzu wenti*) that does not hold up to the evidence contained in recently published archival material.

Connor was not the first scholar to comment on the importance of nationalism in the CCP's rise to power,[3] but his narrow focus suggests that national self-determination was central to CCP handling of the national question. To the contrary, as this chapter demonstrates, from the moment of its inclusion, Chinese Communist leaders—like their Guomindang counterparts—felt uncomfortable with Lenin's principle of national self-determination and its implication for national unity. The Communists and other Chinese nationalists blamed the country's backwardness on the political and ethnic divisions created by domestic warlordism and foreign imperialism and worried more about the effects of foreign intrigue and ethnonationalism on China's frontier than about the legacy of Chinese chauvinist oppression and prejudice. Like members of the Guomindang, they shared Sun Yat-sen's vision of a strong, independent, and unified Chinese state free from foreign interference. To grant political independence to the Mongol, Tibetan, and other former vassal regions of the Qing empire would not only offend these sentiments, but also undermine the party's patriotic credentials and territorial definition of the nation. In contrast to Connor's analysis, this chapter argues that it was Lenin's united front tactic that served as the raison d'être of the CCP's approach to the problem of ethnic diversity within the new nation-state. While the party was not immune to the manipulation of ethnic sentiment on the frontier, its leaders attempted to forge an overarching sense of "Chinese" identity, or what they followed Sun Yat-sen in calling the Zhonghua minzu, that was increasingly defined in opposition to Japanese imperialism. The united front tactic, with its focus on national unity over class antagonism, served as the party's most important state-building tool.

Connor's argument echoes the position of an earlier generation of foreign scholarship on China that held that the CCP's nationality policy was, in the words of George Moseley, a mere "approximation of Soviet orthodoxy."[4] More recently, others such as Ross Terrill have argued that China is an empire masquerading as a nation-state. And the racist distinction between xia (Chinese) and yi (barbarian) that was central to the Chinese imperial worldview had been "baked into the Chinese soul," leading Mao and the Communists to "repackage" the Qing empire's attempts to sinify the frontier barbarian in the name of "an anti-imperialist, revolutionary nation-state."[5] Yet, in his recent book on the ethnopolitics of the CCP, Liu Xiaoyuan follows Benjamin Schwartz in suggesting that CCP policymaking constituted a "third category" between imperial tradition and modern nationalism, one that eclectically combined historical inheritance and modern intervention.[6] Building on this approach, I examine early CCP leaders' discomfort with the cosmopolitan implications of the Comintern's nationality policy, especially its support for Outer Mongolian self-determination and independence from their territorially and historically constructed national imaginary. Mao and the Chinese Communists eventually broke with the Leninist discourse on the national question to fashion their own national minority policy, one that took the "special conditions" of the Chinese revolution—its unique history, shared national character, and common destiny—as its starting point. Much like his Guomindang rivals, Mao crafted a minority policy that stressed the conjoined fate of all Chinese minzus (or "nationalities" in English) under the leadership of a strong, centralized party-state.

The Comintern's Frontier Policy and "Red Imperialism" in Outer Mongolia

The early development of the CCP's frontier program must be understood within the context of Sino-Soviet relations and the role of the Comintern in supporting Bolshevik foreign policy in Asia. In the previous chapter, I discussed the key role played by the Comintern—specifically its adviser, Mikhail Borodin—in establishing a revolutionary united front between the CCP and the GMD in 1924. While Sun Yat-sen saw in the Soviet Union and the Comintern the financial and military support his revolutionary movement desperately needed to gain power in a divided China, Lenin looked to the national liberation movements in Asia to help him consolidate power in Russia. The Comintern cultivated not just Chinese revolutionaries but also other progressive elements along Russia's long border with China in the frontier regions of Xinjiang, Mongolia, and Manchuria. Bolshevik policy encouraged the national self-determination of smaller nationalities, including the right to establish independent satellite states, believing it was yeast for the revolution, both in Russia and globally. As both Walker Connor and Hélène Carrère d'Encausse have demonstrated, "holding out the vision of independence for non-Russian peoples proved very instrumental in the Bolshevik's acquisition of power."[7] In China, however, the strategy ran into obstacles. The right of small frontier minorities, like the Mongols, to break away from the Chinese geo-body violated, in the eyes of nearly all Sinic elites, both the Darwinian principle of social evolution and its spatiotemporal definition of Chinese sovereignty, creating an immediate source of tension in both Sino-Soviet relations and Chinese domestic politics. In fact, the Bolshevik policy of national self-determination played a significant, albeit largely overlooked, role in both the dissolution of the first united front between the CCP and the GMD and the eventual ideological break between the Chinese Communists and Soviet Russia.

Outer Mongolia was, once again, an important site of contention. In what seemed to most Chinese a continuation of Czarist Russia's foreign imperialism, ten thousand Soviet troops marched into the Outer Mongolian capital of Urga (Ulaanbaatar) in 1921 with the aim of establishing an independent People's Government of Mongolia in the name of national self-determination. Criticizing the Soviets for displaying the same "aggressive expansionism" as their Czarist predecessors, the Beijing government of Xu Shichang refused to recognize the new Bolshevik government in Moscow.[8] Sun Yat-sen and his rump Canton government reluctantly agreed to the "status quo" in Outer Mongolia in exchange for Soviet aid, but the Chinese Communists were encouraged to do more in the name of international socialist brotherhood. Influenced by their first Comintern adviser, Hendricus Sneevliet (alias Maring), the Communists incorporated the Bolshevik policy of national self-determination into their political manifesto and launched an aggressive propaganda campaign aimed at legitimating the national aspirations of the Mongolian people.[9]

The CCP's new Comintern-funded mouthpiece, *Xiangdao zhoubao* (*The Weekly Guide*), served as the key organ in this offensive. One of its editors, Gao Junyu, began a September 1922 essay with an unprecedented fait accompli: "Mongolian independence has already been a fact for two years." Gao stressed that "in terms of both its culture and its economy Mongolia is obviously different from China," constituting a separate minzu. These fundamental differences explain Mongolia's independence from China: "We know that political organization is determined by economic form. To place the more backward Mongolia under comparatively more advanced Chinese political control would not suit the needs of the Mongolian people. China's political and economic system would function in a high-handed manner toward Mongolia. It is Mongolia's economic form that has determined its success in establishing a politically independent position [vis-à-vis China]."[10] Moreover, that independence deserved Chinese support. The long period of oppression the Mongols had suffered as an inferior "vassal territory" of the Qing dynasty engendered an implacable resentment that any attempt to regain control of Mongolia by force would only worsen. And China was too weakened by the heavy weight of global capitalism and domestic warlordism to guarantee Mongolia's safety, even if its reconquest should succeed. Gao instead urged the Chinese people to follow the Mongols, who "are rushing ahead of us" in liberating themselves. Yet, in the end, Gao revealed that such forbearance was both strategic and temporary, concluding, "We have faith that in the end China and Mongolia will merge together; however, in order to realize this union, China must first have the power to overthrow warlordism, repel international imperialism, and establish a genuine republican state."[11]

Guided by Maring, the CCP used Lenin's principle of national self-determination to defend Outer Mongolia's temporary independence from feudal China. In his report to the Comintern's Fourth Congress in late 1922, CCP leader Chen Duxiu formally committed his party to the support of Outer Mongolian independence and the propagation of its appropriateness among all revolutionary parties in China.[12] In Moscow, helped by Comintern officials, Chen drafted a new political program that stressed the need to actively assist small and weak nations in gaining self-determination:

> According to the principles governing the organization of states, people with different levels of economic development, national histories, and languages can only hope to adopt a voluntary federal system; it is very difficult to appropriately utilize a centralized political system. Given the reality of the present political situation in China, we must respect the spirit of national self-determination (minzu zijue) and not compel people with different levels of economic development, national histories, and languages to share in our imperialist exploitation and militarist oppression. On these grounds, we must not only recognize the independence of Mongolia in principle, but also render them active support in their efforts to destroy the special privileges of the nobility and the lamas, and lay the economic and cultural foundation for the independence of the Mongolian people.[13]

Chen therefore issued a formal request in the name of the party urging Sun Yat-sen and his Nationalist Party to recognize Outer Mongolian independence—a request that Sun flatly rejected.[14]

Following Sun's death in 1925, more conservative elements within the GMD launched a public counterattack on the CCP, calling its support of Outer Mongolian independence nothing short of lese majesty and a complete renunciation of Sun Yat-sen's principle of minzuzhuyi. The Communists claimed to be upholding the GMD's 1924 manifesto and its pledge to support national self-determination, but their critics asserted that Sun advocated the liberation of the Zhonghua minzu, including the Mongols, as a whole. Members of breakaway elements of the GMD, such as the Western Hills faction (*Xishanpai*) and the Young China Party (YCP), argued that Sun stressed the "fusion" (*ronghe*) of the Manchu, Mongol, Hui, Tibetan, and other small Chinese minzus into a single, great Zhonghua minzu. In the eyes of the YCP's leader, Zeng Qi, Communist advocacy of Mongolian independence proved their failure to understand Sun's political legacy, "causing our country's territory to be torn asunder while turning their backs on Sun Yat-sen's original objective."[15]

The conservatives argued that CCP support for Mongolian self-determination demonstrated its lack of patriotism and support for "red imperialism" (*chise diguozhuyi*) in China. For Hu Hanmin and others, "Outer Mongolia was like an old pig into whose belly they [Soviet Russia] have already bored for a long time,"[16] and CCP support for Russian hegemony was clear evidence of the natural tendency of a dog to follow its master. Thus YCP members often referred to CCP members as the "disciples of the Russian party" (*qin-E-dang*) and "traitorous thieves" (*maiguo zei*).[17] In a series of articles aimed at countering CCP propaganda, Western Hills faction member Zou Lu provided numerous examples of Russian meddling in Xinjiang, Inner Mongolia, Manchuria, Gansu, and Tibet as he sought to prove that the Bolshevik slogan of patronizing small and weak nations was a front for imperialist oppression. "Encroachment," Zou wrote, "is a fundamental part of their national character," unable to be erased by the simple act of political revolution.[18] In disregarding the deep cultural and historical relationship between Mongolia and China proper and supporting the Russian invasions of Outer Mongolia, the Communists, according to the YCP, were guilty of the twin crimes of *maiguo* (treason) and *wuguo* (damaging the national interest).[19] Rather than working for the patriotic "assimilation of the five minzus" in common defense against foreign insult, they were undermining the future fate of the Zhonghua minzu through their attempts to "break up the family of five minzus."

The imputation of lese majesty did not sit well with many Chinese Communists. During the last couple of years of the united front—if articles in *Xiangdao* are an accurate guide—the CCP spent almost as much time defending itself against these charges of treason as advancing its own revolutionary agenda. Though the Soviets had pledged to recognize Outer Mongolia as "an integral part of the Republic of China" in the 1924 Sino-Soviet Accord, normalizing relations between the two countries,[20] the reality of continued Red Army occupation of Mongolia and the repeated delays in their promise to withdraw caused the Chinese Communists to slowly circumscribe their support for Outer Mongolian independence. Their aim, I believe, was to demonstrate their patriotic credentials. In addition to highlighting the accord's clear stipulation that Outer Mongolia was a part of Chinese territory, the CCP went out of its way to stress that it advocated only an interim separation of Mongolia and China.

In a 1924 *Xiangdao* article, Chen Duxiu emphasized the need for the Chinese and Mongolian masses to "jointly rise up" against their common enemies, admitting, for the first time, that the CCP's support for Outer Mongolian independence and its resistance to the dispatching of Chinese troops to retake the region was "a current strategic move" to prevent the region from falling into the hands of the reactionary powers.[21] At the same time, he criticized those "short-sighted people" who questioned the CCP's patriotism. "The current relationship between Russia and Mongolia," Chen stressed, "has already been clearly stated in the Sino-Soviet Accord, and we can all heave a big sigh of relief without the slightest fear [of losing Mongolia], and respect the Mongolian minzu's independent self-rule (*duli zizhi*) while resisting the dispatching of military troops by the Beijing warlords to take back Mongolia."[22] Here Chen Duxiu's language subtly shifts as he replaced his earlier unequivocal support for "Mongolian independence" (*Menggu duli*) with the more ambiguous expression "independent self-rule"—or, in another article that year, "independent resistance" (*duli fankang*).[23] This careful choice of words is clearly meant to highlight the temporary and strategic nature of CCP support for Mongolian independence. In short, Outer Mongolia's "independent resistance" of Chinese warlordism and international imperialism was simply the most expedient method for bringing about a more enduring union of the Chinese and Mongolian peoples.

Others within the party, such as its other cofounder Li Dazhao, stressed the union of the revolutionary movements in China and Mongolia. Li was one of the first Chinese intellectuals to employ the term "national self-determination"; yet for Li, like Sun Yat-sen, the expression referred only to the political independence of the entire multiethnic Zhonghua minzu from foreign imperialism and not, as Chen Duxiu and other Communists had suggested, the liberation of the Mongols and other frontier minorities from China proper.[24] As far back as 1917, Li Dazhao claimed that the evolutionary assimilation of China's five minzus into a single, unified Zhonghua minzu—a process that he referred to as "new Zhonghua nationalism"—had already occurred:

> In the distant recesses of our country's history, the various minzus of Asia smelted together in forming a single Zhonghua minzu, eliminating all previous boundaries and blood lineages and forging our minzu's lofty and effervescent spirit. It is a pity that when the Republic was founded, there were those who still spoke of the five minzus. Those with more foresight, however, realized that under a free and equal Republican system, the cultures of the five minzus had already gradually became one; and thus, the terms Manchu, Han,

> Mongol, Hui, and Tibetan (not to mention Miao and Yao) were now nothing more than residual historical names. The boundaries between them have long ago been replaced with membership in a single Zhonghua Republic, and they now constitute a new Zhonghua minzu.[25]

During the height of the criticism over CCP policy on Mongolia, Li wrote an article describing the "convergence" of China's "national revolutionary movement" and the Mongolian people's "liberation movement," which created an irrevocable "link" between the Mongolian minzu and the Chinese Republic. Li Dazhao's phrasing seems a good indicator of his intent. Instead of referring to the right of "national self-determination" (minzu zijue) and "voluntary federation" (*ziyou lianbang*) set forth in the CCP's political program, he couched his argument in terms of the "liberation movement" (*jiefang yundong*) of the Mongolian people and the "voluntary union" (*ziyou lianhe*) of the Mongolian and Chinese people. Li contended that what was needed was not temporary segregation, as Chen Duxiu had suggested, but rather the "drawing of the liberation movements of Mongolia and China closer together."[26] Li's language, which echoed the rhetoric of the Guomindang, was clearly at odds with the Comintern's handling of the national question. With perhaps a touch of irony, Li mentioned the Sino-Soviet Accord's promise that Russian troops would withdraw from Mongolian territory, expressing China's gratitude for "the Soviet Union's respect for our right to determine our own affairs and the burning desire of the Chinese and Mongolian people for a voluntary union; and thus, it clearly understands this great opportunity for our two minzus to advance together hand in hand under the flag of the Nationalist revolution."[27]

Chiang Kai-shek's bloody purge of the CCP and the collapse of the united front in 1927 sent Comintern policy in China into disarray. With many CCP members arrested or killed, the Comintern's new China adviser, Pavel Mif, decided to hold the party's Sixth National Congress in Moscow, where he oversaw the installation of a new generation of Moscow-trained Chinese Communists (the Twenty-eight Bolsheviks, as they became known) into positions of leadership within the CCP. Though silent about past mistakes, the congress indirectly acknowledged the need to reconsider the party's handling of the national question. Its manifesto skirted the national question altogether, and its political resolution included only a vague and contradictory call for "the unification of China and the recognition of the right of national self-determination." But the congress did issue a four-line Draft Resolution on the National Question that stated the importance of the national question to the Chinese revolution.[28]

Despite its brevity, this document marked an important shift in how the national question in China was framed. It redefined Bolshevik discourse on the national question as "a question concerning the *minority nationals within Chinese territory*"—the first appearance in CCP party documents of the phrase shaoshu minzu.[29] The resolution also limited the scope of the problem—now called the "Chinese national minority question" (*Zhongguo shaoshu minzu wenti*)—to "the Mongols and Hui of the north; the Koreans of Manchuria; the Taiwanese people of Fujian; the Miao, Li, and other primitive minzus of the south; Xinjiang; and Tibet."[30] The party thereby attempted to remove the explosive issue of ethnic relations from the realm of international politics, redefining it as a purely domestic matter pertaining to the ethnic and territorial integration of the former Qing geo-body. Finally, this resolution hinted at the need to completely revamp the CCP's approach to the national question, asking the Central Committee to prepare the materials necessary to develop a new frontier program during the Seventh Party Congress the following summer. In fact, it would be another seventeen years before the CCP held its seventh congress. By that time, Mao Zedong had overseen the drafting of a radically new frontier program for the CCP, one inspired by the nationalism of Li Dazhao and Sun Yat-sen rather than by the internationalism of Chen Duxiu and Vladimir Lenin.

The Circumscribing of National Self-determination

The installation of the Twenty-eight Bolsheviks by Pavel Mif marked what Charles McLane called the "last identifiable instance of outright [Comintern] intervention in the internal affairs of the CCP."[31] When in late 1931 the CCP's Central Committee moved from Shanghai to the isolated Jiangxi Soviet, the party fell out of day-to-day contact with Moscow and its Comintern advisers. This loosening of direct supervision provided the Chinese Communists with enough breathing space to thoroughly examine, for the first time in their history, the Bolshevik discourse on the national question—particularly its central tenet, national self-determination. While our access to documents chronicling the intraparty debates of the 1930s is limited, a careful reading of the available material reveals great ambivalence among top party leaders toward the Comintern's insistence that self-determination must include an explicit right of political independence for marginalized frontier minorities. It appears that a consensus had been reached by the time of the Long March in 1935: the right of temporary secession would apply only to Outer Mongolia—which had already occurred in 1924 with the assistance of the Soviet Red Army—while all other newly defined minority nationals would to be permitted mere political and cultural autonomy within a unitary Chinese state.

This reevaluation of Bolshevik policy needs to be placed within the context of Stalin's own break with proletarian internationalism. Trotsky's forced exile from Russia in 1929 left Stalin in supreme control of the ideological direction of Russian Marxism and opened the way for his theory of "socialism in one country." Unlike Lenin and Trotsky, Stalin argued that it was possible for socialism to take root in Russia prior to a worldwide socialist revolution. But first the Russian state needed to strengthen itself while giving full play to the development of a Soviet national economy and culture. This emphasis on the construction of a new "Soviet nation" made it ever more clear to the Chinese Communists and other non-Russian Marxists that the Comintern was increasingly a tool of Russian national interest, a realization that eventually contributed to its formal dissolution in 1943 at the height of World War II.[32]

The new consensus among CCP leaders on the national question was most evident in their communication with outlying branch committees in the frontier. During the late 1920s, the CCP became suspicious of the patriotic intentions of the Comintern-backed People's Revolutionary Party of Inner Mongolia (*Neimenggu geming remindang* or PRPIM) and attempted to establish its own party cell in the region in order to steer the Mongols away from Soviet-controlled Outer Mongolia and back toward the fatherland. For example, in February 1929 the party center telegraphed its clandestine Inner Mongolian Special Committee urging that PRPIM activists be secretly recruited for membership in the CCP. The telegram also called for opposing the PRPIM's "narrow nationalist thinking," while emphasizing the unity of the Han and Mongolian masses.[33] In the south of China, where the CCP did not have to contend with the strategic interests of its Soviet allies, the party center could afford to more explicitly limit the scope of national self-determination. In a September 1929 directive to its Yunnan Provincial Committee, the party center listed Miao "self-determination" (zijue) as one of the key slogans guiding the party's handling of the "national minority question" (*shaoshu minzu wenti*) in Yunnan but cautioned, "In our work among the Miao and other minorities, national independence (*minzu duli*) is most certainly not an appropriate slogan. Because of the current need for both the Yunnanese worker-peasant masses and the Miao and other minorities to oppose imperial and feudal forces, advocating national independence will only produce an objective split within the united front between the minority nationals and the Yunnanese workers and peasants, resulting in its inevitable use by the French imperialists. National self-determination (minzu zijue) and not national independence is our current propaganda slogan."[34] Here the party makes it explicitly clear that minzu zijue did not include the right of political succession as Lenin had insisted. Though the CCP's alliance with the Soviet Union placed clear limitations on its policy statements toward Outer Mongolia and other large, territorially defined ethnic groups, no one within the party was willing to acknowledge that the numerous but small and widely scattered minority tribes of the South had a right to political independence.

Official pronouncements from the Jiangxi Soviet also reveal a subtle attempt by some within the party to modify the meaning of Lenin's concept of national self-determination. Walker Connor and more recently Liu Xiaoyuan have argued that the policies of the Jiangxi Soviet marked "one of the 'landmarks' in the evolution of the CCP's 'nationality policies'" and the height of its "sovietization" process.[35] In the limited number of Jiangxi Soviet documents that we now have access to, Liu sees a "more elaborate interpretation of the right to secession," explicitly including the Mongols, Tibetans, and other minority nationals of Xinjiang, Yunnan, and Guizhou.[36] However, the iconographic nature of the written Chinese language lends itself to a high degree of ambiguity, and I believe that this interpretive flexibility enabled the Chinese Communists to explicitly include Lenin's principle of national self-determination in the Jiangxi Soviet's 1931 and 1934 constitutions—which would invariably wind their way back to Moscow—while also wording the promise of secession in such a way as to limit its application to the Chinese minority nationals. In any case, the precise wording of the party's nationality platform changed no fewer than four times between 1931 and 1934, as will be discussed, demonstrating great unease (if not open disagreement) among CCP leaders over the meaning and implications of Bolshevik nationality policy.

When party leaders sat down to draft the Jiangxi Soviet's first constitution in late 1931, they made several subtle but important changes to the language of the nationality plank included in the Draft Basic Law drawn up under the direct supervision of Pavel Mif in Shanghai a year earlier.[37] Whereas the Basic Law had unambiguously promised minzu zijue, including the right of political secession, to all "small and weak minzus" (*ruoxiao minzu*) within China, Article 14 of the new constitution returned to the obscure wording of the 1924 Reorganization Congress manifesto: "The Chinese Soviet Government recognizes the right of minority nationals (shaoshu minzu) to self-determination (zijue)," adding, "the Soviet has always recognized the right of small and weak minzus to secede from China and establish their own independent state."[38] Thus a distinction is implied between the "minority nationals," which are entitled only to "self-determination," and "small and weak minzus," which are explicitly promised independence.[39] Finally, a more circumscribed and ambiguous form of self-determination was offered to the "Mongols, Hui, Tibetans, Miao, Li, Gaoli, and other minorities living within Chinese territory": namely, the right to "either join or leave the Federation of Soviet Republics or establish their own autonomous region."[40] This awkward and imprecise wording appears to reflect the leaders' conscious attempt to differentiate between a general right of political secession that would apply to an ill-defined group of "small and weak minzus" (possibly Outer Mongolia) and a more circumscribed right of autonomy for those "minority nationals" who lived intermixed among Chinese settlers (as in Inner Mongolia). The article's inherently contradictory language allowed the party to argue that it was still supporting the Soviet-backed independence of Outer Mongolia, even as it offered a more limited form of autonomy to its "minority nationals."

To complicate matters further, several days before passing the constitution, the Jiangxi Congress approved a separate Draft Resolution on the National Minority Question in China that added two important qualifications to the principle of self-determination. Here, the promise to "categorically and unconditionally recognize the right of the shaoshu minzu to self-determination" was glossed: "This means that within a fixed territory in Mongolia, Tibet, Xinjiang, Yunnan, Guizhou, and other regions, where the majority of the population is non-Han, the toiling masses of each minzu shall have the right to determine for themselves whether they wish to leave the Chinese Soviet Republic and establish their own state, or join the Federation of Soviet Republics, or form an autonomous region within the Chinese Soviet Republic."[41] Thus, the right of political secession applied only to those minzus whose population made up the majority in its own region (such as in Outer Mongolia, Tibet, and Xinjiang). And more importantly, it was open only to the "toiling masses" of each minzu. This second qualification ensured that the CCP alone, as the sole true representative of the toiling masses in "China," had the authority to call for political independence—something, of course, it had no intention of doing. As the resolution made clear, the party's real goal was what Lenin himself had once termed "a state without nationality (minzu) boundaries."[42]

Debate over the precise language of the Chinese Soviet's nationality platform continued at the Second Congress of Soviet Delegates in early 1934. In a significant move immediately before the congress convened, the party's Fifth Plenum—the first since Pavel Mif's departure from China—omitted the term "self-determination" completely from its political resolution. Instead, it called on the party to "lead the minority nationals toward national liberation (*minzu jiefang*), self-sufficiency (*zili*)—including the right to separate (*fenli quan*)—and struggle (*douzheng*)."[43] Although Lenin's concept of national self-determination can easily be inferred from the phrasing, the party's failure to specifically mention minzu zijue is significant. Its omission takes on even greater importance in light of the inclusion of the phrase in every single public resolution dealing with the national question since its first appearance in 1923.

The revised 1934 constitution endorsed by the Second Congress of Soviet Delegates offered yet another locution. Indeed, this modification of Article 14 was one of the few significant changes to the 1931 constitution. The first line of the revised article read: "The Zhonghua Soviet Government recognizes the goal of national freedom (*minzu ziyou*) for all minority nationals within China."[44] The solemn and unconditional pledge of "self-determination" contained in the 1931 constitution was replaced with the more ambiguous "goal of national freedom." Though the term zijue (self-determination) remained, it was now part of the phrase recognizing the right of the minority nationals within Chinese territory to "join or leave the Federation of Soviet Republics or establish their own autonomous region." Finally, the article continued to acknowledge the right of "small minzus" to "break with China and establish an independent state," but it was directly set against the right of Chinese "minority nationals" to self-determination.

Without further access to CCP documents from the Jiangxi Soviet, we cannot be certain of the reasons for the party's desultory and inconsistent nationality discourse. Perhaps it indicates open discord within the leadership over the meaning and necessity of including Lenin's principle of national self-determination in the party's political program, or concern that its exclusion might anger Moscow or undermine the party's legitimacy as a Marxist-Leninist political organization. The repeated reworking of the nationality plank does seem to suggest that party leaders were concerned that the frontier minorities might actually act out the

Leninist right of political secession. Out of deference to its Russian allies and the Russian sphere of influence on the Mongolian steppe, the Jiangxi Soviet recognized the de facto independence of Outer Mongolia as falling under the right of "small and weak minzus" to break away from China and establish their own state. At the same time, the party struggled for the proper phrasing to describe the more limited right of autonomy it was willing to offer those "minority nationals" living firmly within the Chinese geo-body—experimenting with such terms as self-determination (zijue), self-sufficiency (zili), liberation (jiefang), and freedom (ziyou).

Stalin was one of the first Communist leaders to make such a distinction. In his important 1913 tract *Marxism and the National Question*, he clearly distinguished between what he termed "nations"—large, historically stable communities whose language, territory, economy, and culture are well defined—and "minority nationals"—smaller, less stable communities that lived dispersed among larger nations. The former were entitled to the right of national self-determination, but Stalin proposed "to bind the dispersed minorities into a single national union" in a voluntary fashion that guaranteed their right of "regional autonomy."[45] During the course of the Russian revolution, Lenin and Stalin oversaw the creation of a number of independent republics from the embers of the Czarist empire while offering a more limited form of regional and cultural autonomy to the Tatar and German populations of the Volga and the minority peoples in Daghestan and the Crimea. As Carrère d'Encausse points out, "the Bolshevik approach was empirical; policy varied according to circumstance and feasibility," but "the status of nationalities was decided solely by the Bolsheviks, and decisions emanated from the center."[46] And as the Chinese Communists knew well, these independent republics and autonomous regions were ultimately incorporated, some by force, into a single, federated Union of Soviet Socialist Republics that included almost the entire Czarist empire by 1924. Comintern rhetoric aside, it was clear that CCP leaders' expectations were no less ambitious, as they envisioned the eventual creation of a great Zhonghua Republic that would include all the territories of the former Qing empire.

Nevertheless, throughout the early 1930s, the Chinese Communists continued to employ the theoretical framework of the Bolshevik discourse on the national question. Despite the party's fluid language, its public pronouncements still implied the right of Chinese minority nationals to determine their own political destiny without interference from the Han majority. Publicly, at least, the environment was not yet ripe for an open split with Bolshevik ideology. In private communications, however, the party was beginning to chart its own course, emphasizing the joint struggle of all *Chinese* minzus nationalities to carry out collective liberation from foreign imperialism.

It should come as no surprise that Mao Zedong was one of the more influential voices within the party calling for a firmly bounded Chinese nation-state. Speaking before the Second Congress of Soviet Delegates in January 1934, Mao asserted that all Chinese minzus suffered equally from imperialist oppression and feudal backwardness. He urged that this system of mutual exploitation be replaced with what Li Dazhao in 1919 had labeled a "free union of all minzus."[47] As evidence of the party's commitment to national self-determination (minzu zijue), Mao cited the presence at the congress of delegates from Taiwan, Korea, and Annam (Vietnam)—ignoring the Mongol, Tibetan, Miao, and other "minority nationals" whom he viewed as inalienable parts of the Chinese minzu. Echoing the Reorganization Congress Manifesto of 1924, Mao stressed the responsibility of all minority nationals toward the Chinese revolution, alleging that "only by assisting the Chinese Soviet government in obtaining victory *on a national scale* can the government achieve a thorough victory."[48] Like Sun Yat-sen and Li Dazhao before him, Mao believed that "the Chinese" (*Zhongguoren*) could achieve their liberation from foreign imperialism and domestic feudalism only by uniting into a single, unified national entity.

The Long March and the Origins of the United Front Tactic

The CCP's Long March for survival through the southwest frontier region of China deeply impressed on Mao and other party leaders that national unity was essential to the survival of both the party and the minzu. In October 1934, Chiang Kai-shek's Fifth Encirclement Campaign finally forced the CCP out of the Jiangxi Soviet and onto its epic hegira, which eventually ended at its wartime base in Yan'an in northern Sha'anxi province. This more than six-thousand-mile journey on foot took the Red Army through eight provinces, across dozens of mountain ranges, and over scores of major rivers in little more than a year. Much of this time—roughly 33 percent of it, or 125 out of 371 days for Mao's First Route Army—was spent among the Miao, Yao, Yi, Tibetan, and other frontier indigenes of the Southwest.[49] For the first time in its history, the party's minority policy became not just a series of idle ideological considerations, but an important part of its overall strategy for survival and revolutionary success. To ensure the party's safe passage through this hostile and unfamiliar terrain, Mao and the party center were, in the words of Liu Xiaoyuan, "compelled to develop a functional ethnopolitical strategy."[50] The key to this strategy was replacing Lenin's theory of national self-determination with his united front tactic. Class differences among the frontier minorities were to be downplayed, as the emphasis shifted to the revolutionary struggle of the entire Chinese people against their domestic and international enemies.

The concept of a "united front" (*tongyi zhanxian*) arose out of Lenin's 1916 theory of imperialism, which called for national liberation movements in the colonial world to reenergize the fledgling struggle of European workers against the global forces of capitalism. Lenin believed that because of their immaturity, Eastern proletarian parties had to form a temporary and expedient alliance, or united front, with their national bourgeois. Consequently, the revolution in

China and elsewhere in the colonial world would proceed in two stages: a national democratic revolution against foreign imperialism would be followed by a socialist revolution aimed at overthrowing the forces of domestic capitalism. A revolutionary alliance between the national bourgeois and the toiling masses was crucial to the success of the first phrase, during which the communist parties would continue to pursue their own tactical goals while supporting bourgeois democracy.[51] In China, Lenin's united front tactic initially led to an uneasy alliance between the Communists and Sun Yat-sen's Nationalist Party beginning in 1924. Yet following its collapse in 1927 and the rise of Mao Zedong, the policy was transformed into a far more powerful and dynamic tool—one that placed temporary alliances at the very heart of revolutionary strategy.[52] During the Long March, Mao and his party experimented with the united front strategy, realizing that there were times when loyalty was more important than class.

Prior to the Long March, the united front tactic and the national question in China were considered separately. As a part of its broader political program emphasizing class conflict, the party advocated minority resistance to the feudal oppression of their religious and aristocratic leaders. The Resolution on Miao and Yao Liberation, for example, passed by the party's First Congress of Hunan Peasant Representatives in December 1926, called on the delegates to "assist the Miao and Yao in eliminating the cruel oppression of their tribal chieftains."[53] But widespread minority resistance during the Long March forced the party to rethink this approach. Without translators to communicate its policies or minority cadres to mobilize the masses, the strategy did little to advance the party's objectives or ensure its safety on the frontier. As Guomindang troops chased the Communists through Guizhou, Yunnan, and Xikang, the Red Army wasted valuable time and energy fending off the attacks of minority tribesmen while searching for food and other supplies without the assistance of the local population.[54] This situation reached a crisis point in early 1935 when the desperately hungry and tired soldiers of Mao's First Route Army (reduced by more than half to twenty-five thousand since the start of the Long March) reached Huili, a small village in southern Xikang, with Chiang Kai-shek's troops in hot pursuit. At a quickly convened meeting of party leaders, Mao—who had recently assumed de facto control over the party center at the historic Zunyi Conference—called for the Red Army to abandon its heavy equipment and race two thousand li straight through the wilderness home of the dreaded "Lolos" (*Luoluo*).[55] If the Red Army could reach the Luding Bridge across the mighty Dadu River ahead of the Guomindang troops advancing from the southwest, they could join up with Zhang Guotao's eighty-thousand-strong Fourth Route Army in northern Xikang.[56] To ensure the army's safe passage through the land of the fiercely independent Lolos, Mao turned to the united front tactic.

Mao had first put the technique to use during the First Route Army's journey through the territory of the more placid Yao and Miao minorities of southern Guizhou. Echoing his declaration at the Second Congress of Soviet Delegates that "the starting point of the soviet policy on nationalities is the winning over of all oppressed minority nationals,"[57] Mao told all his military commanders before entering Guizhou in November 1934 that "all future field army actions and battles are intimately connected to the problem of winning over the minority nationals, and the solution of this problem has a marked significance to the realization of our battle tactics."[58] He therefore proposed establishing a military and political alliance, or united front, with the Miao and Yao "upper stratum" (*shangceng jieceng*). Despite their open mistrust of the Chinese, the tusi chieftains had a long history of uneasy cooperation with Sinic officials among whom they lived. Furthermore, their familiarity with the Chinese language and customs made them a better target for mobilization than the "ignorant" Yao and Miao masses that the party purported to represent.

In an important directive issued by the Political Department of Mao's First Route Army in late November 1934, the party center argued that the "extreme backwardness" of Yao and Miao economic and cultural development had retarded interclass conflict. As a result, "the Yao [and Miao] tusi and other leaders still possess a high degree of authority and prestige in the minds of the masses, and are thus still the sole representatives of the Yao [and Miao] people's national interests," making it necessary for "our Soviet Red Army" to "develop relations with these representatives." In the current struggle against the national oppression of the Han militarists, bureaucrats, and bourgeois, "the upper stratum obviously still possess a revolutionary function." To win over the Yao and Miao elites, according to the directive, the Red Army must respect their religion, language, and customs, while emphasizing in its propaganda that the Yao and Miao people were "brothers" of the Chinese toiling masses and likewise suffered from imperialist and Guomindang oppression. Finally, the party center urged that Yao and Miao youths be recruited into the CCP and the Red Army and be permitted to form their own Soviet governments or join a united Zhonghua Soviet as an autonomous region.[59]

Mao's new policy helped the Red Army pass through Guizhou without many incidents, but its first real test came in western Sichuan among the warlike Yi people. Upon entering "Lololand," the First Route Army issued an urgent reminder about the "extreme importance" of winning over the Yi upper stratum in order to ensure the Red Army's quick passage northward.[60] In subsequent directives, the party center sanctioned the use of a wide variety of methods—such as offering gifts, money, guns, bullets, or even IOUs—to win over the Yi leaders and gain their assistance in finding food and shelter for the Red Army.[61] What made Mao's united front tactic so successful was that he could always find minority elites willing to cooperate with the Communists in the hope that their weapons or money would alter the balance in the group's own internal struggle for power. At the same time, the united front tactic also helped the Communists gain a foothold among the minorities, from whom they could gradually recruit their own cadres to aid in mobilizing the minorities in the party's struggle against the Nationalist and later the Japanese. Yet some Communists feared that the incorporation of Buddhist lamas, Hui imams, Mongol princes, and Yi chieftains into the party threatened to transform it into a social democratic party. Mao addressed these concerns at the important Wayaopao Party Conference that met following the successful reunion of the First and Fourth Route Armies in northern Xikang. Arguing that ideology and not social composition made the CCP proletarian and revolutionary, Mao—in language reminiscent of Sun Yat-sen—called for the transformation of the party into a "smelting furnace of communism" (*gongchanzhuyi de ronglu*), arguing that the inclusion of minority elites and other feudal elements would result in their "tempering into Bolshevik fighters with the highest class consciousness."[62] Mao, in other words, viewed the united front tactic as a revolutionary strategy for enlarging both the appeal and authority of the CCP.

The Sinification of Marxism and the National Question

Despite the attempts by Mao and other Communist leaders to break with the Comintern's national minority stratagem, CCP policy remained largely wedded to the rhetoric and intent of the Bolshevik theory throughout the early 1930s. But the outbreak of World War II and the ultimate failure of the CCP's Fourth Front Army to "break through" to the Soviet Union changed the international and domestic environment, enabling the CCP to more completely distance itself from Bolshevik theory and develop its own indigenous nationality policy.

Internationally, World War II redirected the attention of the party's Russian advisers and patrons away from China and back toward Europe. As the CCP's Central Committee moved first to rural Jiangxi in 1932 and then into the frontier hinterland of southwest China during the Long March, the Comintern's influence over the party gradually waned. Not surprisingly, the decline in Comintern authority coincided with the diminishing importance of the CCP within the foreign policy objectives of the Soviet Union. After diplomatic relations were established with Chiang Kai-shek's Nationalist Party government in 1935 and the Second United Front was forged between the CCP and the GMD in 1937, the Soviet Union concluded a neutrality and nonaggression pact with Japan in April 1941. Stalin was now free to focus his full attention on Nazi Germany's threatened war in Europe. As long as China did not completely capitulate to the Japanese, Stalin seemed content to ignore its domestic politics. In May 1943 the last formal ties between Moscow and the Chinese Communists were severed when the Presidium of the Central Executive Committee of the Comintern called for the organization's dissolution, claiming that the world's communist parties had matured sufficiently and central supervision was no longer needed. In a resolution accepting the disbanding of the Communist International, Mao stressed that the CCP had "long since been able to determine its political line independently and to carry it out in accordance with the concrete situation and the specific circumstances in its country."[63] Nationality theory was one of the first areas in which the party decided to chart its own course, eager to apply the "unique realities" of China's national unity to the party's handling of the "domestic national question."

Domestically, the full-scale Japanese invasion of China in 1937 fanned the smoldering flames of Chinese nationalism and focused national attention on the struggle for survival. The series of bloody defeats that the Chinese suffered during the early years of the war fostered a sense of national emergency and gave rise to an important shift in CCP's rhetoric and policy. Claiming in their famous declaration of August 1935 that "China is our fatherland" and that "all our compatriots comprise the Zhongguo minzu," the Communists called on "men and women of all walks of life (labor, industry, agriculture, military affairs, politics, commerce, and education)" to put aside their differences and unite together in a broad, anti-Japanese united front.[64] China's "national salvation movement," a November 1936 party document asserted, belonged not solely to the proletariat but to all Chinese classes. The Japanese invasion of China and attempt to turn the entire minzu into a colony had created a special period in which all Chinese classes share a common interest in preventing "the death of the state and the extinction of the race," and now required the party and the nation to subordinate class struggle to the present national struggle against Japan.[65]

Mao and the Chinese Communists stressed the importance of fostering a new "minzu consciousness" (*minzu yishi*) that would bind the sentiments of all nationalities and classes into a single national identity, united against the onslaught of Japanese imperialism. The Japanese, as Mao pointed out in a May 1938 lecture, were not only physically plundering China but also "destroying the national consciousness of the Chinese people (Zhongguoren)," forcing them to become nothing but "docile subjects, beasts of burden forbidden to show the slightest trace of Chinese national spirit (*Zhongguoqi*)."[66] Mao's appeal for the education of a new generation in the national spirit dovetailed closely with Chiang Kai-shek's national spiritual mobilization movement, as both the CCP and GMD attempted to shore up Chinese morale, patriotism, and unity. To Mao and Chiang alike, the desperate struggle for survival seemed to require a new, collective sense of identity, one that would transcend both ethnic and class divisions and join all Chinese in a single composite and indivisible Zhonghua minzu.

This new emphasis on Chinese national identity created a problem for Mao and other self-professed proletarian internationalists (though not for the Nationalists). In urgently calling for the preservation of the Chinese state and minzu, Mao presupposed the existence of a distinct and peculiar Chinese "people" (*renmin*), "race/nation" (minzu), and "culture" (*wenhua*) worthy of protection. Yet the Chinese Communists, like all communists, were supposedly committed to the cause of transnational class revolution, not the preservation of a single national culture or people. While nearly everyone within the party accepted the need for anti-Japanese resistance, some of Mao's colleagues—especially the Twenty-eight Bolsheviks who had been trained in Moscow—felt uncomfortable with Mao's blatantly nationalistic rhetoric. They feared not only his growing hegemony within the party but also his attempt to undermine its ideological foundations.

In order to pave over this theoretical contradiction and consolidate his power within the party, Mao drew on the ideas of Chen Boda (his personal secretary) and others concerning the need to adapt Marxism to suit local Chinese conditions. Mao used the so-called sinification of Marxism to simultaneously strike a blow to the theoretical authority of the Twenty-eight Bolsheviks (especially his main rival, Wang Ming) while shedding Marxism's tag as an "alien ideology" inadequate to meet the revolutionary needs of the Chinese people. Mao and Chen Boda criticized the "formalism" and "dogmatism" of the Twenty-eight Bolsheviks, arguing that they ignored China's unique cultural traditions in their application of Marxist theory, and called instead for the creation of a new strain of Marxism unique to China and its national form.[67] The party's Sixth Plenum in October 1938 (the first since 1934) served as the venue for Mao's bid for ideological preeminence within the CCP. In his marathon three-day report before the Central Committee, Mao boldly declared, "There is no such thing as abstract Marxism, but only concrete Marxism. What we refer to as concrete Marxism is Marxism that has taken on a national form, that is Marxism applied to the concrete struggle in China's concrete environment, and not applied abstractly."[68] In China, Mao argued, Marxism was a meaningless and empty set of concepts and principles unless applied to the individual characteristics and historical conditions of the Chinese minzu: "For the Chinese Communists who are part of the great Zhonghua minzu—flesh of its flesh and blood of its blood—any talk of Marxism in isolation from China's characteristics is merely Marxism in the abstract, Marxism in a vacuum."[69] Thus China's Marxist struggle was recast as the culmination of the historic struggle of Sun Yat-sen and other Chinese revolutionaries to build a "new society and new state for the Zhonghua minzu" free from British, American, Japanese, and Russian hegemony. Similarly, the goal was not to implement an unspecific international proletarian culture, but rather to build a new "national culture" (*minzu wenhua*) that "belongs to our own minzu and bears its national characteristics."[70] In short, Mao appealed for the creation of what Stalin himself had termed, "socialism in one country."

When it came to applying the universal truths of Marxism to the concrete praxis of China's own national question, Mao stressed—above all else—the need for national unity. The protection of the "fatherland" required that "the various minzus unite into a single body to jointly resist the Japanese invaders."[71] Because they were strategically located on the front lines of the War of Resistance and because the Japanese were attempting to splinter Chinese unity by inciting racial and cultural discord, the minority nationals had a special responsibility to unite with the Han majority in this cause. Mao therefore outlined a new, indigenous nationality policy for the party. First, under the principle of jointly opposing the Japanese, the Mongol, Hui, Tibetan, Miao, and other minority nationals would enjoy "equal rights" *(pingdeng quanli)* with the Han majority—namely, "the right to manage their own affairs (*ziji guanli ziji shiwu zhiquan*)while uniting at the same time with the Han nationality in establishing a unified state.[72] Mao sketched a series of general proposals for implementing minority autonomy. In areas where the minority nationals lived intermixed with the Han, the government should establish special political committees made up of minority leaders to advise the local and provincial governments on policies affecting the minority nationals. Moreover, each nationality's culture, religion, and customs should be respected. The state should not only prevent the forced study of the Han language but also help the minorities develop schools that use their own written and spoken languages. Finally, Mao encouraged the Han majority to treat the minorities as equals in order to combat "Han chauvinism" (*dahanzhuyi*) and foster greater intimacy and friendship among China's various nationalities.[73]

Mao's new nationality policy represented a clear departure from the earlier Comintern-inspired program. The Leninist principle of national self-determination, with its explicit right of political secession, was replaced by the vaguer promise of the right to manage one's own affairs. Gone too was the previous aim of minority national liberation, now supplanted by the goal of uniting all minzus into a single body to jointly resist the Japanese invaders. Finally, the party now spoke not of eventually creating a Zhonghua Federated Republic after all frontier nationalities were individually liberated, but rather of immediately establishing a unified state to combat Japanese imperialism. The phrases minzu zijue (national self-determination) and *lianbang gonghe* (federated republic) continued to be used sporadically in local propaganda, but by 1938 Mao had signaled his intention to create a unitary state structure in which the former Qing frontier peoples would be offered autonomy rather than independence. Thus the dissolution of the Comintern and the sinification of Marxism provided the ideological breathing room that the CCP needed to develop its own nationality policy—one that took into consideration the *special characteristics* of Chinese cultural, ethnic, and political unity.

The Northwest Work Committee and Maoist Nationality Policy

After supplying a new ideological framework and broad policy principles, Mao left the details of working out how China's "specific conditions" should affect the party's nationality policy to a group of trusted cadres. Immediately following the Sixth Plenum, the Central Committee created several regional work committees to better coordinate its work outside the central Shaan-Gan-Ning Border Region. The new Northwest Work Committee (*Xibei gongzuo weiyuanhui* or NWC), with authority over all party activities in the frontier regions of Sha'anxi, Gansu, Ningxia, Qinghai, Xinjiang, and Mongolia, assumed responsibility for developing party policy toward the large Hui and Mongol communities that surrounded the party's headquarters in Yan'an. Zhang Wentian, a veteran member of the Twenty-eight Bolsheviks and party secretary-general since siding with

Mao at the 1935 Zunyi Conference, became its head; and daily operations and the committee's national minority work were handed over to Mao's close ally Li Weihan.[74]

To more systematically analyze the peculiarities of the national question in China, Li Weihan set up the National Question Research Office (*Minzu wenti yanjiushi*) in early 1940,[75] and chose twenty-eight-year-old Jiangxi native Liu Chun as its director. Despite his earlier training as an instructor at Shanghai's Mongolian and Tibetan Academy, Liu appeared to have had few qualifications for this important task.[76] Yet his familiarity with minority issues combined with Li Weihan's mastery of the Russian language and Bolshevik theory to create the intellectual wellsprings of China's new nationality policy. Before being reorganized as part of the Central Committee's Northwest Bureau in April 1941, the NWC and its National Question Research Office published a series of detailed analyses of the unique aspects of China's national question. The committee also presented two important policy outlines on the Hui and Mongol questions to the Central Committee in 1940. These papers not only became the foundation of Yan'an-era nationality policy but were selected by Mao for inclusion in the collection of party documents that served as the ideological basis for the party's 1942 Rectification Campaign.[77]

The interconnected destiny of all "Chinese nationalities" (Zhongguo minzu or Zhonghua minzu) became one of the central themes of the NWC's articles and policy papers. Claiming that all nationalities within China suffered equally from Japanese subjugation, Li Weihan and Liu Chun argued that the "fate" (*mingyun*) of all nationalities hinged on their joint resistance to and eventual defeat of Japanese imperialism, which required creating an environment that was conducive to the natural fusion of all nationalities into a single Zhonghua minzu. "If the Hui nationality splits and isolates itself rather than coming together with other nationalities to resist the Japanese and jointly establish a unified state," the NWC's 1941 pamphlet on the Huihui question argued, "they will contravene their own national interest and benefit only the Japanese invaders in destroying China and the Hui nationality."[78] Because of this belief in the common national interests of all Chinese nationalities, the committee concluded in its Central Committee policy paper that "the destiny of the Hui nationality is the same as the entire Zhonghua minzu."[79] Similarly, a pamphlet drafted by Liu Chun on the Mongol question stated that "the fate of the Mongolian nationality cannot be separated from the fate of all Chinese nationalities." Liu contended that since the Japanese invasion, all nationalities must share a "common road" toward liberation.[80]

But a common destiny did not imply an equal ability to attain it. Just as the peculiar conditions of the Chinese revolution bound the various nationalities together, so the "special characteristics" of the frontier minorities prevented them from pursuing their own national liberation without the assistance of their Han "elder brothers." In the NWC's Mongolian policy outline, for example, the Mongolian people's cultural dependency on Lamaism, their political disunity, and their "extremely complex and unequal" socioeconomic structure were listed as "special characteristics" that determined their historical "backwardness." Consequently, "the Mongols lack confidence in their own future and feel that there is no solution to their problems, resulting in a dispirited and dependent nature. These conditions also help to explain why the liberation of the Mongolian people must receive the assistance of an outside revolutionary force. Mongolian liberation must be conjoined with the Chinese revolution in order to succeed."[81]

The burden of impelling the Mongols, Hui, and other "backward minzus" (*luohou minzu*) toward their own liberation fell on the shoulders of China's most advanced minzu—labeled by Li and Liu, the "Han ruling minzu" (*tongzhi minzu de Hanzu*). Furthermore, as the Han nationality's most progressive class, the proletariat (and its political party, the Communists) assumed ultimate responsibility for propelling the reluctant minorities toward their own national liberation.[82] In its analysis, the NWC saw the revolutionary immaturity and inchoate national consciousness of the ethnic minorities as explaining their apparent apathy toward the Japanese invaders, arguing that only the advanced Han proletarian class (read here, the CCP) could spur the toiling masses of the Mongols, Hui, and other minorities into action. Like Sun Yat-sen's discourse of minzuzhuyi, the NWC's version of the Han man's burden denied the minorities any political agency of their own.

In keeping with Mao's policy outline, the Leninist principle of national self-determination was deemed no longer relevant to the special revolutionary situation of collective "Chinese" subjugation and eventual liberation. As early as 1937, the party center suggested that the Japanese invasion required that the right of minority self-determination be temporarily suspended. An internal directive, "The Principle of Independence and Self-rule among the Minority Nationals," recommended "indicating to the Mongolian people that the special steppe region north of the Great Wall shall be handed back to their administration following the victory of Mongolian liberation; however, under the present period of Japanese, GMD, and warlord control and extermination in Mongolia, the handing over [of authority] is not beneficial to any of the Mongolian and Han classes."[83]

The significance of this new revolutionary situation was spelled out in the writings of Li Weihan and Liu Chun. In an important article on the Huihui question, published in the June 16, 1940, issue of the party's theoretical journal *Jiefang* (*Liberation*), Li Weihan admitted that the right of national self-determination—including the right to break away from China and establish an independent state—was a fundamental component of the Bolshevik solution to the national question. But quoting from Stalin's 1913 tract *Marxism and the National Question*, Li argued that "this is not to say that under all conditions they should act in this way; nor is this to say that at all times and in every situation it is advantageous for a nationality to rule itself or split away."[84] Indeed, to do likewise was to "visibly assist the Japanese imperialists in their plot to split apart the Zhonghua minzu."[85]

The emphasis on the congruency of minority-Han liberation was reflected in two subtle, but important, changes in the party's rhetoric. First, the Communists began to employ the autonym Zhonghua minzu. This brilliantly ambiguous term, which was originally popularized in Sun Yat-sen's principle of minzuzhuyi and can simultaneously be rendered as "*the* Chinese minzu" or "the various minzus of China," powerfully aided the imagining of China as a composite yet multiethnic nation-state. First used by Mao in his November 1935 declaration calling for an anti-Japanese national salvation movement, the term Zhonghua minzu—along with others such as "the five Zhonghua minzus" (*Zhonghua wuzu*), "the Zhonghua fatherland" (*Zhonghua zuguo*), and the "mighty Zhonghua minzu" (*weida de Zhonghua minzu*)—became a regular part of the party's discourse throughout the Yan'an period.[86] If the Communists were troubled by the possibility that their usage of Zhonghua minzu could be conflated with the Guomindang's "fascist one-race theory" (see Chapters 4 and 5), that concern was not reflected in their early popular propaganda.

Second, Li Weihan, Liu Chun, and other CCP nationality experts began speaking about China's "domestic national question" (*guonei minzu wenti*).[87] By redefining the heretofore universally applicable national question as a purely domestic political issue, the Chinese Communists signaled their intention to delink the issue of ethnic diversity within China from Bolshevik and Comintern policy. In fact, the party's adoption of this term—much like its subtle replacement of the Leninist phrase "small and weak minzus" (ruoxiao minzu) with the less ambiguous "minority nationals" (shaoshu minzu) during the late 1920s and early 1930s—marked a conscious effort to place the problem of the frontier and its diversity securely under the rubric of *Chinese* nationalism. The party hoped to recast the national liberation struggles of the various frontier minorities against Chinese colonial oppression as the struggle of a single Zhonghua minzu to overthrow foreign imperialism and domestic feudalism while establishing a free and united Zhonghua state.

Inner Mongolia and Regional Autonomy

The new Maoist nationality policy was intended to mobilize all minority classes (especially the so-called upper stratum) under the leadership of the CCP. To this end, the party drew on the united front tactic as it implemented a new policy of limited regional autonomy for the frontier minorities. In a speech before the party's Sixth Plenum, Zhang Wentian stressed that all party work among the frontier people must begin with the upper stratum. While educating and training minority youths, the party should also "do everything humanly possible" to win over their internal traitors and reactionaries.[88] "In carrying out our united front work," a central party directive on work among the Mongols of Suiyuan province similarly declared, "regardless if it is among the Mongols or the Han, we must give an important position to our work among the upper stratum; for unless we handle our work among the upper stratum correctly, our work among the lower stratum will not develop."[89]

Such extension of the united front tactic beyond its expedient uses during the Long March produced some concrete policy changes. For example, the party's treatment of the Inner Mongolian nationalist De Wang shifted markedly. In the past, the party, like its GMD rival, had strongly criticized De Wang and his Inner Mongolian autonomous movement. Following De Wang's open collaboration with the Japanese in April 1936, both political parties branded him a national traitor; and in a July 1936 article, the politburo member Wang Jiaxiang singled out De Wang as a major Japanese collaborator, declaring his so-called independent Mongolian government a mere puppet administration of the Japanese imperialists.[90] Yet, in another article written the same month, Liu Xiao warned that De Wang still enjoyed a good deal of support among the Suiyuan Mongols. His appeal to ordinary Mongols had to be taken seriously if the party hoped to redirect their loyalty back toward China and the Communist Party.[91]

But the revolutionary situation changed following the successful defense of Suiyuan province and the partial defeat of De Wang's Japanese-trained and supplied cavalry during the winter of 1936–37: the party sensed a new opportunity to pull De Wang and his followers over to the side of the Chinese revolution. In a July 1937 directive on Mongolian work, De Wang was recast as a Mongolian nationalist who possessed "a relatively strong national consciousness against Han chauvinist oppression."[92] Because his setbacks had left his support for the Japanese "conditional" and "wavering," the party should adopt a new policy aimed at "winning over De Wang" and establishing a patriotic united front with the Mongolian upper stratum. The directive therefore called for changing the previous slogan, "Strike Down the Mongolian Traitor De Wang," to "Seek De Wang's Resistance to the Japanese."[93]

In its analysis of the Mongolian question, Li Weihan's NWC placed the blame for Mongolian collaboration squarely on the Guomindang's Han chauvinism. Chiang Kai-shek's failure to take De Wang's earnest request for Inner Mongolian autonomy seriously "forcibly shoved the Mongols into the bosom of the Japanese invaders."[94] Rather than being consenting traitors, De Wang and his followers were now described as "accomplices under duress" (*xiecong*). Optimistic about the prospects for winning over the Mongolian upper stratum, the NWC called for a broad united front comprising "all anti-Japanese personal—regardless of their class, party affiliation, religion, and beliefs and irrespective of whether they are princes, lamas, or common folk."[95] Unity was now more important than class struggle, and the party urged the settling of "all disputes among the nationalities according to the principle that 'brothers that quarrel at home should join forces against an attacker from without.'"[96]

The policy of "regional autonomy" (*difang zizhi*) that promised political, economic, and cultural equality with the Han majority was central to the Northwest Committee's plan to unify the Mongols and other frontier minorities under the leadership of the Communist Party. In Inner Mongolia, in the spirit of Mao's Sixth Plenum speech, the NWC proposed creating a Mongolian local government and anti-Japanese base area within the nomadic regions already under Japanese occupation. In the nonoccupied sedentary areas, where the Mongols lived among Han migrant farmers, provincial administrations should set up a special committee of Mongolian leaders to manage all Mongolian political, economic, and cultural affairs and the Mongols' interactions with the Han people. In accordance with Mao's new principle of the right to manage one's own affairs, provincial and county administrations were not to interfere. In particular, the Han chauvinist policy of establishing counties and occupying Mongolian pastureland by force was to cease immediately. Finally, following the principle of "voluntarism and acting on one's own" (*ziyuan yu zizhu*), the party was to assist the Mongols in carrying out democratic reforms—such as reclaiming land, abolishing exorbitant taxes and levies, and reducing rent and interest rates—in order to improve their living standards.[97]

To more effectively mobilize the Mongols in support of the CCP and its struggle against Japanese imperialism, the NWC called for the creation of Mongolian militias, mass organizations, and training academies. According to the Mongol scholar Hao Weimin, the Red Army, despite its limited contact with the Mongols, succeeded in setting up a Mongolian anti-Japanese guerrilla force within the Daqingshan region on the Suiyuan-Sha'anxi border. This small group managed to raise supplies, win over Mongolian collaborators, and protect party organizations behind enemy lies in Suiyuan and Chahar provinces.[98] In order to promote and reform Mongolian culture and language, the party founded the Mongolian Cultural Advancement Society *(Menggu wenhua cujinhui)* in Yan'an during the spring of 1940. More than a thousand Mongolian and Chinese delegates reportedly gathered for its opening congress, where the Mongolian intellectual Ai Siqi called for an "enlightenment movement" using popular Mongolian cultural forms. Two of the society's biggest achievements, according to executive council member Li Weihan, were establishing the Genghis Khan Memorial and the Mongolian Cultural Exhibit in Yan'an.[99] But education was the party's most important avenue for mobilizing the Mongols and other nationalities. Building on the national minority classes created by Li Weihan at the Yan'an Party School in 1939, the party established the Nationalities Institute (*Minzu xueyuan*) during the summer of 1941. During its first year, more than two hundred minorities, representing seven different nationalities, enrolled in its three departments (Hui, Tibetan, and Mongolian). By the summer of 1942, enrollment had grown to three hundred students (40 percent Mongol, 20 percent Hui, and 40 percent others), creating a valuable store of minority cadres on which the party could draw.[100]

The CCP's break with the Bolshevik nationality policy represented an unabashed return to the 1924 minzuzhuyi platform of Sun Yat-sen. Unlike the nationality program originally prescribed by the Comintern, which emphasized class struggle, minority political secession, and the eventual creation of a federated

Zhonghua state, the CCP's new policy of "minzu equality and autonomy" (*minzu pingdeng zizhi*) was consistent with the manifesto of the Guomindang's Reorganization Congress. Having declared in his Sixth Plenum report that there was basically no incompatibility between Marxism-Leninism and the "Revolutionary Three Principles of the People," reinterpreted by Sun Yat-sen during the last years of his life,[101] Mao went a step further in his 1940 essay, "On Democracy." There he announced that these revolutionary principles were "what China needs today" and that the CCP was "ready to fight for their complete realization" because they were "basically similar to the Communist political program for the stage of democratic revolution in China."[102]

This return to the political discourse of Sun Yat-sen can be viewed as strategic moderation, designed to encourage the Nationalist Party and its allies to join the CCP in an anti-Japanese united front. Indeed, as I have already noted, the CCP's nationality policy must be viewed within the context of its struggle with other political organizations in China to gain legitimacy as the patriotic voice of the entire Chinese minzu. At the same time, however, we must remember that the party's attitude toward the frontier minorities never differed significantly from that of Sun Yat-sen (and Chiang Kai-shek, for that matter). Like Sun's discourse of minzuzhuyi, the party's nationality policy ultimately sought the equitable fusion of all Chinese minzus into a strong, independent, and, most important, unified Zhonghua minzu. At times during its development, the party—either because of its reliance on Comintern ideological and financial support or the need to highlight its differences with the reactionary Guomindang—was not in a position to fully articulate Sun's principle of minzuzhuyi. Yet the anti-Japanese united front and Mao's sinification of Marxism-Leninism presented a new opportunity for the party's return to the discourse of minzuzhuyi.

It was within the context of Sun's "Revolutionary Three Principles of the People" that Mao Zedong carefully reintroduced the concept of national self-determination. In his report before the Seventh Party Congress in April 1945, Mao repeated the formal pledge of the Guomindang's First National Congress to recognize "the right of all minzus in China to self-determination and the organization of a free and united Zhonghua Republic (upon the voluntary union of all nationalities) as soon as the revolution achieves victory over the imperialists and warlords." He added, "The CCP is in complete agreement with the nationality policy stated by Mr. Sun above."[103] By resurrecting the principle of national self-determination, the party could simultaneously avoid the appearance of having reneged on a former promise and promote its nationality program as more progressive than the Guomindang's reactionary Han chauvinism, portraying itself as the true inheritor of Sun's revolutionary mantle.

To avoid any confusion, however, Zhou Enlai lectured party members on the proper interpretation of Sun's revolutionary discourse in more detail. Speaking at a Yan'an ceremony marking the nineteenth anniversary of Sun's death, Zhou went through the 1924 Reorganization Congress manifesto line by line to ensure that party members understood its "revolutionary meaning." The "equality of all nationalities within China," for example, should be interpreted as "providing completely equal treatment to the Mongol, Hui, and other nationalities in China and recognizing their right to autonomy."[104] Zhou stressed two meanings of the more controversial pledge of self-determination: first, the recognition of the existence of the Han, Hui, Tibetan, Mongol, and other nationalities "within the confines of the Chinese people (Zhongguoren) or the Zhonghua minzu" and second, the "acceptance that in accordance with the principle of national self-determination, only by uniting together without distinction can we 'organize a free and united Zhonghua Republic (upon the voluntary union of all nationalities).'"[105] Thus the national self-determination of the entire Zhonghua minzu—the equitable union of all Chinese nationalities—represented the ultimate aim of both Sun Yat-sen's discourse of minzuzhuyi and the Communist Party's nationality policy.

Nationalizing the National Question: The Road to CCP State Power?

On the eve of the Communist victory, Mao identified the development of "a united front of all revolutionary classes and groups under the leadership of the party" as one of the CCP's "three principal weapons" that were responsible for the success of the revolution.[106] In its struggle to mobilize the inhabitants of China against the Japanese imperialists and Guomindang reactionaries, the party attempted to broaden its appeal by recasting the revolutionary struggle in the expansive and ambiguous terms of "us" versus "them." It was political loyalty rather than class or ethnic identity that determined membership in the "us group," or what Mao termed "our friends," in the battle against "them," or "our enemies."[107] Drawing on Lenin's united front tactic and the increasing military strength of the Red Army, the CCP gradually brought the frontier and its peoples under Communist control, successfully reunifying most of former Qing territory by late 1950. In the course of its revolutionary mobilization of society, the party sought to persuade the frontier minorities to actively participate, or at the very least to remain neutral, in the *Chinese* revolution. Intentionally downplaying ethnic and class identity, the Communists followed their Nationalist Party rivals in stressing the unity and shared destiny of all "Chinese people" in their struggle for liberation from foreign imperialism. While Communist activists were not immune to the manipulation of frontier minorities' ethnic aspirations, party leaders were careful to stress the conjoined fate of all the inhabitants of the former Qing empire in their collective war against the evil forces of foreign imperialism and domestic feudalism.[108]

From the moment they included Lenin's principle of national self-determination in the party's political program, CCP leaders attempted to circumscribe it. The Comintern's insistence that the CPP support Outer Mongolian independence in the name of socialist brotherhood sharply contradicted the social

Darwinian logic that had come to reinforce the presumed superiority of the age-old Sinic cultural core, and it threatened to undermine the party's patriotic and revolutionary credentials. In their popular propaganda, CCP members went to great lengths to stress that Outer Mongolian independence was only a temporary, tactical withdrawal aimed at strengthening the revolutionary struggle of both the Han and Mongolian peoples before their eventual reunion under CCP leadership. Like Sun Yat-sen, the Communists believed that the frontier minorities lacked the capacity for long-term political independence. The only national entity capable of self-determination and revolution was a Han-led Zhonghua minzu that included all the former peoples of the Qing empire within a new spatiotemporal imagined community. This assumption was made explicit after the party broke with the Comintern and the national question was sinicized under Mao Zedong. As early as 1940, the party asserted that it was the responsibility of the "modern" Han majority, as China's "ruling minzu," to guide the Mongol, Hui, Tibetan, and other "backward minzus" toward their collective liberation and to foster the right environment in which "natural assimilation" (*ziran tonghua*) could forge a new, more evolutionarily robust national people.[109] Again like the Guomindang, the Communist Party offered the frontier minorities political and cultural autonomy in exchange for their incorporation into a multiethnic yet unitary Zhonghua minzu. The Communists also loudly resisted any attempts to "split the minzu," while calling with increasing clarity after the 1949 Revolution for the recovery of those "lost territories," such as Outer Mongolia, Taiwan, Hong Kong, Macau, and others that had been separated from the fatherland.[110] When it came to their policy toward the frontier minorities, Mao Zedong and Chiang Kai-shek shared a common political stratagem, one that sought to accommodate (at least temporary) the desire of the frontier minorities for autonomy, while simultaneously stretching the boundaries of the minzu and its sovereignty firmly over their heads.

Political scientist Germaine Hoston has recently chronicled the "metamorphosis" of the national question as it was transported from Europe to Asia by the Comintern. She argues that in Japan and China, the significance of the national question expanded beyond the narrow focus on "nationality" in European Marxism (namely the attempt by ethnically distinct peoples to construct their own nation-states in the face of rising transnational class consciousness) to embrace such issues as national development, state building, cultural identity, and human agency. By broadening its focus, the CCP—through Mao's sinification of Marxism into a unique brand of Chinese statism—overcame the tension between, on the one hand, loyalty toward one's own cultural tradition and national identity in the face of Western imperial encroachment and, on the other hand, the appeal of proletarian internationalism and its axiom that universal class interest leads to universal freedom.[111]

Though Hoston's argument is helpful in thinking about the adaptation of Marxism to suit China's unique political and cultural traditions, she treats China as an ethnically homogeneous category of analysis in concluding that "the national question [in China] is not primarily a nationalities question," because "Chinese cultural identity has historically overwhelmed the claims of ethnic minorities."[112] As this chapter has shown, the problem of incorporating the frontier minorities of the Qing empire into the new nation-state was central rather than peripheral to the entire Marxist discourse on the national question in twentieth-century China. Despite their small population and comparative economic backwardness, the location of China's minority nationals along the strategic frontier regions greatly enhanced their significance to Chinese political leaders. They took on particular importance during the Republican period when China was struggling to maintain her national independence and territorial integrity in the face of aggressive imperialist encroachment. Here the inherent tension between loyalty and class (which was potentially international) and between loyalty and minzu (which was decisively national) was resolved in favor of the latter, resulting in the eventual *nationalization* of the national question in China. As Liu Chun asserted in a lecture soon after the establishment of the PRC, "In the Chinese revolution the national question has come into being as a *domestic national question*, arising throughout the course of the Chinese revolution, at different stages and circumstances, as one of the fundamental problems of the revolution."[113] Both revolutionary parties in China came to reject the internationalist aspects of Bolshevik ideology on the national question, resisting Comintern attempts to make Lenin's principle of national self-determination government policy while staunchly opposing imperialist plots to tear the minzu asunder in its name. As both parties vied to demonstrate their patriotic intentions, neither could afford to ignore or abandon the frontier and its indigenous population in the struggle to construct a new Chinese state.

An overly narrow focus on ideology in our treatment of Chinese nationalism threatens to obscure the importance of institution building (both political and military) in forging the centralizing technologies through which the nation-state is envisioned, constructed, and ultimately governed. Recent studies on the Republican frontier have tended to emphasize both the importance and limitations of various worldviews, cultures, and religions in forging China's "imagined community." The temptation to overstate the role of ideological structures risks underplaying the centrality of coercive power in Chinese state building. The dramatic arrival of Communist tanks and soldiers in front of the Potala Palace in 1950 vividly demonstrated that the gun ultimately proved more important than the pen in the incorporation of Tibet and other frontier regions into the modern Chinese nation-state. The Communists succeeded were the Nationalists failed, not due to revolutionary rhetoric or a more inclusive and pragmatic nationalism, but rather their superior military strategies and organizational acumen. As the last two chapters have attempted to demonstrate, the Guomindang's frontier policy did not fail due to a lack of commitment to frontier autonomy or understanding about the plight of various minority peoples, but rather due to its failure to rein in regional warlords and the predatory transfrontiersmen associated with them. The Chinese Communists, on the other hand, successfully deployed Lenin's united front tactic in extending its tentacles deep into the frontier, thereby laying the foundations for its future rule. Yet, the ultimate incorporation of the Qing frontiers came only after the CCP's Red Army marched into its furthest corners and forcefully integrated both the frontier nomads and the sedentary colonists into a new authoritarian party-state.

PART II

Narratives of Cultural Innovation

CHAPTER 4

From the Yellow Emperor to Peking Man: The Nationalists and the Construction of Zhonghua minzu

The previous chapters examined the arduous process by which the spatial boundaries of a distinct yet fluid Zhongguo/China toponym came to be fixed in relation to the Chinese state's struggle against foreign imperialism and domestic warlordism. The global system of fully bounded and competing nation-states transformed the overlapping sovereignties of the Qing borderlands into important sites of political intervention as the Republican state (both in its Communist and Nationalist variants) struggled to impose a single centralizing sovereignty over China's newly *bordered* lands and its heterogeneous polities. The following two chapters shift the focus from politics to culture, from state building to nation building, and from space to time. They explore how the newly rediscovered familiar Other came to shape the cultural and temporal frontiers of the modern Chinese nation-state. The reality of their weak and fragmented authority forced GMD and CCP state elites to employ various narratives of cultural innovation aimed at historicizing, naturalizing, and biologizing an ancient yet finite "Chinese" community, one that would explicitly include the non-Sinic peoples of the Qing frontier. Here, Sinic elites sought to reconfigure the meaning of Chineseness, pulling and stretching at its boundaries in the vain hope that it would rather naturally fall into alignment with the rather bloated and fragile sovereighty of the Republican geo-body. It is in this context that I seek to explore the numeric imprecision inherent in the new idiom for the nation, arguing that it was chiefly a matter of timing that determined whether the Zhonghua minzu was rendered as "*the* Chinese minzu" or "the various minzus of China." In other words, the term's ambiguity revolves around the nature and temporality of its imagined unity, whether one chooses to define it primarily as objective or subjective, primordial or emergent, racial or cultural.

In this chapter, I trace the development of several competing narratives of national unity and origin among academics and officials both directly and loosely associated with the Guomindang state. The next chapter continues the discussion, exploring other formations of national belonging used by Communist-affiliated scholars and politicians. Faced with the difficulty of incorporating the heterogeneous population of the Qing empire into the new Chinese nation-state, Chinese intellectuals of all political stripes looked backward into their own history for scientific proof of national unity. It is at times of rapid social transformation, Hobsbawm notes, that nations "invent" new traditions to create a sense of continuity with the past.[1] Yet the process of nation building does not occur in a vacuum. Rather, cultural elites constantly draw on historical memory (in a selective yet coherent fashion) to reconstitute a new national myth, one that emphasizes both continuity with the past and unity among its territorial inhabitants. These two chapters focus on the tension between, on the one hand, a racial formulation that placed the source of Chinese unity in the remote "common origin" (*tongyuan*) of its people and, on the other hand, a cultural formulation that located this unity in the gradual, evolutionary "melding" (*ronghe*) of several distinct cultures into a new national consciousness. Unlike Prasenjit Duara, my reading of the evidence suggests not the gradual displacement of race with culture as the defining marker of national identity in Republican China, but rather their continued imbrication and strategic application as Chinese elites responded to specific scientific and political developments in the domestic and international environment.[2]

While discussing national identity in twentieth-century China, Frank Dikötter makes a useful distinction between racial and cultural nationalism. He speaks of them as two distinct but often overlapping strategies for conceptualizing the nation-state. In both strategies the nation-state is imagined as a unique entity with a common history, territory, culture, and blood. Yet racial nationalism emphasizes the importance of blood ties and the racial bond created through common descent from a shared ancestor, whereas cultural nationalism privileges cultural features that bind individuals together in an organic and dynamic entity.[3] Unfortunately, Dikötter's dichotomy becomes overly essentialized and problematic when he associates cultural nationalism with the attempt to meld tradition and modernity together in an evolutionary vision of the Chinese community, and he links racial nationalism with the iconoclastic rejection of tradition and culture during the process of imagining a uniquely modern sense of national identity.[4] The fluidity of nationalist thought in Republican China defies rigid distinctions between tradition and modernity, religion and science, conservatism and progressivism, and even culture and race. Modernization in China was not a linear and teleological process but rather a complex and relational dialogue between past, present, and future.

In detailing these different narrative strategies for dealing with the problem of ethnic diversity in China, Chapters 4 and 5 highlight the role of nascent scientific disciplines (namely history, archaeology, and ethnology) in authenticating myths of national belonging. My approach steers clear of an overly simplistic distinction between a group of "modern" and "progressive" May Fourth intellectuals and a "traditional" and "regressive" group of conservatives in early twentieth-century China,[5] yet employs the broad political division between the Communists and the Nationalists as an organizational tool for discussing the material. The Republican-era's rich intellectual milieu included a wide variety of strategies for obtaining modernity: some were co-opted by the Chinese state(s) and others were marginalized, becoming what one academic has labeled "repressed modernities."[6] While many of these narratives crossed political divides, the competitive nature of state power forced different actors to modify and differentiate their approaches, reorganizing the heterogeneity of the nation to ultimately arrive at the same unified national imaginary. What was different about early twentieth-century China was not the use of tradition to create different typologies of human variation, but rather the use of new technologies of scientific classification to reorder and historicize humans within the finite and geographically bounded communities that formed the basis of the modern nation-state system. In the case of China, these disciplines helped legitimate the transformation of the formerly marginal barbarians into an integral, albeit still *minority*, component of a unitary body politic. Like others, I find it useful to think about the construction of national identity in modern China as a dynamic process of transmission and dispersion—that is, the transmission of historically based notions of political and cultural communities and the dispersal of these representations over time and space in ways that address present needs.[7]

The Manchurian Incident and the Rising Tide of Chinese Nationalism

The incredible speed and ease with which the Japanese imperial army invaded China's four northeastern provinces following the September 18, 1931, Manchurian Incident swiftly transformed the national mood in China. The event was a source of great embarrassment for the Chinese people as they watched the Kwantung Army occupy this former frontier tributary that now represented nearly one-fifth of the Republic's territory. The cries for armed resistance increased as the Japanese army advanced to within thirteen miles of Beiping in May 1933. Yet Chiang Kai-shek's Nationalist Party government in Nanjing refused to become entangled in a war with the Japanese before it had defeated the Chinese Communists and consolidated its authority over the regional warlords. Seeking to appease the Japanese, Nanjing agreed to the humiliating terms of the Tanggu Truce that granted Japan de facto control over the northern provinces of Hebei and Chahar.

The Manchurian Incident and the sense of national emergency that developed in its wake elicited a series of contradictory responses from the Chinese intelligentsia. Many of the May Fourth intellectuals strengthened their commitment to the "enlightenment project" (*qimeng yundong*), convinced that only Western science and democracy could foster a genuine spirit of national unity and resistance among the Chinese people. Others, however, looked inward toward traditional culture, arguing that China lacked the moral fiber and national identity necessary to withstand the Japanese invasion; many echoed Sun Yat-sen's 1924 call for a revival of China's lost minzuzhuyi.[8] One of the leading voices in this "national salvation movement" (*jiuguo yundong*) was Shao Yuanchong, a veteran of Sun Yat-sen's Tongmenghui and the breakaway Western Hills faction of the Guomindang, which had objected to the first united front between the Nationalists and the Communists. Writing less than a month after the Manchurian Incident, Shao claimed that the invasion provided China with a historic opportunity to cultivate a new "minzu spirit." "We have met with this danger and difficulty," Shao wrote, "because our entire minzu lacks sufficient training and preparation in minzu consciousness."[9]

The growing tide of nationalism in 1930s China needs to be placed within the context not only of Japanese imperialism but also of the political backlash against the cultural iconoclasm of the May Fourth Movement,[10] which Shao blamed for excessive self-indulgence. According to a growing number of academics and state officials, the May Fourth generation's ethic of "self-doubt" had degenerated, in the words of Guomindang insider Chen Lifu, into an unhealthy and exceedingly pessimistic "loathing of the past," "lack of interest in the present," and "lack of concern for the future."[11] Because the Chinese people were what Sun Yat-sen called "a sheet of loose sand," they were easily sundered when faced with a strong and unified Japanese attack. In his 1924 lectures on minzuzhuyi, Sun Yat-sen stressed that the revival of China's unique cultural tradition was the key to restoring national self-confidence and unity. If the Chinese wanted to regain their "minzu spirit," Sun argued, it was crucial to first "reawaken the learning as well as the traditional morality that we once possessed."[12] Throughout the 1930s, officials and intellectuals closely associated with the Guomindang kept Sun's legacy of nationalism alive, repeatedly calling for the arousal of China's lost "minzu consciousness," advocating "minzu thought," and stressing the urgent need for a new "minzu spirit" in the quest for China's "minzu liberation."

For many Chinese nationalists, the Japanese invasion of Manchuria required an urgent shift of attention away from personal enlightenment and toward the troubled fate of the entire minzu. Manchuria had been occupied; and now the Japanese were appealing to the Mongols, Chinese Muslims, and other frontier minorities to "liberate" themselves from the yoke of Chinese domination. Only by fostering a single identity from amongst China's numerous parochial, class, and ethnic identities could the Chinese minzu ensure its continued existence in the Darwinian struggle for the survival of the fittest among nation-states. Shao

Yuanchong and others viewed human evolution through the same Darwinian glasses as Sun Yat-sen. Human history was the story of "minzu competition," with different social groups struggling for evolutionary survival. Because of this struggle, people with similar blood, language, religion, and customs needed to unite together in forming the largest and healthiest minzu possible.[13] The Manchurian Incident demonstrated that the Chinese minzu was debilitated and divided and in desperate need of national reconstruction. If China hoped to reverse its slow walk toward "the death of the state and the extinction of the race," it needed to follow Sun's advice for restoring its national well-being.

What constituted an evolutionary healthy minzu? At times Shao argued that more than a common bloodline, language, and set of customs were needed for a strong and cohesive minzu to unite. Also required was a common consciousness centered on a single minzu culture and minzu education. According to Shao, each minzu possessed its own unique culture, and China's was located in the traditional Confucian values of benevolence (*ren*), knowledge (*zhi*), courage (*yong*), and loyalty (*zhong*). The cultivation of these unique virtues would provide the Chinese people with the self-confidence needed to face their current national crisis.[14] The key to inculcating these values was to implement minzu education. Shao stressed that the purpose of education was to "discipline and cultivate the masses, so as to provide them with a rich national consciousness and morality, and the appropriate knowledge and abilities needed to undertake the responsibility for reconstructing their minzu."[15] It was crucial, however, that a country's educational system have a central focus—the minzu—and that it should lead the people to "understand their own position, their own country, and their own ancestors."[16]

In short, the purpose of education in China was to foster the students' understanding of what it meant to be "Chinese"—their unique culture, long historical tradition, and common destiny. In many ways historical memory was at the center of both "national culture" and "national education." Without a correct understanding of the past, it was impossible to resist the present oppression: "If a majority of [a country's] people do not understand that they have a fatherland, do not know they have a history, do not know the spirit of hardship with which their ancestors built on, and do not know the beauty of their own culture," Shao wrote in 1933, "it becomes easy for country A to look down on country B as their slaves and for country C to have their land occupied and have to follow the orders of country D."[17]

While Shao Yuanchong focused on the reconstruction of China's national spirit, Dai Jitao attempted to draw the attention of the public to its threatened frontier regions. Dai, who served for a while as Sun Yat-sen's personal secretary, had always had a keen interest in the former Qing frontier. Following the establishment of the Nanjing Central Government in 1927, he became one of its top policy advisors on the "frontier question." Echoing his mentor, Dai argued that it was in the frontier region that China's authority was weakest and that the struggle against foreign imperialism would be won or lost. It was pointless to "save the country" while losing the nearly 60 percent of "Chinese territory" that constituted the former frontier regions of the Qing dynasty. "In attempting to save the country today," Dai urged, "we absolutely must not abandon the frontier."[18]

During the 1930s, Dai gathered together a group of like-minded academics and party members to form the New Asia Study Society (Xin Yaxiya xuehui) in Nanjing. The mission statement of the society's journal, *Xin Yaxiya* (*New Asia*), avowed a commitment to promoting research on the Three Principles of the People as they applied both to the frontier question and to the liberation of the "Oriental minzu" (*dongfang minzu*).[19] Following the Manchurian Incident and increased Japanese encroachment in northern China, the journal narrowed its focus to the role of the Chinese frontier (in particular, Mongolia and the rest of the northwest) in revitalizing the Chinese minzu.

For Guomindang nationalists like Dai Jitao and Shao Yuanchong, the Manchurian Incident heightened the importance of persuading all citizens of the fundamental unity of the Chinese nation-state. Nationalist scholars in both China and Japan adopted a variety of strategies to "authenticate" their various claims of sovereignty over the liminal borderland of Manchuria. Drawing on globalized discourses of the modern and their evolving institutionalization as the distinct academic disciplines of history, anthropology, geology, archaeology, and other social sciences, these scholars attempted to nationalize the Manchurian frontier so that it could be incorporated in either a distinctly Chinese or a distinctly Japanese geo-body.[20] In this struggle for legitimacy, Chinese academics admitted that they were far behind their Japanese counterparts, as many of these disciplines were in a nascent stage of development in China. Given the country's rich historical tradition, it was only natural that Chinese nationalists turned to history in their attempts to substantiate Chinese claims over Manchuria.

Following the Manchurian Incident, Tao Xisheng sent an impassioned letter to his fellow historian Fu Sinian, claiming that the Japanese occupation of Manchuria represented the first move in an impending "cultural war."[21] Japanese historians, such as Yano Jin'ichi and Asano Risaburō, were claiming that Manchuria, Tibet, and Mongolia were not originally part of Chinese territory, while Japanese agents working with the Muslim warlord Ma Zhongying in Gansu and various Mongol princes in Inner Mongolia were encouraging the Hui and Mongols to cast off Chinese oppression. Others, such as the influential Japanese ethnologist Torii Ryūzō, were using both race and culture to construct a common Ural-Altaic identity that explicitly excluded the "Han" Chinese from the typology of Northwest peoples.[22] In justifying their interference in Manchuria, the Japanese argued that China's so-called republic of five races (*wuzu gonghe*) was a modern political construct that was being used to forcibly suppress the legitimate national aspirations of the former Qing frontier peoples, who desired self-determination and independence from Chinese rule. By helping to establish the independent state of Manchukuo, with the last emperor of the Qing dynasty as its leader, the Japanese claimed to be unselfishly aiding the small and weak races of Asia in resisting traditional Chinese hegemony. To legitimize these claims about Manchuria, Japanese academics marshaled "scientific evidence" aimed at demonstrating the unique history, geography, economy, and ethnic identity of the Manchurian state and peoples.[23]

Arguing that these false accusations must not go unanswered, Tao Xisheng urged Fu Sinian and other Chinese historians to write their own national histories. Fu Sinian originally intended to create a new, systematic general history of China, but the exigencies of time lead him to quickly compile a short outline of Manchurian history for submission to the Lytton Commission investigating Japan's invasion of Manchuria. The result, *Draft History of Northwest China* (*Dongbei Shigang*), consciously distorted the evidence in its claim that "the northeast" (Dongbei) had been governed by a Chinese bureaucratic system since the beginning of recorded history.[24] This blatant disregard for historical facts drew harsh criticism from not only Japanese nationalists but also, rather surprisingly, the academic community in China. One Chinese critic, Miao Fenglin, asserted that despite its short length, the number of historical errors in Fu's outline would almost certainly break a record. Countering the solid scholarship of Japanese historians with bogus and hollow propaganda was ineffective, the book's critics charged.[25] The chief problem for Chinese historians in responding to the claims of their Japanese counterparts was that throughout China's long recorded history, in fact, few Chinese dynasties had consistently and fully controlled the frontier regions of Tibet, Xinjiang, Mongolia, and Manchuria. In the case of Manchuria, Japanese academics and officials were able to argue rather convincingly that Chinese administration extended throughout the northeast only during the Han and Tang dynasties and then merely in the form of a loose coalition with native rulers. In the end, the Great Wall served as a powerful metaphor for the geographic, ethnic, and political divide between Manchuria and China prior to the fall of the Qing dynasty, making it difficult for Chinese scholars to prove the historical continuity of Chinese sovereignty over the northeast.[26]

Sensing perhaps that China's historical and even geographic claims over the former frontier regions of the Qing empire were weak, a group of Guomindang-affiliated scholar-officials shifted their narrative strategy, focusing instead on the racial ties between the five minzus of the Republic. These racial nationalists, as I will call them, began arguing that China's principal claim over the Qing frontier and its people was based on the racial homology of the Han, Manchu, Mongol, Hui, and Tibetan peoples rather than the territorial or political continuity of the Chinese state. With increasing clarity throughout the 1930s and 1940s, they stressed that all the Republic's citizens, including the Manchus and other frontier indigenes of the former Qing empire, actually constituted an indivisible part of a single Zhonghua minzu—what Sun Yat-sen had termed "the world's largest and most populous people who possess more than four thousand years of civilized history."[27]

The Problem of Sun Yat-sen: Enter the Yellow Emperor

Sun Yat-sen's ambiguous and often contradictory political doctrine actually hampered the racial nationalists' efforts to demonstrate that, in accordance with Sun's own definition, all the peoples of China made up a single minzu.[28] In his famous 1924 lectures on minzuzhuyi, Sun Yat-sen stressed the importance of differentiating between minzu (race/nation) and guojia (state). States, he argued, were created from man-made forces, while minzus developed out of natural forces, specifically common blood, livelihood, language, religion, and customs. While Sun admitted that the Mongols had a different lifestyle than the Han people and the Hui and Tibetans believed in a different religion than the Han, he still insisted that only in China has a "single state developed out of a single minzu, while foreign countries have developed many states from one minzu or have included many minzus within a single state."[29] As a result, the Chinese constituted what Sun termed a single, homogeneous guozu (race-state) in contrast to the hetereogenous nation-states (*minzu guojia*) of the West.

What about the Tibetans, Mongols, Manchus, and other former Qing dynasty frontier peoples that Sun admitted did not share the same minzu characteristics as the Han majority? He dismissed them as numerically insignificant and evolutionarily unfit, arguing that despite the less than ten million "nonnatives" (*wailai*), "we can say that the vast majority of China's four hundred million are entirely Hanzu: sharing a common blood, common language, common religion, and common customs—a single, pure minzu."[30] As for the frontier minorities, it was only a matter of time before they "smelted together in a single furnace" with the Han majority to fashion a new corporate, yet equally pure, Zhonghua minzu.[31]

Japan's occupation of Manchuria and parts of Mongolia and the continued Russian and British meddling along other parts of the Qing frontier made Chinese nationalists (of all political persuasions) more reluctant than Sun Yat-sen to dismiss the minority peoples as insignificant to the Chinese minzu. Their numbers might be small, but the land they occupied contained many of the natural resources necessary for China's national development. Moreover, it was no longer sufficient to simply assert that all the peoples of the Qing dynasty were citizens of the Chinese Republic; rather, scientific proof was now needed to counter Japan's claims about the ethnic diversity of the Republic and the right of its frontier minorities to national self-determination.[32] Here, Sun Yat-sen's definition of minzu did not appear to help.

Shao Yuanchong and Dai Jitao tried rather unconvincingly to demonstrate that taken collectively, all "Chinese people," including the frontier minorities, possessed Sun's fivefold criteria for nationhood.[33] Others, like Chen Guofu, were completely forthright about the fact that the various minzus of China lacked a common livelihood, language, religion, and customs.[34] Officials within the Guomindang found themselves in a quandary: they had elevated Sun Yat-sen's thought to the status of ideological dogma and claimed that China's salvation rested solely with his Three Principles of the People, yet they were unable to use his own theory of national identity to prove that the polyglot peoples of the former Qing dynasty made up a single, homogeneous Zhonghua minzu.

A group of Guomindang scholar-officials found a solution elsewhere in Sun's thought, stressing his emphasis on the role of blood kinship in minzu development. In his 1924 lectures, Sun claimed that of the five forces involved in forming a minzu, common blood was the most important.[35] Zhou Kuntian, a member of the Nationalist government's Commission on Mongolian and Tibetan Affairs, argued that among Sun's five criteria, only blood was "innate" (*xiantian*); the other criteria altered with changes in the natural environment. Indeed, Zhou contended that only a common bloodline was essential for the formation of a minzu. Differences in lifestyle, language, religion, and economic way of life were temporary and would gradually disappear with increased communication and transportation.[36] Dai Jitao and others used a similar rationale in claiming that the Han, Manchu, Mongol, Hui, and Tibetan people belong to a single, ancient race. As Dai declared in a 1934 public letter to his "Qinghai compatriots,"

> The five big minzus and other minzus living today within China were all originally a single race (zhongzu). It is only because they have lived in different places and undergone migration at different times that they have dissimilar languages and religions. The reason why different regions have produced their own sages and religions during the last two to three thousand years has nothing to do with whether or not they belong to a single race (renzhong). It all makes sense when one thinks about it. Not only are all the minzus within our country a single family, our Qinghai compatriots are actually brothers from our ancestral home and relatives living within our ancestral land.[37]

For evidence of this ancient consanguinity, Dai Jitao and the other racial nationalists pointed to the *Shiji* (*Historical Records*), compiled by the Han dynasty court historian Sima Qian in the second century BCE. Unlike previous historical records, this massive 525,000-character work attempted to record the entirety of China's past by imposing moral order and linear continuity on its disparate literary canon. The *Shiji* begins with the Huangdi or Yellow Emperor and progresses through the "five emperors" (*wudi*) and "three dynasties" (*sandai*)—what Sima Qian refers to as the "Golden Age" of Chinese antiquity—to Qinshi Huangdi's unification of all sons and daughters of the Yellow Emperor into a single state.[38] As Shao Yuanchong declared in a 1933 article, "There is almost no doubt that the Yellow Emperor is our minzu's progenitor (*shizu*)."[39]

Shao claimed that the Yellow Emperor was not only the first ancestor of the Zhonghua minzu, but also the creative genius behind the creation of the Chinese state and culture. He was confident that if only the various peoples of China understood their direct racial and historical relationship with the Yellow Emperor, they would naturally unite into a single, indivisible body politic. "If we want to cultivate a national spirit and glorious national culture," Shao wrote, "we must begin by fostering the glorious spirit of the Yellow Emperor; and to accomplish this, we must bear in mind that we must start by eulogizing and exalting the Yellow Emperor."[40] Unlike the often convoluted and contradictory positioning of the frontier minorities in Sun Yat-sen's principle of minzuzhuyi, this notion of shared descent possessed deep cultural meaning and widespread appeal for the Chinese masses, with their strong tradition of ancestor worship and kinship bonds.[41]

Building on the writings of the late Qing anti-Manchuists, such as Zhang Binglin, Chen Tianhua, and others,[42] the Republican-era racial nationalists transformed the ancient saying about the Chinese being the "children of the Yellow Emperor" (*Huangdi zisun*) into a systematic theory of the Zhonghua minzu's antiquity and consanguinity. In honor of the Yellow Emperor's birth, April 4 was declared a national holiday, and party officials (from both the GMD and the CCP) regularly gathered at Huangling in Sha'anxi province to pay their respects to what was thought to be his tomb.[43] There were no fewer than sixteen elegiac addresses between 1911 and 1949 declaring the Yellow Emperor the "progenitor of the Zhonghua minzu," the "progenitor of the Chinese state," and the "progenitor of human civilization," with Sun Yat-sen, Chiang Kai-shek, and Mao Zedong each offering his own homage to the Yellow Emperor.[44] In their popular propaganda, the racial nationalists stressed the linear and unbroken genealogy of Zhonghua racial provenance, arguing that all the peoples of the former Qing empire could trace their ancestors back through the various Chinese dynasties to the inhabitants of the ancient three dynasties, and then ultimately through the five emperors directly to a single, ancient founding father—the Yellow Emperor.

Gu Jiegang and the Doubting of Antiquity

The attempt by the racial nationalists to manipulate Chinese history in the service of political expediency did not go unchallenged by May Fourth intellectuals. While the racial nationalists were using the Yellow Emperor to construct a myth of Zhonghua racial kinship, a group of May Fourth iconoclasts were deconstructing China's historical past. One individual in particular, the Beijing University graduate Gu Jiegang, fiercely opposed the attempts of the Guomindang state to reinvent a history of common ancestry.

As early as 1923, Gu Jiegang began questioning the reliability of the ancient legends used in the construction of Sima Qian's Golden Age chronology. Building on the historical skepticism of his mentor Hu Shi, Gu put forward a "stratification theory" (*jilei de cengci*) to explain the limited and contingent knowledge possessed by contemporary historians about China's distant past. He argued that as time passes, historical myths become longer and more elaborate, and mythical figures take on increasingly heroic and superhuman features. Because of this natural process of mythmaking, it is impossible for us to know the actual truth of ancient historical events and peoples; rather, historians can know only the circumstances of the most recent written examples of these legends. For Gu Jiegang and other "doubters of antiquity" (*yigushi*), the essential question was not, what really happened in ancient China but rather why did past historians write what they did?[45]

In a public letter published in the July 1, 1923, issue of *Dushu zazhi* (*Readers Magazine*), Gu outlined a provocative research agenda for ancient Chinese history. The goal of studying high antiquity should be to destroy a set of commonly held misperceptions: (1) that the Chinese originated from a single minzu, (2) that the scope of Chinese territory has remained unified and unchanged throughout the ages, (3) that the quest for a better life makes it necessary to rationalize ancient myths and historical figures, and (4) that China possessed a Golden Age of antiquity. Gu Jiegang spent the next twenty years gathering philological and historical evidence aimed at challenging these myths.[46]

In 1926 Gu Jiegang began publishing his findings and those of his supporters and detractors in the multivolume *Gushibian* (*Critiques of Ancient History*). In the first volume, Gu stunned China's intellectual establishment by declaring that "properly speaking, there is no history [in China] before the Eastern Zhou dynasty," claiming instead that all historical documents written prior to this period were of spurious origin.[47] Gu contended that Yu the Great, the supposed founder of the Xia dynasty, was the oldest historical figure portrayed in the nonspurious records; all other ancient rulers mentioned in Sima Qian's five emperors chronology—the Yellow Emperor, Zhuanxu, Ku, Yao, and Shun—were mythical figures with no basis in history. Finally, in a move that clearly did not sit well with the racial nationalists, Gu Jiegang argued that all the stories about the Yellow Emperor, the so-called progenitor of the Zhonghua minzu, were groundless legends manufactured sometime during the Qin dynasty.[48]

Gu Jiegang believed that the apologue of Zhonghua racial homogeneity was not only historically inaccurate but also damaging to the state's goal of fostering national unity among the Han majority and the frontier minorities. In the 1933 preface to the fourth volume of *Gushibian*, Gu called the factitious consanguinity of the sage kings a prime example of the "idol of race" (*zhongzu de ouxiang*), which, he argued, was responsible for the erroneous belief in the existence of a racially pure Huaxia people in high antiquity.[49] Historical documents reveal that the so-called Huaxia people and their neighboring tribes all possessed their own blood lineages. During the Zhou dynasty, for example, each of the various minzus worshipped their own ancestors. It was recorded in the *Book of Odes* that the Shang and Zhou minzus considered themselves descendants of two different progenitors. Gu claimed that the idol of race arose only after the forced political unification of the various Zhou kingdoms under the Qin and Han dynasties. Instead of using force to eliminate the strong sense of non-Huaxia "racial consciousness" (*zhongzu guannian*) among the barbarian kingdoms such as Chu and Yue, court officials suggested replacing the horizontal system of ancestors and spirits with a single vertical system, making the ancestor of kingdom A the father of the ancestor of kingdom B and the founder of kingdom C the father of the ancestor of kingdom A. Consequently, Qin and Han officials began declaring, "We are all the sons of the Yellow Emperor; despite differences in sentiment and custom, we are now united into a single country and should eliminate regional prejudices."[50]

Gu Jiegang was also highly critical of the attempts by the Guomindang regime to use the myth of racial consanguinity to buttress its political agenda for national unification. In a 1932 letter to a fellow Yanjing University history professor Hong Weilian, Gu referred to the state's nation-building project as the "manufacturing of ancient history" and argued that a myth claiming that all Chinese are the "children of the Yellow Emperor" was insufficient for fostering a "new conviction of national unity."[51] Gu did not object to the Guomindang's attempts to unify the Chinese people into a single national body or its efforts to improve relations between the Han majority and the frontier minorities; after all, the very survival of the Chinese people depended on their unity in the face of the West's superior material force. Rather, he disagreed with the state's approach and method for fostering this necessary condition of national unity.[52] In Gu's mind and in the minds of other May Fourth intellectuals, there was no conflict between nationalism and iconoclasm. Gu was convinced that disseminating lies about the historical relationship between the minority peoples and the Han majority would hinder rather than help the natural, evolutionary melding of sentiments and cultural practices: "Since we are all Chinese, we have many common interests. If we develop a good method of unifying the nation, we shall have no difficulty in staying together. The government does not need to lie, telling us that we have descended from the same ancestor. Even if the government is successful in unifying the country with lies, this unity will be flimsy. Once the people become intelligent, can this trick still deceive them?"[53]

Gu Jiegang believed that the actual story of the frontier minorities' contribution to the minzu's glorious past would foster the self-confidence and mutual understanding necessary for a truly unified body politic. Moreover, he believed that the minorities had a central role to play in the revival of the Zhonghua minzu as a race, which May Fourth intellectuals claimed was "old and decrepit" (*shuailao*) and on the verge of "extermination" (*miezhong*). Gu argued that the evolutionary youth and virility of the frontier minorities was needed to "infuse a bit of fresh blood" into the veins of the Han majority.[54] Consequently, he frequently advocated intermarriage between the Han majority and the Tibetans, Mongols, and other minority peoples as an effective method for solving China's frontier problem.[55] Blood ties would help strengthen national cohesion, but they needed to be rooted in the actual process of intermarriage rather than spurious myths about racial descent.

A number of politicians and academics in China reacted strongly to Gu Jiegang's violent tearing down of the linear Golden Age chronology. Some maintained that his conclusions were based entirely on a scientifically flimsy and evidentially unsubstantiated "argument from silence" (*mozheng*): one cannot conclude that something never existed (here, China's Golden Age) simply because evidence to prove that it did exist is lacking.[56] "It is a gross fallacy on the part of the historian," Fu Sinian wrote of Gu Jiegang's methodology in 1930, "to mistake what we do not know for what never existed."[57] Fu and others believed that such a mistake was all too easily made during times of cultural insecurity. An element of faith was required to restore national self-confidence in China.

Guomindang officials were far less restrained in their criticism of Gu Jiegang's idol smashing. Racial nationalists within the party worried about the ill effects of the Gushibian movement on the state's nation-building project. They feared that Gu's questioning of the Golden Age narrative could undermine the apologue of racial and cultural homogeneity central to their attempts to construct a single, unified Zhonghua minzu. While there was little they could do to suppress academic freedom in the private institutions in and around Beiping, government officials did attempt to ensure that Gu's "doubting of antiquity" did not spill over into the public realm where it could influence the naive masses.

In 1929 at the insistence of Dai Jitao, the central government banned the high-school textbook that Gu Jiegang had written for the Shanghai Commercial Press.[58] Dai disapproved of how Gu's *Elementary National History* (*Benguoshi jiaokeshu*) questioned the orthodox chronology of the three dynasties and five emperors and cast doubt on the authenticity of the entire Golden Age narrative. In justifying his decision to ban the book, Dai Jitao distinguished between the freedom of academic debate and the need to ban such theories from textbooks; "otherwise, the self-confidence of the minzu will be shaken, which is, of course, harmful for the state. China's ability to unify itself into a single entity depends completely on the people's belief that they come from a single ancestor."[59] Dai was apparently so outraged by the fact that the Commercial Press had already published 250,000 copies of Gu's textbook that he insisted the government fine the company one million yuan and immediately remove all copies of the book from distribution.[60]

In challenging Gu's historical skepticism, many of his critics looked to the new Western sciences of geology, archaeology, and paleoanthropology.[61] They claimed that Gu had intentionally overlooked or slighted evidence provided by recently excavated prehistoric artifacts, preferring to deconstruct rather than reconstruct ancient Chinese history. With its establishment in 1928, the archaeology section of the Guomindang's central research institute, Academia Sinica, became a source of tremendous hope for those who wished to salvage and reconstruct Chinese antiquity. The new director of the archaeology section, the Harvard-trained anthropologist Li Ji, shared many of the critics' concerns about the ill effects of Gu's methodology and conclusions on national morale. Archaeology made it possible, he argued, to conduct scientifically valid, yet nationally sensitive, research on ancient Chinese history. Contending that not all myths were a "tent of lies," Li stressed the importance of recently unearthed artifacts and oracle bones in rebuilding a more positive image of Chinese history.[62]

Indeed, scientific methods of archaeological field research that were first pioneered in the West proved extremely valuable to Chinese nationalists in their attempt to foster a sense of common national identity and pride. They opened the door for the discovery of material remains that would provide, in the words of Li Ji's most famous student K. C. Chang, the "scientifically-authenticated empirical data" necessary to revive traditional Chinese historiography.[63] Fu Sinian, Li Ji's colleague at Academia Sinica, and the new director of its Institute of History and Philology suggested in 1934 that archaeological research could help challenge the so-called Western origin of Chinese civilization (*xilaishuo*). This influential theory, put forward by the French sinologist Albert Terrien de Lacouperie and others, held that the ancestors of the Chinese people had actually migrated to the Yellow River valley from the Mesopotamia region of western Asia. Archaeological research, Fu claimed, had the potential to demonstrate the existence of a native Chinese culture equal in age to those of Babylon and Egypt, thereby promoting a sense of cultural pride among the Chinese people.[64]

In his review of *Gushibian*, the historian Lu Maode criticized Gu's failure to draw on the new science of archaeology. He rejected Hu Shi's claim that because the ancient classics are untrustworthy, it would be foolish to state that Chinese history began more than two to three thousand years ago. According to Lu, this statement ignored the work of archaeologists who were providing a great deal of scientific evidence about prehistoric life. Archaeological research in Egypt, for example, had uncovered numerous details about that country's prehistoric civilization while also enabling scholars, in the words of the British Egyptologist A. H. Keane, "to push Egyptian culture back further and further, so that it now reaches back over eight thousand years."[65] Because they failed to take into consideration recent archaeological discoveries in Asia, Lu questioned whether Gu Jiegang and his fellow Gushibian scholars were really employing a "scientific historiographic method." If Yu the Great and other mythical figures in ancient Chinese history were "prehistoric figures," as Gu Jiegang asserted, what was the point of using the *Shang Hymns*, the *Analects*, the *Shuowen* dictionary, and other "historical documents" to either prove or challenge their existence? "Shouldn't all these questions be handed over to the archaeologists," asked Lu, "who can use the results of their excavations to draw final conclusions [about China's prehistory]?"[66]

In his argument that the various minzus of ancient China "all possessed their own origins and progenitors," Gu Jiegang overlooked recent archaeological evidence in support of the monogenesis of humanity. In fact, Lu declared, China's ancient peoples all descended from a "single race" (*yizhong*) and then evolved into "different groups" (*gelei*) under different environmental conditions. The various creation stories discussed by Gu Jiegang were simply invented by these different clans and then passed down orally from generation to generation. What was spurious, in Lu's eyes, was not the Golden Age narrative or the racial unity of the Chinese people, but the creation myths of these different clans. One day, he believed, archaeologists would prove Gu Jiegang and his fellow doubters of antiquity wrong and demonstrate the fundamental unity of the Chinese people.[67]

The Problem of Gu Jiegang: Enter Peking Man

The wait for Lu Maode and other racial nationalists was not long. On December 2, 1929, while digging in an underground cave west of Beijing, the Chinese archaeologist Pei Wenzhong discovered a nearly intact fossilized cranium of a hominid that appeared to be five hundred thousand years old. Over the next seven years, archaeologists unearthed other hominid remains at Zhoukoudian, enabling scientists to gradually reconstruct the early life and origins of fossil man in "China."[68]

Throughout the 1920s, Western archaeologists digging at Zhoukoudian found a series of fossilized teeth that they claimed represented a new hominid genus—*Sinanthropus pekinensis*, or Peking Man. After a thorough examination of the newly discovered skullcap, the head of the new Cenozoic Research Lab in Beijing, Dr. Davidson Black, concluded from its unique combination of highly original and purely modern features that Sinanthropus appeared to be an older and more generalized type of hominid than either *Pithecanthropus* (Java Man) or *Homo neanderthalensis* (Neanderthal Man), the two oldest hominid remains discovered to date. Black also argued that the Sinanthropus skull appeared to be closely related to the original type of hominid that evolved not only into Java Man and Neanderthal Man, but into all *Homo sapiens*.[69] Yet the scientific community remained divided on the significance of Peking Man; most claimed that Java Man, Peking Man, and Neanderthal Man represented three different and now extinct offshoots from the main line of human evolution.[70]

Most Chinese scientists also approached Black's conclusions with a degree of skepticism. Writing in 1930, Weng Wenhao, an eminent Chinese scientist and the director of the Chinese Geological Survey, seemed uncomfortable with the idea that this "ape-man" (*yuanren*) might prove to be the actual progenitor of the Chinese people, let alone all modern humans. The early drawings and anatomical reconstructions of Peking Man by Black and others depicted a hairy savage, quite unlike the traditional image of the Yellow Emperor as sagacious, cultivated, and resplendent. Weng was clearly proud that Peking Man provided scientific evidence for the existence of primitive man in Asia and possibly a Chinese source for all humankind; but he was also quick to add an important caveat:

> We should not misunderstand Peking Man as the direct ancestor of the Chinese race (renzhong); actually, the difference between Sinanthropus and modern man is far greater than the variation among different races today. . . .

> On the basis of reconstructions [of Peking Man], the most we can say (although we are currently lacking evidence of this) is that Peking Man and contemporary races seem to share a common ancestor (which has yet to be discovered); however, Sinanthropus and our genuine ancestors (who still have not been found) evolved separately: Sinanthropus evolved to the point when it became extinct while our race gradually advanced until it reached its current form.[71]

Regarding the relationship between Sinanthropus and the Zhonghua minzu, Weng Wenhao was willing to state only that "at most we can call Peking Man a very, very distant younger cousin sharing the same father and certainly not our direct lineal ancestor."[72]

The idea that humans, let alone the sagacious Zhonghua minzu, somehow evolved from apes seemed shocking to most Chinese during the 1930s and 1940s and created a general reluctance to directly associate the original Peking Man discovery in 1929 with the origins of the Chinese minzu. A 1939 article in *Science Life* (*Kexue shenghuo*) bluntly put this question to its readers: "Are humans' ancestors monkeys?" The author proceeded to argue that "sensitive people" feel uncomfortable with this notion; he instead insisted that the Chinese people descended from a group of ape-men who have long since become extinct.[73] The excessive hair, dark skin, large nose, and other pongid-like features in early reconstructions of Peking Man not only seemed primitive and inhuman—markers of the lowest level of social evolution that were closely associated with the "black slave race"—but also had a long association with the non-Chinese "barbarians," in sharp contrast to the jade-like complexion and refined rites of the children of the Yellow Emperor.[74]

Western scientists working in China, in contrast, were more willing to highlight the morphological relationship between Peking Man, modern man, and the Chinese race. Following the untimely death of Black in 1934, Franz Weidenreich, a Jewish émigré from Germany, was named the new director of the Cenozoic Research Lab. The discovery of new, more fully evolved human remains in 1935 led Weidenreich to conclude that "Sinanthropus is the ancestor of recent man"—or, at the very least, that "nothing [in the evidence] contradicts the assumption that Sinanthropus is a direct ancestor of recent man."[75] The fact that Peking Man was both older and had a larger cranial capacity than Java Man and Neanderthal Man seemed to suggest that he was Darwin's "missing link" between primitive ape and modern man. Weidenreich also claimed to have discovered two unique features—a thickening of the jaw and shovel-shaped incisors—whose racial morphology resembled that of modern northern Chinese. "Sinanthropus and the Mongoloid of today," Weidenreich wrote in 1936, "must have a direct relationship which can only be the case when Sinanthropus is a direct ancestor of that race and, therefore, also of mankind of today."[76]

Outside the scientific community, Chinese intellectuals saw Peking Man as significant because the fossils demonstrated the native provenance of China's inhabitants. Academia Sinica anthropologist Lin Huixiang and historian Qian Mu, among others, argued that the discovery of Peking Man provided irrefutable scientific evidence that the Chinese people were autochthons.[77] These scholars found the Zhoukoudian discoveries useful in publicly challenging the Western origin thesis, contending that evidence of early man in China invalidated the claims of Lacouperie and other Western cultural imperialists. The historian Zhang Xuguang, in his *Historical Outline of the Zhonghua minzu's Development* (*Zhonghua minzu fazhan shigang*), went a step further. He argued that the unearthing of Peking Man provided "sufficient evidence to prove that, first, the Zhonghua minzu was the original inhabitant of Chinese territory and, second, that today's Zhonghua minzu can be traced back through ancient history to a single progenitor."[78] Zhang contended that contemporary cultural differences among the various "lineage branches" (*zhizu*) of Peking Man reflected the diverse environmental conditions of China rather than the formation of distinct and divergent "races" (zhongzu). Yet most Republican-era intellectuals appeared uncomfortable with this use of the discoveries. Sigrid Schmalzer has recently pointed out that only two of the fourteen early twentieth-century school textbooks she surveyed mentioned Peking Man in telling the story of Chinese origins, and she argues that the omission reflected both the ongoing debate within the scientific community about the significance of Peking Man and a degree of cultural resistance to the idea that this primitive hominid was the ancestor of the Chinese people.[79]

But such uneasiness did not prevent at least a few racial nationalists from using the discoveries to shore up their claims about the racial unity of the Chinese people. Xiong Shili, a self-taught and ultimately reclusive revolutionary-cum-philosopher who became a leading advocate of traditional Confucian morality and culture in Republican China, made Peking Man a star attraction in his 1939 series of lectures on Chinese history at the Guomindang Central Military Academy in Chongqing. He began his first talk on the origin of the Chinese by admitting that they were the product of the nonviolent melding of the Han, Manchu, Mongol, Hui, and Tibetan peoples. Yet he was quick to stress that they represented five racially interrelated *zongzu* (lineages) with a common progenitor rather than five distinct minzus, as most Chinese intellectuals and politicians had argued since the 1911 Revolution. Irrespective of the current debate over human monogenesis versus polygenesis, Xiong claimed that when it came to the "five lineages" (*wuzu*) of the Zhonghua minzu, "logic determines that they all share a common bloodline."[80] The source of Xiong's logic and confidence was the recent discovery of their common ancestor, Peking Man, a rather surprising and ironic admission coming from the man who passionately argued in favor of metaphysics over science while at Beijing University during the 1920s.[81]

For Xiong, the discovery of Peking Man provided irrefutable evidence that the Chinese people originated from a single progenitor who lived in the Yellow River valley some five hundred thousand to one million years ago and then spread out in all directions, populating China and possibly the rest of the world. "If among the five lineages there were a few minzus who migrated into China from other regions and did not disseminate outward from mighty China," Xiong asked his students, "then where are the ancestors of these other people?"[82] In other words, until archaeologists discover evidence of an older fossil man outside the Yellow River valley and China, it is safe—and, more important, scientific—to conclude that all China's people originated from Peking Man.

Xiong Shili argued in his lecture that any differences among the five lineages were temporary and insignificant. He posed and then answered the question that his students were inevitably wondering: "If the five lineages share a common bloodline, then why do their customs (*xi*) and dispositions (*xing*) so obviously differ?"[83] Like Sun Yat-sen and others, Xiong turned to the analogy of the family in explaining these differences, emphasizing the variation among siblings with different "natural endowments" (*tianxing*) and explaining the role of the natural environment in shaping individual communities. "Yet today," he added, "thanks to advances in science and the development of modern technology, man can now control his environment and make his people equal."[84] But Xiong left little doubt in the minds of his students that prior to this great process of equalization, the Han majority would remain the wisest, strongest, and most fecund of the Zhonghua lineages. He referred to the Hanzu as the "grandchildren of the three sage kings and five virtuous emperors" and argued that they have spread not only throughout China, but also throughout Korea, Taiwan, Vietnam, Burma, Thailand, the Ryukyu Islands, the Spratly Islands, and even the Americas via the Bering Strait. Because of their long and glorious culture, "one often refers to the Hanzu when speaking about the Zhonghua minzu," or what others call the *Huazu* (Chinese lineage).[85]

The bulk of Xiong Shili's lecture was spent demonstrating that the frontier minorities were racially related "branches" (*fenzhi*) off the main Han line of evolution. By carefully stitching together a series of quotations, Xiong constructed an intricate ethnogenealogy that linked the original clans of the Yellow Emperor with the contemporary Manchu, Mongol, Hui, and Tibetan lineages, relying on a series of barbarian ethnonyms that appeared throughout the more than three thousand years of written Chinese history. Here, Xiong's methodology differed little from that of his predecessors, as China has a long tradition of fictive ethnogenealogies. Since Sima Qian first pioneered the method in his *Shiji*, generations of Chinese historians have created historical genealogies aimed at incorporating the recalcitrant frontier barbarians into the heavenly cosmology (tianxi). Xiong Shili went a step further, however, adding a new layer of modern, "scientific" proof of this racial unity: "From the distribution of our Huazu, we can infer that our prehistoric ancestor was Peking Man (this is based on the similar racial morphology of Beijing people and Sinanthropus). . . . It is from the discovery of Peking Man by archaeologists that we now know that our five lineages originally come from a single source. Simply put, the five lineages share a common blood lineage with Peking Man. This evidence is solid and cannot be disputed."[86]

While much of Xiong Shili's historical evidence was flimsy and based on texts, like the *Shiji*, that Gu Jiegang claimed were either spurious or unreliable, his archaeological evidence carried with it a new aura of scientific credibility.

In their important volume examining the link between archaeology and politics, Philip Kohl and Clare Fawcett argue that a close relationship exists between archaeology, nationalism, and the construction of national identities. They point to the intertwined history of the development of archaeology as a scientific discipline in the nineteenth century and the formation of nation-states in Europe and America. Archaeological evidence has long played an important role in the construction and naturalization of national and racial identities, they contend. Moreover, the inherent ambiguity of archaeological and prehistoric data "paradoxically strengthens this role or, more accurately, enhances the potential for abusing it."[87]

For Xiong Shili, the discovery of Peking Man seemed to provide the type of irrefutable scientific evidence needed not only to silence Gu Jiegang and the other doubters of antiquity, but also to prove once and for all the antiquity and racial unity of the Chinese people. Xiong concluded his lecture by claiming that he was convinced of the monolithic (*yiyuande*) and monophyletic (*tonggende*) origin of the Zhonghua minzu: "The discovery of Peking Man by archaeologists has made it even more certain that this primitive race (renzhong) was the common ancestor of all our five lineages, who only later split into different branches and are today known as the so-called five lineages."[88]

Rethinking Minzu: Enter the Ethnologists

While Xiong Shili and others within the Guomindang were using archaeological evidence to reconstruct the myth of Zhonghua minzu consanguinity, Gu Jiegang was encouraging a group of foreign-trained ethnologists to reexamine the entire concept of minzu. Drawing on the nascent disciplines of anthropology, sociology, and ethnology, these academics developed a new methodology and language for discussing ethnic identity, one capable of conceptualizing the unity of the Chinese people without ignoring the reality of their diverse historical, linguistic, and cultural traditions. In particular, they looked to challenge the scientific validity of race (zhongzu or renzhong) as an analytical category and rethink the meaning and significance of minzu.[89] The narrowness of Sun Yat-sen's definition of minzu became one of their central concerns. As discussed earlier, during his 1924 lectures on minzuzhuyi, Sun Yat-sen set forth a rigidly formalistic definition of minzu as a group of people who share a set of five common traits—blood, livelihood, language, religion, and customs—and identified blood as the most important. Racial nationalists latched onto his claims about blood, arguing that the entire Zhonghua minzu shared an objective and innate unity in its common bloodline. By offering a more subjective—and, they believed, more scientific—definition of minzu, these cultural nationalists (as I will call them) hoped to promote Chinese political unity without neglecting the importance of ethnic and cultural pluralism within both China's past and its present.

During the inaugural seminar of the Frontier Study Society, a group established by Gu Jiegang in 1936, the young ethnologist Fei Xiaotong spoke about his field research among the Yao people of Guangxi. In place of Sun Yat-sen's rigid definition of minzu, Fei proposed the concept of an "ethnical unit" (*zutuan*), first developed by his Russian mentor S. M. Shirokogoroff, as a more useful tool for analyzing ethnic diversity in China. According to Shirokogoroff's theory, Fei told his audience, all communities that share a common culture, language, consciousness, and endogamous kinship constitute a distinct ethnic unit. Fei stressed, however, that because ethnic identity is both subjective and situational, Shirokogoroff's concept needed to be applied flexibly. Ethnic identity was based not on a static set of objective criteria, as Sun Yat-sen's theory of minzuzhuyi would have us believe, but rather on a constantly evolving network of relationships in specific local conditions. During his research in Guangxi, Fei discovered a growing sense of common identity among the geographically isolated and culturally distinct Yao communities. He argued that rather than fostering a sense of common Zhonghua minzu identity, the state's civilizing mission had actually united the different Yao communities, thereby encouraging rather than undermining a distinct *Yaozu* ethnic identity.[90]

Lü Simian, a member of another of Gu Jiegang's newly established study societies, the Yugong Study Society, began his trailblazing 1934 history of ethnic diversity in China by distinguishing between minzu and zhongzu (race), claiming that the former refers to differences of language, religious beliefs, and customs while the latter refers to differences in skin color and physiology. Declaring that "the ethnic groups of a state should be neither too heterogeneous nor homogeneous," because they would be too difficult to govern if they were completely heterogeneous and too difficult to develop if they were completely homogeneous, Lü argued that China (Zhonghua) was unique in its "integrated ethnic heterogeneity" (*heji cuoza zhi zu*).[91] He identified twelve distinct minzus that constituted the Chinese people, which he preferred to call the Huaxia, and argued that the Han were at its cultural and racial core. Like both Sun Yat-sen and Xiong Shili, Lü credited the demographic weight and cultural luster of the Han majority with drawing these different ethnic groups together throughout the long course of Chinese history.

Several years later, another member of the Yugong Study Society, Qi Sihe, offered an even more systematic critique of Sun Yat-sen's definition of minzu. In an essay written in honor of the twelfth anniversary of Sun's death in 1937, Qi followed Lü Simian in stressing the importance of differentiating zhongzu and minzu. Since the late Qing dynasty, an entire generation of scholars, including Liang Qichao, Zhang Binglin, and Sun Yat-sen, had been using these two Chinese terms interchangeably without distinguishing between their distinct

English meanings of "race" (zhongzu) and "nation" (minzu). Qi acknowledged the important shift in Sun Yat-sen's thinking from the "narrow racism" (*zhaixia de zhongzuzhuyi*) associated with his prerevolutionary anti-Manchuism to his post-1911 call for the "five races" (wuzu) of the Republic to be assimilated into a single Zhonghua minzu. Yet though this aspect of Sun's theory revealed "enormous foresight," its weaknesses also needed to be acknowledged.[92]

A graduate of Harvard University, Qi Sihe believed that the major flaw in Sun's theory of minzuzhuyi lay in his excessive emphasis on "common blood." "Viewed from today's perspective," Qi wrote, "the biggest shortcoming of Sun Yat-sen's minzuzhuyi is his obsolete view of minzu and his failure to distinguish between nation (minzu) and race (zhongzu)."[93] Qi claimed that Sun's formalistic understanding was based on the outdated ideas of an older group of Western intellectuals (such as Ernest W. Burgess and Arthur de Gobineau) who stressed the importance of consanguinity in group formation. The new generation of American academics, led by Carlton J. H. Hayes and Franz Boas, had demonstrated that human characteristics once thought to be inherited are actually the result of differences in environment.

Qi contended that years of racial mixing and interbreeding made it impossible to rely on race to distinguish between one group of people and another. In other words, since "pure races" no longer existed, the entire concept of race was a meaningless and unscientific category of analysis. "From the perspective of anthropology," Qi argued, "race was originally grounded in superstition and thus cannot be scientifically analyzed."[94] From the perspective of biology, race has to do with the "innate" (*xiantian*) characteristics of skin color, physical makeup, and bone structure, while the characteristics of language, religion, and customs are "acquired" (*houtian*) and relate to changes in environment and culture. The idea that there somehow exist "pure races" is a myth because all human races have been melding for hundreds of thousands of years. Although humans descended from the same pair of primate ancestors, environmental differences have produced innumerable differences in culture and habits.

Qi echoed Fei Xiaotong in calling for a more dynamic and situational understanding of minzu to replace Sun's rigid, race-based notion of identity formation. He argued that membership in a minzu, or "nation" as he chose to translate it, was determined by a subjective sense of unity and difference and not a laundry list of objective criteria. A minzu, he declared, was founded on consciousness rather than substance, making it a mental rather than physical phenomenon. Similarly, political rather than biological factors establish the acquired characteristics that fashion minzu identity. For China, Qi located this common spirit in its joint history of past calamities and achievements and its current struggle against foreign imperialism. In short, the minzu, as defined by Qi Sihe and other cultural nationalists, was a group of people who possessed a sense of common history and shared destiny. The formation of what Sun Yat-sen had called a "country with a single minzuzhuyi" could proceed only on the basis of a common feeling of national belonging, not on unscientific theories of biological descent.[95]

The development of this new more subjective definition of minzu was closely associated with the emergence of ethnology (*minzuxue*) as a modern discipline and mode of representation. China has a long and rich tradition of representing, both visually and rhetorically, the Other living along its cultural margins. Yet it was not until the creation of the late Qing "Miao albums" that Chinese scholar-officials started to base their representation on "the rigor of direct observation and empirical method."[96] The merging of this novel methodology with the budding Western disciplines of sociology and anthropology and their notion of unmediated scientific field research produced a new discursive practice for representing and categorizing human variation. After seeking training abroad in these disciplines, Chinese ethnologists began calling for a systematic survey of ethnic diversity in China to create a taxonomy of human diversity and assist the state in its efforts to unify the nation-state. This process was greatly accelerated when most Chinese academics were forced to follow the Guomindang state to the southwest following the Japan's invasion of China proper in 1937. To many ethnographers, China's southwest, with its rich cultural and ethnic diversity, seemed like the perfect laboratory to experiment with this new scientific methodology and discursive category of minzu.[97]

During the late 1930s, a series of new academic institutions were established to carry out ethnographic research along the frontier. Southwest Union University in Kunming, for example, set up the Southwest Frontier Cultures Research Section (*Xinan bianjiang wenhua yanjiushi*) where Wen Yu, Wu Han, Tian Rukang, Luo Changpei, and other ethnographers carried out research under the leadership of the Naxi sociologist Fang Guoyu. After returning from some time abroad, leading sociologist Wu Wenzao founded the Research Station for Sociological Research (*Shehuixue shidi diaocha gongzuozhan*) with Rockefeller Foundation funding in 1939. With well-established researchers such as Fei Xiaotong, Lin Yaohua, and Tian Rukang, the station became another hotbed of ethnographic research during the early war years. Under the leadership of Wu Zelin, a student of Franz Boas, the Social Research Center affiliated with Daxia University launched a massive ethnographic field research project on the indigenous peoples of Guizhou. Xu Yitang, a member of the sociology department at Jinling University, set up the Chinese Ethnographic Study Society (*Zhongguo minzuxue hui*) in November 1938 and began editing the journal *Xinan bianjiang* (*Southwest Frontier*) in Kunming before it moved to Chengdu in 1941. Xu's journal soon became one of the more important mediums for discussing ethnographic research along the southwest frontier and, before long, a target of Guomindang concern.[98]

The growing professionalization of ethnology, sociology, and anthropology as academic disciplines, combined with the mass migration of Chinese universities to the southwest frontier in 1938, momentarily expanded the scope of the Chinese discourse on ethnic diversity. During the Qing and early Republican periods, the political discourse had been largely limited to the wuzu: the Han, Manchu, Mongol, Tibetan, and the Hui peoples of the Northwest. These five main constituencies of the Qing empire served as the basis for reimagining the new Republican state as a republic of five races in 1912. While state and local officials in the southwest had long possessed a detailed knowledge of the ethnic and cultural contours of the region, outsiders tended to collapsed this mosaic into blanket categories such as "Miao," "Yao," or "Yi" with nearly everyone following Sun Yat-sen in declaring them either completely "assimilated" (tonghua) or well on their way.[99] The explosion of ethnographic research on the southwest frontier during the late 1930s helped to complicate the Republic's five-zu taxonomy while calling into question the supposed racial unity of the Zhonghua minzu. As they struggled to develop a more scientific and "standardized gaze," Chinese ethnographers (with the assistance of both foreign and indigenous researchers) uncovered a complex and fluid tapestry of human diversity that seemed to defy static categorization and called for a thoroughgoing reconsideration of the origin, nature and meaning of ethnic identity in China.[100] Deep in the Yunnan forest and high on the Xikang plateau, researchers discovered numerous isolated and distinct peoples who spoke mutually unintelligible languages and observed a multiplicity of cultural, economic, and religious practices. The pages of *Xinan bianjiang* were literally filled with a multitude of traditional and newly invented ethnonyms—the Bai, Li, Dong, Luoluo, Maxie, Va, and Shan-Tai minzus to name but a few—as Chinese ethnologists attempted to identify, categorize, and analyze the rich diversity they encountered.[101]

The Problem of the Japanese: Enter the Ideologues

The controversial historian Gu Jiegang was arguably the biggest champion of cultural diversity in Republican China. Like many other academics, he followed the Guomindang into exile in the southwest. But before taking up a position at Yunnan University in Kunming, Gu accepted an invitation from the Boxer Indemnity Education Fund to conduct research on Hui education in Gansu, Ningxia, and Qinghai. The nearly five months Gu spent traveling throughout the Northwest reinforced his belief that national unity among the various ethnic groups of China, based on a genuine feeling of national belonging rather than a myth of racial propinquity, was crucial for the future survival of the Chinese minzu.[102]

In his lectures among Muslim educators and officials of the Northwest, Gu stressed the importance of understanding the difference between zhongzu/race and minzu/nation. The Chinese state, Gu explained to his audience, was composed of peoples with different physical and cultural attributes; yet the incomplete process of their amalgamation into a single Zhonghua minzu or nation had begun with Qinshi Huangdi's unification of China in 221 BCE. The

Guomindang state's continued existence—now more than ever, in the face of the Japanese invasion—depended on the cultivation of a broad nationalist or minzu sentiment, which was capable of incorporating all these racial and cultural elements while eliminating the narrow racial hatred that had torn the late Qing dynasty asunder. The so-called Zhonghua minzu was the product of thousands of years of mutual mixing and assimilation among the various peoples; consequently, from a very early date in its history, China lacked a single pure race or culture. "Even the so-called Hanzu," Gu argued, "actually includes not only Manchu, Mongol, Hui, and Tibetan blood, but also Malay blood (such as in the Fukienese and Cantonese); . . . [thus] what we call the Hanzu are actually the result of the gradual fusion (ronghua) of various races in East Asia."[103] Although Gu called into question the usefulness of zhongzu as a category of analysis in China, he did not gloss over the importance of cultural and ethnic differences. Unlike some within the Guomindang government, Gu did not advocate the forced assimilation of Hui and other minority cultures into the Han majority—a process he likened to "cutting the foot to fit the shoe" (*xuezu shilu*). Instead he urged that minority cultures be modernized so that they could more fully contribute to strengthening the Chinese state and nation.

For Gu Jiegang, at least initially, there was no tension between the May Fourth ideal of *qimeng* (enlightenment) and the urgent need to *jiuguo* (save the country) from the destructive force of the Japanese imperialists. The best way to preserve the Chinese nation and culture was to advance scientific knowledge and communication. It was the sacred duty of the scholar to carefully guard his intellectual autonomy from the temptations and constraints of politics in order to ensure that truth and not propaganda, science and not religion, diversity and not homogeneity served as the foundation of China's national unity. Moreover, Gu Jiegang did not share the racial nationalists' fears about the continuity of Chinese culture. For Gu the continuity of tradition meant not *persistence*—a transcendent, unchanging Chinese essence—but rather *gradual evolution and change*, the continual mixing and melding of China's various peoples and cultures.[104] Gu believed that the racial virility and vitality of the minority peoples was crucial for the renewal of the Chinese minzu, and he aggressively called for the "infusion of fresh blood" into the veins of the Han majority through racial intermarriage with the frontier minorities.[105]

Yet, other intellectuals found it more difficult to separate politics from scholarship, especially when confronted with the immediate threat of foreign imperialism. Gu Jiegang's old roommate at Beijing University, Fu Sinian, was one of the leading May Fourth intellectuals to develop a very different view on the role of ethnic and cultural diversity in China's struggle for national salvation. One finds a deep tension between patriotism and iconoclasm running throughout Fu's professional life. As a northerner, he was deeply distressed by the 1931 Japanese invasion of Manchuria and felt that the bending of historical facts in his *Draft History of Northwest China* was necessary (or at least unavoidable) to counter Japan's attempts to detach the region from the fatherland.[106] His growing patriotic sentiments led him in December 1935 to publish a short article in the popular national newspaper *Dagongbao* declaring that "the Zhonghua minzu is one." Fu argued that despite periodic political disunity due to the invasion of northern barbarians, China's unique natural environment had produced a single national identity. "Our Zhonghua minzu," Fu Sinian wrote, "possesses a single spoken and written language, common culture, and collective ethic, just like a single clan (*jiazu*)."[107]

The Sino-Japanese War placed tremendous pressure on Chinese academics to reexamine their commitment to self-emancipation and intellectual autonomy.[108] The war seemed to require a temporary postponement of the enlightenment project for the sake of national survival. Patriotic "faith" now came to be seen as more important than the self-indulgent search for pure intellectual "reason." As China suffered defeat after defeat at the hands of the Japanese between 1937 and 1939, confidence in enlightenment waned, and many intellectuals heeded the increasingly urgent call for all Chinese citizens to rally behind either the GMD or the CCP in resisting the Japanese invaders. Collective identity, not individual consciousness, mattered most. As the acculturated Mongolian intellectual Ai Siqi put it, "The cultural movement before May Fourth had been grounded in self-transformation. Patriotism then began with the emancipation of the self. Now, however, with the enemy attacking us so directly, so viciously, the leisure for self-transformation is no more."[109]

The need to construct a new national identity that would incorporate all the peoples of the former Qing empire was made all the more urgent by Japan's strategy for defeating the Chinese. The Japanese army and pro-militarist intellectuals attempted to manipulate the national aspirations of the non-Chinese minorities in order to weaken and eventually annihilate the Nationalist Party government. Tokyo set itself forward as the liberator of the small and weak peoples of Asia, calling for their "national self-determination" from Chinese domination and protection as a part of a Japanese-led Greater East Asia Co-prosperity Sphere. As the war drew to a stalemate during the 1940s, Japanese planes began dropping propaganda leaflets announcing their government's support for the creation of an independent Huihui state throughout Xinjiang and the Gansu corridor with a Tokyo-backed pan-Islamism serving as a "citadel against communism."[110] At the same time, Japan's troops in Southeast Asia actively supported the Thai leader Phibun Songkhram's call for reviving the ancient Kingdom of Sipsong Panna among the Tai peoples of southern China. There was even talk of Japanese troops marching through Assam directly into Tibet. On the ground, Japanese secret agents played up the racial differences between the frontier minorities and their Chinese overlords, promising to support tribal and religious leaders in their efforts to break away from Chinese control.[111] The Guomindang Central Government reacted to Japan's strategy by intensifying its efforts to erase all signs of ethnic or cultural diversity in Chinese society and history. The Guomindang racial nationalists, through their control of the Education Ministry and secret security apparatuses, attempted to force the myth of Zhonghua minzu consanguinity on the academy. Anyone who now dared to suggest that the minorities were a distinct minzu or possessed an unrelated culture was likely to be called unpatriotic or, even worse, a traitor to his or her people (*hanjian*).

The quiet, largely background struggle between the racial and cultural nationalists over the position of ethnic diversity in Chinese society burst into the public discourse during the winter of 1938–39. As the struggle with Japan intensified and the public mood swung decidedly toward national unity, conservative Guomindang ideologues lost patience with the exiled academic community and their research on the Chinese frontier. In their view, during China's current national emergency, no discussion—academic or not—that ran counter to the national unity of the Chinese people could be tolerated. In particular, they were livid with Gu Jiegang's new *Bianjiang* (*Frontier*) supplement to the highly popular Kunming newspaper *Yishibao* (*Social Welfare*) that he began editing on December 15, 1938.[112] Though in its avowed purpose *Bianjiang* differed little from many of the prewar publications of the Guomindang's Commission on Mongolian and Tibetan Affairs, some state officials felt the new political situation required a more circumspect approach to frontier affairs. And when Gu claimed in one of its early issues that the Guomindang state was carrying out a policy of forced assimilation and colonization along the frontier and called for the creation of new nonderogatory names for its various minzus, Academia Sinica president, Zhu Jiahua, urged Fu Sinian to write a letter to his old friend urging him to choose his words more carefully.[113]

In his strongly worded letter, written in early February 1939, Fu Sinian played to Gu Jiegang's sense of patriotism and academic responsibility. He began by urging Gu to be more careful when using the terms minzu and bianjiang: referring to the various peoples of the southwest frontier as minzus not only contradicted Sun Yat-sen's definition of the term but, more importantly, aided the imperialists attempting to divide the Chinese nation-state. Fu contended that Thailand, urged on by the Japanese, was now claiming that Guangxi and Yunnan provinces were the original homeland of the Tai people and was encouraging its people to recover their lost territory. Similarly, the English in Burma were inciting the tribal chieftains of southern Yunnan while the Buddhists in Tibet were now speaking in unison about their desire for an independent country. Fu warned Gu Jiegang that "making up all of these [minority] names not only invites division, it also causes one to seem unacademic and unpatriotic;"[114] and he gave Gu three pointed pieces of advice. First, the term bianjiang in his weekly *Yishibao* supplement should be replaced with "Yunnan," "Guizhou," "geography," and the like. Second, the supplement should join other nonspecialized publications in limiting topics treated during this time of national crisis to geography, economics, native production, and political conditions and stop discussing the invention of new minzu names. Third, he should spare no effort in stressing that history can prove that "the Zhonghua minzu is one," and the Han and Yi (southern barbarians) are a single family. "Who dares," Fu Sinian wrote, "to guarantee that there is no Hu blood among the northerners or no Bai, Yue, Miao, or Li blood among the southerners. Yunnan today is not different from the lower Yangtze River valley or Sichuan several thousand years ago. This is not crooked scholarship."[115] Dismissing Gu Jiegang's theory about the importance of continued infusions of minority cultures and races into the Chinese minzu, or what he termed "fresh blood history" (*xinxueshi*), as completely "absurd," Fu ended his letter by calling on his "elder brother" to "bow down and submit" in the interest of the minzu.[116]

Although it is uncertain whether Gu Jiegang directly responded to Fu's letter, we do know that he addressed some of the issues it raised during a long article, "The Zhonghua minzu Is One" (*Zhonghua minzu shi yige*), first published in the February 9, 1939, issue of *Bianjiang* and reprinted in nearly all the major newspapers in unoccupied China. Gu wrote that he had received a letter from "an old friend" expressing concern about his indiscriminate use of the term minzu and arguing that the claim, "the Zhonghua minzu is one," is historically true—an "earnest letter" that spurred his desire to "offer a sympathetic response."[117] In fact, his reply was far from sympathetic to the political concerns of Fu Sinian and other Guomindang racial nationalists. Though Gu did not argue against the need to unite all Chinese peoples into a single political and territorial state or even the historical reality of a unitary Chinese minzu, he continued to challenge the ahistorical myth of a culturally and racially pure people descended from a single, ancient progenitor (be it the Yellow Emperor or the Peking Man).

In order to unravel what he called the "self-spun cocoon" of Chinese homogeneity, Gu turned to the long tradition of Confucian culturalism. Gu contended that since ancient times, the Chinese have possessed only a concept of wenhua (culture) and not one of zhongzu (race). Those who observed Chinese cultural practices were considered Chinese, while those who did not were considered uncivilized and barbaric outsiders. Indeed, his Han surname, Gu, could actually be traced back to the barbaric Yue minzu; but his ancestors had agreed to submit to the authority of the Han dynasty and became Chinese. And the Zhonghua minzu mixed not just blood but also a variety of cultural traditions. Gu provided numerous examples of "Chinese" cultural customs—from music to dress—that had actually originated with the non-Chinese barbarians and argued that such openness to "alien" races and cultures is characteristic of the Han: "We have always felt that if an old custom is no longer as good as a new one, it should be abandoned and the new one adopted so as to advance."[118]

Gu defended his terminology and faulted those who fail to distinguish between zhongzu and minzu: races are created naturally through a common bloodline and language while nations are man-made and entail only a shared lifestyle, interests, and feeling of unity. The Chinese people constitute a single Zhonghua minzu, not a single zhongzu. Moreover, Gu contended that the term sowing disunity among the various peoples of the Zhonghua minzu was not bianjiang but rather "China proper" (*Zhongguo benbu*), whose popularization had caused those in the Chinese heartland to perceive themselves as more important, and hence superior, to those living along the frontier. More fundamentally, he blamed the Japanese and other imperialist powers that were using the slogan minzu zijue (national self-determination) to encourage the frontier minorities to break with the Chinese state, not careless Chinese scholars or their analytical categories, for the strains threatening to sunder the nation-state.[119]

Gu concluded his essay by warning once again against distorting historical truths to achieve temporary political gains:

> There are overly cautious people who believe that it is best not to talk about the situation of our country's various races and lineages, as if just talking about it is enough to summon the disaster of division. I remember that several years ago someone said to me: "The frontier people will be easier to control if they do not know their own history; as soon as they know, they will be uncontrollable." However, this attitude, I believe, is like hiding one's sickness for fear of treatment and is inappropriate for us to adopt. If one hides a sickness for fear of treatment and the illness gets a bit better, what good is it if it only gets worst in the future![120]

The best method for countering Japanese propaganda and resisting the imperialist onslaught was to tell the truth—both about the Zhonghua minzu's past glories and about the current state of oppression. In addition, the state should encourage the center and the periphery to "meld together into a single body," both by improving the flow of information between them and by promoting intermarriage between Han and frontier peoples, so that "the racial boundaries will thin from generation to generation and national consciousness will increase from one to the next—leading to the absorption of new blood from each group and the increased strength of our descendants."[121]

Gu Jiegang clearly was not an advocate of multiculturalism in its modern, liberal sense (defined by Will Kymlicka as the inalienable right of different ethnic and cultural groups to peacefully coexist within a unified political state).[122] He continued to conceptualize diversity within the social evolutionary framework of Sun Yat-sen and Liang Qichao: the gradual and nonviolent melding (ronghe) of human diversity into growing unity through the Darwinian principle of natural selection. The goal was the American melting pot, championed by the Chicago School of Sociology and the American School of Historical Particularism during the early twentieth century. Chinese intellectuals of all political stripes accepted the minzu as a collective subject of history but disagreed on its racial and cultural composition. Gu forcefully rejected attempts to read the history of the minzu backwards, transposing an evolving and future state of racial unity on the past in the hope that it would paste over all signs of diversity and disunity. In contrast, he argued that the frontier minorities were destined to once again culturally and racially reinvigorate the decrepit Han majority. This would ensure the Zhonghua minzu's survival and eventual victory over the imperialists.

Gu Jiegang's provocative essay found little favor with the Guomindang government. In a letter to Zhu Jiahua, Fu Sinian expressed his frustration with it and with Gu's persistent refusal to modify his opinions.[123] Fu continued to blame Gu and others for undermining national unity in their academic research and public writings. He contended that before these so-called scholars were exiled from the northeast and began incessantly talking about minzu while "sitting on their asses," the people of the southwest frontier did not consider themselves Luoluo, Miao, or any other minzus distinct from the Zhonghua minzu. Fu singled out Gu Jiegang as the ringleader of those "scholars" who claimed that "scholarship is scholarship and has nothing to do with politics."[124] In reality, this meaningless debate about minzu had badly damaged the assimilation process, causing the national spirit of the Chinese guozu to be replaced with "tribal consciousness"; and those minorities who had already been assimilated were now talking about Han oppression rather than their common origin.[125]

Around this time, others within the party started to pressure Chinese ethnologists to bring their research findings into accord with the state's national salvation movement. Take, for example, the strongly worded rebuke of Zhang Tingxiu, personal secretary to Education Minister Chen Lifu, which was published in *Xinan bianjiang* in early 1939. According to Zhang, the recent explosion of ethnographic research on the problem of the Miao and Yi peoples of the southwest was based on the erroneous premise that these two peoples were distinct minzus separate from the Han majority. Thus his essay was intended "to correct this mistake and to clarify that the Yi [southern barbarians] and Han are a single family—essentially a single minzu with a common origin."[126] The term Zhonghua minzu was simply another name for the Han people, with whom the various peoples of the southwest were racially one and the same. To prove this point scientifically, Zhang cited foreign and Chinese research in arguing that the Yi and Han belonged to a common language family; he also cited several creation myths that he claimed tied the origin of the Yi people to that of the Han majority, and finally noted the similarity between the physical appearances of the two peoples. Zhang also pointed to the findings of a Japanese scholar who had conducted anthropometric research among the Miao during the Qing dynasty and discovered that the nose shape, cranial size, and eyes of the Miao people matched those of the Mongoloid race, leading him to conclude that the Miao were members of the Mongoloid race who exhibited special South Asian characteristics.

To explain the obvious differences in culture, religion, and dialect between the Yi and Han uncovered by the Chinese ethnologists, Zhang followed others in emphasizing the impact of different environments following their migration throughout China. Because of the great distances separating them, members of the same minzu evolved differently, causing the formation of different "branches" or "tributaries" of a single racial stock. In time, these distinctions begot the different names Miao, Yi, and Han. More recently, however, these different branches had come back into contact with one another; and racial and cultural mixing had naturally resulted. "In sum," Zhang wrote, "the Han and Yi initially shared a common origin, and then, after splitting, melded back together, so the saying that the Yi and Han are a single family is as solid as fact."[127] Zhang praised researchers for publicizing the plight of the frontier minorities and enabling them to "resume their original family name and return to their ancestral lineage" (*fuxing guizong*).[128] More to the point, however, he expressed his concern "that many of the essays examining this question still like to use the two characters minzu, describing this Miao and Yao minzu and that Yi minzu, even to the extent that a group of scholars has recently created a new name by calling ffor research on the "Yunnanese minzu.". There is only one Zhonghua minzu and the people of Yunnan, regardless of whether they are Yi or Han, are all a part of this Zhonghua minzu; there are absolutely no Yunnanese minzu."[129] Not only does this "excessive and abusive use" of the label minzu ignore historical facts; it is reckless at a time of war. By speaking about this and that minzu, Chinese ethnographers were actually aiding the Japanese in spreading their potentially destructive lies. Though he claimed to "deeply admire" those scholars who endured great risk and much personal discomfort to study these peoples, Zhang urged them to highlight the spirit of national unity and foster a single Zhonghua minzu spirit among all China's peoples.[130]

The growing political consensus on the urgent need for national unity was reflected in some of the resolutions passed by the Chinese government's special wartime parliament, the People's Political Council (*Guomin canzhenghui*, or PPC). Before being reorganized in 1942, the PPC was a remarkably representative body; most of its two hundred members represented non-GMD political parties (including the Chinese Communists) and independent, nonpartisan constituencies.[131] A month before Zhang Tingxiu's article appeared in *Xinan bianjiang*, the PPC passed a resolution entitled "On the Necessity of Unifying the Mongol, Tibetan, Hui, Miao and other Lineages Prior to Opening Up the Northwest and Southwest Frontiers" at its Third Congress in Chongqing.[132] It outlined crucial work to be done in four specific areas: propaganda, language, lifestyle, and customs. First, the government should compile historical evidence of the common racial lineage shared by the Manchu, Mongol, Hui, Tibetan, and Miao peoples and then disseminate this message among the masses so that they realize their membership in a single Zhonghua minzu and resist the attempts by foreigners to tear them away from the fatherland. Second, use of a single "national spoken and written language" would unify the various minority languages and strengthen the fusion of their sentiments and consciousness with the Han majority. Third, calling the lifestyle of the frontier minorities "prehistoric" and "simple and crude," the document urged the state to improve their economic conditions so that they might advance into the modern era. Finally, the resolution called for mass education to reform the harmful and evil customs of the minority peoples. In short, this document reflected the growing agreement among not only GMD members but also the Chinese Communists and other progressive elements that China's survival as a state and people hinged on the rapid assimilation of the frontier minorities and the development of a single, unified national sentiment among all its peoples.

Narrative Convergence: *China's Destiny*

These concerns were most clearly articulated in the Guomindang's new political manifesto, *China's Destiny* (*Zhongguo zhi mingyun*) that, as noted in Chapter 2, was ghostwritten in early 1942 by Guomindang historian Tao Xisheng and published in Chongqing on March 10, 1943, under Chiang Kai-shek's name.[133] After important revisions were made to the book, a revised edition appeared in January 1944. Following its publication, the book became required reading for students, civil servants, army officers, and party members. With a price tag of only ten cents, by 1947 it had sold more than a million copies, with several hundred printings. Because it was so widely distributed and caused such a political stir, one contemporary commentator referred to *China's Destiny* as the "political bible of the Guomindang."[134]

In its first chapter, "The Growth and Development of the Zhonghua minzu," Tao Xisheng contended that the Chinese, including the frontier minorities, were both racially and culturally one. But in a gesture toward those who argued that the Chinese represented a composite national people, Tao claimed not that the Zhonghua minzu was racially pure, but rather that the various Chinese "lineages" (zongzu) "were *either* descendants of a common ancestor *or* interrelated through marriage."[135] In other words, he boldly declared, "the main and branch lineages (*da xiao zongzhi*) all belong to the same bloodline," albeit a mixed one as Gu Jiegang had long insisted.[136] In the revised edition, Tao Xisheng went a step further, maintaining that "throughout its lengthy historical development, [the Zhonghua minzu's] lineages, on the occasion of the contact and blending of their cultures, often discovered their common origin. . . . In short, our various lineages belong to not only the same minzu but also to the same zhongzu."[137]

Although Tao Xisheng did not make direct mention of Peking Man or the Yellow Emperor, both figures were invoked as "scientific" proof of the Zhonghua minzu's common origin in one of the official primers that accompanied the publication of *China's Destiny*. Yu Jianhua's *History of the Zhonghua minzu* (*Zhonghua minzushi*), which was published in 1944 as part of the Propaganda Department's *China's Destiny* Research Collection, contended that the recent discovery of Peking Man and Sima Qian's historical research on the Yellow Emperor provided irrefutable scientific evidence of the Zhonghua minzu's racial genealogy.[138] *China's Destiny* institutionalized the diamond-shaped paradigm of Chinese racial evolution first championed by Guomindang racial nationalists during the 1930s. The Zhonghua minzu originated from a single progenitor, either Peking Man or the Yellow Emperor, during high antiquity. Amid the decay and chaos of the feudal period, the Zhonghua minzu's various lineages migrated to the four corners of the Middle Kingdom, where they adopted different customs, dialects, and religious practices as suited the diverse environmental conditions of the frontier. But the growth and expansion of the modern Chinese state over the past two thousand years facilitated greater intercourse, communication, and the continuous blending of these different lineages into a single, homogeneous guozu—restoring the original state of unity and authenticity. Running throughout these three periods is the continuity of bloodline and culture on which the unity and sovereignty of the minzu has been constituted.

The publication of *China's Destiny* and the growing intensity of the conflict with Japan had a chilling effect on the academic community in the southwest. As most academics, including Gu Jiegang, came to accept the temporary postponement of the enlightenment project, many started to echo the Guomindang state in stressing the consanguinity of the Zhonghua minzu. At the least, they either ceased or modified their research agendas to accommodate this new narrative of racial and national unity.[139] Acculturated indigenous elites also appeared to have buckled under the pressure. Despite their active appropriation and manipulation of state discourse, many came to accept the legitimacy and urgent need for national integration, with one Miao ethnographer, Shi Qigui, even providing "evidence" of the common origin of the Miao and Han in order to stress that the differences between these two peoples were cultural and economic rather than racial.[140] For state elites of nearly every political persuasion, the increasingly violent nature of the Japanese invasion highlighted the urgent need to incorporate the former Qing frontier regions and their peoples into the new Chinese nation-state. Faced with the potential "death of the state and extinction of the race," they began to think of both themselves and other former subjects of the Qing empire as an organic whole, ordering the rich ethnic diversity of the new Republic into a single national community labeled the Zhonghua minzu, and replacing the various minority ethnonyms with the more generic categories of *bianbao* (frontier compatriots) or *bianmin* (frontier peoples). Convinced that Sun Yat-sen was right when he described the people of China as "a sheet of loose sand," they marshaled scientific evidence to prove the fundamental unity of the Zhonghua minzu in the face of the obvious differences among its citizens.

Edward Said has underscored the role of science—as institutionalized in academic disciplines like history, archaeology, ethnology, and linguistics—in fashioning an "ontogenetic explanation" of racial origins. By presenting "empirically analyzable data" that is based on systematic reasoning and a logical methodology, these discourses reinforce and naturalize speculative myths of historical belonging.[141] Yet, unlike the tianxia (all-under-heaven) cosmology of imperial China, these new sciences derived their political authority from what Nancy Leys Stepan has identified as their "conceptual claim to be a neutral, empirical, secular, and uniquely authoritative (because uniquely objective) form of knowledge."[142] At the same time, the spread of these new scientific disciplines in China helped weaken state control over ideology and cosmology. Having lost their monopoly on the interpretation of rites (not to mention the apparatuses of state coercion), representatives of the Guomindang state had to compete with other political actors and independent intellectuals, situated both nationally and transnationally, as they sought to legitimate their version of the national imaginary with scientifically verifiable data.

It was a disagreement over the source of national unity in China that differentiated two of the more popular narratives of national belonging among

Republican-era elites. On one side, a group of racial nationalists closely affiliated with the conservative wing of the Guomindang anchored Chinese unity in the distant past, arguing that all Chinese people (including the frontier minorities of the Qing empire) shared a common ancestry and thus constituted a single homogenous yet composite minzu. Unwilling and unable to wait for nature to run its evolutionary course, they manufactured a myth of shared descent, suggesting that the Yellow Emperor or Peking Man was the ancient progenitor of the entire Zhonghua minzu. In the tradition of Zhang Binglin and other turn-of-the-century anti-Manchuists, they constructed a racial genealogy demonstrating the historical continuity of the Chinese people and their unbroken line of descent from a single ancient ancestor. Insisting that the threat of foreign imperialism required immediate action, they projected Sun Yat-sen's future state of minzu unity backward in time to the very origin of Chinese history.

On the other side, a group of cultural nationalists resisted this distortion of history and chose to locate the unity of the Chinese people in a subjective and emergent national consciousness that, they claimed, accompanied the natural evolutionary process of racial and cultural melding. They rejected the attempt by the racial nationalists to erase all traces of ethnic and cultural diversity in China, contending that only the truth of the Zhonghua minzu's shared history and common plight could spur the continued development of national sentiment. Here, in the tradition of Liang Qichao, "Chineseness" was rooted in the organic unfolding of a composite yet politically-defined national people rather than the persistence of a single race and cultural tradition.

Prasenjit Duara has pointed to the deep ambivalence within nationalist discourse over the historicity of the nation: "While on the one hand nationalist leaders and the nation-states glorify the ancient or eternal character of the nation, they simultaneously seek to emphasize the unprecedented novelty of the nation-state, because it is only in this form that the 'people' have been able to realize themselves as the subjects or masters of their history."[143] This ambiguity is readily apparent in the two narratives I have been discussing. Yet, unlike other "imagined communities" that flowed out of the collapse of the Qing empire—such as an independent Tibetan or Mongolian nation-state, regional or provincial autonomy set within a loose federalist framework, or the transnational Greater East Asia Co-prosperity Sphere—these two formulations were both firmly set within a bounded and fully demarcated geo-body. In other words, taking the spatial boundaries of the Qing empire as its starting point, Chinese intellectuals came to either look past the heterogeneity of the frontier to an emergent cultural and political imaginary or collapse it backward onto a single consanguineous "embryo" rooted in the distant past.[144] Either way, the problem of diversity remained.

CHAPTER 5

Han Man's Burden: The Communists and the Construction of Zhonghua minzu

In *The Invention of Tradition*, Eric Hobsbawm argued that traditions that appear or claim to be old, especially those that have to do with the supposed antiquity of national identity, are often of quite recent origin.[1] China might appear to be a natural exception to this current historiographic axiom. With more than three thousand years of written history—progressing from ancient ideographs inscribed on animal bones through the numerous official and unofficial dynastic histories—Chinese historians, unlike their counterparts in Australia, France, or the United States, seem immune from the need to invent a historical legacy for their nation. But because of the sheer size and complexity of this documentation, historians in China have assumed the important responsibility of creating continuity from the dissonance of the historical record—inventing order where none exists. So, too, early twentieth-century historians, answering the nationalist appeal to save the nation, attempted to project a desired state of national unity onto China's historical past. In imagining a unified and homogeneous national community, Chinese historians imposed a linear and unbroken narrative of racial and cultural continuity on the rich ethnic mosaic of Chinese history—creating an arabesque of temporal and spatial connections that tightly bound the diversity of the Chinese minzus, or "nationalities," together in a shared myth of national unfolding.

This chapter continues the examination of how history, archaeology, and ethnology were used to produce knowledge in early twentieth-century China, shifting the focus to the role played by CCP officials and scholars in the construction of national identity. The outbreak of the Sino-Japanese War caused Mao and others within the party to reevaluate their uniformly negative judgment of China's feudal historical legacy. The need to revive national self-confidence in the wake of the Japanese occupation and instill an overarching sense of national unity among the heterogeneous peoples of the former Qing empire compelled Communist, no less than Guomindang, historians to reconsider China's rich historical tradition and impose order and uniformity on the geo-body.

Rather than emphasizing class as before, this new nationalist historiography chose the entire Zhonghua minzu as its subject. Communist leaders could no longer simply claim that China's various minzus were bound together in a common destiny of national liberation and independence from the global forces of imperialism; they now felt compelled to trace this unity backwards in time to the very origin of the Chinese people. In other words, to make the unity of the Zhonghua minzu seem organic and innate, Communist intellectuals needed to engage in what Benedict Anderson termed "the process of reading nationalism *genealogically*—as the expression of an historical tradition of serial continuity."[2] In this process, Communist historians drew on many of the same tropes of national wholeness—the Yellow Emperor, Peking Man, and Qinshi Huangdi—as their Guomindang counterparts. Historians affiliated with both political parties manufactured intricate ethnogenealogies linking the contemporary frontier minorities with the numerous ethnonyms appearing in China's historical canon, fashioning a linear narrative of Zhonghua minzu evolution and scientifically "proving" the interconnected history, culture, and blood of the Chinese people.

A major concern of this chapter is to explore the narratives of cultural innovation adopted by Communist historians in demonstrating the oneness of the Zhonghua minzu. In positioning themselves within the larger ideological and political struggle against the Guomindang, Communist historians were forced to adopt different discursive strategies than their Nationalist Party rivals in constructing what was essentially the same myth of national unity. In the previous chapter, we examined how racial nationalists closely associated with the Guomindang, such as Dai Jitao and Xiong Shili, promoted a myth of common descent, arguing that the Han, Mongol, Manchu, Hui, and Tibetan people shared a similar progenitor—either the Yellow Emperor or Peking Man. This common origin thesis (*tongyuanlun*) became official Guomindang policy in 1943 when the polemic *China's Destiny* declared that all non-Han people were actually lineage branches (zongzhi) of a single, ancient and consanguineous Zhonghua minzu. All Chinese people formed not just a single nation (minzu) but a single race (zhongzu)—what Liang Qichao and Sun Yat-sen had termed a guozu or race-state.

Communist historians reacted against this so-called fascist myth of shared descent by using recent archaeological and ethnographic research to demonstrate the polyphyletic origins of the Zhonghua minzu. Rather than pointing to a single ancient progenitor, Communist historians contended that the Chinese descended from a series of racially distinct hominids, including Ordos Man, Peking Man, and Java Man. In constructing their own myth of Chinese antiquity and consanguinity, Communist historians shifted their attention away from racial descent and refocused on the interconnected historical evolution of a composite yet organically unified Zhonghua minzu. By the 1940s, Communist historians were echoing Gu Jiegang in arguing that the entire scope of Chinese history revealed the gradual concrescence of different lineages into a single national people. But unlike Gu, the Communists located the source of the Zhonghua minzu's national strength in the superior culture and fecundity of its majority Hanzu (typically gloss as the "Han nationality" in English) rather than in the virility and fresh blood of the frontier minorities. Through its intermingling with and gradual assimilation of minority cultures and blood, the five-thousand-year-old Hanzu had transformed itself into a biological microcosm of the Zhonghua minzu's current pluralistic unity; and its unbroken and linear evolution functioned as the primary source of the minzu's historical inclusiveness rather than any single point of origin.

The Zhonghua minzu and the Problem of Minzu

As already noted, the outbreak of the Sino-Japanese War in 1937 and the rapid series of defeats suffered by the Chinese at the hands of the advancing Japanese army sparked a renewed wave of nationalism in China. Moreover, the Japanese were deliberately manipulating the national aspirations of the frontier dependencies of the former Qing empire, claiming that the Republic of China was an unnatural territorial construct that denied the legitimate national aspirations of the frontier minorities. In the eyes of all Chinese nationalists, Japan's exploitation of ethnic divisions along the Republican frontier threatened the "death of the state and extinction of the race," causing officials from both the Nationalist and Communist parties to call for a new collective identity—one capable of binding all "Chinese people" (including the frontier minorities) into a single body politic.

In articulating this new collective identity, Mao Zedong, like his rival Chiang Kai-shek, turned to Sun Yat-sen's discourse of minzuzhuyi. Following the 1911 Revolution, Sun Yat-sen claimed that all the peoples of China, namely the so-called five races of the republic, formed a single national entity, which he termed the Zhonghua minzu. China's ongoing struggle against outside invaders and shared destiny of national independence bound the Han majority and its ethnic minorities together into a single, organic, and indivisible race-state (guozu).[3] As Japanese hegemony grew, Mao Zedong and the Chinese Communists began employing the term Zhonghua minzu when referring to the Chinese people, regardless of class or ethnic identity, as a national collective.[4] Yet the term remained largely undefined until the publication of Mao Zedong's important 1939 essay, *The Chinese Revolution and the Chinese Communist Party*. In the first section, "The Zhonghua minzu," Mao echoed Sun Yat-sen in declaring that more than 90 percent of China's population belongs to a single "Han people" (Hanren or Hanzu), while adding a number of new ethnonyms (the Uyghurs, Miao, Yi, Dong, Zhongjia, and Koreans along with the more frequently mentioned Mongols, Hui, and Tibetans) to the Comintern's category of minority nationals (shaoshu minzu).[5] As the Red Army's political education textbook that accompanied the publication of Mao's essay put it: "China is a multi-minzu state and all the minzus within Chinese territory are collectively referred to as the Zhonghua minzu."[6] Mao's insistence that the people of China embodied a single national entity appealed to the patriotic sentiments of most party cadres who felt that national unity was one of the important keys to victory over both the Japanese invaders and the Guomindang reactionaries.

As observed in earlier chapters, the inherent ambiguity of the neologism Zhonghua minzu—simultaneously a single homogeneous race-state and a composite multi-minzu state—helped transform the term into a powerful nationalist trope among twentieth-century Chinese intellectuals. Here, the implied process of becoming *hua* (Chinese) in the term *Zhonghua* opened up the possibility of incorporating cultural and ethnically diverse populations into a single minzu while accepting a temporary state of heterogeneity. For the Chinese Communists, however, Mao's use of the term Zhonghua minzu to incorporate a hodgepodge of different social communities (at distinctly different stages of economic development) into a single national body created a theoretical problem for party intellectuals. It seemed to contradict Marxist theory—more precisely, Stalin's specific definition of "nation," which had already been translated into Chinese as minzu.

Li Da, one of Republican China's leading Marxist philosophers, was responsible for introducing much of Marxist thought on the national question to the Chinese intellectual community during the 1920s and 1930s. In his landmark 1929 pamphlet, *The National Question* (*Minzu wenti*), he outlined the Marxist laws behind human socioeconomic development. In man's struggle with nature, technological and economic changes shape the nature of human societies. "Thus," Li Da wrote, "the organizational form of human society parallels each stage of economic development."[7] Though humans adopt different types of sociocultural structures depending on their specific stage of economic development, in each case the economic base always determines the social superstructure. Drawing on Engels' *The Origins of the Family, Private Property and the State*, Li Da outlined three distinct stages of human social organization: clans (shizu), races (zhongzu), and finally, with the arrival of industrialization, unified nations (minzu).[8]

In his 1926 Shanghai University lectures on the national question, future party leader Qu Qiubai drew closely on Stalin's 1913 tract, *Marxism and the National Question*, in discussing the genesis of a minzu. After commerce develops within a country, the dominant race (zhongzu) initiates a movement to unify the heterogeneous peoples, languages, customs, and laws into a single political state. With the rise of industrial capitalism, the bourgeois of the dominant race, seeking to monopolize the domestic market and protect all profits from foreign intruders, melds the minority races into a single national people. The eventual result is a unified nation-state (*minzu guojia*). Like Stalin, Qu argued that a nation (minzu) was a "stable community" and thus its existence required several special criteria: a common economy, territory, language, and culture.[9] Likewise relying on *Marxism and the National Question*, Li Da directly quoted Stalin's "objective and scientific" definition of a nation as "a historically evolved, stable community of language, territory, economic life, and psychological makeup manifested in a community of culture."[10] Both Li and Qu stressed that "a nation (minzu) is not merely a historical category but a historical category belonging to a definite epoch, the epoch of rising capitalism."[11] Stalin had argued that the proper economic base for the formation of a nation comes into existence only after feudal isolation is destroyed, commercial production rises, and a national market develops. Thus the inevitable destruction of capitalism would also end national antagonism and eliminate both national and state boundaries.

Their pedantic and Stalinist reading of the national question left Li Da and Qu Qiubai with little to say about the specific implications of Marxist nationality theory for China. Li devoted a chapter to Soviet Russia's national question but said next to nothing about China's own national form. Qu's lectures contained repeated attacks on the national chauvinism of Dai Jitao and the Guomindang racial nationalists, which he compared to the "revolutionary nationality policy" contained in Sun Yat-sen's minzuzhuyi,[12] but were silent about the origins and development of social communities in China.

In fact, Stalin's firm link between national identity and the rise of capitalism made it difficult for the Chinese Communists to theorize about the nation/minzu in what Mao himself called "semi-feudal, semi-colonial" China. If China had yet to reach the capitalist stage, how could the Chinese people make up the single, composite Zhonghua minzu described by Mao in *The Chinese Revolution and the Chinese Communist Party*? Not only was the Han majority struggling to develop its own national bourgeois class, but some of the "backward" minority nationals were mired in a slave or primitive stage of economic development. By Stalin's fourfold criteria, neither the individual ethnic communities in China nor the entire Zhonghua minzu could be considered a nation/minzu.

Yang Song was the first Communist intellectual to directly grapple with the inherent contradiction between Stalin's precise theoretical definition of nation and Mao's utilitarian usage of the term minzu. Having spent more than seven years in Russia, including a stint studying the national question at Sun Yat-sen University in Moscow, Yang was uniquely qualified to tackle the issue.[13] Yang arrived in Yan'an in 1938 after several years spent working underground in Manchuria, where he witnessed firsthand Japan's efforts to split the Chinese nation-state apart by manipulating ethnic sentiment. After taking up a position at the newly created Marxist-Leninist Institute in Yan'an, Yang delivered a series of important lectures—eventually published in the party's theoretical journal *Jiefang* (*Liberation*)—in which he attempted to reconcile Stalin's definition with the urgent need in China to construct an overarching sense of Chinese national identity.

Yang Song began by asking a simple question: "What is a minzu?"[14] Like his predecessors Li Da and Qu Quibai, Yang echoed Stalin's insistence that it is "a historical category" that arises from the union of various tribes, clans, and races during the transition from feudalism to capitalism. But unlike them, Yang attempted (rather unconvincingly) to demonstrate that "the Chinese" (Zhongguoren), or what he followed Mao in calling the Zhonghua minzu, met all four of Stalin's criteria for modern nationhood. According to Yang, the various dialects in China each form part of a single Chinese language. Overlooking the waxing and waning of past dynasties and their ethnic diversity, Yang Song argued that the Chinese had occupied a single, common territory for the past four to five millennia, exhibiting a history that demonstrates their shared national essence (*minzu xing*), national culture (*minzu wenhua*), and national customs (*minzu fengsu*). Moreover, Yang claimed that China already had a reasonably well-developed capitalist economy with a national transportation and communication system. Though he admitted that the Chinese minzu possessed its own special characteristics (*minzu de texing*)—namely, the semi-feudal, semi-colonial condition described by Mao—he went to great lengths to stress that in its development, the Zhonghua minzu had followed the same scientific laws as all the world's nations. The difference in China was simply timing; Stalin's universal historical processes still applied.

The Zhonghua minzu—like France, America, Germany, Italy, and other Western countries—grew from the organization of different tribes and races into a single national community. As Mao had stated in *The Chinese Revolution and the Chinese Communist Party*, the Zhonghua minzu included not only the Han majority, but also the Manchu, Hui, Fan, Miao, Mongol, and other minority nationals. Yet living among the Han majority for many generations had caused the minorities to become assimilated and "lose the special characteristics for forming a minzu." The retention of a few distinctive customs and habits did not prevent them from belonging to "a single, new modern minzu—the Zhonghua minzu."[15] Much like Sun Yat-sen, Yang Song attempted to eliminate the problem of the ethnic minorities through redefinition. The evolutionary logic underlying both men's thought precluded the possibility that one of China's minority nationals might actually develop into its own independent minzu.

Yet Mao also insisted in *The Chinese Revolution and the Chinese Communist Party* that the various ethnic components of the entire Zhonghua minzu constituted distinct minzus, a stance that presented Yang Song with an even more difficult theoretical problem. How could the backward minority nationals meet Stalin's fourfold criteria for nationhood? In struggling to reconcile Mao's pragmatic usage of minzu with Stalin's narrow definition of nation, Yang simply contradicted himself:

> That is to say, towards outsiders, the Zhonghua minzu represents all the nationalities (minzus) within Chinese territory, and thus serves as the nucleus of all these nationalities within China and unites them into a single modern state. Yet, inside China, there also exist minority nationals. . . . These minzus—besides a large portion of the Manchus who have already been assimilated by the Han—still maintain their own national territory, language,

> customs and economic life, and thus . . . from the standpoint of nationality (minzu), still represent distinct minzus. Yet, with regards to citizenship (*guoji*), they are all citizens of the Zhonghua Republic, compatriots of the same fatherland and the common target of the Japanese enemy's invasion.[16]

As Yang Song's lectures attempted to demonstrate, the Japanese invasion made the definition of minzu more than an abstract theoretical issue. Forming a new, overarching national identity was central to the revolutionary strategies of both the Guomindang and the Chinese Communists. One manifestation was the heated debate among Chinese intellectuals and politicians as to whether the Sino-Muslims (the *Huizu*, *Huimin*, or *Huihui*) were a minzu or simply a religious group. To counter Japanese propaganda, which was inciting some Sino-Muslims leaders to declare their independence from China, Chiang Kai-shek declared that the so-called Huizu were merely Han who practiced Islam. "Despite a portion who came from the Western regions," Chiang contended in 1938, "the vast majority of China's Huizu compatriots are innately people of the interior, who in reality differ only in terms of their religious belief and not their racial (zhongzu) identity."[17] In September 1940, Chiang's new classification became law: the Executive Yuan banned the term Huizu from public use. "Besides their religious ceremonies," the new law read, "they [the Sino-Muslims] are no different from the Han people and those religious disciples who believe in Catholicism; thus we should only call them Muslims (*Huijiaotu*) and not Huizu."[18]

Since the 1920s, the Chinese Communists had been referring to the Sino-Muslims, without much thought, as either the Huizu or the Huihui minzu. But given the Japanese invasion and the new focus on the precise definition of minzu, some intellectuals within the party—notably a leading expert on religious matters, Ya Hanzhang—began to openly embrace the Guomindang view of the Hui as a religious group. Others within the party, such as Ma Yin and Li Yinmin, resisted this reinterpretation and continued to defend the minzu status of the Sino-Muslims.[19] Thus Li Yinmin argued that the Hui of the Northwest, with their distinct physical and cultural features, were the true embodiment of the Hui minzu. Those party cadres who questioned Hui nationality were conflating the largely assimilated southern Hui with the vast majority living in Ningxia, Gansu, and Xinjiang.[20] But none of the defenders of Hui nationality attempted to apply Stalin's fourfold definition of the nation to the Sino-Muslims. As the party's National Question Research Office was forced to admit in an important 1940 policy paper, "The Huihui are not a *modern* minzu and have only begun to enter this developmental process."[21] At the same time, the Central Committee accepted Mao's claim in *The Chinese Revolution and the Communist Party* that the Hui were a minority national in semi-colonial, semi-feudal China and a minzu within Chinese territory. Ignoring these contradictions, the Central Committee approved the National Question Research Office's report, which sharply criticized the GMD's policy of Han chauvinism toward the Sino-Muslims and upheld their status as a distinct minzu.

In a June 1940 essay on the Hui question, published in the party journal *Jiefang*,[22] Central Party School chancellor Li Weihan proposed a way to resolve the contradiction between the narrowness of Stalin's nation and the breadth of Mao's minzu. He divided those who questioned Hui nationality into two camps: the deniers and the doubters. The deniers, such as Chiang Kai-shek and others within the Guomindang, either held that the Hui were basically members of the Han nationality who believed in Islam or admitted that the Hui used to be a minzu but have long been assimilated by the Han. To counter both claims, Li drew on the research of the Hui scholar Jin Jitang,[23] who argued in a 1936 article that Islam was an entire "social system," not just a religion. Consequently, the Hui maintained special national characteristics in their language, politics, and economy. The doubters in the CCP, such as Ya Hanzhang, who argued that the Hui do not conform to Stalin's definition of minzu, also erred. For although the Hui did not meet Stalin's four criteria for "a complete minzu," that definition refers "only to a modern minzu"[24]—not to premodern national communities or incipient minzus like the Hui.

According to Li Weihan, the Hui and other Chinese minorities represented a special type of "incomplete minzu" that he later termed "backward minzus" (*luohou minzu*).[25] Ignoring Stalin's unequivocal assignment of nationhood to the epoch of rising capitalism, he cited four rather ambiguous passages from *Marxism and the National Question* that seemed to suggest that precapitalist national communities might exist. Li Weihan claimed that China, unlike the homogeneous nation-states of Europe, was a unique "multi-minzu state" (*duo minzu guojia*). Its history of ruling class oppression had slowed the economic development of some of its minority nationals, preventing them from fully evolving into a modern minzu. But despite their underdevelopment, the Hui and other minority nationals were an integral part of China's multi-minzu state; thus, Li Weihan contended, they could still be considered distinct, albeit incomplete, minzus. By claiming that Stalin's fourfold criteria applied only to fully developed nations, the Chinese Communists could simultaneously hold that the Zhonghua minzu (and its Hanzu core) constituted a modern nation, and its various "backward" or "incomplete" minzus were still in the process of evolving toward full nationhood.[26] At the same time, CCP scholars downplayed (but never completely abandoned) Stalin's definition, as a common economy, territory, language, and culture became less important than a subjective national consciousness and written historical record. Now that minzu identity was being read genealogically, empirical evidence was needed from the newly emerged social sciences of history, archaeology, and ethnology to demonstrate Mao's claims about the fundamental unity of the Zhonghua minzu.

The Zhonghua minzu and the Problem of History

In addition to arguing that the various Chinese nationalities made up a single, modern Zhonghua nation, Mao Zedong also claimed in *The Chinese Revolution and the Chinese Communist Party* that they shared a long history of national unity. Reading the nation backwards, Mao asserted that China was one of the oldest civilizations in the world with a recorded history of nearly four thousand years. While admitting that the historical record primarily reflected the accomplishments of the Han majority, he maintained that the minority nationals had their own long histories, though at different levels of cultural development. They made the Zhonghua minzu unique, as they repeatedly united to resist foreign encroachment even as they also resisted the oppression of one minzu by another.[27]

The Chinese Revolution and the Chinese Communist Party marked an important turning point in the development of CCP historiography. Prior to the Long March, Mao and other Communist leaders unequivocally condemned China's historical legacy, dismissing its traditional culture and philosophy as mere impediments to social development. Marxist historians spent most of the late 1920s and early 1930s on a highly abstract question, debating whether Marx's holistic schema of human development was appropriate for analyzing Chinese history.[28] To counter the Guomindang assertion that class revolution was unnecessary in China, Communist historians mechanically overlaid Marx's entire paradigm of historical development (with its stages of primitive communism, slavery, feudalism, and capitalism) onto Chinese history—hoping to demonstrate that Marx's depictions of the bourgeois-democratic and then socialist revolutions applied to Chinese society. One of the most striking features of this high profile debate over the periodization of Chinese social history was the denial that China's past had any unique features. Chinese history was put forward as a mirror image of Western social development, as Communist scholars attempted to free China from a unique form of "Oriental despotism."[29]

But the sinification of Marxism, described in Chapter 3, sparked a reevaluation of China's historical legacy among Communists intellectuals. Mao now placed what he called the "glorious revolutionary tradition and outstanding historical legacy" of the Zhonghua minzu,[30] at the center of his call for the scientific and objective laws of Marxism-Leninism to be applied to the concrete and unique conditions of the Chinese revolution. In his 1938 address before the party's Sixth Plenum, Mao advocated a critical reexamination of Chinese tradition because "today's China is a development from historical China, and as Marxist historicists we should not cut ourselves off from history."[31] Mao reversed his previous criticism of China's reactionary past, declaring in 1940 that "a splendid old culture was created during the long period of Chinese feudal society."[32] He stressed the importance of studying its development in order to "reject its feudal dross and assimilate its democratic essence" in the process of fostering a "new national culture and self-confidence."[33] As a result, Chinese history became one of the central topics of study during the 1942–43 Rectification Campaign, when Mao lashed out at party members for failing to understand the legacy and sacrifices of their own ancestors.

During the debate on social history, Marxist historians had focused on the role of class revolution in propelling society from one stage to another. In Yan'an, however, Mao began calling for a new type of history. In a January 1939 letter to the CCP historian He Ganzhi, Mao praised He's attempt at writing "national history" (*minzu shi*). In particular, Mao praised his reorganization of the entire scope of Chinese history around the struggle between two competing national groups: the patriotic "minzu resisters" and the reactionary "minzu capitulationists"[34] During the 1940s, the construction of a new historical metanarrative became a central component of Chinese nationalism, as both CCP and GMD intellectuals attempted to convince the citizens of the Republic that they belonged to a single, organic Zhonghua minzu. In China, like the rest of the world, states (and their elites)—to paraphrase Eric Hobsbawm—created the nation and not the reverse.[35] But simply claiming, as Yang Song and Li Weihan had done, that the various nationalities within China constituted a single, contemporary Zhonghua minzu was no longer enough. In order to make this modern construct seem natural and immutable, Chinese historians needed to document the Zhonghua minzu's antiquity and historical inclusiveness. As they rewrote history, Communist historians followed the lead of GMD racial nationalists in projecting a desired future state of national unity back onto prehistoric China.

The Office for Research on Chinese History (*Zhongguo lishi yanjiushi*) attached to the Yan'an Central Research Institute became the new center of CCP's nationalist historiography. First established in early 1938 as a part of the Marxist-Leninist Academy, the office quickly grew in size and importance; in late 1941, it was reorganized as part of the Central Research Institute.[36] Key to its growth was Fan Wenlan, who at the request of Liu Shaoqi became its director in 1939. A classmate of Gu Jiegang and Fu Sinian at Beijing University who joined the CCP in 1926, Fan became one of the party's leading historians. As a professor of history at Beijing and Beijing Normal universities, he made a name for himself during the debate on Chinese social history. He eventually rose to the position of president of the Central Research Institute and served as a trusted party ideologue during the Rectification Campaign.[37]

Increasing concern over the incessant Japanese propaganda asserting Chinese racial and cultural diversity led Mao Zedong to personally request in early 1940 that Fan Wenlan and his Office for Research on Chinese History make the writing of a new general history of the Zhonghua minzu their top priority. Fan pooled the severely limited resources of his office to complete a nearly half-million-character history in little over a year's time.[38] The textbook, *A Concise General History of China* (*Zhongguo tongshi jianbian*), took the Zhonghua minzu as its lead subject. Fan declared in the preface that "if we want to understand the future of the Zhonghua minzu, we must understand its past history."[39]

To demonstrate the organic unity of the Han, Mongol, Manchu, Hui, Tibetan, and other Chinese nationalities, Fan fashioned a new, shared past—one that folded the individual histories of the contemporary minorities into the linear evolution of the five-thousand-year-old Han people.

In undertaking his national history of China, Fan Wenlan needed to address the problem of his old Beijing University classmate Gu Jiegang. As discussed in Chapter 4, Gu Jiegang had challenged the authenticity of the classical canon in China and its linear narrative of Chinese ethnogenesis. According to Gu, the myths about the Yellow Emperor, Yu the Great, and other ancient leaders were manufactured by later generations of Chinese historians for purely political reasons and thus were utterly unreliable. Fan Wenlan dismissed these concerns and came to share the view of Guomindang racial nationalists who argued that Gu's radical historical skepticism was incompatible with nationalist historiography. Indeed, Fan contended that these ancient legends, if treated critically, could serve as sources of historical knowledge as valuable as new archaeological and oracle bone evidence: "If one scrubs away the factitious myths and uncovers the exaggerations of later generations and then compares this material with more recent factual material, these legends maintain considerable weight."[40] Even inconsistencies—for example, in the genealogy of the Yellow Emperor set out in Sima Qian's *Shiji* that Gu Jiegang rejected as entirely spurious—could be seen as demonstrating authenticity. "If the entire thing was concocted by later generations," Fan rationalized, "wouldn't the genealogy be orderly so as to make it naturally plausible?"[41] For him and other nationalist historians, the need to preserve an unbroken connection with the past made abandoning China's rich store of historical legends inconceivable.

Like Liang Qichao before him, Fan Wenlan began his history of China with the intense Darwinian struggle between different races (zhongzu) and cultures (wenhua) in the fertile Yellow River valley. The historical unity of the Zhonghua minzu, in this account, depended on placing contemporary Chinese minzus firmly on the historical stage of prehistoric China. The Yizu, who originated in Manchuria, were said to have been led by their legendary leader Taihao into the eastern reaches of the valley, where their Longshan culture flourished. In the south, the barbarian chieftain Chiyou was described as the leader of the Manzu, who carried their Annamese culture into the valley from present-day Vietnam. The Qiangzu and their primitive nomadic assemblage originated in the west before migrating with their leader, the mythical Yandi or Fire Emperor, into the Yellow River valley. Finally, traces of the ancient dwellers on the northern fringes of the valley, the savage Dizu (little discussed in the historical record), had been recently uncovered by archaeologists.[42] Although Fan never spelled out the link, his readers would have recognized the homology between these ancient ethnonyms and the most prominent frontier minorities within contemporary China: the Manchus as the descendants of the Yizu, the numerous southern minorities as the progeny of the Manzu, the Tibetans (and possibly the Hui) as the offspring of the Qiangzu, and the Mongols as the sons and daughters of the ancient Dizu. Fan Wenlan thus stretched the existence of China's minority nationals, and the history of Chinese ethnic and cultural unity, back to the very dawn of Chinese civilization.

The delicate balance among the indigenous inhabitants of the Yellow River valley was upset around 2700 BCE when a new, more advanced culture entered the region. Traces of this advanced Neolithic assemblage—called the Yangshao culture after the location of its initial discovery—had been found by Swedish geologist Johan Gunnar Andersson. Building on Albert Terrien de Lacouperie's original Western origin thesis, Fan married the venerable legends of the Yellow Emperor with Andersson's recent scientific findings: the ancient stories about the Yellow Emperor's westward migration into the Yellow River valley 'proved,' in Fan's words, that "Yangshao culture was actually the culture of the Yellow Emperor's clan."[43] As the Yellow Emperor's people (the so-called Huazu) came into the valley, the powerful Qiangzu initially blocked their entry. According to Fan, Xiaohao, who is listed in the *Shiji* as one of the sons of the Yellow Emperor, led a portion of the clan eastward, where they gradually assimilated the Yizu. The remaining followers of the Yellow Emperor forged an alliance with Yandi to attack their common enemy, the barbaric Manzu. After the Yellow Emperor had personally slain their chieftain, Chiyou, he became the undisputed leader of the valley and gradually introduced his clan's civilized Yangshao culture throughout the region. In the process the Qiang, Man, Di, and Yi barbarians were either assimilated by the advanced Hua people or chased out of the Yellow River valley, which became the home of China's first dynasty, the Xia. The story of Xiaohao's assimilation of the Yizu seems at first to be a minor thread in Fan Wenlan's historical narrative, with little hard evidence behind it—Andersson's discovery of Yangshao-style painted pottery in southern Manchuria and a rather ambiguous reference in the *Shiji* to Xiaohao making his home in the region of present-day Shandong. Yet the prehistoric intermingling of the proto-Han and Yi peoples was crucial to Fan's carefully woven narrative of Zhonghua racial and cultural unity.

While scholars in early twentieth-century China continued to debate the actual birthplace of Chinese civilization, few questioned its monophyletic origin—until a distinctly non-Yangshao black painted pottery was discovered in 1928 by the Chinese archaeologist Wu Jinding in the Shandong village of Longshan.[44] The Guomindang historian Fu Sinian seized on the discovery of Longshan culture to challenge the myth of the linear descent of the Chinese people from a single ancestor. In his skillfully argued East Yi West Xia theory (*yixia dongxi shuo*), Fu claimed that the Xiazu (represented by its Yangshao culture) and the Yizu (represented by its Longshan culture) had a horizontal interrelationship in prehistoric China. Originally devised as a critique of the Orientalist Western origin thesis,[45] Fu's plural origins thesis was premised on the possibility that the Xia people might have migrated into China from the West—as Andersson's archaeological evidence seemed to suggest—while putting forward the Yi people and their Longshan assemblage as autochthonously Chinese.

However, the Japanese occupation of Manchuria altered the political landscape in which Fu's thesis was originally constructed, causing his book to come under intense criticism from Chinese scholars. The Japanese imperialists seized on Fu's argument as evidence that the Manchus—who, they claimed, were the descendants of the Yizu—were racially and culturally distinct from the Chinese and their Xiazu ancestors and therefore deserved an independent state of their own. Thus, when Chinese archaeologists discovered stratified layers of Yangshao, Longshan, and Shang dynasty Bronze Age cultures at a single site near Anyang in Henan province, some began to argue that these three supposedly distinct cultures actually represented successive phases in a single, unbroken "Chinese" cultural and racial development.[46] For his part, Fan Wenlan appeared to have constructed the myth of Hua-Yi intermingling in the form of the Yellow Emperor's son Xiaohao to counter Japanese claims about the independent racial origins of the Manchu people and to reinforce his contention that the Longshan and Yangshao assemblages "belong to the same cultural system."[47]

By giving full weight to the ethnic diversity in the historical and archaeological evidence and then carefully constructing a seamless nexus of interrelationships, Fan Wenlan traced the contemporary Zhonghua nationalities back into China's prehistoric past. "The modern Zhonghua minzu absorbed (*xishou*) countless races (zhongzu)," Fan asserted, "and on the basis of a particular culture and race underwent four to five thousand years of struggle and fusion before gradually coming into being."[48] That *basis* was none other than the progeny of the Yellow Emperor—the so-called Huazu or Chinese clan—and their advanced Yangshao culture. Thus, like Dai Jitao, Shao Yuanchong, and other Guomindang racial nationalists, Fan Wenlan constructed the unity and antiquity of the Zhonghua minzu around the Yellow Emperor. His narrative of ancient Chinese history highlighted the unilinear transmission of a single Chinese culture and people from the Yellow Emperor to the legendary rulers through the historical dynasties and down to the present. Along the way, all ethnic and cultural diversity was gradually subsumed under a single Huazu-cum-Hanzu core, whose sheer size and cultural effervescence attracted and then gradually assimilated all non-Chinese elements.

Despite the fluency of Fan's claims about the apparent antiquity of Zhonghua cultural and ethnic unity, the Communist Party's first attempt at writing nationalist history was not without problems. Chief among them was its failure to describe either the culture of the Huazu or its progenitor—the Yellow Emperor—as indigenous to the Yellow River valley. Given the scientific weight of Andersson's archaeological discoveries and the appropriation of Fu Sinian's plural origins thesis by the Japanese imperialists, Fan Wenlan felt compelled in his general history of China to admit that "the Yangshao culture's race developed from the West toward the East," and that "antiquarians have proven that China's Yangshao-style painted pottery belongs to the same family as the white sand pottery of Babylon and the earthen pottery of Anau, Tripolje, and other Central Asian regions."[49] Unlike Xiong Shili and other racial nationalists, Fan seemed reluctant or uncomfortable in using the Peking Man discoveries or other archaeological evidence to demonstrate the indigenous origins of Chinese civilization. Though he began his general history of China with the discovery of ancient hominid remains at Zhoukoudian and the Ordos region of Inner Mongolia, Fan downplayed their significance to the development of the Chinese minzu and culture. As noted in Chapter 4, no consensus existed among the scientific community about the anatomical relationship between these early hominids and modern *Homo sapiens*. As his graphic descriptions of the bestial physiognomy of Chiyou, Taihao, and other ancient barbarian leaders reveals, Fan Wenlan, like many other Chinese nationalists, appeared uncomfortable with claiming that the apelike Peking Man was the progenitor of the regal and mighty Zhonghua minzu. "Chinese history," Fan boldly declared in *A Concise General History of China*, "should begin with the Yellow Emperor."[50] And the possibility that the Yellow Emperor might have migrated into China from the West, as Lacouperie and other Western imperialists had argued, apparently was of little significance to Fan. His concern was to draw a racial and cultural link between the present-day Chinese, including the Han majority and its minority nationals, and the Yellow Emperor's descendents.

The Zhonghua minzu and the Problem of Zhongzu

Communist historians, of course, were not the only Chinese intellectuals engaged in this nationalist enterprise. As discussed in Chapter 4, researchers closely affiliated with the Guomindang were fashioning their own narratives of Zhonghua minzu antiquity and historical unity. As early as 1939, Xiong Shili and other Nationalist Party historians were using Paleolithic fossils to construct a myth of Chinese consanguinity. Xiong Shili made the discovery of Peking Man the central component of his 1939 lectures on the origin of the Chinese race at the Guomindang's Central Military Academy in Chongqing.[51] In these lectures, Xiong claimed that the "five lineages" (wuzu) of the Zhonghua minzu—the Han, Manchus, Mongols, Tibetans, and Hui—all descended directly from that single, ancient progenitor. Consequently, the Zhonghua minzu was a single race, with its various branches—like children from the same parents—differing only in "natural endowment" (tianxing) and their adaptation to different environmental conditions.

In Yan'an, many Communist scholars and officials had long been hostile to what they saw as the unscientific use of race to construct the historical unity of the Zhonghua minzu. Orthodox Marxism identifies race as a form of false consciousness that hinders the development of a transnational class consciousness among the workers of the world. As early as 1926, Qu Qiubai warned his fellow intellectuals against conflating zhongzu (race) with minzu (nation/nationality). Racial characteristics—such as facial features—are slow to alter, while changes in the economic base always affect the superstructural conditions of a minzu.[52] In his 1938 lectures at the Marxist-Leninist Institute, Yang Song asserted that minzu, as defined by Stalin, was fundamentally a nonracial category. Like the English, American, French, and Italian minzus, all modern nationalities were formed through the union of nonconsanguineous tribes, clans, and races. Yang criticized the unscientific racial theories of German scholars, claiming that the fascists were attempting to supplant Stalin's scientific and nonracial concept of the nation with an ahistorical theory of race that fraudulently used a biological concept to explain the complex social processes of human development. In actuality, Yang argued, the German fascists were relying on these "utterly absurd theories" to justify the invasion and subjugation of the "inferior" Czech, Slavic, and Soviet nationalities by the supposedly "superior" Aryan race.[53]

Following Gu Jiegang, Li Weihan and his National Question Research Office pointed out in 1941 that many Chinese scholars were making unscientific and ahistorical claims about race in China. In particular, Li highlighted the abuses of race in categorizing the Hui nationality. Guomindang scholars and officials denied that the Hui were a distinct minzu, claiming instead that they shared a common progenitor and common race with the Han majority, differing only in their religious beliefs. Li argued that by insisting that the Hui and the Han belong to a single race, the Guomindang was ignoring historical facts.[54] Far from sharing a common ancestry, the Hui were the descendants of Arab and Persian traders who entered China during the Yuan dynasty; as such, they could not possibly belong to the same race as the Han people.[55]

Outside the narrow confines of the Yan'an academy, however, a group of Communist historians found recent archaeological discoveries, and the conclusions they could draw from it about the racial origins and continuity of the Zhonghua minzu, useful as they sought to heed Mao's call for a more positive and patriotic view of the Chinese past. The discovery of the world's earliest known hominids in China seemed to offer the type of irrefutable scientific evidence that was necessary both to counter Japanese propaganda and to demonstrate the indigenous origins and ancient consanguinity of the entire Chinese people. In their early attempts at national history, the Communist historians Jian Bozan, Lü Zhenyu, and Yin Da grafted a myth of racial continuity onto the material evolution of the Zhonghua minzu as presented in Fan Wenlan's *A Concise General History of China*.

In a 1943 essay, Jian Bozan revisited the 1922 discovery by French archaeologists Emile Licent and Pierre Teilhard de Chardin of a single upper incisor from what appeared to have been a Paleolithic hominid in the Ordos region of Inner Mongolia. Jian, a member of a small, acculturated Uyghur community in Hunan province, had secretly joined the CCP in 1937. He spent the war working as an editor and independent scholar in the Guomindang capital of Chongqing, where he maintained close ties with Nationalist Party scholars.[56] Sidestepping Andersson's argument about the cultural links between Yangshao cultural remains and those of Central Asia, Jian asserted that the remains of "Ordos Man"

(*Hetaoren* or *E'erduosiren*), now largely forgotten, provided scientific evidence of the indigenous origins of the Chinese race. They demonstrated that rather than migrating into the Yellow River valley from the West, the ancient Xiazu descended from the Ordos region and then, following the recession of the ice age, moved outward in several directions before becoming the Zhuxia, or various Xia people, of the Zhou dynasty. Unlike Fan Wenlan, Jian concluded that judging from "the existing archaeological and historical evidence, not only did the culture of the Xia originate in the Ordos, but so did its race (zhongzu)."[57]

For many Chinese historians, the discovery of late Paleolithic human remains in the newly excavated Upper Cave at Zhoukoudian in 1933 seemed to offer a more convincing story of the Zhonghua minzu's origin. Unlike the original Peking Man skullcap unearthed in 1929, the three fully intact skulls found in the Upper Cave were more fully evolved and humanlike. Lü Zhenyu was one of the first Communist historians to seize on this discovery in asserting the indigenous origins of the Chinese race. Lü, who also taught in the wartime capital of Chongqing after having secretly joined the CCP in 1936 under Zhou Enlai's patronage,[58] placed the Zhoukoudian archaeological dig, and in particular the Upper Cave discoveries, at the center of his revised 1940 *Studies on Prehistoric Chinese Society*. Rejecting the monogenesis of mankind, Lü contended that the human remains dug up at Zhoukoudian provided irrefutable scientific evidence of the indigenous provenance of the Chinese people; and he cited Pei Wenzhong in support of his position.[59] Pei, who had led the team of Chinese archaeologists in the Upper Cave excavation, concluded in his 1934 preliminary assessment that the skulls shared a physical morphology with not just modern *Homo sapiens* but also the Mongoloid race (*Menggu renzhong*). Pei concluded that the so-called Upper Cave Man (*shanding dongren*), as a more fully evolved species of the original Peking Man, represented "the earliest Chinese man," or what Lü Zhenyu termed "the progenitor of the Chinese people" (*Zhongguoren de zuxian*).[60]

In his treatment of early Chinese cultural developments, Lü Zhenyu did not directly challenge Fu Sinian's plural origin thesis. Unlike Fan Wenlan, Lü believed that the Yangshao culture of the Western Xia people and the Longshan culture of the Yi people "compose the two main branches of the ancient Chinese minzu," that is cultural systems that developed independently of one another in different parts of China.[61] At the same time, Lü stressed that the Yi and Xia people were both "offspring of the Mongoloid race." By connecting these two distinct peoples with a layer of racial propinquity—in the form of the ancient progenitor Upper Cave Man—Lü Zhenyu cleverly surmounted the ethnic discontinuity of Fu Sinian's thesis. In place of Fan's rather forced genealogy of the Yellow Emperor, he put forward "hard, scientific" evidence from the fields of anatomy and archaeology to demonstrate the racial unity of both the Yi and Xia during antiquity and by extension the biological kinship of all "fraternal nationalities" (*xiongdi minzus*) in contemporary China.

This focus on race and the search for Chinese origins received its most systematic treatment in the work of Yin Da, one of the few Communist historians to have received formal archaeological training. While studying at Henan University, Yin Da was selected by Academia Sinica as a field researcher for their excavations at Anyang, where he spent almost ten years learning archaeological methods firsthand. Following the Japanese invasion, Yin fled to Yan'an where he joined the Communist Party in 1938 and became a section chief in its Central Publishing Bureau.[62] In a 1940 essay, "On the Origins of the Zhonghua minzu and Its Culture," Yin Da stressed the renewed importance of this old question in the context of China's life and death struggle against Japanese imperialism. By refocusing attention on the genesis of the Chinese race, he hoped to "strengthen national self-confidence and cause the grandchildren of the Zhonghua minzu to understand their glorious and magnificent historical legacy, while opposing the shameful activities of those national scum who 'treat a thief as their father.'"[63] Proposing to reexamine the prehistoric record from a contemporary and nationalistic point of view, Yin sidestepped Gu Jiegang's attack on ancient Chinese mythology by arguing that recent archaeological and anatomical evidence provided a more reliable route for constructing a positive and accurate story of Chinese origins.

Yin Da pointed to the common racial elements found among all the human remains thus far unearthed in China as proof that "the cultural legacy of our vast land of China is ten to one hundred times as old as our over five-thousand-year-old historical footprint."[64] He claimed that the highly original morphology Weidenreich identified among the original Sinanthropus remains—a shovel shaped incisor and thickening of the jaw—were found not only in the Ordos Man and Upper Cave Man fossils, but also in the Neolithic human remains found at Yangshao and Shaguotun, as well as the more than five hundred skulls recently unearthed at Anyang. Yin saw the ongoing Anyang dig as "the crucial link in the course of the Zhonghua minzu's development."[65] Preliminary analysis revealed the same shovel-shaped incisor among the human remains found in the Shang and Zhou dynasty deposits, enabling historians to now draw a direct racial link back to the five-hundred-thousand-year-old Peking Man. "Somewhere between the Shang and the Zhou dynasties," Yin concluded, "historical legends already tell us there existed the ancestors of the Zhonghua minzu. In the future, research on the [Anyang] human remains will certainly prove that the story of our minzu's continuous development in these legends is a matter of historical fact rather than some calumny meant to patch over gaps in the historical narrative."[66] Like Xiong Shili a year earlier, Yin Da claimed that this ongoing scientific research "should strongly convince us that Sinanthropus is most likely the forerunner (*qianshen*) of the Mongoloid people."[67]

As noted in the previous chapter, the publication of *China's Destiny* in 1943 dramatically altered the political and ideological landscape in China. Its criticism by CCP leaders forced Communist historians to adopt new narrative strategies for demonstrating the ancient unity of the Zhonghua minzu. In the book's opening chapter, the Zhonghua minzu was presented as racially one, with different "lineages branches" (zongzhi) described as "either descendants of a common ancestor or interrelated through marriage"; and thus "the main and branch lineages all belong to the same bloodline."[68] In contrast to Mao's claim about the existence of numerous minzus within China, *China's Destiny* declared that all inhabitants of China were organically part of a single, consanguineous Zhonghua minzu. Though Mao and the Communists envisioned a similarly bounded and ancient Chinese people, the politics of the time required them to distance themselves from GMD rhetoric.

In Yan'an, Mao Zedong mobilized the entire CCP in attacking *China's Destiny*. Sensing that Japan's defeat was now inevitable, Mao viewed the publication of Chiang's book as the opening salvo in the impending CCP-GMD struggle for national leadership in China. During a June 16, 1943 politburo meeting, Mao called for an immediate reversal of the party's united front tactic as it related to the Guomindang and the ban on public attacks of its "reactionary ideology." Stressing the urgent need to expose the "fascist policies" of the Guomindang, he placed Liu Shaoqi personally in charge of rallying the party in a thorough critique of *China's Destiny*. Liu quickly convened a cadres conference in Yan'an, during which Fan Wenlan, Ai Siqi, Lü Zhenyu, and other Communist intellectuals criticized *China's Destiny* as the "Bible of Chinese fascism." Chen Boda, Mao's personal secretary and chief ideologue, wrote a long essay systematically refuting each argument in the book. On July 19, having reviewed and revised Chen's article, Mao wrote a personal letter to the director of the Xinhua News Agency requesting that the entire piece not only be published in *Jiefang Daily* but also broadcast repeatedly on the Communist radio network. In addition, Mao ordered the Central Publishing Office to print fifteen hundred copies of Chen's essay to aid the study and criticism of *China's Destiny* in all political education classes.[69]

In his *Critique of "China's Destiny,"* Chen Boda argued that Chiang's version of the genesis and development of the Zhonghua minzu was not supported by the facts. In claiming that "our Zhonghua minzu was formed through the amalgamation of many different lineages who shared the same descent," the book was echoing the facile and unscientific "racial blood-lineage theories" (*minzu xuetong lun*) of the German, Italian, and Japanese fascists. "The term Zhonghua minzu, as we commonly use it," he added, "actually refers to the various Zhonghua nationalities (or various minzus): our China is a multi-minzu state."[70] The argument in *China's Destiny* that there is only one minzu in China not only contradicted Sun Yat-sen's own claims in the manifesto of the Guomindang's Reorganization Congress about the "various minzus within Chinese territory," but also violated history itself. Chen Boda declared that it required only "common sense and not profound knowledge" to realize that all China's nationalities were not the offspring of a single progenitor. Similarly, it was ridiculous to argue that intermarriage between the Han majority and the minority nationals had transformed the Tibetans or any other minority group into a branch of the Han nationality. "If it did," Chen mocked, "the Zhonghua minzu would have already become a branch of the Japanese minzu, because many Chinese—including many prominent Guomindang leaders—have married Japanese women!"[71] Chen Boda concluded his attack in a tone reminiscent of Gu Jiegang's critique of the Guomindang racial nationalists:

> Science is flourishing in today's world; thus, national history should be approached scientifically. The trick of distorting, altering, and fabricating national history, which is practiced by the fascists, cannot be an example for us; and to place such things in our national textbooks is simply a case of fooling the people. The reason why the big landlord and capitalist classes in China have fabricated this single minzu theory (*danyi minzulun*) is so that they can propagate Han chauvinism and oppress the weak minorities within China. Since our Han minzu was originally also a weak people, we should unite with all the minorities within our country—democratically and on an equal footing—so that we can resist the invaders together.[72]

The Zhonghua minzu and Its Han Biological Microcosm

With the direct authority of Mao Zedong behind it, Chen Boda's condemnation of the Guomindang's single minzu theory forced Communist historians like Jian Bozan and Lü Zhenyu to rethink their previous narratives of Chinese history. They could no longer afford to rely on a single progenitor—the Yellow Emperor, Ordos Man, Upper Cave Man or Peking Man—in constructing a myth of Zhonghua minzu unity and antiquity. Their new strategy was to emphasize the polyphyletic or multiracial origins of the Zhonghua minzu, while continuing to weave a linear and unbroken narrative of historical and biological interaction between the various minzus of contemporary China. Taking a page from Gu Jiegang's notebook,[73] the Communists began arguing that the unity of the Zhonghua minzu was located in its long history of cultural and racial fusion (ronghe) around a single Hanzu nucleus. China was a multi-minzu state, but it also constituted a single consanguineous yet composite people.

Lü Zhenyu was the first Communist historian to suggest that the origins of the Zhonghua minzu might be multiracial. In his 1941 *A Concise General History of China*,[74] which was written as a college-level textbook at the behest of Zhou Enlai, Lü introduced a new, distinctly non-Chinese hominid to the story of Chinese origins: Java Man (*Pithecanthropus*), whose ancient remains were found on the island of Java in 1891 by the Dutch geologist–cum–amateur archaeologist Eugène Dubois. When the fossilized skull of Peking Man was discovered in 1929, paleoanthropologists quickly recognized the similarities in age and essential structure between these two Asian hominids; but its larger brain capacity and more fully evolved human morphology won Peking Man the lion's share of attention, as scholars' focus shifted away from comparisons between the two hominids and toward the relationship between these early hominids and modern humans.[75]

In his textbook, Lü Zhenyu attempted to redirect the attention of his students toward the significance of Java Man to the evolution of the Chinese race (*Zhongguo renzhong*), calling into question the idea that the Chinese descended from a single ancient hominid. He argued that a more careful examination of the racial morphology and historical development of the various Chinese nationalities revealed that the Zhonghua minzu arose in two different regions and from two different races: "Of the fraternal minzus of China, the Han, Manchu, Mongols, and others originated in Mongolia and constitute part of the North China Mongoloid race, the Tibetan, Miao, Tong, and other southwestern minorities within our territory are primarily composed of the Melanesoid race and originated in Malaya—the former descended from Peking Man while the latter are the offspring of Java Man."[76] The discovery of Peking Man, Java Man, Heidelberg Man, and other early hominids provided irrefutable evidence, Lü Zhenyu contended, of the polyphyletic provenance of both individual minzus as well as all of humanity.

Yet the Zhonghua minzu's polyphylesis was not necessarily an argument against the contemporary nationalities of China sharing a common racial identity. According to Lü, in a claim he made more explicit in a 1943 article printed in *Jiefang Daily* immediately following the publication of *China's Destiny*, the long history of intermingling among the various peoples of China fused them together into a single, new race. After enumerating the racial composition of the various Zhonghua nationalities (mainly the Mongoloid race, followed by the Melanesoid race, the Caucasoid race, and a few still unknown races), Lü insisted, "However, this only refers to the origins of the various Zhonghua nationalities: after having undergone thousands of years of mutual intermingling, everyone's blood (*xue*) is today mixed together."[77] Despite admitting that there were no longer any pure races in China, or elsewhere in the world for that matter, Lü continued to employ the term "Zhonghua minzu race" (*Zhonghua minzu renzhong*) to highlight the racial propinquity of the Chinese people. Among Communist historians, the term Zhonghua minzu came to function as a powerful nationalist trope, capturing not only the biological, cultural, and political unity of the contemporary inhabitants of the Republic of China, but also its long history of racial interbreeding. Today's Zhonghua nationalities might not have descended from a single ancestor, but they still possessed a common bloodline and culture that could be traced back through thousands of years of Chinese history, as the GMD did in *China's Destiny*.

In *An Outline of Chinese History*, published in late 1943, Jian Bozan—who in earlier writings had narrowly focused on Ordos Man and the Xiazu—adopted this new, multiracial paradigm to explain the genesis of the Zhonghua minzu. In the first chapter, "The Origins of the Chinese Race and Its Historical Setting," Jian divided the Chinese race (*Zhongguo renzhong*) into two major phyla: the "Mongolian steppe branch" (*Menggu gaoyuan xi*) and the "South Pacific branch" (*Nan taipingyang xi*). Archaeologists had found Stone Age assemblages both on the eastern fringes of the Mongolian steppe, at the now famous

Zhoukoudian cave of Peking Man, and in the Ordos region of western Inner Mongolia. According to Jian, the end of the ice age brought climatic changes that forced these primitive peoples off the steppe in search of new sources of food. One of the bands associated with Peking Man drifted west into the Bohai coastal region, where it evolved into the Yinzu or Shang clan; another Zhoukoudian band moved north into Manchuria, becoming known as the Dongyi or eastern barbarians. The Ordos group split into four different bands: one migrated southeast into the Lower Yellow River valley (Shanxi and Henan), where their offspring were referred to as the Eastern Xia; another moved southwest into the Upper Yellow River valley (Sha'anxi, Gansu, and Qinghai), later evolving into the Western Xia and eventually the Qiangzu or Qiang clan; yet another group, which became known as the various races of the western regions (*xitu zhu zhongzu*), journeyed due west into the Tarim Basin of present-day Xinjiang; and a final group wandered north into the vicinity of Lake Baikal, where they became known as the Beidi or Northern Di.[78]

At the same time that these primitive bands were spreading throughout northern China, another racially distinct group of hominids entered southern China from the Malay Archipelago. Jian pointed to the discovery of a new Paleolithic culture in Guangdong by the Hong Kong missionary Daniel J. Finn as scientific evidence of a South Pacific branch of the Chinese race. The distribution of its Neolithic remains in South China led Jian to speculate that the South Pacific branch entered China along two main routes: up the Mekong River into Yunnan and eventually Sichuan, and along the Vietnamese coast and into southeast China. Members of the former group became known as the Dongnanyi or southwestern barbarians and were the ancestors, Jian argued, of today's Miao and Yi nationalities. Those in the latter group, referred to as the Baiyue in the Chinese historical canon, were the ancestors of today's Yao and Tong nationalities, the Yi of Hainan Island, and the Fan nationality of Taiwan. According to Jian, the prehistoric traces of a distinct South Pacific racial branch disproved the GMD's monophyletic thesis of Chinese provenance; and because these two racial branches later mixed, the search for a single pure race in China today was a vain quest.[79]

The long process of cultural and racial melding that formed the Chinese race began in what Jian termed the first period of "great racial and cultural interchange," during the legendary era of the Yellow Emperor. According to legend, the migrating Xia people, led by the Yellow Emperor, clashed with and then defeated the Miao people who had been led into the Yellow River valley by their chieftain, Chiyou. To Jian Bozan, the distinct patterns of Mongolian steppe and South Pacific Neolithic cultural assemblages in the Yellow River valley proved that this ancient myth was actually evidence of the racial melding of two peoples.[80] In his account, much as in Gu Jiegang's, the entire story of Chinese history revolved around an endless series of racial and cultural transfusions between the ancient clans and racial branches of the Chinese race, which eventually consolidated in the form of a single, organic and indivisible national entity—the Zhonghua minzu.

This narrative was a new approach to demonstrating the historical unity of the Zhonghua minzu. Rather than viewing the Chinese nationalities as political categories constructed to describe ethnic diversity in contemporary China, Communist scholars began arguing that they represented distinct, historically evolved minzus that could be traced back through the written record to the earliest beginnings of Chinese history. China's twenty-five dynastic histories contain literally hundreds of different ethnonyms referring to non-Chinese barbarians living along the frontiers of the Middle Kingdom. Communist historians used these ancient ethnonyms to construct a seamless ethnogenealogy for each of the state's contemporary minzus—inventing not only a rich historical tradition for each of the Zhonghua nationalities but also an unbroken, linear history of their cultural and racial interactions.

As noted in Chapter 4, the writing of ethnogenealogies has a long history in China. Beginning with Sima Qian's *Shiji*, all the dynastic histories contained a section dedicated to *liezhuan* (biographies, genealogies) that chronicled the exploits of famous individuals and barbarian tribes and their leaders. In their accounts of the origins and development of non-Chinese peoples, historians often conjectured about the relationship between different ethnonyms in order to construct a sense of continuity with the past, thereby participating in the Confucian project of *zhengming* or rectification of names. The tradition of ethnogenealogies continued into the early twentieth century with classically trained historians, including Lü Simian, Lin Huixiang, Xiong Shili, and eventually even Gu Jiegang himself, analyzing the historical evolution of the minority nationals within the framework of more systematic examinations of national history.[81] Lü Zhenyu and Jian Bozan were two of the first Communist historians to engage in this type of speculative ethnohistoriography.

Jian Bozan's "Chart of the Chinese Racial Family," attached to his 1943 *An Outline of Chinese History*, is a graphic example of this genealogical project. His Y-shaped taxonomy begins with the two main branches of the Chinese race, the Mongolian steppe branch and the South Pacific branch, and then winds its way down through scores of different historical ethnonyms to the major contemporary nationalities (Manchus, Han, Hui, Tibetans, Mongols, and southwestern minorities minzus) before finally ending with a single Zhonghua minzu. The key elements of Jian's ethnogenealogy are the lines of interaction he draws at the top and bottom of the chart between its different racial elements—creating a historical stemma of cultural and racial homology between the various Zhonghua nationalities. Nevertheless, his chart looked more like a series of fragile racial strains loosely tied together at each end than a tightly woven rope, leaving open the possibility that broken and independent strains might threaten the organic integrity of the Zhonghua minzu. What was required was a more central role for the Zhonghua minzu's racial core, the Hanzu: it had to be placed at the very center of the Chinese race's evolution.

Lü Zhenyu's *A Concise History of the Chinese Minzu* (*Zhongguo minzu jianshi*) is probably the CCP's single most important pre-1949 ethnogenealogy.

Written during the height of the CCP-GMD civil war in February 1947 and revised immediately after the Communist victory in May 1950, the book provides the most systematic taxonomy of the Zhonghua minzu's historical unity. According to Lü, the very concept of Zhonghua minzu or Zhongguo minzu—with its simultaneous reference to the various nationalities of China and the entire Chinese nation/race—arose in the context of CCP translation of Marxist works on the national question. Unfortunately, the "Chinese fascists" (read Guomindang) "stole this sacred term away" to support their own "chauvinist and unscientific aims."[82] Twisting and distorting historical facts, they claimed that only the Han are a minzu and that the Manchu, Mongol, Hui, Tibetan, Miao, and other minority nationals were simply "branch lineages" of a single, homogeneous Hanzu. Since "the fascist chauvinists are completely ignorant about the origins, historical evolution, and current conditions of the various nationalities in China," Lü Zhenyu proposed to write a new, systematic history of the Zhongguo minzu.[83] By using a scientific Marxist methodology to reveal the actual development and interaction of all its ethnic components, he aimed to free the sacred term Zhonghua minzu from the unscientific grips of the Guomindang reactionaries.

In *A Concise History of the Chinese Minzu*, Lü also continued to argue in favor of the polyphyletic origins of the Chinese people; but I am most interested here in his intricately constructed ethnogenealogy of the Zhonghua minzu. For the purpose of analysis, Lü's argument can be divided into two sections: first, he crafts a detailed history of the Zhonghua minzu's cultural and racial nucleus—the Hanzu; second, he traces the long history of interaction and fusion between the Han core and the major minority communities of contemporary China.

In the first part of his ethnogenealogy, Lü Zhenyu constructed a long, unbroken narrative of the Han nationality's historical evolution. Throughout its long history, the Han functioned as the "leading component" (*lingdao chengfen*) and "backbone" (*gugan*) of the Chinese people's struggle to maintain their independence against outside invaders.[84] In answering the questions, Where did the Hanzu come from? and How did it form and develop? Lü Zhenyu outlined three distinct stages. In the first period, the heterogeneous clans of the Yellow River valley fused together to form a single Huazu (Chinese clan). In 1766 BCE, the Dongyi (eastern barbarians), because of their superior production force, defeated the Xiazu, Qiangzu, Miaozu, and other primitive bands living in the Yellow River valley, establishing the slave Shang dynasty. During the ensuing struggle against their new masters, the Xia and other slaves slowly merged with the Shang people. Finally, when the King Wu Rebellion overthrew the Shang slave system and established the feudal Zhou dynasty in 1200 BCE, "this long period of mutual struggle and melding produced—with the Xia and Shang clans as its backbone—the Huazu or Huaxiazu."[85] In the second stage, additional barbarian groups were folded into the Huazu nucleus, producing what became known as the Hanzu around 140 BCE. Because of its economic, political, cultural, and demographic strength, the Huazu were able to fuse with the various northern nomadic tribes, such as the Hunyi, Guifang, Quanrong, and Xirong, during the Warring States and Spring and Autumn periods. With Qinshi Huangdi's unification of the six Zhou kingdoms, the Huazu incorporated several other barbarian tribes living south of the Yellow River valley, such as the Wu and Yue peoples, preparing the foundation for the Han dynasty and the newly named Hanzu or Han nationality. In the final stage of its development, marked by a long series of invasions by "alien minzus," the Hanzu transformed itself into the nucleus of a multiethnic Zhonghua minzu. The military superiority of the Tibetan, Mongol, Manchu, and other nomadic invaders enabled them to temporarily occupy and rule the Middle Kingdom; but they were inevitably assimilated and incorporated into the Zhonghua minzu, no match for the Hanzu's superior production methods. As Lü Zhenyu concluded, "The result of this great period of minzu assimilation and the interlocking relationship among the various minzus was that the Hanzu added new elements from different minzus not only to their racial features, production techniques, and social customs but also to their philosophy, science, arts and religion, producing quite a bit of change. At the same time, these other minzus also absorbed varying degrees of the Han's racial and cultural composition."[86] In the end, the mestizo-like Zhonghua minzu had the blood and culture of a single Han nationality at its core.

In the second part of *A Concise History of the Chinese Minzu*, Lü Zhenyu constructed an ethnogenealogy for each of the contemporary Chinese nationalities, tracing their evolution and interaction with the Han racial and cultural nucleus back through time. Whenever possible, Lü drew a direct link between the ancestors of China's contemporary minority nationals and their Han forefathers. The Manchus, for example, were followed back through the Nüzhen (Jurchen) and then the Donghu (Eastern Hu) to the Suzhen clan of the Xianbei people, who, Lü claimed, helped form the Huazu. Other nationalities, such as the Mongols, Tibetans, and Miao, were traced to the Huazu's ancient nomadic neighbors—the Xiongnu, Tujuezu, Qiangzu, and Miaozu.

Take, for example, Lü's detailed historical pedigree of the Hui nationality (Huizu or Hui minzu). In his landmark study on the Hui, Dru Gladney has convincingly demonstrated that the Huizu, as a distinct ethnic or national community, was a purely modern construct, arising only with the transition from empire to nation-state in China.[87] But to counter the claims of Guomindang racial nationalists (discussed earlier in this chapter) that the Hui were simply Hanzu who practiced Islam, Hui historians invented their own national tradition.[88] By locating the origin of the Huizu outside of China in Central Asia and the Middle East, Sino-Muslims hoped to legitimatize their claim as a distinct national people or minzu. Li Weihan and other top-ranking Communist officials sympathized with the Hui in their struggle against the Nationalist Party. The GMD's so-called Hui-Han common origin thesis (*Hui-Han tongyuan*), Li declared, was "without any contemporary or historical basis"; he instead maintained that the Hui were descended from Arab and Persian traders.[89] Although Li Weihan's argument about the nonindigenous origin of the Huizu was effective in countering the theories of the Guomindang, it also threatened to undermine Chinese national unity. During the 1940s, Sino-Muslim "separatists" in Xinjiang pointed to their non-Chinese racial identity in justifying their right for an independent East Turkestan.[90] Consequently, the pressure mounted on Chinese historians to demonstrate the historical unity of the Hui and Han people.

One approach was to construct an autochthonous ethnogenealogy of Hui provenance. In his 1941 *A Concise General History of China*, Lü Zhenyu followed Guomindang historians in tracing the genesis of the Huizu back through the Huihe and Huihu to the Tujuezu. Lü contended that the Hui, like their Tujuezu forefathers and their Han brothers, were primarily Mongoloid in racial classification, while admitting that a portion were Caucasoid (from Central Asia).[91] In his 1950 history, he went a step further, directly linking the Hui ancestors to the actual origin of the Huazu nucleus of the Zhonghua minzu.

Yet postulating such a link created a couple of problems for Lü. First, he needed to avoid any direct association with the Guomindang's common origin thesis. He therefore claimed, as he had in 1941, that the Hui were "not of a single racial origin," pointing to the obvious physical differences among not only the Hui people themselves but also the Hui and Han nationalities.[92] Then, despite an admitted lack of dependable historical evidence, he speculated about the origins of the so-called *Ganhui*, or those Hui living in Gansu and Ningxia, while ignoring the other, possibly nonindigenous racial branches of the Hui. Second, the Tujuezu ethnonym to which Lü Zhenyu linked the Hui in 1941 could be traced only as far back as the Tujue Khanate, established southwest of the Altai Mountains around the sixth century CE. Further etymological speculation was required for the Hui genealogy to reach the twelfth-century BCE origin of the Huazu. In their own ethnogenealogies of the Hui, Guomindang historians frequently cited a line in the *Beishi* (*History of the Northern Kingdoms*) claiming that the Tujuezu were the descendants of the Xiongnu, which could then be easily linked through Sima Qian's *Shiji* to the Yellow Emperor.[93] Lü Zhenyu, needing to distance himself from the "fascist historiography" of the Guomindang, constructed an alternative stemma—through an exercise of etymological gymnastics—that nevertheless led back to the same Han racial core.

Arguing that the rulers of the Zhou dynasty used to refer to all the nomadic tribes west of their territory with the general ethnonym *Qiang* (western barbarians), which later split into the Di and Qiang barbarians, Lü claimed that the proto-Hui designation, Tujuezu, was actually a "linguistic transmutation" (*zhuanyin*) of the Zhou term *diqiang*. Thus the Diqiang were actually the "forerunners" (*qianshen*) of the Tujuezu. The Zhou ethnonym Diqiang, he maintained, was itself a transmutation of the Shang dynasty term *liangqiang*, which referred to a group of slaves living in present-day Gansu and Ningxia. Because they participated in the slave rebellion overthrowing the Shang dynasty, a portion of the Liangqiang "formed part of the Huazu's composition," following the fall of the Shang and the establishment of the feudal Zhou dynasty.[94] In this way, through a series of essentially unrelated ethnonyms—Huihu, Huihe, Tujuezu,

Diqiang, and Liangqiang—Lü traced the historical evolution of the contemporary Hui nationality back to the original Han core of the Zhonghua minzu.

In the end, Lü Zhenyu's ethnogenealogy of the Chinese minzu was remarkably similar to Xiong Shili's racial taxonomy of the Zhonghua minzu. Despite their opposing views on the political future of China, the Communist Lü and the Nationalist Xiong shared a common faith in the unity and antiquity of the Chinese race-state. By constructing an elaborate mosaic of historical interconnections, both men hoped to demonstrate the fundamental consanguinity of the Zhonghua minzu—what Xiong Shili termed a "common blood lineage" (*tongyi xuetong*) and Lü Zhenyu called the "mutual fusion and absorption of racial bloodlines" (*renzhong xuetong de xiangmu ronghe yu shenxiu*).[95] The two historians differed only in their narrative strategies for demonstrating this central point. Though both manufactured individual histories to link the minorities culturally as well as racially to the Huazu-cum-Hanzu core, Xiong Shili went a step further in claiming that all Chinese "lineages" (zongzu) descended from a single ancient progenitor, Peking Man. As the political, cultural, and demographic nucleus of the Chinese people, the Han absorbed countless racial and cultural strains in the course of its five thousand years of uninterrupted development, eventually fusing all the peoples of the former Qing empire into a single, organic and indivisible national form: the Zhonghua minzu.

Narrative Convergence: "The Development of the Zhonghua minzu"

As the executive vice chairman of the PRC's new Historical Research Society and director of the Academy of Sciences' Institute of Modern History, Fan Wenlan was responsible for institutionalizing Lü Zhenyu's new historical paradigm after the PRC was founded. By 1955, Fan incorporated this new Han-centered paradigm into a revision of his *A Concise General History of China*, producing what became the standard interpretation of Chinese history until Mao's death in 1976.[96] In an October 1950 article, published in the party journal *Xuexi* (*Study*), Fan foreshadowed the positioning of China's minority nationals in this new general history of China. Entitled "The Development of the Zhonghua minzu," Fan's article was part of a series of essays to assist party cadres in studying Mao Zedong's classic 1939 work, *The Chinese Revolution and the Chinese Communist Party*, and drew on Lü Zhenyu's research to clarify Mao's usage of the term Zhonghua minzu while codifying the party's new orthodoxy on the national question.[97]

Fan Wenlan began his survey of the Zhonghua minzu's development with Peking Man. Unlike previous Communist interpretations, he treated the prehistoric fossils as evidence of a *group* of proto-Chinese rather than a single individual or progenitor, arguing that these primitive hominids were responsible for the widespread development of China's Stone Age culture. To Fan, the extensive distribution of the remains suggested that these prehistoric ape-men "subsequently became the ancestors of each of the Zhonghua minzu nationalities, or in other words, the collective ancestors of the Zhonghua minzu."[98] In marked contrast to Xiong Shili, Fan Wenlan made it clear that China's early clans and lineages all had different progenitors; yet the Communist party-state was also eager to retain Peking Man as a nationalist trope or archaeological mascot for the collective diversity and antiquity of the Zhonghua minzu.[99] The centrality of Peking Man to the story of Chinese origins was institutionalized during the 1950s and eventually took physical form with the construction of the first permanent museum at Zhoukoudian in 1953.[100]

Because of China's huge territory, Fan contended that no single minzu could open up and develop all of China. While crediting the Hanzu with being the first to develop the central plains region along the Yellow River valley, he maintained that the ancestors of today's minority nationals were chiefly responsible for opening up China's vast frontier regions: the Dongyizu developed the Bohai coastal regions; the Miaozu and Yaozu opened up the Yangtze, Min, and Pearl river valleys; the Zangzu were the first to exploit Qinghai and Tibet; the Yizu and other southwest lineages opened up the southwestern frontier; the Donghuzu took care of Manchuria; the Xiongxu and other proto-Mongolian peoples the Mongolian steppe; the Huizu and other northwest lineages were the first to explore the Northwest, and so on.[101] In his narrative, Fan projected the ethnic diversity of twentieth-century China onto the imagined spatial unity of an ancient "fatherland."

In spite of its conjoined heterogeneity at birth, the Zhonghua minzu was not without a nucleus. As Mao pointed out in 1939, a single Han nationality constituted more than 90 percent of China's population, with the remainder divided among the numerous minority peoples. Fan believed that two interrelated factors explain Han dominance: "first, its population propagated owing to the continuous development (albeit slow and gradual) of its production forces; second, it gradually assimilated those minority nationals with relatively low cultures owing to the continuous expansion of its cultural influences."[102] Thus, over the course of five thousand years, a single Hanzu gradually grew from the Yellow Emperor's clan to the center of the multiethnic Zhonghua minzu. Through the process of this racial and cultural envelopment, the Han absorbed countless different clans, tribes, races, and cultural groups. The Han nationality thereby transformed itself into a microcosm of the Zhonghua minzu's collective diversity: its geographic spread became the unified territory of the Chinese nationalities; its national culture embodied all local and ethnic cultures; and its mongrel blood flowed through the veins of each and every member of the mighty Zhonghua minzu. In other words, its inherent superiority led the Han nationality to assume the Han man's burden of absorbing the blood and traditions of the inferior ethnic minorities so that they might, in the words of Liang Qichao and then Sun Yat-sen, be "smelted together in a single furnace," creating a single and indivisible Zhonghua minzu.[103]

In his pioneering work on the discourse of race in China, Frank Dikötter overlooks the importance of the ethnic minorities in early twentieth-century narratives of biological continuity in China, arguing that "there was a physical continuity [between the minorities and the Han] that precluded the elaboration of racial theories."[104] Because his analysis is focused on the supranational tensions between a white or black alien Other and a yellow, indigenous Self, Dikötter misses key aspects of the republican-era discourse and wrongly assumes that Sinic elites always perceived of their ethnic minorities only in terms of "sociocultural differences." In practice, racial and cultural typologies often overlapped, and the inherent ambiguity of the central concept of minzu lent itself to the blurring of the boundary between the various markers of difference. In the eyes of early Chinese nationalists, the very real differences between the Hui of Xinjiang, the Miao of Yunnan, and the Han of the central plains—be they linguistic, physical, economic, or cultural—were seen as major barriers to the independence and modernization of the Chinese nation-state. In this context, narratives of blood and descent were not only used to justify struggles against the white imperialists and the Japanese invaders, but were also inverted into a type of "Oriental Orientalism" or "internal Orientalism" aimed at domesticating a more familiar yet equally barbarian Other in order to incorporate them (both people and territory) into a bounded and homogeneous geo-body.[105] In constructing a myth of Zhonghua cultural antiquity and racial propinquity, Sinic intellectuals transposed the Orientalist discourse of white racial superiority onto China's own minority nationals—rationalizing a paternalistic nationality policy and a Darwinian narrative of Chinese historical development with a single, dominant Han majority at its center.

As already noted, Sun Yat-sen's discourse of minzuzhuyi intentionally blurred the lines between racial and cultural differences. The concept of minzu was first introduced into China in the context of the Han minzu's struggle against an alien and barbarian Manchu imperial court. Yet, following the 1911 Revolution, the lines of Chinese cultural and racial identity were redrawn to incorporate the territory and peoples of the old Qing empire. Inverting the Orientalist discourse of the Darwinian struggle among the world's race-states, Sun argued that China's very survival as a people depended on its own internal struggle for national unity. In his view, the evolutionarily unfit minorities were fated for assimilation into an organic and indivisible Zhonghua minzu that had the more advanced Han people at its core—transforming China's racial and cultural heterogeneity into a single homogeneous guozu. Unwilling and unable to wait for the slow workings of nature, nationalist intellectuals among both the Communist and Nationalist parties drew on history, archaeology, ethnography and other scientific disciplines to both construct and authenticate a myth of Zhonghua minzu antiquity and consanguinity, projecting Sun's future state of unity into the distant past. By fashioning a long history of racial and cultural interconnectedness among the peoples of the former Qing empire, Chinese nationalists hoped to reify the spatial and temporal boundaries of the nation as it struggled against foreign imperialism and domestic warlordism.

This effort to write the history of the nation persists. Historians in the PRC continue to construct elaborate webs of historical and racial interrelations aimed at discursively binding the current inhabitants of the country together, much as Xiong Shili and Lü Zhenyu did sixty years earlier. Like the racial nationalists, they trace the source of this unity to the beginnings of Chinese civilization, claiming that the advanced culture, productive forces, and population of the Han majority enabled it to absorb and assimilate the frontier minorities as far back as the Zhou dynasty (if not earlier) and led to the formation of a unified, multiethnic Zhonghua minzu as early as the Qin dynasty. At the same time, in their academic writings, PRC scholars echo Gu Jiegang in rejecting the monophyletic thesis of Chinese origin as unscientific and chauvinistic, claiming that the Zhonghua minzu has multiple yet indigenous origins and was formed, in the words of Fei Xiaotong, like a "snowball" as different minzus were added and molded around a single Han "coagulate core" (*ningju hexin*) as it rolled back and forth over the massive Chinese geo-body.[106] Here an arabesque of physical connections overshadows any single point, as this continual process of sinicization creates, in the words of the great twentieth-century historian Qian Mu, "a rope that never ends"—a braided, kernmantle rope wrapped around a solid Han racial and cultural core.[107]

Looking past Marx's theory of historical materialism and Stalin's rigid definition of a "nation," PRC scholars stress that the unity of the Zhonghua minzu is rooted in more than five thousand years of racial and cultural melding. "Despite China's vast territory and some inevitable conflict between feudal minzus," the historian Chen Yuning argues, "the process of racial intermixing is an irrefutable historical pattern on which the coagulability (*ningjuli*) of the Zhonghua minzu has been built."[108] In other words, the unity of the Chinese people is more than a subjective consciousness (as argued by Qi Sihe), a product of rising capitalism (Stalin), or a common evolutionary trajectory (Sun Yat-sen); it is fundamental to the very fabric of each Chinese family's history and racial makeup. In locating the source of this unity in China's glorious past, the Communist party-state has built on Republican-era narratives of the Yellow Emperor and Peking Man in its popular propaganda, repeatedly referring to them both as the progenitor of today's racial homogeneous Zhonghua minzu.[109] Though its vocabulary is now slightly different, the PRC has not changed the goal of its discourse on national unity (minzu tuanjie): to construct a myth of national belonging rooted in the perception of a common history, soil, and blood.

Conclusion

In his chapter in the authoritative *Cambridge History of China*, Joseph Fletcher perceptively outlined three important eighteenth-century changes that "set the course of China's subsequent history": the arrival of Western imperialism, the doubling of China's population, and the dramatic expansion of its territory under the Manchu Qing empire.[1] This book has attempted to demonstrate how these three interrelated developments shaped the form and structures of modern Chinese nationalism. These radical transformations helped fashion a spatially defined Chinese geo-body set firmly within the boundaries of the Qing empire and placed internal and external pressures on the new state to politically and culturally incorporate the once marginal frontier and its indigenous population into a more encompassing national imaginary.

Examining the strategies of political intervention and narratives of cultural innovation adopted by Sinic male elites, I have highlighted the significance of the frontier in the revolutionary agendas of the two major political parties in early twentieth-century China and analyzed how a political consensus on the boundaries, form, and meaning of Chinese sovereignty was forged by the GMD and the CCP over the course of the Republican period. By invoking the umbrella-like phrase, Zhonghua minzu, Chinese political leaders from Sun Yat-sen and Liang Qichao to Mao Zedong and Chiang Kai-shek signaled their intention to construct a firmly bounded and uniform community from the polyethnic embers of the Qing empire. But the messy reality of a divided and weak Republican state forced political leaders to accommodate (at least temporarily) the nation's ethnic variations while actively drawing on new technologies, categories, and practices of translated Asian modernity to weave together an inclusive narrative of national unfolding and belonging. Here the numeric imprecision of the term Zhonghua minzu assisted Sinic elites in subsuming the heterogeneity of the empire into the homogeneity of the nation-state. That said, it must be remembered that this imagined community has lived under a constant state of threat from the moment of its formation. To this day, many non-Han peoples reject their inclusion within the Chinese state while others ascribe to an array of subnational or transnational identities, which challenges the very substance and boundaries of the nation.

Here, by way of conclusion, I want to return briefly to the unusual resilience of China's national form. As noted in Chapter 1, among the large agrarian empires of the nineteenth-century, China alone survived the transition from empire to nation-state with its territory largely intact. The novel principle of national self-determination—with its insistence that state boundaries match ethnic and cultural boundaries—contributed to the breakup of the Austro-Hungarian and Ottoman empires into a series of small, ethnically based nation-states following the end of World War I. The Prussian and Russian empires met a similar fate, although each was temporarily reconstituted under the Nazi Third Reich and the Soviet Union, respectively. Yet the borders of the PRC are nearly identical to those of the Manchu Qing empire at the height of its power in 1800. Thus, despite its internal weakness and fragmentation, Republican China managed to somehow maintain the impression if not the reality of Chinese sovereignty over the vast territory of the Qing empire—one of the greatest accomplishments of the twentieth-century Chinese state. This apparent accident of history rests on a series of related but independent contingencies that belie the sense of inevitability conveyed in Chinese nationalist historiography, making the question of how the Chinese state managed to accomplish what no other agrarian empire could both a complex and intriguing one.

Many have dodged the question by claiming that the PRC is a "new Chinese empire," merely "garbed in the costume of a nation."[2] Others have argued that the collapse of the Qing empire produced not one, but several competing and inchoate visions of "China" held together rather awkwardly by an autocratic "nationless state" in desperate search of the "missing referent" for Zhongguo/China.[3] Yet, one is left wondering whether nation-states must always be constructed from the bottom up through popular will and shared vision, or whether there is an alternative model of nation building that can be fashioned, or more precisely hegemonically negotiated, from above by a transformative and totalitarian state complex—ultimately creating a "common sense" identity rooted in quotidian life, language, and emotion.[4] Perhaps it is time to bring the state (in all its complexity and diversity) into sharper focus in our discussions of nationalism, bearing in mind both Eric Hobsbawm's famous dictum—"nations do not make states and nationalism but the other way round"—and Anthony Smith's important reminder that "modern nations are not created ex nihilo" but rather rest on premodern antecedents, which in the case of China took the form of a strong bureaucratic and centralizing state.[5] Unlike the fragmented, aristocracy-based political system that developed in Europe after the fall of the Roman Empire, China, in the words of one historian, "sustained the vision and repeatedly recreated the reality of unified empire" based on a common set of institutional and ideological instruments of rule.[6] I have suggested that the modern nation-state in China came to be spatially constituted out of the historical memory of this common Sinic political community. Born in the era of high imperialism, when the ideologies of territorial sovereignty and imperial expansionism combined to gradually enclose once marginal borderlands, the Republican state chose to define Zhongguo/China as an eternal and bounded geo-body within the territorial boundaries of the last Qing empire. And it urgently devised strategies for the extension of state structures over the formally autonomous borderlands while widening its core Sinic identity to include the newly *nationalized* minorities in a shared myth of victimization and heroic resistance to foreign imperialism.

This spatial and temporal imaginary could not have survived the twentieth century if outsiders had not accepted its authenticity. While the West quibbled over (and nibbled at) its margins (and in the case of Japanese imperialism, its very core), the foreign powers also reinforced and codified the Chinese geo-body. In fact, the very principle of "territorial integrity," with its grounding in international law, was first introduced into China by foreign powers seeking to prevent any single country from dominating the Chinese landmass and triggering international instability.[7] The precise boundaries of the Chinese geo-body were disputed throughout the Republican period, but the Republic of China (despite its numerous changes in government) was widely viewed as the legitimate successor of "the Chinese Empire," as the Manchu Qing empire had long been known in the West. Such acceptance was formalized in 1922 when America, England, France, Italy, and five other powers (including Japan) agreed to "respect the sovereignty, the independence, and the territorial and administrative integrity of China" in an international treaty signed in Washington DC. Broad international support for Chinese sovereignty in Tibet, Xinjiang, and other frontier regions continues to this day even in the face of spirited opposition from (and strong popular support of) the Dalai Lama and other exiled minority leaders who oppose Beijing's rule.[8]

The failed attempt by Japan to create an independent Manchurian nation-state is evidence of how contested yet durable this Zhongguo/China super-sign was. As the traditional homeland of the Manchu people (the so-called Willow Palisade), Manchuria seemed to have a strong claim to historic nationhood outside the Chinese geo-body. Indeed, as Mark Elliott has shown, "Manchuria" was firmly entrenched as an independent toponym, region, and identity in the minds of most people (Chinese and Westerners alike) before its 1931 invasion by Japan.[9] Yet the Lytton Commission and subsequent League of Nations' resolution unambiguously recognized Chinese sovereignty, concluding that the region was "unalterably Chinese" and condemning Japan's imperial ambitions.[10] In other parts of the former Qing borderland, England, Russia, and other imperialist powers came to accept Chinese sovereignty, though it was sometimes couched in the more constrained language of "suzerainty." The political independence of Outer Mongolia, the one major exception, did not come easily. Although it was granted its independence in 1945 following a UN plebiscite, many Chinese nationalists continue to believe that it was unfairly stolen away from China by the Soviet Union. Mao repeatedly pushed Soviet leaders for its return during the 1950s and 1960s, and until recently maps issued by the Republic of China on Taiwan included Outer Mongolia within Chinese territory.[11] Today, the PRC has overseen the successful "return" (*huigui*) of Hong Kong and Macau to the "fatherland" and continues to isolate the Republic of China from the international community. Despite Taiwan's democratic revolution, Chen Shui-bian and other Taiwanese nationalists have found it exceedingly difficult to separate the island from the Zhongguo/China super-sign in the face of widespread international support for a "one China policy."

Yet international recognition alone does not prevent territorial disintegration. The dramatic collapse of the Soviet Union in 1991 produced fifteen new nation-states and made some wonder if China was fated to the same course. In *The New Chinese Empire*, Ross Terrill draws a number of comparisons between the PRC and the USSR, suggesting that China is "quite likely" to follow the Soviet Union in an "involuntary breakup" that would separated Tibet, Xinjiang, and possibly other frontier regions from China proper.[12] I am less certain, for a couple of factors that help explain the continued durability of the Chinese geo-body also make likely its reconstitution even if the CCP should implode.

As fictive as the static and primordial Chinese nation imagined in Beijing might be today, we cannot ignore the recurrence and continuity of a distinct Sinic political community and its largely successful appropriation (albeit in a fragmented and highly mythologized fashion) by the current Chinese state and many of its inhabitants. The modern category of Hanzu, with its bounded and racial overtones, was constituted from the shared political and cultural traditions of the sedentary inhabitants of what is today referred to as "China proper." As the work of numerous scholars has demonstrated, the perception of a common political and cultural identity in China can be traced back at least as far as the tenth century, if not earlier, and was forged over the *longue durée* at both an elite and popular level through the recurrence of a common ideographic script, centralized bureaucracy and education system, and shared set of cultural and religious rituals closely associated with a sedentary, patrilineal kinship system. This dynamic and fluid sense of community accommodated a rich variety of beliefs and practices at a popular level while remaining linked to a statewide elite discourse through the examination system and its local officials.[13] And though the Manchu Qing dynasty complicated this Sinic identity, it persisted and even strengthened. The useful yet slightly misleading debate over sinicization has shifted our focus away from the Manchu court's strong support for Confucian institutions and values. As John Shepherd has pointed out, it has also prevented us from distinguishing between "'acculturation' (the adoption of the customs and ways of life of another group) and 'assimilation' (an individual's identification with another group)."[14] The Manchus employed distinctly non-Sinic models of rulership in expanding the boundaries of their empire into Central Asia, but they also adopted Confucian institutions and ideology in ruling over the territories of the former Ming dynasty and even associated their empire with the

Zhongguo/China super-sign they inherited from the Ming. Indeed, late imperial China seemed to exhibit the type of "anonymous solidarity" that others have associated with the postindustrial state in Europe and America, forcing us to rethink the origins of modern Chinese nationalism.[15]

But we must look elsewhere to explain the heretofore successful incorporation of the non-Sinic populations into the new Chinese nation-state. Here, the major factor, I believe, is the demographic strength of this Sinic political community and its ability to rapidly overwhelm and forcefully colonize the far-flung borderlands following the collapse of the Qing empire in 1911. Numerically, the sedentary Sinic population has always hugely outnumbered the nomadic and semi-nomadic communities of the frontier; and today 92 percent of the PRC's population is officially classified as members of this Chinese or Han majority. In sharp contrast to the Czarist empire and its Soviet successors, most of whose inhabitants were identified as *inorodtsy* or non-Russian natives,[16] the Qing empire-cum-Zhonghua Republic were built on the perception (if not reality) of a demographic homogeneity, as commonly noted by its political leaders. On several occasions, Sun Yat-sen dismissed the frontier minorities as numerically insignificant, declaring in 1924 that despite the roughly ten million "nonnatives" (*wailai*), "the vast majority of China's 400 million people are entirely Hanzu: sharing a common blood, common language, common religion, and common customs—a single, pure minzu."[17] In 1939, Mao Zedong echoed this sentiment when he declared that more than 90 percent of China's 450 million people were ethnically Han.[18] The relatively small size of China's minority population led first the Guomindang and then the Chinese Communists to reject Lenin's federalist model as inappropriate for China's "unique" national form. Zhou Enlai explained in his report before the People's Political Consultative Conference on the eve of the PRC's establishment that a Soviet-style federation was unnecessary in China because the minority nationals represented less than 10 percent of the new state's entire population.[19] China's rejection of federalism, with its potential for "institutionalized multinationality," removed what several analysts have recently identified as one of the principal sources of the Soviet Union's collapse.[20] Roger Brubaker has convincingly shown that the "ethno-territorial federalism" of the Soviet Union provided "a ready-made template" for alternate claims to sovereignty after political autocracy eroded under Gorbachev.[21] But the PRC has constructed a more encompassing and totalitarian Zhonghua identity while implementing a far more circumscribed form of regional autonomy that leaves little room for any alternative claims of sovereignty.

Though the Guomindang Central Government and the CCP failed to exercise direct control over the frontier region during the Republican era, transfrontiersmen and their warlord patrons rapidly pushed a hybridized form of Sinic culture into the furthest corners of the former Qing borderlands, gradually allowing Chinese political and economic institutions to establish in their wake. Aided by what Owen Lattimore has astutely identified as the two principal technologies of modern territorial expansion—the rifle and the railway—Chinese pioneers permanently altered the centuries-old equilibrium between frontier nomads and sedentary farmers, establishing permanent Chinese communities and institutions on the former "wastelands" of the steppe and desert. After restrictions on frontier migration were removed during the late Qing, Chinese peasants, merchants, soldiers, and adventurers flowed into the borderlands. They quickly overwhelmed the indigenous inhabitants of Manchuria, Inner Mongolia, and Xinjiang, who were forced either to flee further into ecologically marginal land or to stay put and adapt to a sedentary or semi-sedentary lifestyle.[22] For obvious strategic and political reasons, the PRC continues to actively encourage and facilitate large transfers of Chinese settlers onto the frontier, dramatically altering the demographic shape of its geo-body. They are aided in this process by an increasingly sophisticated and comprehensive transportation network, which will include one hundred and ninety airports, two million kilometers of roads and one hundred thousand kilometers of rail track by 2010.[23]

Between 1890 and 1942, Manchuria experienced one of the largest inward migrations in human history. More than 8 million Chinese settlers and sojourners moved into the region—at a rate of half a million per year—completely transforming the ethnic profile of this once marginal borderland. Today, nearly 94 million Han live in the three northeastern provinces of Manchuria with a mere 7.4 million Manchus.[24] In Inner Mongolia, the Han to non-Han ratio rose from 4:1 to 9:1 during the first three decades of Communist rule; and in 2000 the 18.5 million Han represented 79 percent of the autonomous region's total population.[25] The story has been much the same in Xinjiang, where the Han population swelled to 7.5 million in 2000, making up 40.6 percent of the province's population (compared to only 6 percent in 1949). With the region's population divided among twelve different nationalities, only the Uyghurs at 45.2 percent still outnumber the Han; and that situation is likely to be reversed in the coming years. The paramilitary Xinjiang Production and Construction Corps has actively promoted Chinese colonization since its establishment in 1954, contributing to the doubling of the Han population during the 1990s.[26] Moreover, these PRC census figures, it is important to note, do not include military personnel and their families nor China's large floating population of itinerant labors; and thus the total Chinese population of each of these frontier regions is actually much higher.

At present, Xinjiang and Tibet remain the only territorial units where the Chinese do not constitute an outright majority. Yet the Tibetan government in exile, pointing to incomplete census data, claims that ethnic Tibetans are now a minority in "Greater Tibet" (the three historic Tibetan provinces of Amdo, Kham, and U-Tsang), where 7.5 million Chinese outnumber 6 million Tibetans.[27] According to government census figures for 2000, Tibetans still comprise 92.8 percent of the population of the Tibetan Autonomous Region (TAR), but only 49.8 percent in the territory claimed by the exile community, where the Han now represent 34.5 percent and other nationalities 15.7 percent.[28] Despite Beijing's claims that it restricts Han migration to the TAR, the recent completion of the world's highest railway, linking Lhasa with China proper, is likely to permanently tip the demographic balance in favor of the Chinese, making them the majority in every region of the country. Dubbed the "railway to new riches" by the Beijing media, the $3.7 billion line is expected to bring 2.5 million tons of goods and a million international and domestic visitors each year to this once-isolated mountain kingdom. With the resulting decline in the cost of living, better television and Internet connectivity, and more modern comforts of home, many of these Chinese sojourners will undoubtedly decide to stay over the coming years.[29]

The modern technologies of state building have given full play to the demographic hegemony and cultural cohesiveness of the Sinic majority, ensuring that today every square inch of PRC territory is carefully guarded by Chinese peasants, politicians, schoolteachers, entrepreneurs, and, most importantly, soldiers, while simultaneously decreasing the likelihood that China will disintegrate along similar lines as the Soviet Union. It would seem that with each passing day, China is becoming more "Chinese," and the *mythomoteur* of the frontier is fading into the red sun of the center. Yet, the past is not always a reliable guide to the future, and national and ethnic identity, as we have seen, can be a chameleon-like creature.

Notes

Introduction

1. Hobsbawm 1990, 66.
2. Diamond 1998, 322–33.
3. Fairbank 1992, 44–45.
4. Fei Xiaotong 1989, 1–2.
5. Diamond 1998, 323, original emphasis.
6. Crossley 1999; Di Cosmo 1998; Purdue 2005a; Lavely and Wong 1998, 717.
7. Richards 2003, 112–47; Lattimore 1937; Pan Chia-lin and Taeuber 1952.
8. My usage of the term "geo-body" follows Thongchai 1994.
9. B. Anderson 1991, 86.
10. Purdue 2001, 304.
11. Dreyer 2006, 279–80; Fei Xiaotong 1981, 23–25.
12. Jiang Ping 1994, 16.
13. Morris-Suzuki 1998, 4; Duara 2003; Handler 1988, 6–9.
14. Duara 1995; Duara 2003.
15. Turner 1962, 3.
16. Adelman and Aron 1999, 816.
17. M. Anderson 1996, 4, Anderson's italics.
18. Fitzgerald 1996a: 136.
19. Ibid., 107.
20. Tsu Jing 2005.
21. R. Wong 2006, 95.
22. Chatterjee (1986) was the first to theorize colonial nationalism as a "derivative discourse" of Western Orientalism.
23. Gladney 1994, 92–95; Harrell 1995a; Schein 2000.
24. Fei Xiaotong 1989, 1.
25. Cohen 1991, 114–25; Schwarcz 1986; Tu Wei-ming 1994.
26. Harrison 2000, 240–43, 83–85; Harrison 2001.
27. Harrison 2000, 83–85; Cohen 1991, 126.

28. Duara 2003, 9–40.
29. See, for example, Lattimore 1940 and 1962; Forbes 1986; Goldstein 1989; Benson 1990; Lipman 1998; Millward 1998; Purdue 2005a; Mitter 2000; Atwood 2002; Tighe 2005; Reardon-Anderson 2005; Giersch 2006; Crossley, Siu, and Sutton 2006; Gladney 1991, 1994, and 1996; Harrell 1995a and 2001; Brown 1996 and 2004; Cheung Siu-woo 1995 and 2003; Schein 2000; Kulp 2000; Bulag 2002 and 2006; Rossabi 2004.
30. L. Liu 1995, 1–42.
31. Ibid., 26.
32. Keyes 2002, 1182; Lin Yaohua 1963; Dikötter 1992, 108–10; Crossley 1990b, 19–20.
33. Morris-Suzuki 1998, 204; Duara 1995, 36n10.
34. Chatterjee 1986, vii.
35. Furth 1976; Crossley 1990b, 19.
36. Chen Liankai [1988] 1994, 27–69.
37. Chow Kai-wing 1997, 39. During the 1900s, Zhang and other revolutionaries used the terms *Hanzu*, *Hanren*, *Hanzhong*, and *Han renzhong* interchangeably to refer to their more circumscribed Sinic identity, one that explicitly excluded the Manchus. By the 1911 Revolution, Hanzu emerged as the neologism of choice, allowing for the distinction between a larger "yellow race" (*huangzhong*) and the Hanzu as a branch or lineage of the yellow race (see Chow Kai-wing 2001, 54–55).
38. Gladney 1991, 82–83; Chow Kai-wing 2001, 47–48, 76.
39. Zhao Gang 2006, 6; Chen Liankai [1988] 1994, 32–34; L. Liu 2004, 75–81.
40. Zhao Gang 2006, 10–14. See also the language employed in the international treaties signed between the Qing dynasty and the West that are contained in Tian Tao 1999.
41. Liang Qichao 1901, 3, as cited in L. Liu 2004, 76–77.
42. The earliest usage of Zhonghua minzu that I have been able to locate is Liang Qichao's 1907 essay investigating the role of the Chinese minzu in history (see Liang Qichao 1907, 2). Here Liang employs the term as a synonym for the Hanzu, which nearly all turn-of-the-century Chinese intellectuals used to refer to the Sinic cultural and political community. Yet, unlike the anti-Manchuists, Liang went to great lengths in other essays to demonstrate the inclusive, racially composite nature of the Zhonghua minzu and how it fused together a number of different lineages living within the territorial confines of Qing China. In doing so, he paved the way for the term's widespread usage among Republican-era elites and the repositioning of the Hanzu as the racial "backbone" (*gugan*) of a territorially bounded yet multiethnic Zhonghua minzu (see Liang Qichao 1922, 1–34).
43. Chen Liankai [1988] 1994, 66–69; Lipman 2002, 117–18.
44. Dikötter 2002, 496.
45. B. Anderson 1991, 19.
46. Adelman and Aron 1999, 814–16.
47. Luo Zhufeng 1997, 3: 6467; Ma Ruheng and Ma Dazheng 1994, 85–101; Purdue 2005a, 409–61.

48. Thierry 1989, 77.
49. My translation of guozu, a term that literally means "state lineage,"as "race-state" is an attempt to articulate the widespread semantic convergence of race, nation, and state among turn-of-the-century intellectuals. Numerous scholars have pointed out how these concepts were used interchangeably among Western elites prior to the end of World War I (see Duara 1995, 22). The same was true of Chinese intellectuals who used what is today rendered in English as "race" (*zhongzu*), "nation" or "nationality" (*minzu*), and "state" (*guojia*) interchangeably to refer to a group of territorially and genealogically distinct peoples locked in a battle for evolutionary survival with other race-states.
50. Liang Qichao 1903a, 12; Hobsbawm 1990, 31–45.
51. Liang Qichao 1903a, 11.
52. Jin Binggao 1987, 47.
53. Crossley 2005.
54. Eley and Suny 1996, 8.
55. Sun Yat-sen 1921a, 24.
56. Harrell 1996, 4.
57. Cited in Hobsbawm 1990, 12.
58. B. Anderson 1991, 204–6.

Chapter 1

1. Kaldor 2004, 161–77.
2. Gellner 1983; Smith 2000; Hobsbawm 1990; Greenfeld 1992.
3. Hobsbawm 1990, 66.
4. Ibid., 137, 66n37.
5. Gellner 1983, 16, 108, 109n1, 141.
6. B. Anderson 1991, 113.
7. B. Anderson 2001, 31.
8. Chatterjee 2000, 940.
9. Purdue 1998a, 285. Also see Purdue 2005b, 183–86.
10. Crossley 1990b, 1–34. See also Fairbank and Teng 1954; and Levenson 1964–65 (with recent criticism of the "impact/response" model of sinology in Cohen 1984; and Farquhar and Hevia 1993).
11. Fiskesjö 2006, 19.
12. Fairbank 1968.
13. Levenson 1964–65.
14. Hsiao Kung-chuan 1979, 24.
15. Ibid., 25.
16. Ibid. The culturalism-to-nationalism thesis remains influential, albeit in a qualified fashion, with James Townsend (1996) and Zhao Suisheng (2004, 40–44) recently rearticulating its significance.
17. Lattimore 1932; Lattimore 1937.

18. Eberhard 1982; Fletcher 1995; Franke and Twitchett 1994; Rossabi 1975 and 1988; Wakeman 1985; Barfield 1989.
19. Chen Yinke 1977; Xiang Da 1979.
20. Harrell 1995a; Millward 1996. Also see Millward 1998; Di Cosmo 2002; Di Cosmo and Wyatt 2003; Mair 2005; Crossley, Siu, and Sutton 2006; Giersch 2006.
21. Langlois 1981, 15; Also see Serruys 1987, 137–90.
22. Elliott 2001, 5–6; Crossley 1990a; Rhoads 2000.
23. Crossley 1990b, 2. See also Brown 2004, 30–34.
24. Gladney 1991; Elliott 2006, 32–35; and Duara 1995, 49–54. On ethnicity as a boundary process, see Barth 1969.
25. Levenson 1964–65, 96.
26. Duara 1995, 8.
27. Ibid., 57.
28. Duara 1995, 60. Also see Dow Tsung-I 1982; Dikötter 1992; Huang Guangxue 1995, 51–92; Q. Wang 1999; Ebrey 1996; Poo Mu-chou 2005.
29. Yang Lien-sheng 1968, 26.
30. Legge 1961, 355. The exclusivist representation in the Zuo commentary is closely associated with the unique form of environmental determinism that grew out of the proto-Sinic yin-yang, and five-element epistemologies of the Zhou period (see Henderson 1984). This system of "correlative thought" that came to underpin imperial Confucianism during the Han dynasty linked celestial phenomena, climatic conditions, human physiognomy, and nature in a cosmology that situated differences in regional qi (psycho-physical energy) that produced distinct xing (nature). While in the inclusivist narrative of political community, one's xing was transformable, the exclusivist tradition argued that the differences in nature and lifestyle associated with different climatic zones created an unbridgeable chasm between the frontier and the harmonious qi of the central plains. As the *Book of Rites* (*Liji*) states, "The Chinese and the barbarians of the five directions all have their own xing which cannot be transposed (*tuiyi*)" (Liu Dianjue and Chen Fangzheng 1992, 34).
31. Cited in Yang Lien-sheng 1968, 28. See also Yu Ying-shih 1967; Barfield 1989; Di Cosmo 2002.
32. Cited in Pusey 1983, 322.
33. Cited in Huan Kuan 1931, 77.
34. Ebrey 1996, 26.
35. We must resist the temptation, however, to read modern taxonomies of race backward into premodern markers of difference (see Dikötter 1992, 3; Dikötter 2002, 497). While the imperial tradition of ethnocentrism contributed to the modern discourse of race, these markers operated within a separate episteme in which qi (psycho-physical energies) differed from *xue* (blood), and *zulei* (kinship) was distinct from *zhongzu* (race).
36. See the writings of Emile Durkheim, Edmund Leach, and Fredrik Barth; on the rich genealogy of "ethnicity" as an analytical concept, see S. Jones 1997.
37. Cited in Gladney 1996, 471.

38. Duara 1996, 49-54. For a discussion of the various elements of this Sinic cultural complex, see Ng-Quinn 1993, 53–61; Watson 1993, 80–103; Ho Ping-Ti 1976, 547–54; Ebrey 1996; R. Wong 2006, 93–4; Harrison 2001, 10–25. Fitzgerald refers to imperial China's "proto-nation" as "the wedding of internal differentiation with formal unity." He goes onto to explain: "That is, it consisted of a series of distinct vertical communities within large regional blocs which were integrated internally by ties of customs and commerce, which were associated with one another through common ritual practices and a common textual tradition, and which were bound to the state through the working of the imperial bureaucracy and the placement of imperial garrisons" (Fitzgerald 1994, 27).
39. Johnson, Nathan, and Rawski 1985; Watson and Rawski 1988; Watson 1993; Tu Wei-ming 1994.
40. R. Wong, Huters, and Yu 1997; Sutton 2007; and other contributors to the January 2007 special issue of *Modern China.*
41. Melissa Brown's recent article is an important exception. However, I believe she underestimates the role of culture in identity formation, treating Han, or Chinese identity, more broadly as a type of false consciousness forcefully imposed by state elites for coldly calculated political and economic gain. To my mind, this does not help to explain the unique durability, recurrence, and lived social reality of a distinctly Sinic identity, especially when faced with the numerous changes in the political and economic foundations of Chinese society over the centuries, nor the popular basis and raw emotion of modern Chinese nationalism (see Brown 2007).
42. Millward and Dunnell 2004, 1–12; Rawski 1996, 833; Waley-Cohen 2004.
43. See the various essays gathered together in Struve 2004, including Jack A. Goldstone's critique of the Qing state as early modern in "Neither Late Imperial nor Early Modern: Efflorescences and the Qing Formation in World History," 242–302.
44. Crossley 1999, 55–88.
45. Cited in de Bary and Lufrano 2000, 34.
46. Cited in Li Guoqi 1981, 22. Also see Dikötter 1992, 1–30.
47. Crossley 1999, 248.
48. Cited in de Bary and Lufrano 2000, 34.
49. Cited in Li Guoqi 1981, 22; Also see Liu Xianxiao 1965, 418–19.
50. Mair 1985.
51. Langlois 1980.
52. Purdue 2005a, 122–27. Compare here Morris Rossabi's comment, "Khubilai succeeded admirably in charting a cultural policy that affirmed the Mongol heritage, accepted certain Chinese practices, and strove for universalism. As with his religious policy, Khubilai presented himself in different guises to the different audiences he faced" (1988, 175), with Crossley's 1999 account of Manchu rule.
53. Elliott 2001, 39–171.
54. Millward 1998, 194-203; Crossley 1999, 1–52; Purdue 2005a, 15–299. Yet as Millward and Newby point out, this five-fold multiethnic empire was "never

fully developed or unambiguously propagated" (Millward and Newby 2006, 128).

55. Zhao Gang 2006, 3–10. Emperor Qianlong stated in 1755, "There exists a view of China (Zhongguo), according to which non-Han people cannot become China's subjects and their land cannot be integrated into the territory of China. This does not represent our dynasty's understanding of China, but is instead that of the earlier Han, Tang, Song and Ming dynasties" (Cited in Zhao Gang 2006, 4).
56. Hostetler 2001, 74; Also see Purdue 1998b and 2005a, 409–61; Struve 2004; Karl 2002.
57. Millward 1998, 194-203; Crossley 1999; Rawski 1996.
58. Millward and Dunnell 2004, 2; Rawski 1996, 835.
59. Di Cosmo 1998, 294–96; Ning Chia 1993, 60–62.
60. Rawski 2004, 19; Crossley 1999, 9–18 passim; Rawski 1996, 835.
61. Millward 2004, 101.
62. On Qing policies towards the south, see Cheung 1995; Hostetler 2001, 101–57; Rowe 2001; Atwill 2005; Giersch 2006; Sutton 2006.
63. Elliott 2001, 275–333.
64. Crossley 1989; Elliott 2001, 333–44.
65. Crossley 1999, 222. See also Rhoads 2000; Elliott 2001, 345–61.
66. Spence 1996, 160–63, 181–82.
67. Zarrow 2006, 114–16. Also see Duara 1995, 20–21, 139–44; Chow Kai-wing 2001.
68. Duara 1995, 17–23; Hobsbawm 1990, 31–45; Connor 1984, 5–20. On the impact of the "Darwinian revolution" in Europe, see Stocking 1968.
69. Quotation adapted from Pusey 1983, 64. Long before Darwin, the Chinese philosopher Xunzi (ca. 310–237 BCE) had argued that it was man's ability to group that marked him off from animals and other barbarians (see Pusey 1983, 239; Schwartz 1964; Chang Hao 1972, 105–12).
70. Sun Yat-sen 1894b and 1895; Leibold 2004, 166–67.
71. See Chow Kai-wing 1997, 39–40; Dikötter 1992, 61–96; Onogawa Hidemi 1981, 246–52; Laitinen 1990; Chow Kai-wing 2001.
72. Tsou Jung [1903] 1968, 108–9. On the Subao affair, see Lust's introduction, pp. 3–17 in the former; Bergère 1998, 110–11; Schiffrin 1968, 265–74.
73. Rhoads 2000, 114–16 passim; Zhao Gang 2006, 18–23.
74. Tuttle 2005, 59, drawing on the research of Rhoads 2000, 114–16.
75. Liang Qichao 1903a, 11–20.
76. Liang Qichao 1901, 2; Liang Qichao 1903a, 6; Liang Qichao 1907, 2.
77. Liang Qichao 1901, 3–7.
78. Liang Qichao 1922, 4.
79. Liang Qichao 1901, 3–7.
80. Zhao Gang 2006, 15–18; Tang Xiaobing 1996, 43–74; Hostetler 2001, 51–80; Ishikawa Yoshihiro 2004.
81. Cited in Rhoads 2000, 3.
82. Liang Qichao 1903b, 76.
83. Zarrow 2006, 132.

84. Liang Qichao 1903b, 76. In terms of the non-Han inhabitants of China, Liang's political thought could hardly be described as "deeply anti-hegemonic" (cf. Zarrow 2006, 113 passim). Liang favored unity among the races of China—with the superior Hanzu at its center—rather than their equality as a modern policy of multiculturalism would assert.
85. Crossley 1999, 353; Crossley 2005, 146.
86. Two classic examples of this tendency are Scalapino and Yu (1985), in which Chapter 3 is titled "Liang Qichao and the Defense of Reform" (pp. 109–47) and Chapter 4, "Sun Yat-sen and the Revolutionary Movement" (pp. 148–230), and the extremely influential textbook of Fairbank and Reischauer (1978) that portrays Sun and Liang as the two competing "protagonists" of the 1911 Revolution (see pp. 406–11).
87. Leibold 2004, 166–78.
88. Sun Yat-sen [1900] 1990, 17–28. The map was completed by Sun in 1899 and eventually published in Tokyo in late 1900. On the context of the map's usage of *Zhina* for China, see L. Liu 2004, 78–79.
89. Sun Yat-sen 1894b: 20.
90. Cited in Chong Key Ray 1969, 262. For the original text, see Sun Yat-sen 1894a, 14.
91. Sun Yat-sen 1917–19, 157–493. It was first published in English in 1922 under the title, *The International Development of China* (New York: G. P. Putnam's Sons and London: Knickerbocker, 1922).
92. Sun Yat-sen 1905, 288–89. Sun describes minzuzhuyi in the foreword as some vague evolutionary force that transformed the Roman Empire into the various independent countries of Europe and would now eliminate the evil Manchu dictatorship and revitalize China.
93. Sun Yat-sen 1906b, 296–318.
94. Cited in Zhang Yong 2002, 107.
95. Cited in Pusey 1983, 331. For the original text, see Zhang Binglin [1907] 1982, 333.
96. Admitting, like many other commentators, that Zhang Binglin's polemics were "difficult to explain," Crossley suggests that his anti-Manchu racism was more than a political strategy, while Peter Zarrow has described anti-Manchuism as "signs of uncontrolled anger and hurt," a type of "traumatized historical memory" (see Crossley 1999, 356–57; Zarrow 2004, 69). In a similar vain, Chang Hao refers to Zhang Binglin's conception of "perfect nationalism" as a "moral vision of universal racial-ethnic liberation," a concept that not only applied to the Chinese Muslims but also the Indians, Burmese, Vietnamese, and other Asian peoples who had traditionally suffered under Chinese hegemony and were now being colonized by the Western powers (see Chang Hao 1987, 113). Others, however, have pointed to a marked tension in Zhang's thought between the desire to construct, on the one hand, an ethnically pure Han republic and to maintain, if not expand, Qing territorial boundaries on the other hand. Take, for example, Zhang's assertion in his 1907 article, "Explaining the Republic of China" (*Zhonghua minguo jie*), that "from the standpoint of regulating the borders of the Republic of China, the two prefectures Vietnam and

Korea must be recovered and the district Burma follows slightly behind in priority; as for Tibet, the Hui areas and Mongolia, let them decide themselves if they want to be incorporated or rejected" (Cited in Lodén 1996, 281). Wong Young-tsu has noted that while Zhang was "sympathetic to the aspirations of self-determination for all races, including the Manchus," he also realized that it was impractical to identify all Manchu people and send them back to Manchuria. At different times Zhang suggested everything from their extermination to the creation of an autonomous state of Manchuria or their naturalization and assimilation into a homogeneous Han republic (see Wong Young-tsu 1989, 61–66).

97. Liang Qichao 1903b, 76. On Liang's impressions of America, see Liang Qichao [1903c] 1957.
98. Zhang Yong 2002, 108; Yu Xintun 1981, 501–16.
99. Sun Yat-sen 1906a, 325.
100. Ibid., 324.
101. Michael Gasster was one of the first scholars to pick up on this predicament, referring to it as a choice between Scylla and Charybdis, or what Pamela Crossley has more recently labeled, the "conceptual crisis" of late Qing nationalism (see Gasster 1969, 82; Crossley 1999, 344).
102. Wang Jingwei [1905] 1977, 82–114.
103. Sun Yat-sen 1924c, 187.
104. Ibid., 239.
105. Rhoads 2000, 173–30; Esherick 1976.
106. Zhang Yong 2002, 110. On the five-color flag and other alternatives, see Fitzgerald 1996a, 181–90; Harrison 2000, 100–102.
107. Sun Yat-sen 1912c, 2.
108. "Waiwubu zhi geguo gongshi zhaoan" [1912] 1996, 7–8; "Zhonghua minguo linshi xianfa" 1912, 327.
109. Rhoads 2000, 205–28.
110. Cited in Ibid., 226.
111. "Yuan dazongtong ling gonghe zhengfu bushe lifan zhuanbu, Meng, Zang, Huijiang, shiyi guibing neiwubu jieguan" 1912, 453.
112. Harrison 2000, 16–24.
113. "Yuan dazongtong banfa chuanyu" 1912, 441.
114. See Onon and Pritchitt 1989; Paine 1996, 288–90; Mehra 1974, 132–38.
115. Goldstein 1989, 59; "Mengzangju nicheng 'daiyu Xizang tiaoli dagang'" 1913, 49.
116. Mehra 1974, 131–32; Paine 1996, 290–92; Young 1977, 182; Tighe 2005, 197–200.
117. Paine 1996, 292–95.
118. B. Anderson 1991, 7.
119. On the anti-Russian, anti-Mongolian independence movement of the winter of 1912–13, see Pavlovsky 1949, 50–54; Young 1977, 182–83; Li Yushu 1968, 42–50.
120. Song Jiaoren [1913] 1981, 449–50.

121. Sun Yat-sen 1912a: 544–49. The translation has been adapted from Wei, Myers, and Gillian 1994, 111–17.
122. Dai Jitao [1912] 1991, 1252.
123. Duara 1995, 184.
124. Pavlovsky 1949, 52.
125. Chiang Kai-shek [1912] 1937, 13.
126. Zhonggong zhongyang wenxian yanjiushi, ed. 1993, 1: 24. Cited in Liu Xiaoyuan 2004, 27.
127. Li Dazhao 1917, 288.
128. On the development of popular sovereignty and concepts of citizenship in China as they relate to nationalism, see Fitzgerald 1996a; Fogel and Zarrow 1997; Crossley 2005.
129. Noting a similar shift in Meiji Japan, Tessa Morris-Suzuki speaks about "the transfer of difference from geography ('foreignness') to history ('backwardness')" (see Morris-Suzuki 1998, 29).
130. Sun Yat-sen 1912b, 399.
131. Sun Yat-sen 1919, 187–88. Here Sun was echoing Frederick Jackson Turner: "In the crucible of the frontier the immigrants were Americanized, liberated, and fused into a mixed race, English in neither nationality nor characteristics" (see Turner [1893] 1962, 23).
132. From its inception, Sun Yat-sen fought against the five-color national flag and the notion of a republic of five races (see Leibold 2004, 179–81).
133. Sun Yat-sen 1921b, 475.
134. Goldstein 1989, 68–88; Richardson 1962, 107–13.
135. Paine 1996, 298–305.
136. Cited in Elleman 1997, 85.
137. Duara 2003, 51–59.
138. Kirby 1997, 437. The recognition of Outer Mongolian independence in 1945, of course, is the one glaring exception (see Liu Xiaoyuan 2006).
139. Maier 2000. Yet, as Prasenjit Duara (1997) rightfully points out, the territorial nation was continually challenged by, and at times forced to, "domesticate" a variety of "transnational imaginings," such as pan-Asianism or communism.
140. R. Wong 2000, 109–10; Kirby 2005, 105.
141. Crossley 2005, 139; Terrill 2003, 9. See also Purdue 2005b, 188–90. In the words of Lucian Pye, China remains a "civilization pretending to be a nation" (Pye 1990, 58).
142. Crossley 1999: 33.
143. R. Wong 1997, 174–77; R. Wong 2006, 98.
144. Fitzgerald 1996b, 57 (original emphasis).
145. Esherick 1976, 153–58; Duara 1993, 9–35; Chesneaux 1969, 96–137; Zhang Yong 2002, 106–9; Karl 1998, 1096–1118; Duara 1997, 1030–51.
146. Purdue 2005a, 335–36 passim.
147. Karl 2002; Duara 1995, 3–82; Tang Xiaobing 1996.
148. Zhao Suisheng 2004, 49.
149. Tang Xiaobing 1996, 38 passim. See also Ishikawa Yoshihiro 2004.

150. L. Liu 2004, 75–81; Zhao Gang 2006. It is important to note, however, that there were some exceptions to this growing acceptance, such as the great late Qing scholar-official Wei Yuan who limited his definition of Zhongguo to the seventeen provinces of China proper and the three eastern provinces of Manchuria, but specifically excluded Mongolia, Tibet, and Xinjiang from Zhongguo in his nineteenth-century *Shengwuji* (*Record of Military Accomplishments*) (see Wei Yuan 1984, vol. 2, 93).

Chapter 2

1. Jiang Ping 1994, 110. Not surprisingly, Sun Yat-sen's principle of minzuzhuyi is a good deal more nuanced than this depiction would lead us to believe. I have argued elsewhere that a persistent social evolutionary logic dominated Sun's positioning of the ethnic minorities in his principle of minzuzhuyi (see Leibold 2004).
2. Notable exceptions include So Wai-chor 2003; Tuttle 2005; Lin Hsiao-ting 2002 and 2006.
3. Crossley 2005, 149–50.
4. Mackerras 1994, 59.
5. Zhao Suisheng 2004, 172. For another highly influential example, see the widely cited Dreyer 1976, 15–41; and for a more recent examples, Rhoads 2000, 275–76; Bulag 2002, 110; Harrell 2001, 29–31.
6. Elleman 1997, 60–63. Also see Huang Guangxue 1995, 90–92; Kindermann 1989, 55–56; Duara 1995, 142; Li Shiyue and Zhao Shiyuan 1984; and Gregor and Chang 1979.
7. Chiang Kai-shek [1944] 1986, or as translated, Chiang Kai-shek 1947. On Tao Xisheng's authorship, see Dirlik 1976, 305.
8. Liu Xiaoyuan 2004, 24. Liu slightly modifies this position in his latest book, acknowledging a degree of "political realism" in GMD policy during the 1930s and 1940s, but still finds its government "wanting" and "unimaginative" in its efforts to maintain the inclusive ideology and policies of the Qing court (See Liu Xiaoyuan 2006, 30, 42, 197).
9. The term "transfrontiersmen" was coined by Philip Curtin during the 1960s to refer to those frontier communities who adopt a hybrid cultural and economic way of life at the intersections of major civilizations. Frederic Wakeman (1986) employed the term in his analysis of the Chinese settlers in Liaodong who assisted the Manchus in seizing power in 1644. In contrast, my usage of the term refers to both Chinese and minority members of a uniquely plural frontier society that was more clearly identified by its commitment to agricultural development and the economic modernization of frontier space than it was with a fixed cultural, ethnic, or linguistic identity.
10. Harrell 1995b, 3–36, quote from p. 7.
11. Lenin [1920] 1960–70.
12. Sun Yat-sen 1924d, 118–19.

13. For example, Colin Mackerras states, "Sun Yat-sen's policies in the latter part of his life were based rather closely on those of the Soviet Union, which meant that he was inclined to accept notions of self-determination and autonomy for the minorities" (Mackerras 1995, 9). For other notable examples, see Benson 1990, 11–12; Wei, Myers, and Gillin 1994, xxi; Dreyer 1976, 17.
14. See Connor 1984, 67–68; Hong Quanhu 1980, 117–50.
15. Sun Yat-sen 1921b, 480.
16. Ibid.
17. See, for example, Sun Yat-sen 1924d, 118–19.
18. On Wilson's and Lenin's interpretation and usage of the term national self-determination, see Heater 1994; Connor 1984, 118–19.
19. Sun Yat-sen 1923, 458. Sun revealed this information in reply to the charge by veteran GMD party member Deng Zeru that CCP leader Chen Duxiu had drafted the manifesto.
20. "Gongchan guoji shining weiyuanhui zhuxituan guanyu Zhongguo minzu jiefang yundong he Guomindang wenti de jueyi" 1923, 342–45.
21. Borodin 1924, 448–50.
22. Borodin 1924, 471.
23. Sun Yat-sen 1924a, 127.
24. Sun Yat-sen 1924d, 119. See also Jin Binggao 1987, 47.
25. Sun Yat-sen 1924d, 119. Both Borodin and Soviet ambassador to Beijing, Leo Karakhan, expressed their frustration with the vaguely worded and contradictory nature of the GMD pledge. Although, Karakhan believed the final language already represented a tremendous victory for the Comintern in shaping the ideological direction of the GMD (see Borodin 1924, 425; Karakhan 1924, 418).
26. Borodin 1924, 465–66.
27. Elleman 1997, 68.
28. On the Sun-Joffe Accord and the negotiations leading up to Comintern support for the Guomindang, see Whiting 1953; Tang 1959; Elleman 1997, 85–113. Prior to his death in 1925, Sun had good reason to trust the intentions of the Soviet Union toward Outer Mongolia. Not only had Moscow unconditionally renounced all Czarist unequal treaties and territorial concession in China, but its Beijing emissaries made repeated promises to return Outer Mongolia to Chinese rule following the cessation of White Russian hostilities in the region. This promise was personally conveyed to Sun on a number of occasions between 1923 and 1924 by Borodin and other Moscow representatives and was eventually confirmed when the Soviet Union formally agreed that Outer Mongolia was "an integral part of the Republic of China" and promised to respect "China's sovereignty therein" in the Sino-Soviet Treaty of May 31, 1924 (see Weigh 1959, 349–53; Liu Xiaoyuan 2006, 26–27). Liu Xiaoyuan (45–77) also provides a detailed analysis of the Soviet Union's "two-Mongolia" policy, which aimed to eventually create an independent Outer Mongolian satellite while preventing pan-Mongolian nationalism and preserving Inner Mongolia as an autonomous region under Chinese rule.
29. Zou Lu 1938, 636n9.

30. Sun Yat-sen 1924b, 107; Karakhan 1923, 389.
31. Sun Yat-sen 1924c, 200.
32. Sun Yat-sen 1921b, 473.
33. Sun Yat-sen 1921a, 24.
34. See Eastman 1991, 1–19; McCord 1999; McCord 1993.
35. "Disanci quanguo daibiao dahui xuanyan" 1929, 624.
36. "Guomin zhengfu Mengzang weiyuanhui zuzhifa" 1928; "Guanyu Mengzang zhi jueyi an" 1929; "Xiuzheng Mengzang weiyuanhui zushifa" 1932. Also see Zhang Xingtang 1962, 125–26.
37. Ma Ruheng and Zhao Yuntian 1991, 1–14; Ma Ruheng and Ma Dazheng 1994.
38. A survey of the numerous administrative plans and regulations drafted by the CMTA reveals a striking similarity in both language and policy with the Qing's Lifanyuan. Take, for example, the series of laws created to codify, regulate, and administer the systematic visits of minority princes, headmen, and religious personnel to the capital, or the regulations governing the bestowing of state titles and awards on loyal frontier princes and officials, or the countless laws meant to ensure state supervision of the banners, Lamaist temples, and other frontier institutions. See "Mengzang Xinjiang huibu laijing zhenjin renyuan zhaodai guize" 1934; "Meng Zang Huijiang ge difang changguan ji ge zongjiao lingdao renyuan laijing guanjian lijie dan" 1934; "Mengzang Huijiang ge difang changguan ji ge zongjiao lingdao renyuan laijing zhanguan shanglai banfa" 1935; "Guanli lama simiao tiaolie" 1935; "Lama jiangzheng banfa" 1936; "Mengzang bianqu renyuan renyong tiaolie" 1937.
39. Lattimore 1938, 245 passim.
40. Zhang Ji 1928.
41. Wei Xiaotao 1928, 37.
42. See the documents and explanations included in the entry on the "Menggu dahui bihui" 1930, 754–58; Hao Weimin 1997, 170.
43. "Guomin zhengfu gongbu Mengguo meng-bu-qi zuzhifa" 1931.
44. Zuo Zuohua 1929, 7.
45. Lattimore 1932, 321.
46. In my reconstruction of the Bailingmiao autonomous movement, I have drawn on recently reprinted Nanjing government documents from the Second Historical Archive and the following secondary and primary sources: Tan Tiwu 1934, 117–92; Chen Jianfu 1934; Huang Fengsheng 1935; Lu Minghui 1980; Hao Weimin 1997, 159–85; Lattimore 1936a, 427–39; Lattimore 1936b, 440–55; Tighe 2005, 229–55. The analysis of Sechin Jagchid, who at the time was a young follower and soon-to-be secretary of De Wang, is also particularly valuable, although not free from bias (see, in particular, Jagchid 1999; Jagchid 1979, 229–45; Jagchid 1954, 2: 251–66).
47. De Wang 1933a, 89–91.
48. "Zizhi zhengfu zuzhi dagang" (Outline for the organization of an autonomous government), October 1933, in Chen Jianfu 1934, 36–38.
49. De Wang 1933b, 108–10.

50. See Lu Minghui 1980, 39–42; Ni Wang 1933, 95; Zhuo Wang 1933, 96; Fu Zuoyi 1933a, 103–4; Fu Zuoyi 1933e, 105.
51. Fu Zuoyi 1933b, 105–7; Fu Zuoyi 1933d, 107; Fu Zuoyi 1933c, 107–8.
52. Wen Tingxiang, et al., "Diyici jianyi shu" (First petition), October 1933?, in Chen Jianfu 1934, 25–36. Also see Tighe 2005, 232–55.
53. Wen Tingxiang, et al., "Dierci jianyi shu" (Second petition), November 1933?, in Chen Jianfu 1934, 36–42.
54. Fu Zuoyi 1933g, 91–94; "Mengzang weiyuanhui guanyu Menggu zizhi zhibiao zhiben yijuean" 1933, 64.
55. "Neizhengbu deng guanyu Menggu zizhi an huigao" 1933, 63–64. The plan was signed by the heads of the Ministry of Interior, CMTA, and Central Military Staff.
56. On the Nanjing government's struggle to gain control over the provinces, see Eastman 1991, 9–15.
57. Fu Zuoyi 1933f, 100–101.
58. See "Xingzhengyuan guanyu gaige Menggu difang xingzheng xitong fangan" in Chen Jianfu 1934, 77–79.
59. See Lu Minghui 1980, 43–44.
60. "Xingzhengyuan wei guanyu Menggu zizhi wenti bugao" 1933, 68–69.
61. "Huang buzhang Zhao fuweiyuanzhang zai Bailingmiao yu Neimeng zizhi huiyi shangding Menggu zizhi banfa" 1933, 116–18; Lu Minghui 1980, 54–57.
62. Eastman 1974, 112.
63. Hao Weimin 1997, 184.
64. For a copy of the Taiyuan plan, see "Guomin zhengfu wenguanchu wei niding Neimeng zizhi banfa zhi Xingzheng Yuan gonghan" 1934, 69–72.
65. "Neimeng zizhi banfa shiyi xiang" (Eleven Methods for Inner Mongolian Autonomy), January 17, 1934, in Chen Jianfu 1934, 68–69.
66. Lu Minghui 1980, 63–64.
67. Eastman 1974, 130–39.
68. Chen Jianfu 1934, 68–73; Lu Minghui 1980, 61–62; Hao Weimin 1997, 184; Jagchid 1999, 92–93.
69. Chiang Kai-shek was said to have exercised final approval on Wu Heling's eight-point plan, insisting only on the insertion of "local" between the words "Mongolian" and "autonomy" in the title of the new law and autonomous organization (see Jagchid 1999, 94).
70. Chiang Kai-shek 1934, 108.
71. Ibid., 107.
72. Sun Tzu 1963, 83.
73. Lattimore 1936a, 436–38; Jagchid 1954, 2: 270; Tighe 2005, 240–47.
74. Lu Minghui 1980, 77–86; Jagchid 1999, 103–5, 106–7.
75. Lattimore 1936a, 438. After the end of World War II, Fu Zuoyi blocked yet another attempt by the GMD to implement regional ethnic autonomy for the Inner Mongols (see Liu Xiaoyuan 2006, 216–18).
76. Kapp 1973, 62.

77. For a short biography of Liu Wenhui, see Boorman and Howard 1967, 2: 417–19.
78. Chen Zhiming 1933, 88–91.
79. On Kesang Tsering, see Goldstein, Sherap, and Siebenschuh 2004, 10; Tuttle 2005, 147–48.
80. On the establishment and composition of the Xikang Special Administrative Committee, see *Xikang tequ zhengwu weiyuanhui zhounian zhuankan* 1929.
81. Feng Youzhi 1992, 115–20; Chen Zhiming 1933, 103.
82. On the supposed accomplishments of Liu's regime as of late 1929 and its future plans, see Du Xiangrong 1929, 69–82. With a population density of only two people per square li, one writer claimed that at least one million starving Sichuan peasants could farm "virgin land" in Xikang over the next ten years (Chen Zhongwei 1930, 99). A 1929 report released by Liu's administration outlined extensive opportunities for *kenhuang* (the opening up of wasteland) in Xikang (see Mei Xinfu [1934] 1970, 230–37).
83. Feng Youzhi 1992, 299; Lin Hsiao-ting 2006, 58–59. On Liu Wenhui's encouragement of opium cultivation and other aspects of his Xikang regime, see Barnett 1963, 215–29.
84. The population figures are from Sichuan sheng kangding xian zhi bianzuan weiyuanhui 1995, 73; Mei Xinfu [1934] 1970, 13–14.
85. Hu Horu 1929, i–ii.
86. For other examples, see Lipman 1997, 175 passim; Bulag 2002, 29–62.
87. Dong Tiaofu 1929, 1–18 and 1–46.
88. Ibid., 1.1: 1–18,1.2: 1–32, with quotes from 1.2: 31, 32.
89. Ibid., 1.2: 32–46.
90. On Zhao Erfeng, see Sperling 2003. In a number of ways, Zhao Erfeng's attempts to colonize Kham serve as a useful precedent and base on which Liu Wenhui's Xikang regime developed.
91. On the Simla Conference and events leading up to it, see Li Tieh-Tseng 1956, 135–42; Goldstein 1989, 68–88; Richardson 1962, 107–13.
92. On premodern Tibet's relations with China, see Van Walt van Praag 1987, 1–25.
93. On the transition between premodern and modern notions of space and national sovereignty, see Thongchai 1994, 62–112 passim; and on how it played out in the context of Manchuria, see Elliott 2000, 603–46.
94. Mehra 1974, 162–244; Chen Zhiming 1933, 72–82.
95. On the Targye Monastery incident, see Mei Xinfu [1934] 1970, 97–99; Goldstein 1989, 221–24; Lin Hsiao-ting 2006, 61.
96. See Chen Zhiming 1933, 102–9; Feng Youzhi 1992, 109–11.
97. See the letter from CMTA chairman Shi Qingyang to the Dalai Lama cited in Chen Zhiming 1933, 104–5. The Dalai Lama also sought the mediation of the British, who dispatched Lieutenant Colonel J. L. R. Weir, political officer in Sikkim, to Lhasa to consult on the matter. Believing that the border issue remained "the outstanding obstacle to a permanent settlement between the two countries," Weir redrafted the McMahon line to recognize the "existing rights" of the Tibetan government to Derge, Nyarong, and Sangen, now

including them as part of "Outer Tibet." Yet, the British decided that "the time was not opportune for pressing the Chinese government," and Weir's draft was never presented to the Chinese. As British official Hugh Richardson admitted, "the influence of Liu Wen-hui prevented the Central Government from getting a footing there [Xikang]" (see Richardson 1998, 573; McGranahan 2003, 282).

98. On Liu Wenhui's counter-offensive and the October 10, 1932, Truce Agreement, see Feng Youzhi 1992, 121–26.
99. McGranahan 2003, 282.
100. Du Xiangrong 1929, 80–81.
101. Tuttle 2005, 172–76.
102. Fan Xiaofang, Bao Dongbo, and Li Chuanli 1992, 342–43.
103. Lin Hsiao-ting 2002, 329–30.
104. Liu Manqing [1933] 1987, 119; Goldstein 1989, 213–21, 223–24.
105. On Huang Musong's mission to Tibet, see Sun Zihe 1995, 235–78; Lin Hsiao-ting 2002 and 2006, 71–85; Goldstein 1989, 213–51; Li Tieh-Tseng 1956, 168–72.
106. Huang Musong 1935, 262.
107. Huang Musong 1934b, 211; Huang Musong 1934d, 211–12.
108. Wang Jingwei 1934a, 220.
109. Huang Musong 1934f, 223–24. Also see Huang Musong 1934g, 222–23.
110. According to Lin Hsiao-ting, "In early October, in a telegram to Huang from Nanking, Chiang Kai-shek instructed him to exercise extreme caution in dealing with the border issues and strongly suggested that, if necessary, he should shelve the issue" (see Lin Hsiao-ting 2002, 335).
111. Wang Jingwei 1934e, 226; Wang Jingwei 1934d, 226–27.
112. For a summary of the National Assembly's response, see Huang Musong 1934c, 229–30. For the complete text, see Huang Musong 1934a, 232–33. On Huang Musong's orders to leave Lhasa, see Wang Jingwei 1934f, 234.
113. Huang Musong 1934h, 238–39.
114. Wang Jingwei 1934c, 240. Along with the border issue, one of the other sticking points in the negotiations was the return of the Panchen Lama to Tibet, who had been in exile in China since 1923. The Tibetans were worried that the Panchen Lama would force his way back into Tibet (potentially with a large Chinese military escort) and thus insisted that he return via India where the British could monitor his entrance rather than overland through China. The Chinese repeatedly ensured the Tibetans that the Panchen Lama would not need a large military escort if he return overland from China. In this cable, Wang Jingwei gives General Huang the authority to negotiate the exact nature of the Panchen Lama's return. On the politics of the Panchen Lama's return, see Lin Hsiao-ting 2006, 86–104.
115. Wang Jingwei 1934b, 241.
116. Goldstein 1989, 238–39; Sun Zihe 1995, 267–68.
117. Cited in Goldstein 1989, 236–39.
118. Huang Musong 1934e, 242–43.
119. Lin Hsiao-ting 2006, 85, x.

120. Ibid., 85.
121. Liu Xiaoyuan 2004, 89–90.
122. Duara 1995, 159.
123. Chatterjee 1986 and 1993; Bhabha 1990; Duara 1995.
124. Duara 1995, 177–204; Duara 1993, 9–35; Fitzgerald 1994, 39–42; Fitzgerald 1996a, 147–79.
125. Duara 1993, 9.
126. Bulag 2002, 29–62; Bulag 2006, 9; Mitter 1999.
127. Lipman 1997.
128. Friedman 1979; Friedman 1987.
129. Tambiah 1976, 102–31 and as also cited in Tuttle 2005, 52.
130. White 1991. David Bello and Pat Giersch have pointed to the existence of a similar middle ground in Southern Yunnan as the Qing state came face to face with the fiercely independent tribal cultures on its remote frontier (Bello 2005; Giersch 2006), while Prasenjit Duara has recently explored competing narratives of sovereignty and authenticity in the Manchurian borderland of the early twentieth century (Duara 2003). The concept of a liminal borderland that is historically positioned in between the premodern imperial frontier and the clearly defined territorial boundaries of the modern nation-state was developed by Adelman and Aron 1999, 814–41
131. Ma Ruheng and Zhao Yuntian 1991, 1.
132. See, for example, Liu Wenhui's entry in Ren Yimin 1986, 1: 101–7; Zhang Xinwu 1995. Also see Bulag 2006, 18–28. This oversimplification of Guomindang national minority policy has been perpetuated in Western language scholarship on China with June Teufel Dreyer, for example, claiming in her now classic *China's Forty Million* that Liu Wenhui and Fu Zuoyi "had a reputation for equal treatment of minorities and for making an honest attempt to deal with their grievances," while, in comparison, the Guomindang's "inept" minority policy greatly contributed to its poor reputation along the frontier (Dreyer 1976, 40). Similarly, Liu Xiaoyuan has dubbed Fu Zuoyi a "'frontier mandarin' who dutifully carried out the GMD's policies" and reflected *its* "Great Hanism" (Liu Xiaoyuan 2004, 135).

Chapter 3

1. Connor 1984, 67–100.
2. Ibid., 6.
3. See, for example, the now classic Johnson 1962.
4. Moseley 1965, 17.
5. Terrill 2003, 41–43, 184, 202 passim.
6. Liu Xiaoyuan 2004, 3–4.
7. Connor 1984, 45; Carrère d'Encausse 1992, 71–98.
8. Paine 1996, 321–22; Elleman 1997, 85–116.

9. The manifesto and political programme of the CCP's Second National Party Congress, which was written under Maring's guidance in 1922, described the Mongols, Tibetans, and Hui as "distinct minzus" and called for their temporary "autonomy" (*zizhi*) from feudal China. Following the liberation of the Chinese people, the party called for the creation of a "voluntary federation" (*ziyou lianbang*) to bring the frontier and China proper together in a Federated Zhonghua Republic (*Zhonghua lianbang gongheguo*). By the following year, at the party's Third National Congress, the creation of a Federated Republic was removed from the party's program and replaced with an insistence that China's relationship with Tibet, Mongolia, Xinjiang, Qinghai, and other frontier regions must be guided by the principle of national self-determination (minzu zijue). See Leibold 2003, 112–16, 127; Liu Xiaoyuan 2004, 27–50; Liu Xiaoyuan 2006, 80–89.
10. Gao Junyu 1922, 19.
11. Ibid., 20.
12. Chen Duxiu 1922b, 6. I question the listed date of this document, June 30, 1922. It seems unlikely that Chen's report to the Fourth Comintern Congress, which did not meet until late November, was written during the middle of the CCP's Second Party Congress. More likely, it appears that it was written after Chen's arrival in Moscow. It is also interesting to note that this controversial document is not included in any of Chen Duxiu's collected works.
13. Chen Duxiu [1922a] 1993, 424.
14. Zou Lu 1938, 636n9.
15. Zeng Qi 1925a, 1–3; On Zeng Qi and the YCP, see Levine 1992 and Chan Lau Kit-ching 1972. See also "Zhongguo guomindang dierci quanguo daibiao dahui xuanyan" [Western Hills clique] 1926, 1: 399.
16. Hu Hanmin [1929] 1980, 2: 461.
17. "Zhongguo guomindang xuanyan xuanbu Zhongguo gongchandang zuizhuang" 1927, 480; Zeng Qi 1925b, 1; Chen Qitian [1929] 1988, 56–69; Liu Zhangda 1926, 1–2; Hu Guowei 1925b, 2.
18. Zou Lu 1930, 3: 28. Also see Ibid., 3: 29–32, 39–41.
19. See, for example, Hu Guowei 1925a, 2.
20. On the protracted negotiations over the Sino-Soviet Accord and its eventual signing on May 31, 1924, see Elleman 1997, 85, 103–4, 162, 206; Paine 1996, 321–32.
21. Chen Duxiu 1924a, 597.
22. Ibid.
23. Compare Chen Duxiu 1924b, 673; Chen Duxiu 1924a, 597; Chen Duxiu [1922a] 1993, 424.
24. Li first used the term minzu zijue in his January 1, 1919, attack on Japanese "pan-Asianism" (*dayaxiyazhuyi*). In substitution of the "encroachism" (*qinlüezhuyi*) central to Japan's pan-Asianism, Li called for the creation of a "new Asianism" (*xinyaxiyazhuyi*) that advocated the "national self-determinism" (*minzu zijuezhuyi*) of all Asian countries (see Li Dazhao 1919a, 253–55; also see Li Dazhao 1919b, 74–78). For a more detailed discussion of Li Dazhao's treatment of the national question and how he diverged significantly from Chen

Duxiu and Qu Qiubai, the two leaders of the party during the 1920s, see Leibold 2003, 164–74.

25. Li Dazhao 1917, 302–3.
26. Li Dazhao 1925, 41.
27. Ibid.
28. "Zhongguo gongchandang diliuci quanguo daibiao dahui tongguo de zhengzhi jueyian" 1928, 86; "Zhongguo gongchandang diliuci quanguo daibiao dahui guanyu minzu wenti de jueyian" 1928, 87.
29. Ibid. On this being the first usage of shaoshu minzu, see Jin Binggao 1987, 47.
30. Ibid.
31. McLane 1958, 9.
32. Carrère d'Encausse 1992, 173–94; Pipes 1993, 436–89.
33. "Zhonggong zhongyang gei Mengwei de xin" 1929, 103–4. On the organization of the Inner Mongolian Special Committee, see Hao Weimin 1997, 196–99. On the PRPIM, see Atwood 2002.
34. "Zhonggong zhongyang gei Yunnan shengwei de zhishixin" 1929, 110.
35. Connor 1984, 73–77; Liu Xiaoyuan 2004, 51–75, esp. 70–71. In a 1931 cable to the party, the Comintern demanded "the [Chinese] soviet government ought to implement a Bolshevik nationality policy toward the minority nationalities in accordance with the principles of equality and national self-determination" (Liu Xiaoyuan 2004: 70-71).
36. Liu Xiaoyuan 2004, 72.
37. "Zhonghua suweiai gongheguo guojia genbenfa (xianfa) dagang caoan" 1930, 123.
38. "Zhonghua suweiai gongheguo xianfa dagang" 1931, 166. Much of this ambiguity has been ironed out of English translations of the 1931 constitution. See, for example, the translation included in Brandt 1952, 220–21, where no distinction is made between the terms ruoxiao minzu and shaoshu minzu, and the right of the minority nationals to form their own zizhi quyu (autonomous region) is incorrectly translated as "their own state."
39. The careful and deliberate choice of words here and their marked departure from Mif's 1930 draft seems to contradict Liu Xiaoyuan's assertion that the CCP has a "primitive" understanding of Soviet Russia's important distinction between large, territorial-based "nations" or "nationalities" (*narod, narodnost', natsional'nost,'* or *natsiia* in Russian and *minzu, ruoxiao minzu,* or *xiao minzu* in Chinese), who were more fully developed and thus theoretically had the right to national secession, and smaller (diasporic or highly primitive and marginalized) groups of "minority nationals" (*nacional'noe men'shinstvo* in Russian and *shaoshu minzu* in Chinese) who lived scattered among other demographically dominate peoples and thus deserved cultural autonomy at best. See Hirsch 2005, 35–45, 282–92 and Carrère d'Encausse 1992, 71–98, 173–94 on the process by which this distinction was worked out in the Soviet Union. In contrast to Liu's claim that the CCP used the blanket term "minority nationality" for "all the non-Han groups of China," other terms were clearly employed during the 1920s and 1930s, suggesting an understanding, perhaps incomplete, of the types of distinctions that Soviet ethnologists were employing back in the USSR (see Liu Xiaoyuan 2004, 68).

40. "Zhonghua suweiai gongheguo xianfa dagang" 1931, 166.
41. "Guanyu Zhongguo lingnei shaoshu minzu wenti de jueyi'an" 1931, 169–70.
42. Ibid., 170. Carrère d'Encausse 1992, 112.
43. "Zhonggong zhongyang liujie wuzhong quanhui zhengzhi jueyi'an" 1934, 205.
44. "Zhonghua suweiai gongheguo xianfa dagang" 1934, 209.
45. Stalin [1913] 1940, 5–7, 50–51.
46. Carrère d'Encausse 1992, 92.
47. Li Dazhao 1919a, 253.
48. Mao Zedong 1934, 210–11, emphasis added.
49. See Lin Huaming 1996, 2046.
50. Liu Xiaoyuan 2004, 78.
51. See Pantsov 2000, 41–52; Lenin [1920] 1960–70.
52. Van Slyke 1967.
53. "Hunansheng diyici nongmin daibiao dahui jiefang Miao-Yao jueyi'an" 1926, 52. Also see Zhou Xiyin 1996, 2040–46.
54. On some of the difficulties the Red Army faced among the minorities, see "Zhongguo gong-nong hongjun erfangmian jun zhengzhibu guanyu er-liu juntuan changzheng de zhengzhi gongzuo zongjie baogao" 1936, 436–40; Snow 1968, 194–204; Salisbury 1985, 106-8, 196-200.
55. In referring to the Lolos, the CCP also used *Yimin* (Yi people) and *Yizu* (Yi race). Note here that the Communists are still using the "Yi," or "barbarian" character, that beginning in the Ming dynasty was used as a generic term for the non-Sinic peoples of southwestern China. After the Communists came to power in 1949, a new homophonous character, meaning a sacrificial wine vessel, was used to identify the newly invented and bounded Yi nationality. See Bradley 2001, 201.
56. Salisbury 1985, 188–97.
57. Mao Zedong 1934, 210.
58. Cited in Lin Huaming 1996, 2047.
59. "Zhongguo gong-nong hongjun zhengzhibu guanyu Miao-Yao minzu zhong gongzuo yuanze de zhishi" 1934, 244–46.
60. "Zhongguo gong-nong hongjun zong zhengzhibu guanyu zhuyi zhengqu yimin de gongzuo" 1935, 258.
61. See "Qiangdu Daduhe de xuanchuan gudong gongzuo" 1935, 265; "Nuli shixian zhong zhengzhibu tichu de sida haozhao" 1935, 267. One of the more colorful legends of the Long March—the so-called Chicken-Blood Oath between Sichuan native Liu Bocheng, the Red Army's "one eyed dragon," and Xiao Yedan, a Lolo chieftain—represented one of the successes in implementing the united front tactic. According to Long March lore, as the Red Army was racing north toward the Dadu River, they ran smack into several hundred wildly chanting Yi tribesmen armed with homemade guns, sticks, spears, and clubs. When they refused to allow the Communists safe passage, the "chieftain" of the Red Army's vanguard regiment, Liu Bocheng, asked to meet with the Yi chieftain. At the edge of a crystal mountain lake, Liu Bocheng drank a bowl full of cock's blood to seal an alliance of sworn brotherhood between himself

and Xiao Yedan, thereby ensuring the Red Army's rapid march northward and successful crossing of the Dadu River ahead of Chiang's troops (see Salisbury 1985, 196–200; Wilson 1971, 136-50; and its use in CCP propaganda in Chen Changfeng 1986, 40–43). Once stripped of its mythology, however, the incident takes on a more prosaic significance. As Karen Gernant has demonstrated, Liu Bocheng essentially bought the allegiance of the Guji faction of the Yi people with dozens of guns and nearly one thousand silver dollars, while Xiao Yedan, for his part, found the money and guns useful in his struggle against the rival Luohong faction, while also hoping that the Red Army might even assist him in attacking his enemy (Gernant 1980, 278–81).

62. Mao Zedong 1935, 38. Part of the split between Mao and Zhang Guotao, whose First and Fourth Route Armies reunited in Western Sichuan in 1935, was the perceived ability of the party to mobilize and work among the Tibetan masses of Western Sichuan. While Zhang Guotao called for the construction of a revolutionary base area among the Tibetans, Mao asserted that the party's "relationship with the Fan [Tibetan] people [was] extremely bad" and called instead for the Red Army to continue its march northward in order that it might link up with the Soviet Union in the far northwest (see Liu Xiaoyuan 2004, 91–99).
63. Cited in McLane 1958, 160.
64. "Zhongguo gongchandang zhongyang weiyuanhui he Zhonghua suweiai zhongyang zhengfu wei kangri jiuguo gao quanti tongbao shu" 1935, 301–4.
65. "Minzu tongyixian de jiben yuance" 1936, 525; Mao Zedong 1938c, 215.
66. Mao Zedong 1938b, 129.
67. Wylie 1980.
68. Mao Zedong 1938a, cited in Ibid., 90.
69. Mao Zedong 1938d, 603.
70. Mao Zedong 1940, 663, 706.
71. Mao Zedong 1938a, 219.
72. Ibid., 219-20.
73. Ibid.
74. For a short bio of Li Weihan and discussion of his relationship with Mao, see Klein and Clark 1971, 1: 534–40.
75. On the NWC and the National Question Research Office, see Li Weihan 1986, 451–59; Liu Chun 1988, 228–46.
76. After joining the party in 1936, Liu Chun studied under Li at the Central Party School and then worked for him in the Organization Department of the CCP. See the short bio in the preface to Liu Chun 1996, 1–2.
77. See Li Weihan 1986, 455. The collection of documents was entitled *Daliu Yilai* (*Since the Six Party Congress*). According to Liu Chun, Mao personally read and made some revisions to both documents before stating that he "agreed with [their] principles" and before having the party secretariat distribute them among Central Committee members for their approval. See Liu Chun 1996, 296, 307.
78. Minzu wenti yanjiushi 1941, 910. According to *Minzu wenti wenxian huibian*, the pamphlet was first published on April 15, 1941; yet both its version and

the one published by the Nationalities Publishing Bureau in 1980 are based on an October 4, 1946, reprint published by the CCP's Southern Shandong Hui Advancement Society.

79. "Zhonggong zhongyang xibei gongzuo weiyuanhui guanyu Huihui minzu wenti de tigang" 1940, 652.
80. Minzu wenti yanjiushi [1941?] 1993, 29–30. Liu Chun drafted this pamphlet sometime during early 1941; but for reasons that are not entirely clear, the manuscript was not printed until 1946 when it was published by the Inner Mongolian Printing Press in Zhangjiakou.
81. "Zhonggong zhongyang xibei gongzuo weiyuanhui guanyu kangzhan zhong Menggu minzu wenti tigang" 1940, 659.
82. Minzu wenti yanjiushi [1941?] 1993, 27; Li Weihan 1940, 851.
83. "Zhonggong zhongyang guanyu shaoshu minzu duli zizhu de yuanze de zhishi" 1937, 579.
84. Li Weihan 1940, 852. For original see Stalin [1913] 1940, 18.
85. Ibid., 851.
86. See, for example, "Zhonghua suweiai gongheguo zhongyang zhengfu, Zhongguo gongnong hongjun geming junshi weiyuanhui kangri jiuguo xuanyan" 1935, 320; "Zhonghua suweiai zhongyang zhengfu dui Huizu renmin de xuanyan" 1936, 366; Yang Song 1938, 766; "Zhonggong zhongyang wei gongbu guogong hezuo xuanyan" 1937, 548.
87. See, for example, Minzu wenti yanjiushi 1941, 913; Minzu wenti yanjiushi [1941?] 1993, 29.
88. Zhang Wentian 1938, 605–6.
89. "Guanyu Sui-Meng gongzuo de jueding" 1938, 612–13.
90. Wang Jiaxiang 1936, 506. See also "Zhonggong zhongyang guanyu Neimeng gongzuo de zhishixin" 1936, 416.
91. Liu Xiao 1936, 511–13.
92. "Zhonggong zhongyang guanyu Menggu gongzuo de zhishixin" 1937, 546.
93. Ibid.
94. See "Zhonggong zhongyang xibei gongzuo weiyuanhui guanyu kangzhan zhong Menggu minzu wenti tigang" 1940, 663; Minzu wenti yanjiushi [1941?] 1993, 38.
95. Minzu wenti yanjiushi [1941?] 1993, 57.
96. "Zhonggong zhongyang guanyu Menggu gongzuo de zhishixin" 1937, 545.
97. See "Zhonggong zhongyang xibei gongzuo weiyuanhui guanyu kangzhan zhong Menggu minzu wenti tigang" 1940, 664–67.
98. Hao Weimin 1997, 391–92. Liu Xiaoyuan (2006, 104) quotes one CCP commander as stating that the establishment of the base area cost "countless people's lives" and argues that it failed in its original objective of opening up a supply and communication channel with the Soviet Union and the MPR.
99. Li Weihan 1986, 462–64.
100. On the Nationality Institute, see both Hao Weimin 1997, 387–89 and Li Weihan 1986, 459–61.
101. Mao Zedong 1938a, 225–27.
102. Mao Zedong 1940, 689.

103. Mao Zedong 1945, 1084.
104. Zhou Enlai 1944, 729.
105. Ibid., 730–31. National self-determination (minzu zijue) seems to have reappeared as a useful propaganda slogan in the CCP's mobilization work among the minorities following the defeat of the Japanese in 1945. In its internal communication, the party continued to insist on the share destiny of the entire Zhonghua minzu, arguing the current civil war against the GMD, like the previous struggle against the Japanese, did not favor the splitting apart of different Zhonghua peoples. See, for example, "Zhonggong zhongyang guanyu Neimeng minzu wenti yingqu shenzhong taidu de zhishidian" 1946. Yet in their face-to-face negotiations with local minority elites, the CCP still held out the possibility of a future state of independence when conditions permitted. See, for example, "Neimeng renmin daibaio huiyi kaimu dianli kongqian shengda" 1947; "Zhonggong Guizhen bianqu dangwei guanyu xuanchuan fan Jiang tongyi zhanxian qishiwu tiao kouhao de zhibiao" 1947. Only after the victory of the CCP became apparent did the party center explicitly prohibit its members from using the slogan, with the Central Party Propaganda Office of the New China News Agency issuing the following warning in October 1949: "Today the question of each minority's 'self-determination' should not be stressed any further. . . . In the past, during the period of the civil war, for the sake of strengthening the minorities' opposition to the Guomindang's reactionary rule, we emphasized this slogan. This was correct at the time. But today the situation has fundamentally changed. . . . For the sake of completing our state's great purpose of unification, for the sake of opposing the conspiracy of imperialists and other running dogs to divide China's nationality unity, we should not stress this slogan in the domestic national question . . ." (cited in Gladney 1991, 89–90; see also Liu Chun 1951–52, 87).
106. Mao Zedong 1949, 422. The other two weapons were the party and the army.
107. See Mao Zedong 1925.
108. For examples of the party's post-1945 efforts in Inner Mongolia, see Leibold 2003, 348–73; Liu Xiaoyuan 2006, 115–282. And in Tibet, see Goldstein, Sherap, and Siebenschuh 2004; Lin Hsiao-ting 2006, 159–98.
109. Minzu wenti yanjiushi [1941?] 1993, 27; Li Weihan 1940, 851; and as summarized in Liu Chun 1950–51, 75–76.
110. The story of the PRC's efforts to regain sovereignty over Taiwan, Hong Kong, and Macau after the 1949 Revolution is well documented. Yet, the Communist party-state's attitude toward Outer Mongolian independence has received less scholarly attention in English. Aiming to redress this imbalance, Liu Xiaoyuan's path-breaking new study examines the role of Mongolia in China's domestic and international affairs. He details a marked shift in CCP discourse on Outer Mongolia during the Sino-Japanese War. In his 1936 interview with Edgar Snow, Mao echoed previous party policy in stating, "When the People's Revolution has been victorious in China, the Outer Mongolian republic will automatically become a part of the Chinese federation, at its own will" (Snow 1968, 444). Yet, Liu demonstrates how after 1937, "the MPR was

not only linked to a Communist China in the future but also to the GMD's official China at present" (Liu Xiaoyuan 2006, 108). Following the Communist victory in 1949, Mao used Outer Mongolia as a bargaining chip in his negotiations with Stalin for a new treaty of friendship between China and the Soviet Union (happy, in Liu's words, to "leave the credit for 'losing' Mongolia entirely to his Nationalist predecessors"). But the issue of Outer Mongolia continued to serve as an irritant in Sino-Soviet relations with Mao famously declaring in 1964 that the Soviet Union had used the ploy of Outer Mongolian independence to unjustly sever the region from Chinese sovereignty—a point reiterated by Deng Xiaoping during his historic 1989 summit with Mikhail Gorbachev and today kept alive on Chinese internet sites (see Liu Xiaoyuan 2006, 376–421 and Radchenko 2003).

111. Hoston 1994, 3–17, 361–401.
112. Ibid., 8.
113. Liu Chun 1950–51, 81, emphasis added.

Chapter 4

1. Hobsbawm 1983, 4–5.
2. Duara 2003, 17, 191–93. Mu-chou Poo (2005, 157) and others have argued the reverse: that "ethnicity and racial consciousness, with its intense emphasis on physical features (yellow, white, black, etc.) has taken precedence over cultural factors such as language, religion, or customs" in the construction of modern Chinese identity. Like prewar Japan (see Weiner 1997, 99–100), the increased popularity of minzu in early twentieth-century intellectual discourse in China did not reduce the importance of physiological markers or notions of biological consanguinity in the construction of ethnic and national identity.
3. Dikötter 1996, 590–91.
4. Ibid., 591.
5. Hon Tze-ki 2004, 506–8; Q. Wang 2000; A. Schneider 2002.
6. D. Wang 1997.
7. Duara 1995, 51–82.
8. Schwarcz 1986, 195–239.
9. Shao Yuanchong 1931, 235.
10. Guo Yingjie 2004, 21–23; Schwarcz 1986, 214–22.
11. Chen Lifu [1934] 1935, 177.
12. Sun Yat-sen 1924c, 247.
13. Shao Yuanchong 1933a, 365–69; 1932b, 254–305.
14. Shao Yuanchong 1930, 211–18; 1936, 421–27.
15. Shao Yuanchong 1934a, 392.
16. Shao Yuanchong 1934b, 218–19.
17. Shao Yuanchong 1933b, 377.
18. Cited in Li Juanli 1992, 337.
19. "Xin Yaxiya zhi shiming" 1930, n.p.

20. Duara 2003, 171–243.
21. Wang Fan-sen 2000, 149.
22. Asano Risaburō 1928; Yano Jin'ichi 1931; Wang Jianmin 2002, 180; Jagchid 1999, 60–124; Duara 2003, 182–83.
23. Shao Dan 2002, 16–68; Duara 2003, 53–59; 180–88.
24. Li Ji 1932. Li Ji's abridged summary of Fu Sinian's report was published in English in 1932 as *Manchuria in History: A Summary*. The original Chinese language version, titled *Dongbei shigang: gudai zhi Dongbei* (*A Draft History of the Northeast: The Ancient Northeast*), was never published. See Wang Fan-sen 2000, 149–50; Shao Dan 2002, 42.
25. Wang Fan-sen 2000, 150–52.
26. East-Asiatic Economic Investigation Bureau 1932, 16–38; Kawakami 1933.
27. Sun Yat-sen 1924c, 188.
28. Leibold 2004.
29. Sun Yat-sen 1924c, 184–85.
30. Ibid., 188.
31. Sun Yat-sen 1919, 187.
32. Hu Boxuan 1932.
33. See Shao Yuanchong 1932; Dai Jitao 1931.
34. See Chen Guofu [1943] 1965.
35. Sun Yat-sen 1924c, 187.
36. Zhou Kuntian 1941, 10.
37. Dai Jitao 1934, 89.
38. In a fashion remarkably similar to the Republican-era racial nationalists, Sima Qian employed a narrative of descent to incorporate the non-Chinese "barbarians," chiefly the nomadic Xiongnu federation, into Chinese history and its moral cosmology. He began his chapter on the Xiongnu in the *Shiji* by highlighting the Sinic origin of these nomadic barbarians: "The ancestor of the Xiongnu was a descendant of the ruling clan of the Xia dynasty, named Shunwei." Thus creating an ethnogenealogy that united the Han and Xiongnu people in a bond of fictive kinship. See Di Cosmo, 2002, 294–304.
39. Shao Yuanchong 1933c, 369.
40. Ibid.
41. Dikötter 1996, 592–94; Chow Kai-wing 1997, 38–40 and 2001.
42. In attempting to construct a racially distinct Hanzu, the anti-Manchu revolutionaries were the first group of modern Chinese intellectuals to use the Yellow Emperor in fashioning a narrative of common descent. The major difference between the uses of the Yellow Emperor by the late Qing revolutionaries and by Republican-era racial nationalists was the scope of this myth of common origin. For the Qing revolutionaries, the Manchus were purposefully excluded from the nation, while post-1911 intellectuals stretched the boundaries of the nation to explicitly include the Manchus and other frontier minorities of the former Qing dynasty (see Shen Shun-Chiao 1997; Chow Kai-wing 1997 and 2001; Liu Li 1999; Leibold 2003, 381–94; Zarrow 2006, 132–44). As Frank Dikötter (1996, 591) has pointed out, this discourse of race in Republican China should not be misconstrued as a "derivative discourse" of a more

"authentic" discourse in the West, but rather viewed as "the active reconfiguration of indigenous modes of representation," such as ancestor worship and lineages groups, that were central to the construction of social identity in premodern China. It is also interesting to note that some reformers within the late Qing dynasty also employed the myth of racial descent to rationalize their construction of China as a unitary yet multiethnic empire. Zhao Gang (2006, 22) cites a 1907 memorial from Dong Fangsan (a licentiate from Fulu county in Hubei) that stated, "The Manchu, Mongols, and Han are different branches of a single tree. Originally, they came from the same ancestor and they will develop into a unity (*yi er shu, shu er yi*)."

43. Shen Shun-Chiao 1997.
44. Liu Li 1999.
45. L. Schneider 1971, 188–217; Tay Lian Soo 1987, 3–11; Hon Tze-ki 1996, 323–26.
46. Gu Jiegang 1923a.
47. Gu Jiegang 1921, 35.
48. Gu Jiegang 1923b, 59–60.
49. Gu Jiegang 1933, 5–7.
50. Ibid., 6.
51. Cited in Gu Hong 1998, 3.
52. L. Schneider 1971, 261.
53. Cited in Hon Tze-ki 1996, 323.
54. Gu Jiegang 1926, 89.
55. Gu Jiegang 1938, 21.
56. Zhang Yinglin 1925.
57. Cited in Wang Fan-sen 2000, 118.
58. Gu Chao 1994, 172; Hon Tze-ki 1996, 321–23.
59. Dai Jitao, cited in Gu Chao 1994, 172.
60. Ibid.
61. During the Republican period, the distinction between these disciplines was blurred in China—particularly in the case of archaeology (today translated as *kaoguxue*) and paleoanthropology (*gurenleixue*), with the term *kaoguxue* used for both. It was the use of the Western scientific methods of field excavation and surveying that characterized kaoguxue and geology (*dizhixue*) rather than the type of materials being examined. For a history of the development of *kaoguxue* in China, see Chen Xingcan 1997.
62. Li Ji [1934] 1977, 191–92.
63. Chang Kwang-chih 1981, 161–66.
64. Fu Sinian [1934b] 1996, 352; Lacouperie 1894.
65. Cited in Lu Maode 1926, 371.
66. Ibid., 375.
67. Ibid., 373, 380.
68. Jia Lanpo and Huang Weiwen 1990; Chen Xingcan 1997, 76–263.
69. Black 1927, 733-34; Andersson [1934] 1973, 94–126.
70. Bowler 1986, 31–40.
71. Weng Wenhao [1930] 1989, 270.

72. Ibid.
73. Cited in Schmalzer 2004, 111–12.
74. Dikötter 1992, 2–17, 126–60.
75. Weidenreich 1935, 467.
76. Weidenreich 1936, 38.
77. Lin Huixiang [1936] 1996, 1: 45–67; Qian Mu [1939] 1989, 3–4.
78. Zhang Xuguang 1942, 4.
79. Schmalzer 2004, 106–13.
80. Xiong Shili [1939] 1984, 33.
81. On Xiong's intellectual background, see Tu Wei-ming 1976; Ding Weixiang 1999.
82. Xiong Shili [1939] 1984, 33.
83. Ibid.
84. Ibid.
85. Ibid., 2.
86. Ibid., 18–19.
87. Kohl and Fawcett 1996, 13.
88. Xiong Shili [1939] 1984, 34–35.
89. Tay Lian Soo 1987; Liu Qiqian 1986, 221–48; Gu Chao 1994, 214–77.
90. Fei Xiaotong [1936] 1996, 131–44.
91. Lü Simian [1934] 1987, 6.
92. Qi Sihe 1937, 26–27.
93. Ibid., 28.
94. Ibid.
95. Ibid., 30–34.
96. Hostetler 2001, 5.
97. On the development of ethnology in Republican China, see Wang Jianmin 1997; Guldin 1994; Wong Siu-lun 1979; Cheung Siu-woo 2003, and Mullaney 2004.
98. Wang Jianmin 1997, 215–56; Guldin 1994, 57–62; Wong Siu-lun 1979, 19–36; Cheung Siu-woo 2003, 103.
99. See, for example, Sun Yat-sen 1924c, 239.
100. Cheung Siu-woo 2003; Mullaney 2004, 214–25.
101. See, for example, Ling Chunsheng 1938; Wang Xingrui 1939; Rui Yifu 1938; Tao Yunkui 1940; and others as discussed in Mullaney 2004.
102. On Gu's northwest tour, see Gu Chao 1994, 276–84; L. Schneider 1971, 285–88; Lipman 2002, 121–24.
103. Gu Jiegang 1937, 1–3. Also see Gu Chao 1994, 280.
104. L. Schneider 1971, 14–15.
105. See, for example, Gu Jiegang 1938, 21.
106. Wang Fan-sen 2000, 140–63. Following the 1937 Marco Polo Bridge Incident, Fu Sinian grew increasingly active in the Guomindang government and its efforts to mobilize national unity. At the request of Chiang Kai-shek, Fu joined the government's Council of National Defense (*Guofang canyihui*) and went on to become a prominent member of its successor organization, the People's Political Council (*Guomin canzhenghui*). Despite his often spirited criticism

of Chiang and his regime, Fu remained confident that the Guomindang represented China's best hope for national salvation (Wang Fan-sen 2000, 164–96).

107. Fu Sinian 1935, 985–86.
108. Schwarcz 1986, 230–36.
109. Cited in Ibid., 231.
110. See Yang Ce 1997; Li Ziyuan 1995, 309–50; Esenbel 2004.
111. Lin Hsiao-ting 2002a, 485–510.
112. It is unclear whether a complete copy of Gu's *Bianjiang* supplement survived the war. A preliminary check of major collections of Chinese newspapers in the United States, Europe, Beijing, Nanjing, Shanghai, and Hong Kong failed to produce a complete run of the Kunming edition of *Yishibao*. Consequently, the following discussion is based on an incomplete copy held by the Shanghai Municipal Library. There is little doubt, however, over the high profile nature of this debate. Writing in 1942, anthropologist Rui Yifu referred to "over ten" participants in what he called an important and highly public discussion of ethnic and cultural diversity in China (Rui Yifu [1942] 1972, 1–2).
113. See Fu Sinian's comments about Gu's essays in *Bianjiang* in Fu Sinian 1939b, 1215–16.
114. Fu Sinian 1939a, 1213.
115. Ibid., 1214.
116. Ibid.
117. Gu Jiegang [1939] 1996, 773.
118. Ibid., 777, see also 775–76.
119. Ibid., 777–79.
120. Ibid., 784.
121. Ibid., 785.
122. Kymlicka 1995.
123. Fu Sinian 1939b, 1215–16.
124. Ibid., 1216.
125. Ibid.
126. Zhang Tingxiu 1939, 501.
127. Ibid., 508.
128. Ibid.
129. Ibid.
130. Ibid.
131. Shyu 1972.
132. Cited and reprinted in Ma Yi 1939, 608–9.
133. See Dirlik 1976, 305.
134. Jaffe 1947, 18–23.
135. Chiang Kai-shek [1944] 1986, 2, emphasis added.
136. Ibid.
137. Ibid., 8–9.
138. Yu Jianhua 1944, 1–17.
139. For a fuller discussion of this, see Leibold 2003, 491–509.
140. Cheung Siu-woo 2003, 95.

141. Said 1979, 231–33.
142. Stepan 1991, 63.
143. Duara 1996, 42.
144. Compare Wei Hunlin 1945 and Rui Yifu [1944] 1972. While admitting that the *Zhonghua guozu* (Zhonghua race-state) arose from a "single embryo," Rui Yifu was quick to stress that in addition to this "collective appearance," its "individual appearance" exhibited extensive racial, linguistic, and cultural diversity. He went on to identify sixty-six distinct "lineage branches" (*zu* or *zhixi*), providing an important empirical basis for the formal identification of national minorities under the PRC's ethnic identification campaign during the 1950s (see Mullaney 2004). On the other hand, sociologists Wei Hunlin and other contributors to *Bianzheng gonglun* (*Frontier Affairs*), which was published from 1941 until 1948, were less interested in the taxonomy or origins of China's various peoples than exploring concrete methods for exercising Chinese sovereignty over the vast frontier and solving the frontier question through specific policy initiatives, including different types of regional and cultural autonomy.

Chapter 5

1. Hobsbawm and Ranger 1983, 1.
2. B. Anderson 1991, 195.
3. Sun Yat-sen 1924c, 186–88. Also see Chapter 1.
4. As far as I have been able to determine, the first usage of the term by the Communists occurred in November of 1935. See "Zhonghua suweiai gongheguo zhongyang zhengfu, Zhongguo gongnong hongjun geming junshi weiyuanhui kangri jiguo xuanyan" 1935, 320.
5. Mao Zedong 1939b, 626. For an English translation, see Mao Zedong 1964 2, 306.
6. Balujun zhengzhibu 1939, 808.
7. Li Da [1929] 1980, 561.
8. Engels 1972; Li Da [1929] 1980, 562.
9. Qu Qiubai [1926] 1987, 488–90; Stalin [1913] 1940, 5–8.
10. Li Da [1929] 1980, 564; Stalin [1913] 1940, 8.
11. Qu Qiubai [1926] 1987, 490; Li Da [1929] 1980, 565; Stalin [1913] 1940, 13.
12. Qu Qiubai [1926] 1987, 495.
13. For a short biography of Yang Song, see Xu Youchun 1991, 1211.
14. Yang Song 1938, 763–68.
15. Ibid., 766–67.
16. Ibid., 767.
17. Cited in Yu Zhengui 1996, 314.
18. Cited in Yang Huiyun 1993, 28.
19. See Gladney 1991, 89.
20. Li Yimin 1936, 518.

21. "Zhonggong zhongyang xibei gongzuo weiyuanhui guanyu Huihui minzu wenti de tigang," 1940, 648 (emphasis added).
22. Li Weihan 1940, 850–52.
23. See Jin Jitang 1936, 29–39.
24. Li Weihan 1940, 850–51.
25. Li Weihan 1940, 851; "Zhonggong zhongyang xibei gongzuo weiyuanhui guanyu kangzhan zhong Menggu minzu wenti tigang" 1940, 658.
26. Li Weihan 1940, 851-52. In spite of Li Weihan's clever solution, Stalin's narrow and formalistic definition of minzu remained problematic for the Chinese Communists and became a major source of debate during the 1950s. It was not until 1962 that a high-level party conference settled on the appropriateness of the term minzu for all China's minority nationals regardless of their level of economic development. See Leibold 2003, 532n29. On the PRC's ethnic classification campaign and its Republican-era roots, see Mullaney 2004.
27. Mao Zedong 1939b, 625–27.
28. Dirlik 1978.
29. Hoston 1994, 273-324.
30. Mao Zedong 1939b, 627.
31. Mao Zedong 1938a, 260.
32. Mao Zedong 1940, 707; or as translated in Mao Zedong 1964, 2, 381.
33. Mao Zedong 1941, 797; or as translated in Mao Zedong 1964, 3, 19.
34. Mao Zedong 1939a, 620.
35. Hobsbawm 1990, 44.
36. Ye Huosheng 1984, 69–76; Ma Jinke and Hong Jingling 1994, 387–88.
37. Zhu Ruiyan 1985, 1473–1502; Klein and Clark 1971, 264–67.
38. See the revised preface in Fan Wenlan 1955, 5.
39. Zhongguo lishi yanjiushi [1941] 1944, ii.
40. Ibid., 5.
41. Ibid., 8.
42. Ibid., 4.
43. Ibid., 8.
44. Wu Chin-ting 1938.
45. See Wang Fan-sen 2000, 101–14 and Chapter 5.
46. Chang Kwang-chih 1963, 78–79. Despite the Anyang findings, Fu Sinian's plural origins thesis (see Fu Sinian 1934) continued as the dominant scholarly paradigm for Neolithic archaeology during the 1930s and 1940s. Chang argues that new archaeological discoveries in northern China during the 1950s rendered Fu's thesis "obsolete" while demonstrating conclusively the interconnectedness of Longshan and Yangshao culture.
47. Zhongguo lishi yanjiu [1941] 1944, 8.
48. Ibid.
49. Ibid., 5.
50. Ibid., 15.
51. Xiong Shili [1939] 1984, 1–35.
52. Qu Qiubai [1926] 1987, 491.
53. Yang Song 1938, 763.

54. Minzu wenti yanjiushi 1941, 869.
55. Ibid., 870; Li Weihan 1940, 841.
56. On Jian Bozan, see Zhang Zhuanxi 1985, 1528–61.
57. Jian Bozan [1943b] 1969, 37.
58. Ye Guisheng and Liu Maolin 1985, 1581–1603.
59. Lü Zhenyu [1940] 1961, 176.
60. Ibid.; Pei Wenzhong 1934, 327–58. Pei's findings were not shared by the director of the Peking Cenozoic Laboratory, Dr. Franz Weidenreich, who argued in 1939 that the skulls exhibited "three different racial elements . . . to be classified as primitive Mongoloid, Melanesoid and Eskimoid." He rejected the significance of the discovery to the origin of the Chinese race and continued to argue that the original and more primitive Sinanthropus remains were the earliest traces of the Chinese race while the Upper Cave remains probably represented "a migrating tribe foreign to the country" before they were attacked and killed by "the real representatives" of the Chinese race (Weidenreich 1939, 69).
61. Ibid., 176.
62. Lin Ganquan and Ye Guisheng 1985, 1645–63.
63. Yin Da [1940] 1989, 301–18.
64. Ibid., 311.
65. Ibid.
66. Ibid.
67. Ibid., 305.
68. Chiang Kai-shek [1944] 1986, 1.
69. See Zhonggong zhongyang wenxian yanjiushi 1993, 2, 446, 458; Zhonggong zhongyang wenxian yanjiushi 1996, 1, 427–28.
70. Chen Boda 1943, 945. For a loose English translation, see Chen Pai-ta 1944, 1–9.
71. Ibid., 945.
72. Ibid., 946–47.
73. Gu Jiegang [1939] 1996, 773–85.
74. Lü Zhenyu 1941.
75. Weidenreich 1946, 93 and passim; Bowler 1986, 31–40, 107–11. The discovery of new *Pithecanthropus* remains during the 1930s by G. H. R. von Koenigswald brought renewed scholarly attention to Java Man, as Koenigswald and Weidenreich teamed up to demonstrate the supposed affinity between these two hominids and their relationship to modern man.
76. Lü Zhenyu 1941, 10.
77. Lü Zhenyu 1943, 4.
78. Jian Bozan [1943] 1950, 1, 12–18.
79. Ibid., 19–24.
80. Jian Bozan [1943] 1950, 1, 84.
81. Lü Simian [1934] 1987; Lin Huixiang [1936] 1996; Xiong Shili [1939] 1984.
82. Lü Zhenyu 1950, 1-2.
83. Ibid., 2.
84. Ibid., 15.

85. Ibid., 16.
86. Ibid., 23.
87. Gladney 1991, 96ff.
88. See, for example, the special issue on the Hui edited by Hui historian Bai Shouyi in Gu Jiegang's journal *Yugong banyuekan* 5.11 (August 1, 1936).
89. Minzu wenti yenjiushi 1941, 864–70, quote from p. 870; Li Weihan 1940, 841–42.
90. See Forbes 1986. Also see the two pamphlets from the East Turkestan Republic included as Appendix E and F in Benson 1990, 200–208.
91. Lü Zhenyu 1941, 11.
92. Lü Zhenyu 1950, 100–101.
93. See Xiong Shili [1939] 1984, 12–14. Interestingly, Xiong questions the authority of the *Beishi* passage, claiming that while it is not without reason to assume that the Xiongnu were the ancestors of the Hui, it only represented conjecture. Xiong's own reconstruction of Hui origins traced them back through the *Tujuezu* to the so-called *Di* barbarians, mentioned in the *Book of Poetry*, who he claimed were actually the descendants of the Hu princely clan of the Hanzu. See pp. 19–20.
94. Lü Zhenyu 1950, 102. Lü Zhenyu's speculative genealogy of the Hui did not go unchallenged by Communist historians. Following the establishment of the PRC, the highly respected Hui historian, Bai Shouyi, reasserted Li Weihan's initial claim about the foreign origin of the Hui, going so far as claiming in 1957, "The Huihui minzu, or Huizu, did not meld, develop and form from clans and tribes within China; rather it melded, developed and formed on the basis of foreigners. The initial provenance of the Huihui minzu, that is its primary origin, was from the early thirteenth century westward migration of Central Asian Persians and Arabs" (Li Weihan [1957] 1992, 155). A year later, Bai Shouyi's work on Hui history was questioned by a young Hui scholar named Luo Lan. Arguing that Bai's "foreign origin thesis" was "not only unhelpful for raising the patriotic consciousness of the Hui people but was also being used to foment their propensity towards local nationalism," Luo contended that "racially speaking, the Han people comprise more [of the Huihui minzu] than any single Central Asian, Persian, Arab or other [foreigner] element" (Luo Lan 1958, 62). The young Hui scholar's critique did not go unanswered. Firing right back at Luo Lan, Bai argued that "it did not make any sense" to assume that because the Han minzu lived intermixed among the Hui for several generations, that "the Han people abandoned their own nationality and formed the primary component of the Hui nationality" (Bai Shouyi [1960] 1992, 181).
95. Xiong Shili [1939] 1984, 18; Lü Zhenyu 1950, 205.
96. Fan Wenlan 1955.
97. Fan Wenlan 1950, 45–47.
98. Ibid., 45.
99. Ibid. Also see Fan Wenlan 1955, 90.
100. Schmalzer 2004, 205–16.
101. Fan Wenlan 1950, 45.

102. Ibid., 46.
103. Liang Qichao 1903b, 76; Sun Yat-sen 1924c, 187.
104. Dikötter 1992, x. Also see Dikötter 1997, 12–33.
105. On "Oriental Orientalism," see Gladney 1994, 113–14, and on "Internal Orientalism," see Schein 1997, 70–74. In contrast to the exotic and erotic representations of minority cultures identified by Gladney and Schein during their recent anthropological field research in China, Republican-era depictions tended to be much more prosaic and dark. Unlike the "array of polychromatic and titillating forms" in which the minorities are presented today, the early twentieth-century frontier and its peoples were more likely to be described as "barren," "backward," and "vulnerable" rather than "colorful," "alluring," and "promiscuous." As Gladney and Schein point out, the recent valorization of the frontier is closely tied to the commodification of minority cultures in post-Mao China but, as this chapter and the previous have attempted to demonstrate, it is not without precedent in Republican-era ethnography.
106. Fei Xiaotong 1989, 1–8.
107. Cited in Poo Mu-chou 2005, 157.
108. Chen Yuning 1994, 5.
109. Sautman 1997, 76; Sautman 2001; L. Liu, 1999; Schmalzer 2004, 498–574.

Conclusion

1. Fletcher 1978, 35, as cited in Millward 1996, 113.
2. Terrill 2003, 202. Also see Crossley 2005; Purdue 2005b; Pye 1990.
3. R. Wong 1997, 174–77; R. Wong 2006, 98; Fitzgerald 1996b; L. Liu 2004, 75–81; Townsend 1996, 16–17; Pye 1996; Zhao Suisheng 2004, 8–36.
4. Gramsci 1985, 416–21; Lustick 2002, 22-28; Landy 1986. Referring to this "common sense" form of nationalism in a distinctly Western context, Michael Billig coined the term "banal nationalism" to demonstrate how national identity can be "found in the embodied habits of social life" (1995, 8).
5. Hobsbawm 1990, 10; Smith 2000, 62–77, quote from p. 63. John Breuilly presents one useful model for a state-centered approach in exploring how nationalism relates to "the objective of obtaining and using state power" (1985, 2), while anthropologists Stevan Harrell and Dru Gladney have long stressed the centrality of the state in the construction of individual ethnic identities in contemporary China (see Gladney 1991 and 1994; Harrell 1995a and 2001).
6. R. Wong 1997, 73.
7. Kirby 2005, 107.
8. "A Treaty Between All Nine Powers" 1922, 66.
9. Elliott 2000.
10. Duara 2003, 41–86.
11. Liu Xiaoyuan 2006, 376–432; Radchenko 2003.

12. Terrill 2003, 250–52.
13. Harrison 2001, 10–25. Ho Ping-Ti 1976, 547–54; R. Wong 2000, 109–22; Watson 1993, 80–103; Cohen 1991, 114–25; Fitzgerald 1994; Ebrey 1996.
14. Shepherd 1993, 362–63, in contrast to Crossley 1990b; Rawski 1996; Ho Ping-Ti 1998.
15. R. Wong 1997, 175; B. Anderson 1991; Gellner 1983.
16. In the 1897 All-Russian Census, only 45 percent of the 126,368,000 people identified were classified as "Russian" (Carrère d'Encausse 1992, 3). Using "mother tongue" as the maker of nationality, the 1897 census identified some 130 different groups—a number that grew to nearly 190 by the time of the USSR's 1926 census and the adoption of more "scientific" methods of classification, only to be whittled down to 60 after Stalin decreed in 1936 that "there are about sixty nations, national groups, and *narodnosti* in the Soviet Union," forcing Soviet ethnologists to dramatically reduce the number of ethnic categories in the USSR (see Hirsch 2005, 101–44, 282–325).
17. Sun Yat-sen 1924c, 188.
18. Mao Zedong 1939b, 626.
19. Zhou Enlai 1949, 1266–67.
20. See, for example, Brubaker 1996, 23–54; Tuminez 2000, 42–45; Suny 1993.
21. Brubaker 1996, 23-54.
22. Lattimore 1938, 245 and passim; Lattimore 1937, 97–119; Lattimore 1932, 307–24.
23. Fu Jing 2006; Wang Hui 2006; "China Outlines Future Plans for Expansion of Road Network" 2002.
24. Gottschang 1987, 461; Duara 2003, 44; Guojia tongjiju renkou he shehui keji tongjisi 2003, 4, 8.
25. Li 1989, 528; Guojia tongjiju renkou he shehui keji tongjisi 2003, 4.
26. Toops 2004, 1 and passim; Becquelin 2004, 55 and passim; Guojia tongjiju renkou he shehui keji tongjisi 2003, 4.
27. Tibet Online 1996-2007; Hao Yan 2000.
28. Guojia tongjiju renkou he shehui keji tongjisi 2003, 4, 590–689.
29. Liu Jun and Zhu Yuan 2006; M. Liu 2006; Watts 2006.

References

Abbreviations

FSQJ: Fu Sinian. 1980. *Fu Sinian quanji* [*Complete works of Fu Sinian*]. 7 vols. Taipei: Lianjing chuban shiye gongsi.

GSB: Gu Jiegang, ed. 1982. *Gushibian* [*Critiques of ancient history*]. 7 vols. Shanghai: Shanghai guji chubanshe.

LDW: Li Dazhao. 1999. *Li Dazhao wenji* [*Collection of essays by Li Dazhao*]. 5 vols, comp. Zhongguo Li Dazhao yanjiuhui. Beijing: Renmin chubanshe.

LGZY: Zhonggong zhongyang dangshi yanjiushi diyi yanjiu bu, trans. and comp. 1997. *Liangong (bu), gongchanguoji yu Zhongguo guomin geming yudong, 1920–1925* [*Russian Bolshevik party, Comintern and the Chinese national revolutionary movement, 1920–25*]. 10 vols. Beijing: Xinhua shudian.

MZDJ: Mao Zedong. 1970–72. *Mao Zedong ji* [*Collected works of Mao Zedong*]. 10 vols., comp. Takeuchi Minoru. Tokyo: Hokubosha.

MZWT: Zhonggong zhongyang tongzhanbu, ed. 1991. *Minzu wenti wenxian huibian: 7/1921—9/1949* [*Collection of documents on the national question, July 1921 to September 1949*]. Beijing: Zhonggong zhongyang dangxiao chubanshe.

MZXJ: Mao Zedong. 1991. *Mao Zedong xuanji* [*Select works of Mao Zedong*]. 4 vols. Jiangsu: Renmin chubanshe.

SW: Mao Zedong. 1964. *Selected works of Mao Tse-tung*. 4 vols. Peking: Foreign Language Press.

SYXW: Shao Yuanchong. 1983. *Shao Yuanchong xiansheng wenji* [*Collected works of Mr. Shao Yuanchong*]. 4 vols. Taipei: Zhongguo guomindang zhongyang weiyuanhui dangshi weiyuanhui.

SZSQJ: Sun Yat-sen. 1981–86. *Sun Zhongshan quanji* [*Complete works of Sun Yat-sen*]. 11 vols. Comp. Zhongguo shehui kexueyuan jindaishi yanjiusuo. Beijing: Zhonghua shuju.

XMWZ: Gansusheng tushuguan shumu cankaobu, comp. 1984. *Xibei minzu zongjiao shiliao wenzhai* [*Collection of historical materials on nationality and religion in the northwest*]. 5 vols. Lanzhou: Gansusheng tushuguan.

YBSHJ: Liang Qichao. 1941. *Yinbingshi heji* [*Complete works from the Ice Drinker's studio*]. 40 vols. Shanghai: Zhonghua shuju.
YBSWJ: Liang Qichao. 1960. *Yinbingshi wenji* [*Collected writings from the Ice Drinker's studio*]. 16 vols. Taipei: Taiwan Zhonghua shuju.
ZGQZ: Rong Mengyuan, ed. 1985. *Zhongguo guomindang lici daibiao dahui ji zhongyang quanhui ziliao* [*Documents from the Guomindang's national party congresses and central committee plenums*]. 2 vols. Beijing: Guangming ribao chubanshe.
ZMSD: Zhonghua minguo shi yanjiushi, et al. 1994. *Zhonghua minguo shi dang'an ziliao huibian* [*Collection of archival documents on Republican history*]. 11 vols., comp. Zhongguo dier lishi dang'anguan. Beijing: Zhonghua shuju; Nanjing: Jiangsu guji chubanshe.
ZMSS: Zhonghua minguo shishi jiyao bianji weiyuanhui, comp. 1974– . *Zhonghua minguo shishi jiyao (chugao)* [*Chronology of historical events from the Republic of China (draft)*]. Multi-vols. Taipei: Zhonghua minguo shiliao yanjiu zhongxin.
ZSP: Chen Qingquan, et al. 1985. *Zhongguo shixuejia pingzhuan* [*Critical biographies of Chinese historians*]. 3 vols. Zhengzhou: Zhongzhou guji chubanshe.

Works Cited

Adelman, Jeremy, and Stephen Aron. 1999. "From borderlands to borders: Empires, nation-states and the peoples in between in North American history." *American Historical Review* 104 (June): 814–41.
Anderson, Benedict. 1991. *Imagined communities: Reflections on the origin and spread of nationalism*. Rev. ed., New York: Verso.
———. 2001. "Western nationalism and Eastern nationalism: Is there a difference that matters?" *New Left Review* 9 (May/June): 31–42.
Anderson, Malcolm. 1996. *Frontiers: Territory and state formation in the modern world*. Oxford: Polity Press.
Andersson, J. Gunnar. [1934] 1973. *Children of the yellow earth: Studies in prehistoric China*. Repr., Trans. E. Classen. Cambridge, MA: MIT Press.
Asano Risaburō. 1928. *Manmo no rekishi chiriteki kenkyu* [*Research on Manchurian and Mongolian history and geography*]. Tokyo: Sekai Kaizo Sosho Kankokai.
Atwill, David. 2005. *The Chinese sultanate: Islam, ethnicity, and the Panthay Rebellion in Southwest China, 1856–1873*. Stanford, CA: Stanford University Press.
Atwood, Christopher. 2002. *Young Mongols and vigilantes in Inner Mongolia's interregnum, decades, 1911–1931*. 2 vols. Leiden: Brill.
Bai Shouyi. [1957] 1992. "Huihui minzu de xingcheng he chubu fazhan" [The origin and initial development of the Huihui nationality]. In *Bai Shouyi minzu zongjiao lunji*, 155–68. Beijing: Beijing shifan daxue chubanshe.
———. [1960] 1992. "Guanyu huizu shi de jige wenti" [Several problems concerning the Hui nationality's history]. In *Bai Shouyi minzu zongjiao lunji*, 176–87. Beijing: Beijing shifan daxue chubanshe.
Balujun zhengzhibu. 1939. Kangri zhanshi zhengzhi keben [Political textbook for War of Resistance soldiers]. In *MZWT*, 807–8.

Barfield, Thomas. 1989. *The perilous frontier: Nomadic empires and China.* London: Basil Blackwell.
Barnett, A. Doak. 1963. *China on the eve of Communist takeover.* New York: Praeger.
Barth, Fredrik. 1969. "Introduction." In *Ethnic groups and boundaries*, ed. Fredrik Barth, 9–38. Bergen: Universitets-forlaget.
Becquelin, Nicolas. 2004. "Staged development in Xinjiang." In *China's campaign to "open up the west": National, provincial and local perspectives*, ed. David S. G. Goodman, 44–64. Cambridge: Cambridge University Press.
Bello, David. 2005. "To go where no Han could go for long: Malaria and the Qing construction of ethnic administrative space in frontier Yunnan." *Modern China* 31.3 (July): 283–317.
Benson, Linda. 1990. *The Ili rebellion: The Moslem challenge to Chinese authority in Xinjiang, 1944–1949.* Armonk, NY: M. E. Sharpe.
Bergère, Marie-Claire. 1998. *Sun Yat-sen.* Trans. Janet Lloyd. Stanford, CA: Stanford University Press.
Bhabha, Homi. 1990. *Nation and narration.* London: Routledge.
Billig, Michael. 1995. *Banal nationalism.* London: Sage.
Black, Davidson. 1927. "Tertiary man in Asia: the Chou Kou Tien discovery." *Nature* 118: 710-36.
Boorman, Howard, and Richard Howard, eds. 1967. *Biographical dictionary of Republican China.* 4 vols. New York: Columbia University Press.
Borodin, Mikhail. 1924. Bao-luo-ting de zhaji he tongbao [Reading notes and reports of Mikhail Borodin]. In *LGZY*, vol. 1, 419–87.
Bowler, Peter. 1986. *Theories of human evolution: a century of debate, 1844–1944.* Oxford: Blackwell.
Bradley, David. 2001. "Language policy for the Yi." In *Perspectives on the Yi of Southwest China*, ed. Stevan Harrell, 195–213. Berkeley: University of California Press.
Brandt, Conrad, et al. 1952. *A documentary history of Chinese communism.* London: Allen and Unwin.
Breuilly, John. 1985. *Nationalism and the state.* Chicago: University of Chicago Press.
Brown, Melissa, ed. 1996. *Negotiating ethnicities in China and Taiwan.* Berkeley: Institute of East Asian Studies, University of California, Center for Chinese Studies.
———. 2004. *Is Taiwan Chinese? The impact of culture, power and migration on changing identities.* Berkeley: University of California Press.
———. 2007. "Ethnic identity, cultural variation, and processes of change: Rethinking the insights of standardization and orthopraxy." *Modern China* 33.1 (January): 91–124.
Brubaker, Roger. 1996. *Nationalism reframed: Nationhood and the national question in new Europe.* Cambridge: Cambridge University Press.
Bulag, Uradyn. 2002. *The Mongols at China's edge: History and the politics of national unity.* Lanham, MD: Rowman & Littlefield.
———. 2006. "The yearning for 'friendship': Revisting 'the political' in minority revolutionary history in China." *The Journal of Asian Studies* 65.1 (Feburary): 3–32.

Carrère d'Encausse, Hélène. 1992. *The great challenge: Nationalities and the Bolshevik state, 1917–1930.* Trans. Nancy Festinger. New York: Holmes & Meier.

Chan Lau Kit-ching. 1972. *The Chinese youth party, 1923–1945.* Hong Kong: Centre of Asian Studies.

Chang Hao. 1972. *Liang Ch'i-ch'ao and intellectual transition in China.* Cambridge, MA: Harvard University Press.

———. 1987. *Chinese intellectuals in crisis: Search for order and meaning (1890–1911).* Berkeley: University of California Press.

Chang Kwang-chih. 1963. *The archaeology of ancient China.* New Haven, CT: Yale University Press.

———. 1981. "Archaeology and Chinese historiography." *World Archaeology* 13.2: 156–69.

Chatterjee, Partha. 1986. *Nationalist thought and the colonial world: A derivative discourse.* London: Zed Books.

———. 2000. "Whose imagined community?" In *Nationalism: Critical concepts in political science,* vol. 3, ed. John Hutchinson and Anthony D. Smith, 940–45. London: Routledge.

Chen Boda. 1943. "Ping 'Zhonguo zhi mingyun'" [Critique of "China's destiny"]. In *MZWT,* 945–49.

———. *See also* Chen Pai-ta.

Chen Changfeng. 1986. *On the Long March with Chairman Mao.* Beijing: Foreign Language Press.

Chen Duxiu. [1922a] 1993. "Zhongguo Gongchandang duiyu muqian shiji wenti zhi shihua" [The immediate tactics of the CCP]. In *Chen Duxiu zhuzuoxuan,* vol. 2, ed. Ren Jianshu, et al., 422–27. Shanghai: Shanghai renmin chubanshe.

———. 1922b. "Zhonggong zhongyang shiweihui shuji Chen Duxiu gei gongchan guojide baogao" [Report of CCP Central Executive Committee Secretary Chen Duxiu to the Comintern]. In *MZWT,* 6.

———. 1924a. "Meiguo yinlue yu menggu duli" [The American invasion and Mongolian independence]. *Xiangdao zhoubao* 75 (July 23): 597–98.

———. 1924b. "Women de huida" [Our reply]. *Xiangdao zhoubao* 83 (September 17): 673–74.

Chen Guofu. [1943] 1965. "Minzuzhuyi de jianshe" [Reconstruction of minzuzhuyi]. In *Guofu sixiang lunwenji,* 2 vols. Taipei: Zhonghua minguo kejie jinian guofu bai nian dan zhenzhoupai weiyuanhui.

Chen Jianfu. 1934. *Neimeng zizhi shiliao jiyao* [*Compilation of important historical documents on Inner Mongolian autonomy*]. Nanjing: Nanjing fati shudian chuban.

Chen Liankai. [1988] 1994. "Zhongguo, huayi, fanhan, zhonghua, zhonghua minzu—yige zai lianxi fazhan bei renshi de guocheng" [One method for recognizing the developmental relationship between the terms Zhongguo, Huayi, Fanhan, Zhonghua, and Zhonghua minzu]. In *Zhonghua minzu yanjiu chutan,* 27–91. Beijing: Zhishi chubanshe.

Chen Lifu. [1934] 1935. "Sanminzhuyi yu jiaoyu" [The three principles of the people and education]. In *Chen Lifu xiansheng yanlunji,* 177–204, n.p.

Chen Pai-ta [Chen Boda]. 1944. *Critique of "China's destiny": Review of Marshall Chiang Kai-shek's book.* Bombay: People's Publishing House.

Chen Qitian. [1929] 1988. "Jindai guojiazhuyi yundong shi" [Contemporary history of the *guojiazhuyi* movement]. In *Zhongguo qingniandang*, ed. Zhongguo dier lishi dang'anguan, 56–69. Nanjing: Zhongguo dierci lishi dang'anguan.

Chen Xingcan. 1997. *Zhongguo shiqian kaoguxue shi yanjiu, 1895–1949* [*Research on the history of prehistoric archaeology in China, 1895–1949*]. Beijing: Sanlian shudian.

Chen Yinke. 1977. "Sui Tang zhidu yuanyuan luelun" [Rough theory on the origins of the Sui and Tang systems]. In *Chen Yinke xiansheng quanji*, vol. 1: 1-150. Taipei: Jiusi gongsi.

Chen Yuning. 1994. *Zhonghua minzu ningjuli de lishi tansuo* [*Exploration into the historical coagulability of the Zhonghua minzu*]. Kunming: Yunnan renmin chubanshe.

Chen Zhiming. 1933. *Xikang yange zhi* [*Record of Xikang's development*]. Nanjing: Boti shudian.

Chen Zhongwei. 1930. *Xikang wenti* [*The Xikang problem*]. Shanghai: Zhonghua shuju.

Chesneaux, Jean. 1969. "The federalist movement in China, 1920–1923." In *Modern China's search for a political form*, ed. Jack Gray, 96–137. London: Oxford University Press.

Cheung, Siu-woo. 1995. "Millenarianism, Christian movements, and ethnic change among the Miao in Southwest China." In *Cultural encounters on China's ethnic frontiers*, ed. Stevan Harrell, 217–47. Seattle: University of Washington Press.

———. 2003. "Miao identities, indigenism and the politics of appropriation in Southwest China during the Republican period." *Asian Ethnicity* 4.1 (February): 85–114.

Chiang Kai-shek. [1912] 1937. "Mengzang wenti zhi genben jiejue" [Fundamental solution to the Mongolian and Tibetan problems] In *Jiang weiyuanzhang quanji*, vol. 3, ed. Shen Fenggang, 12–16. Shanghai: Shanghai guotai shuju.

———. [1934] 1984. "Zhongguo zhi bianjiang wenti" [China's frontier problem]. In *Zongtong Jiang gong sixiang yanlun zongji*, vol. 12, ed. Jin Xiaoyi, 105–110. Taipei: Zhongguo guomindang zhongyang weiyuanhui dangshi weiyuanhui.

———. [1944] 1986. *Zhongguo zhi mingyun* [*China's destiny*], 2nd rev. ed. Taipei: Zhongzheng shuju.

———. 1947. *China's destiny and Chinese economic theory*. Notes and commentary by Philip Jaffe. London: D. Dobson.

"China outlines future plans for expansion of road network." 2002. *People's Daily* [Online]. http://english.people.com.cn/200210/22/eng20021022_105463.shtml (accessed June 4, 2007).

Chong Key Ray. 1969. "Cheng Kuan-yin (1841–1920): A source of Sun Yat-sen's nationalist ideology?" *The Journal of Asian Studies* 28.2 (February): 247–68.

Chow Kai-wing. 1997. "Imagining boundaries of blood: Zhang Binglin and the invention of the Han 'race' in modern China." In *The construction of racial identities in China and Japan*, ed. Frank Dikötter, 34–52. Hong Kong: Hong Kong University Press.

———. 2001. "Narrating nation, race and national culture: Imagining the Hanzu identity in modern China." In *Constructing nationhood in modern East Asia*, ed.

Kai-wing Chow, Kevin Doak, and Poshek Fu, 47–83. Ann Arbor: University of Michigan Press.

Cohen, Myron L. 1991. "Being Chinese: The peripheralization of traditional identity." *Daedalus* 120.2 (Spring): 113–34.

Cohen, Paul A. 1984. *Discovering history in China: American historical writing on the recent Chinese past.* New York: Columbia University Press.

Connor, Walker. 1984. *The national question in Marxist-Leninist theory and strategy.* Princeton, NJ: Princeton University Press.

Crossley, Pamela Kyle. 1989. "The Qianlong retrospect on the Chinese-martial (*hanjun*) banners." *Late Imperial China* 10.1 (June): 63–107.

———. 1990a. *Orphan warriors: Three generations and the end of the Qing world.* Princeton, NJ: Princeton University Press.

———. 1990b. "Thinking about ethnicity in early modern China." *Late Imperial China* 11.1: 1–35.

———. 1999. *A translucent mirror: History and identity in Qing imperial ideology.* Berkeley: University of California Press.

———. 2005. "Nationality and difference in China: The post-imperial dilemma." In *The teleology of the modern nation-state*, ed. Joshua Fogel, 138-58. Philadelphia: University of Pennsylvania Press.

Crossley, Pamela Kyle, Helen Siu, and Donald Sutton, eds. 2006. *Empire at the margins: Culture, ethnicity and frontier in early modern China.* Berkeley: University of California Press.

Dai Jitao. [1912] 1991. "Zhengmeng yu jue" [Attack Mongolia and resist Russia]. In *Dai Jitao xinhai wenji: 1909–1913*, vol. 2, comp. Sang Bing et al., 1251–58. Hong Kong: Chinese University of Hong Kong Press.

———. 1931. "Zhongguo zhi tongyi yu fuxing" [The unity and revival of China]. *Xin Yaxiya* 2.6 (September): 1–10.

———. 1934. "Xiaoyuan zhiqiao" [Sketches from the garden of filial piety]. *Xin Yaxiya* 7.5 (May): 89.

de Bary, William Theodore, and Richard Lufrano, comp. 2000. *Sources of Chinese traditions.* 2nd ed., 2 vols. New York: Columbia University Press.

De Wang [Demchugdongrob]. 1933a. "De Wang deng wei tuixing Menggu gaodu zizhi zhenxiang zhi zhongyang dangbu shixing weiyuanhui deng dian" [The cable of De Wang and others to the Guomindang Central Executive Committee and others concerning the actual facts of promoting a high degree of Mongolian autonomy]. In *ZMSD*, 5.1.5, 89–91.

———. 1933b. "De Wang wei zuzhi neimeng zizhi zhengfu shixing zizhi zhi zhongyang shixing weiyuanhui tongdian" [Circular telegram from De Wang to the Guomindang Central Executive Committee concerning the organization of the Inner Mongolian Autonomous Government for carrying out autonomy]. In *ZMSD*, 5.1.5, 108–10.

Di Cosmo, Nicola. 1998. "Qing colonial administration in Inner Asia." *The International Historical Review* 20.2 (June): 287–309.

———. 2002. *Ancient China and its enemies: The rise of nomadic power in East Asian history.* Cambridge: Cambridge University Press.

Di Cosmo, Nicola, and Don Wyatt, eds. 2003. *Political frontiers, ethnic boundaries, and human geographies in Chinese history*. London: RoutledgeCurzon.

Diamond, Jared. 1998. *Guns, germs and steel: a short history of everybody for the last 13,000 years*. London: Vintage.

Dikötter, Frank. 1992. *The discourse of race in modern China*. Stanford, CA: Stanford University Press.

———. 1996. "Culture, 'race' and nation: the formation of national identity in twentieth century China." *Journal of International Affairs* 49.2: 590–605.

———. 1997. "Racial discourse in China: Continuities and permutations." In *The construction of racial identities in China and Japan*, ed. Frank Dikötter, 12–33. Hong Kong: Hong Kong University Press.

———. 2002. "Race in China." In *A companion to racial and ethnic studies*, ed. David Theo Goldberg and John Solomos, 495–510. Oxford: Blackwell.

Ding Weixiang. 1999. *Xiong Shili xueshu sixiang pingzhuan* [*A critical biography of Xiong Shili*]. Beijing: Tushuguan chubanshe.

Dirlik, Arlif. 1976. "T'ao Hsi-sheng: The social limits of change." In *The Limits of change: Essays on conservative alternatives in Republican China*, ed. Charlotte Furth, 305–31. Cambrige, MA: Harvard University Press.

———. 1978. *Revolution and history: Origins of Marxist historiography in China, 1919–1937*. Berkeley: University of California Press.

"Disanci quanguo daibiao dahui xuanyan" [Manifesto of the Guomindang's Third National Congress]. 1929. In *ZGQZ*, vol. 1, 624.

Dong Tiaofu. 1929. "Dao biandi qu" [To the frontier]. *Bianzheng* 1.1–2 (September–October): 1–18, and 1–46.

Dow Tsung-I. 1982. "The Confucian concept of a nation and its historical practice." *Asian Profile* 10.4: 347–62.

Dreyer, June Teufel. 1976. *China's forty millions: Minority nationalities and national integration in the People's Republic of China*. Cambridge, MA: Harvard University Press.

———. 2006. *China's political system: Modernization and tradition*. 5th ed. New York: Pearson Longman.

Du Xiangrong. 1929. "Zuijin duiyu xikang de kaocha yu yijian: yu bianzheng shunlian suo Liubu ge tongzhi tanhua" [Recent investigation and opinion on Xikang: a talk given to the comrades of the 24th Army at the Frontier Training Institute]. *Bianzheng* 1.1 (September): 69–82.

Duara, Prasenjit. 1993. "Provincial narratives of the nation: Centralism and federalism in Republican China." In *Cultural nationalism in East Asia: Representation and identity*, ed. Harumi Befu, 9–35. Berkeley: Institute of East Asian Studies, University of California, Center for Chinese Studies.

———. 1995. *Rescuing history from the nation: Questioning narratives of modern China*. Chicago: University of Chicago Press.

———. 1996. "De-Constructing the Chinese nation." *Chinese nationalism*, ed. Jonathan Unger, 31-55. Armonk, NY: M. E. Sharpe.

———. 1997. "Transnationalism and the predicament of sovereignty: China, 1900–1945." *The American Historical Review* 102.4 (October): 1030–51.

———. 2003. *Sovereignty and authenticity: Manchukuo and the East Asian modern*. Lanham, MD: Rowman & Littlefield.

East-Asiatic Economic Investigation Bureau, comp. 1932. *The Manchurian year book, 1932–1933*. Tokyo: Japan Times Printing Office.

Eastman, Lloyd. 1974. *The abortive revolution: China under Nationalist rule, 1927–1937*. Cambridge, MA: Harvard University Press.

———. 1991. "Nationalist China during the Nanking Decade, 1927–1937." In *The Nationalist era in China, 1927–1949*, ed. Lloyd Eastman et al., 1–52. Cambridge: Cambridge University Press.

Eberhard, Wolfram. 1982. *China's minorities: Yesterday and today*. Belmont, CA: Wadsworth.

Ebrey, Patricia. 1996. "Surnames and Han Chinese identity." In *Negotiating ethnicities in China and Taiwan*, ed. Melissa J. Brown, 19–36. Berkeley: Institute of East Asian Studies, University of California, Center for Chinese Studies.

Eley, Geoff, and Ronald Suny. 1996. "Introduction: From the moment of social history to the work of cultural representation." In *Becoming national: a reader*, ed. Geoff Eley and Ronald Suny, 3–37. Oxford: Oxford University Press.

Elleman, Bruce A. 1997. *Diplomacy and deception: The secret history of Sino-Soviet diplomatic relations, 1917–1927*. Armonk, NY: M. E. Sharpe.

Elliott, Mark. 2000. "The limits of Tartary: Manchuria in imperial and national geographies." *The Journal of Asian Studies* 59.3: 603–46.

———. 2001. *The Manchu way: The Eight Banners and ethnic identity in late imperial China*. Stanford, CA: Stanford University Press.

———. 2006. "Ethnicity in the Qing Eight Banners." In *Empire at the margins*, ed. Pamela Kyle Crossley, Helen Siu, and Donald Sutton, 27–57. Berkeley: University of California Press.

Engels, Frederick. 1972. *The origins of the family, private property and the state: In the light of the researches of Lewis H. Morgan*. Edited and intro by Eleanor Burke Leacock. New York: International.

Esenbel, Selçuk. 2004. "Japan's global claim to Asia and the world of Islam: Transnational nationalism and world power, 1900–1945." *The American Historical Review* 109.4: 1140–70.

Esherick, Joseph. 1976. *Reform and revolution in China: The 1911 revolution in Hunan and Hubei*. Berkeley: University of California Press.

Fairbank, John, ed. 1968. *The Chinese world order*. Cambridge, MA: Harvard University Press.

———. 1992. *China: a new history*. Cambridge, MA: Belknap Press of Harvard University Press.

Fairbank, John, and Edwin Reischauer. 1978. *China: Tradition & transformation*. Boston: Houghton Mifflin.

Fairbank, John, and Ssu-yü Teng. 1954. *China's response to the West: A documentary survey 1839–1923*. Cambridge, MA: Harvard University Press.

Fan Wenlan. 1950. "Zhonghua minzu de fazhan" [The development of the *Zhonghua minzu*]. *Xuexi* 3.1 (October 1): 45–47.

———. 1955. *Zhongguo tongshi jianbian* [*A concise general history of China*]. Rev. ed. Beijing: Remin chubanshe.

Fan Xiaofang, Bao Dongbo, and Li Chuanli. 1992. *Guomindang lilunjia Dai Jitao* [*Guomindang theoretician Dai Jitao*]. Zhengzhou: Henan Renmin chubanshe.

Farquhar, Judith, and James Hevia. 1993. "Culture and postwar American historiography of China." *Positions* 1.2: 486–525.

Fei Xiaotong. [1936] 1996. "Hualan yao shehui zuzhi—shehui renleixue diaochao de chuci changshi" [The organization of Hualan Yao society: A preliminary experiment in social anthropological field research]. In *Fei Xiaotong xuanji*, 83–147. Fuzhou: Fuzhou xinhua shudian.

———. 1981. *Toward a people's anthropology*. Beijing: New World.

———. 1989. *Zhonghua minzu duoyuan yiti geju* [The plurality and organic unity of the *Zhonghua minzu*]. Beijing: Zhongyang renmin xueyuan chubanshe.

Feng Youzhi. 1992. *Xikang shi shiyi* [*Supplementary collections of Xikang history*]. Kangding: Ganzi zangzu zizhizhou zhengxie wenshi ziliao weiyuanhui.

Fiskesjö, Magnus. 2006. "Rescuing the empire: Chinese nation-building in the twentieth century." *European Journal of East Asian Studies* 5.1: 15–44.

Fitzgerald, John. 1994. "'Reports of my death have been greatly exaggerated': The history of the death of China." In *China deconstructs: Politics, trade and regionalism*, ed. David S. G. Goodman and Gerald Segal, 21–58. London: Routledge.

———. 1996a. *Awakening China: Politics, culture, and class in the Nationalist Revolution*. Stanford, CA: Stanford University Press.

———. 1996b. "The nationless state: The search for a nation in modern Chinese nationalism." In *Chinese nationalism*, ed. Jonathan Unger, 56–85. Armonk, NY: M. E. Sharpe.

Fletcher, Joseph. 1978. "Ch'ing Inner Asia c. 1800." In *The Chambridge history of China: Late Ch'ing, 1800–1911*, vol. 10, pt. 1, ed. John King Fairbank, 35–106. Cambridge: Cambridge University Press.

———. 1995. *Studies on Chinese and Islamic Inner Asia*. Ed. Beatrice Manz. Aldershot: Variorum.

Fogel, Joshua, and Peter Zarrow, eds. 1997. *Imagining the people: Chinese intellectual and the concept of citizenship, 1890–1920*. Armonk, NY: M. E. Sharpe.

Forbes, Andrew. 1986. *Warlords and Muslims in Chinese Central Asia*. Cambridge: Cambridge University Press.

Franke, Herbert, and Denis Twitchett, eds. 1994. *The Cambridge history of China: Alien regimes and border states, 907–1368*, vol. 6. Cambridge: Cambridge University Press.

Friedman, Jonathan. 1979. *System, structure and contradiction: The evolution of "Asiatic" social formations*. Copenhagen: The National Museum of Denmark.

———. 1987. "Generalized exchange, theocracy and the opium trade." *Critique of Anthropology* 7.1: 15–31.

Fu Jing. 2006. "Spending on airports to soar in 5 years." *China Daily* [Online] http://www.chinadaily.com.cn/china/2006-05/09content_584844.htm (date accessed June 4, 2007).

Fu Sinian. 1934. "Yi xia dong xi shuo" [East-West theory of Yi and Xia]. In *FSQJ*, vol. 3, 823–93.

———. [1934b] 1996. "'Chengziya' xu" [Preface to 'Chengzi cliff']. In *Fu Sinian juan*, ed. Lei Yi, 351–55. Shijiazhuang: Hebei jiaoyu chubanshe.

———. 1935. "Zhonghua minzu shi zhengge de" [The Zhonghua minzu is one]. In *FSQJ*, vol. 6, 985–86.

———. 1939a. "Zhi Gu Jiegang shu" [Letter to Gu Jiegang]. In *FSQJ*, vol. 7, 1213–14.

———. 1939b. "Zhi Zhu Jiahua Hang Liwu" [Letter to Zhu Jiahua and Hang Liwu]. In *FSQJ*, vol. 7, 1215–16.

Fu Zuoyi. 1933a. "Fu Zuoyi guanyu De Wang zizhi huiyi qingxing ji zizhi dagang zhi mengzang weiyuanhui dian" [Fu Zuoyi's cable to the CMTA about the conditions of De Wang's autonomous conference and its autonomous outline]. In *ZMSD*, 5.1.5, 103–4.

———. 1933b. "Fu Zuoyi guanyu xinmeng faqi zizhi qiyin yi xuanhua qingxing zhi mengzang weiyuanhui dian" [Fu Zuyoyi's cable to the CMTA about the reasons for the origins of the autonomous movement among the Silinghol league and pacification conditions]. In *ZMSD*, 5.1.5, 105–7.

———. 1933c. "Fu Zuoyi wei baogao De Wang yunong Menggu ge qi shixing zizhi deng zhi mengzang weiyuanhui dian" [Fu Zuoyi's cable to the CMTA about how De Wang has hoodwinked all the Mongolian banners into carrying out autonomy and other matters]. In *ZMSD*, 5.1.5, 107–8.

———. 1933d. "Fu Zuoyi wei baogao De Wang zizhi chouhua bingli ji ge meng daibiao taidu zhi mengzang weiyuanhui dian" [Fu Zuoyi's cable to the CMTA concerning De Wang's plans to use military force and the attitude of all the Mongolian league delegates]. In *ZMSD*, 5.1.5, 107.

———. 1933e. "Fu Zuoyi wei baogao Sha mengzhang dui De Wang zizhi taidu zhi mengzang weiyuanhui dian" [Fu Zuoyi's cable to the CMTA reporting league chieftain Sha's attitude towards De Wang's autonomous movement]. In *ZMSD*, 5.1.5, 105.

———. 1933f. "Guomin zhenggu xingzheng yuan mishu chuwei chaosong Fu Zuoyi guanyu De Wang zizhi qingxing ji chuli banfa zhi mengzang weiyuanhui" [A duplicate copy of Fu Zuoyi's description of De Wang's autonomous movement and methods for dealing with it sent by the secretary of the Executive Yuan to the CMTA]. In *ZMSD*, 5.1.1, 100–1.

———. 1933g. "Suiyuan sheng zhengfu zhuyi Fu Zuoyi baogao De Wang zai Bailingmiao kaihui qingxing zhi mengzang weiyuanhui" [Suiyuan provincial government chairman Fu Zuoyi's cable to the CMTA reporting De Wang's convening of a conference at Bailingmiao]. In *ZMSD*, 5.1.5, 91–94.

Furth, Charlotte. 1976. "The sage as rebel: The inner world of Chang Ping-lin." In *The Limits of change: Essays on conservative alternatives in Republican China*, 113–50. Cambridge, MA: Harvard University Press.

Gao Junyu. 1922. "Guoren duiyu menggu wenti ying chi de taidui" [What the attitude of our country's people should be toward the Mongolian question]. *Xiangdao zhoubao* 3 (September 27): 19–20.

Gasster, Michael. 1969. *Chinese intellectuals and the revolution of 1911: The birth of modern Chinese radicalism*. Seattle: University of Washington Press.

Gellner, Ernest. 1983. *Nations and nationalism*. Ithaca, NY: Cornell University Press.

Gernant, Karen. 1980. "The Long March." PhD diss., University of Oregon.

Giersch, C. Pat. 2006. *Asian borderlands: The transformation of Qing China's Yunnan frontier*. Cambridge, MA: Harvard University Press.

Gladney, Dru. 1991. *Muslim Chinese: Ethnic nationalism in the People's Republic.* Cambridge, MA: Council on East Asian Studies, Harvard University.

———. 1994. "Representing nationality in China: Refiguring majority/minority identities." *The Journal of Asian Studies* 53.1 (February): 92–123.

———. 1996. "Relational alterity: Constructing Dungan (Hui), Uygur, and Kazakh identites across China, Central Asia, and Turkey." *History and Anthropology* 9.4: 445–77.

Goldstein, Melvyn. 1989. *A history of modern Tibet, 1913–1951: The demise of the Lamaist state.* Berkeley: University of California Press.

Goldstein, Melvyn, Dawei Sherap, and William R. Siebenschuh. 2004. *A Tibetan revolutionary: the political life and times of Bapa Phüntso Wangye.* Berkeley: University of California Press.

"Gongchan guoji shining weiyuanhui zhuxituan guanyu Zhongguo minzu jiefang yundong he Guomindang wenti de jueyi" [The resolution of the Presidium of the Comintern's Central Executive Committee concerning China's national liberation movement and the question of the Guomindang]. 1923. In *LGZY*, vol. 1, 342–45.

Gottschang, Thomas. 1987. "Economic change, disasters, and migration: The historical case of Manchuria." *Economic Development and Cultural Change* 35.3 (April): 461–90.

Gramsci, Antonio. 1985. *Selections from cultural writings.* Cambridge, MA: Harvard Unversity Press.

Greenfeld, Liah. 1992. *Nationalism: Five roads to modernity.* Cambridge, MA: Harvard University Press.

Gregor, A. James, and Maria Hsia Chang. 1979. "Nazionalfascismo and the revolutionary nationalism of Sun Yat-sen." *The Journal of Asian Studies* 39.1 (November): 21–37.

Gu Chao. 1994. *Gu Jiegang nianpu* [*Chronicle of Gu Jiegang*]. Beijing: Zhongguo shehui kexue chubanshe.

Gu Hong, comp. 1998. *Gu Jiegang xueshu wenhua suibi* [*Gu Jiegang's informal academic and cultural writings*]. Beijing: Zhongguo tiedao chubanshe.

Gu Jiegang. 1921. "Zishu zhengli Zhongguo lishi yijianshu" [Letter expressing my own opinion on reorganising Chinese history]. In *GSB*, vol. 1, 34–37.

———. 1923a. "Taolun gushi da Liu Hu liang xiansheng shu" [Discussion of ancient history: A reply to Mr. Hu and Mr. Liu]. In *GSB*, vol. 1, 99–102.

———. 1923b. "Yu Qian Xuantong xiansheng lun gushi shu" [Letters discussing ancient history with Mr. Qian Xuantong]. In *GSB*, vol. 1, 59–82.

———. 1926. "Zixu" [Preface]. In *GSB*, vol. 1, 1–103.

———. 1933. "Gu yu" [Gu Jiegang's preface]. In *GSB*, vol. 4, 1–24.

———. 1937. "Ruhe keshi Zhonghua minzu tuanjie lai?" [What can cause the Zhonghua nation to unify?] In *XMWZ*, vol. 1, 1–3.

———. 1938. "Zhongguo bianjiang wenti ji qi duice" [China's frontier question and policy]. In *XMWZ*, vol, 1, 13–22.

———. [1939] 1996. "Zhonghua minzu shi yige" [The Zhonghua nation is one]. In *Gu Jiegang juan*, ed. Gu Chao and Gu Hong, 773–85. Shijiazhuang: Hebei Jiaoyu chubanshe.

"Guanli lama simiao tiaolie" [Regulations governing the management of Lamaist temples]. 1935. In *ZMSD*, 5.1.5, 13.

"Guanyu mengzang zhi jueyi an" [Resolution on Mongolia and Tibet]. 1929. In *ZGQZ*, vol. 1, 765–67.

"Guanyu Sui-Meng gongzuo de jueding" [Decision on our work among the Mongols of Suiyuan Province]. 1938. In *MZWT*, 612–17.

"Guanyu Zhongguo lingnei shaoshu minzu wenti de jueyi'an" [The draft resolution on the national minority question in China]. 1931. In *MZWT*, 169–71.

Guldin, Gregory Eliyu. 1994. *The saga of anthropology in China: From Malinowski to Moscow to Mao*. Armonk, NY: M. E. Sharpe.

Guojia tongjiju renkou he shehui keji tongjisi, comp. 2003. *2000 nian renkou pucha Zhongguo minzu renkou ziliao* [*Tabulation on nationalities of 2000 population census of China*]. Beijing: Minzu chubanshe.

"Guomin zhengfu gongbu mengguo meng-bu-qi zuzhifa" [The national government announces the Organizational Law for Mongolian Leagues, Banners and Tribes]. 1931. In *ZMSD*, 5.1.5, 45-48.

"Guomin zhengfu mengzang weiyuanhui zuzhifa" [Organizational law of the CMTA]. 1928. In *ZMSD*, 5.1.5, 1–2.

"Guomin zhengfu wenguanchu wei niding neimeng zizhi banfa zhi xingzheng yuan gonghan" [Public circular on the methods for Inner Mongolian autonomy drafted by the national government's Civil Officials Department and presented to the Executive Yuan]. 1934. In *ZMSD*, 5.1.5, 69–72.

Handler, Richard. 1988. *Nationalism and the politics of culture in Quebec*. Madison: University of Wisconsin Press.

Hao Weimin. 1997. *Neimenggu gemingshi* [*Revolutionary history of Inner Mongolia*]. Hohhot: Neimenggu daxue chubanshe.

Hao Yan. 2000. "Tibetan population in China: Myths and facts re-examined." *Asian Ethnicity* 1.1 (March): 11–36.

Harrell, Stevan, ed. 1995a. *Cultural encounters on China's ethnic frontiers*. Seattle: University of Washington Press.

———. 1995b. "Introduction: Civilizing projects and the reaction to them." In *Cultural encounters on China's ethnic frontiers*, 3–36. Seattle: University of Washington Press.

———. 1996. "Introduction." In *Negotiating ethnicities in China and Taiwan*, ed. Melissa J. Brown, 1–18. Berkeley: Institute of East Asian Studies, University of California, Center for Chinese Studies.

———. 2001. *Ways of being ethnic in Southwest China*. Seattle: University of Washington Press.

Harrison, Henrietta. 2000. *The making of the Republican citizen: Political ceremonies and symbols in China 1911–1929*. Oxford: Oxford University Press.

———. 2001. *China*. London: Oxford University Press.

Heater, Derek. 1994. *National self-determination: Woodrow Wilson and his legacy*. New York: St. Martin's.

Henderson, John B. 1984. *The development and decline of Chinese cosmology*. New York: Columbia University Press.

Hirsch, Francine. 2005. *Empire of nations: Ethnographic knowledge and the making of the Soviet Union*. Ithaca, NY: Cornell University Press.

Ho Ping-Ti. 1976. "The Chinese civilization: A search for the roots of its longevity." *The Journal of Asian Studies* 35.4 (August): 547–54.

———. 1998. "In defense of sinicization: A rebuttal of Evelyn Rawski's 'Reenvisioning the Qing.'" *The Journal of Asian Studies* 57.1 (February): 123–55.

Hobsbawm, Eric. 1990. *Nations and nationalism since 1780: Programme, myth, and reality*. Cambridge: Cambridge University Press.

Hobsbawm, Eric, and Terence Ranger, eds. 1983. *The invention of tradition*. Cambridge: Cambridge University Press.

Hon Tze-ki. 1996. "Ethnic and cultural pluralism: Gu Jiegang's vision of a new China in his studies on ancient history." *Modern China* 22.3 (July): 315–39.

———. 2004. "Cultural identity and local self-government: a study of Liu Yizheng's history of Chinese culture." *Modern China* 30.4 (October): 506–42.

Hong Quanhu. 1980. *Zhongshan xiansheng minzu zijuelun zhi yanjiu* [*Research on Mr. Sun Yat-sen's theory of self-determination*]. Taipei: Guoli zhengzhi daxue sanminzhuyi yanjiusuo yanshi lunwen.

Hostetler, Laura. 2001. *Qing colonial enterprise: Ethnography and cartography in early modern China*. Chicago: The University of Chicago Press.

Hoston, Germaine. 1994. *The state, identity, and the national question in China and Japan*. Princeton, NJ: Princeton University Press.

Hsiao Kung-chuan. 1979. *A history of Chinese political thought*, vol. 1. Trans. F. W. Mote. Princeton, NJ: Princeton University Press.

Hu Boxuan. 1932. "Dongbei sisheng zhi jianzhi lishi yu minzu yuanliu—wei bi riren 'Dongbei fei Zhonguo lingtu' shuo er zuo" [Establishing the historical and national origin and development of the four Northeastern provinces—refuting the Japanese claim and actions that "Manchuria is not part of Chinese territory"]. *Xin Yaxiaya* 3.4 (January): 39–56.

Hu Guowei. 1925a. "Minzu zijue yu guojia duli" [National self-determination and state independence]. *Xingshi zhoubao* 41 (July 18): 2.

———. 1925b. "'Qinshan zhuyi' yu 'waijiao zhengce'" ["Good-will-ism" and "diplomatic policy"). *Xingshi zhoubao* 27 (April 11): 2.

Hu Hanmin. [1929] 1980. "Yongbao wo guojia minzu de duli ziyou pingdeng" [Forever protect our country's national independence, freedom and equality]. In *Hu Hanmin shiji ziliao huiji*, vol. 2, ed. Zunzui xuehui, 458–65. Hong Kong: Datong tushu gongsi.

Hu Horu. 1929. "Bianyan" [Preface]. *Bianzheng* 1.1 (September): i–ii.

Huan Kuan. 1931. *Discourse on salt and iron: A debate on state control of commerce and industry in ancient China*. Trans. Esson Gale. Leiden: E. J. Brill.

"Huang buzhang Zhao fuweiyuanzhang zai Bailingmiao yu neimeng zizhi huiyi shangding menggu zizhi banfa" [Methods for Mongolian autonomy negotiated between Minister Huang and vice-chairman Zhao and the Bailingmiao Inner Mongolian Autonomous Congress]. 1933. In *ZMSD*, 5.1.5, 116–18.

Huang Fengsheng. 1935. *Neimeng mengqi zizhi yundong ji* [*Record of actual events from the Inner Mongolian league and banner autonomous movement*]. Shanghai: Zhonghua shuju.

Huang Guangxue, ed. 1995. *Zhongguo de minzu shibie* [*Distinguishing China's nationalities*]. Beijing: Minzu chubanshe.

Huang Musong. 1934a. "Huang Musong chenbao shiqi ri kaxia han quanwen zhi xingzheng yuan deng dian" [Huang Musong's cable to the Executive Yuan and others with the complete text of the Kashag's October 17 letter]. In *ZMSD*, 5.1.5, 232–33.

———. 1934b. "Huang Musong guanyu rezheng deng jiejue zhongyan yu xizang wenti taidu zhi xingzheng yuan deng midian" [Secret cable of Huang Musong to the Executive Yuan and others concerning the Reting's attitude about the solution of Sino-Tibetan questions]. In *ZMSD*, 5.1.5, 211–12.

———. 1934c. "Huang Musong jiang kaxia han yaodian bao xingzheng yuan" [Huang Musong's cable to the Executive Yuan reporting the main points of the Kashag's letter]. In *ZMSD*, 5.1.5, 229–30.

———. 1934d. "Huang Musong mibao sikalun tichu cuoshang zhongyang yu xikang wenti erhou juxing dianli zhe xingzheng yuan deng dian" [Huang Musong's secret cable to the Executive Yuan and others concerning the four Shapes' desire to first discuss Sino-Tibetan problems before holding the memorial ceremony]. In *ZMSD*, 5.1.5, 211–12.

———. 1934e. "Huang Musong wei chenbao kaxia lai han suoti shi xiang tiaojian bing niji hui jing shi zhi xingzheng yuan deng dian" [Huang Musong's cable to the Executive Yuan and others reporting the Kashag's ten-point proposal and his intentions to immediately return to the capital]. In *ZMSD*, 5.1.5, 242–43.

———. 1934f. "Huang Musong wei kalun tichu zhongyang yu xizang wei tanyue guanyu bing yaoqiu jiejue kang-zang chuan-zang jiewu shi zhi xingzheng yuan deng dian" [Huang Musong's cable to the Executive Yuan and others about the Shapes' proposal for priest-patron relations between Tibet and the Central Government and their desire to resolve the Xikang-Tibet and Sichuan-Tibet border issue]. In *ZMSD*, 5.1.5, 223–24.

———. 1934g. "Huang Musong wei kaxia biangua bu tichu zhongyang yu xizang guanxi shi zhi xingzheng yuan dian dian" [Huang Musong's cable to the Executive Yuan and others concerning the Kashag's going back on its word to discuss Sino-Tibetan relations]. In *ZMSD*, 5.1.5, 222–23.

———. 1934h. "Huang Musong wei wanju kaxia shisan xiang koutou jianyi shi zhi xingzheng yuan dian" [Huang Musong's cable to the Executive Yuan stating his tactful refusal of the Kashag's thirteen-point oral proposal]. In *ZMSD*, 5.1.5, 238–39.

———. 1935. "Huang Musong fengshi ru zang cefeng bing zhicha shisanjie dala dashi baogaoshu" [Huang Musong's report on his mission to Tibet to confer a title and express condolence to the Thirtheeth Dalai Lama]. In *ZMSD*, 5.1.5, 261–357.

"Hunansheng diyici nongmin daibiao dahui jiefang miao-yao jueyi'an" [The resolution of the First Congress of Hunan Peasant Representatives on the liberation of the Miao and Yao]. 1926. In *MZWT*, 52.

Ishikawa Yoshihiro. 2004. "Liang Qichao, the field of geography in Meiji Japan, and geographical determinism." In *The role of Japan in Liang Qichao's introduction of modern Western civilization to China*, ed. Joshua Fogel, 156–76. Berkeley: Institute of East Asian Studies, University of California, Center for Chinese Studies.

Jaffe, Philip. 1947. "Introduction." In *China's destiny and Chinese economic theory*, notes and commontary by Philip Jaffe, 1–25. London: D. Dobson.

Jagchid, Sechin. 1954. *Menggu zhi jinxi* [*Mongolia yesterday and today*], 2 vols. Taipei: Zhonghua wenhua chubanshi weiyuanhui.

———. 1979. "The failure of a self-determination movement: The Inner Mongolian case." In *Soviet Asian ethnic frontiers*, ed. William McCagg and Brian Silver, 229–45. New York: Pergamon.

———. 1999. *The last Mongol prince: The life and times of Demchugdongrob, 1902–1966*. Bellingham: Center for East Asian Studies, Western Washington University.

Jia Lanpo, and Huang Weiwen. 1990. *The story of Peking Man from archaeology to mystery*. Trans. Yin Zhiqi. Beijing: Foreign Language Press.

Jian Bozan. [1943] 1950. *Zhongguo shigang* [*An outline of Chinese history*]. 2 vols. Repr. Beijing: Sanlian shudian.

———. [1943b] 1969. "Xiazu de qiyuan yu shiqian zhi ouerduosi" [The origin of the Xiazu and the Ordos]. In *Zhongguoshi lunji*, vol. 1, 35–47. Hong Kong: Longmen shudian.

Jiang Ping. 1994. *Zhongguo minzu wenti de lilun yu shixian* [*Theory and practice of China's national question*]. Beijing: Zhonggong zhongyang dangxiao chubanshe.

Jin Binggao. 1987. "'Shaoshu minzu' yici zai wo guo heshi chuxian" [When does the term "minority nationals" first appear in our country?]. *Minzu tuanjie* 6: 47.

Jin Jitang. 1936. "Huijiao huizu shuo" [On the differences between Islam and the Hui nationality]. *Yugong banyuekan* 5.11 (August 1): 29–39.

Johnson, Chalmers. 1962. *Peasant nationalism and Communist power: The emergence of Revolutionary China, 1937–1945*. Stanford, CA: Stanford University Press.

Johnson, David, Andrew Nathan, and Evelyn Rawski, eds. 1985. *Popular culture in late imperial China*. Berkeley: University of California Press.

Jones, Siân. 1997. *The archaeology of ethnicity: Constructing identities in the past and present*. London: Routledge.

Kaldor, Mary. 2004. "Nationalism and globalization." *Nations and Nationalism* 10.1–2: 161–77.

Kapp, Robert. 1973. *Szechwan and the Chinese Republic: Provincial militarism and central power, 1911–1938*. New Haven, CT: Yale University Press.

Karakhan, Leo. 1923. "Jia-la-kan gei Bao-luo-ting de xin" [Letter from Leo Karakhan to Mikhail Borodin]. In *LGZY*, vol. 1, 386–94.

———. 1924. Jia-la-kan gei Bao-luo-ting de xin [Letter from Leo Karakhan to Mikhail Borodin]. In *LGZY*, vol. 1, 417–19.

Karl, Rebecca. 1998. "Creating Asia: China in the world at the beginning of the twentieth century." *American Historical Review* 103.4 (October): 1096–1118.

———. 2002. *Staging the world: Chinese nationalism at the turn of the twentieth century*. Durham, NC: Duke University Press.

Kawakami, K. K. 1933. *Manchoukuo: Child of conflict*. New York: Macmillan.

Keyes, Charles. 2002. "Presidential address: 'The peoples of Asia': Science and politics in the classification of ethnic groups in Thailand, China, and Vietnam." *The Journal of Asian Studies* 61.4 (November): 1163–1203.

Kindermann, Gottfried-Karl. 1989. "An overview of Sun Yat-sen's doctrine." In *Sun Yat-sen's doctrine in the modern world*, ed. Cheng Chu-yuan, 52–78. Boulder, CO: Westview Press.

Kirby, William. 1997. "The internationalization of China: Foreign relations at home and abroad in the Republican Era." *China Quarterly* 150 (June): 433–58.

———. 2005. "When did China become China? Thoughts on the twentieth century." In *The teleology of the modern nation-state*, ed. Joshua Fogel, 105–14. Philadelphia: University of Pennsylvania Press.

Klein, Donald, and Anne B. Clark, comps. 1971. *Biographical dictionary of Chinese communism, 1921–1965*. 2 vols. Cambridge, MA: Harvard University Press.

Kohl, Philip, and Clare Fawcett. 1996. "Archaeology in the service of the state: theoretical considerations." In *Nationalism, politics, and the practice of archaeology*, 3–18. Cambridge: Cambridge University Press.

Kulp, Katherine. 2000. *Creating the Zhuang: Ethnic politics in China*. Boulder, CO: Lynne Rienner.

Kymlicka, Will. 1995. *Multicultural citizenship: A liberal theory of minority rights*. New York: Oxford University Press.

Lacouperie, Albert Terrien de. 1894. *Western origins of the early Chinese civilization from 2300 B.C. to 200 A.D., or, chapters on the elements derived from the old civilizations of West Asia in the formation of the ancient Chinese culture*. London: Asher.

Laitinen, Kauko. 1990. *Chinese nationalism in the late Qing Dynasty: Zhang Binglin as an anti-Manchu propagandist*. London: Curzon.

"Lama jiangzheng banfa" [Methods for rewarding and punishing lamas]. 1936. In *ZMSD*, 5.1.5, 13–18.

Landy, Marcia. 1986. "Culture and politics in the work of Antonio Gramsci." *Boundary 2* 14.3 (Spring): 49–70.

Langlois, John D. 1980. "Chinese culturalism and the Yuan analogy: Seventeenth-century perspectives." *Harvard Journal of Asiatic Studies* 40.2: 355–98.

———. 1981. *China under Mongol rule*. Princeton, NJ: Princeton University Press.

Lattimore, Owen. 1932. "Chinese colonization in Manchuria." In *Studies in frontier history: Collected papers, 1928–1958*, 307–38. London: Oxford University Press.

———. 1936a. "The eclipse of Inner Mongolian nationalism." In *Studies in frontier history: Collected papers, 1928–1958*, 427–39. London: Oxford University Press.

———. 1936b. "The historical setting of Inner Mongolian nationalism." In *Studies in frontier history: Collected papers, 1928–1958*, 440–55. London: Oxford University Press.

———. 1937. "Origins of the Great Wall of China: a frontier concept in theory and practice." In *Studies in frontier history: Collected papers, 1928–1958*, 97–118.

———. 1938. "The georaphical factor in Mongol history." In *Studies in frontier history: Collected papers, 1928–1958*, 241–58. London: Oxford University Press.

———. 1940. *Inner Asian frontiers of China*. New York: American Geographical Society.

———. 1962. *Studies in frontier history: Collected papers, 1928–1958*. London: Oxford University Press.

Lavely, William, and R. Bin Wong. 1998. "Revising the Malthusian narrative: The comparative study of population dynamics in late imperial China." *The Journal of Asian Studies* 57.3 (August): 714–48.

Legge, James, trans. 1961. *The Chinese Classics: The Ch'un Ts'ew with the Tso Chuen*, vol. 5. Hong Kong: Hong Kong University Press.

Leibold, James. 2003. "Constructing the Zhonghua minzu: The frontier and national questions in early twentieth-century China." PhD diss., University of Southern California.

———. 2004. "Positioning 'minzu' within Sun Yat-sen's discourse of minzuzhuyi." *Journal of Asian History* 38.2: 163–213.

Lenin, Vladimir. [1920] 1960–70. "Preliminary draft theses on the national and the colonial question for the Second Congress of the Communist International." In *Works*, vol. 31, 144–51. Moscow: Foreign Language Publishing House.

Levenson, Joseph R. 1964–65. *Confucian China and its modern fate: A trilogy*. Berkeley: University of California Press.

Levine, Marilyn. 1992. "Zeng Qi and the frozen revolution." In *Roads not taken: the struggle of opposition parties in twentieth-century China*, ed. Roger Jeans, 225–40. Boulder, CO: Westview.

Li Da. [1929] 1980. "Minzu wenti [The national question]." In *Li Da wenji*, vol. 1, 560–605. Beijing: Renmin chubanshe.

Li Dazhao. 1917. "Xin zhonghua minzuzhuyi" [New Zhonghua nationalism]. In *LDW*, vol. 1: 287–89.

———. 1919a. "Dayaxiyazhuyi yu xinyaxiyazhuyi" [Pan-Asianism and new Asianism]. In *LDW*, vol. 2, 253–55.

———. 1919b. "Zailun xinyaxiyazhuyi" [Another discussion of new Asianism]. In *LDW*, vol. 3, 74–78.

———. 1925. "Menggu minzu de jiefang yundong" [The liberation movement of the Mongolian nationality]. In *LDW*, vol. 5, 40–42.

Li Guoqi. 1981. "Zhongguo jindai minzu sixiang" [Nationalist thought in modern China]. In *Jindai Zhongguo sixiang renwu lun: minzuzhuyi* [*Essays on modern Chinese thought and personalities: nationalism*], ed. Li Guoqi, 19–43. Taipei: Shibao wenhua chuban shiye youxian gongsi.

Li Ji [Li Chi]. 1932. *Manchuria in history: A summary*. Peiping: Peking Union Bookstore.

———. [1934] 1977. "Zhongguo kaogu baogao jizhiyi chengziyai fachu baogao yu" [Chinese archaeological report: Preface to a report on the excavation of Chengzi cliff]. In *Li Ji kaogu xuelun wenji*, 189–205. Taipei: Lianjing chubanshe yegongsi.

Li Juanli. 1992. *Guomindang lilunjia Dai Jitao* [*Guomindang theoretician Dai Jitao*]. Hebei: Henan Renmin chubanshe.

Li, Rose Maria. 1989. "Migration to China's northern frontier, 1953–82." *Population and Development Review* 15.3 (September): 503–38.

Li Shiyue, and Zhao Shiyuan. 1984. "Sun Zhongshan de minzuzhuyi he 'fanman' wenti" [The problem of Sun Yat-sen's minzuzhuyi and "anti-Manchuism"]. In *Sun Zhongshan yu Zhongguo minzu geming*. Shenyang: Liaoning renmin chubanshe.

Li Tieh-Tseng. 1956. *The historical status of Tibet*. New York: King's Crown.

Li Weihan. 1940. "Huihui wenti yanjiu" [Research on the Huihui question]. In *MZWT*, 841–56.

———. [1957] 1992. "Huihui minzu de xingcheng he chubu fazhan" [The origins and initial development of the Huihui nationality]. In *Bai Shouyi minzu zongjiao lunji*, 155–68. Beijing: Beijing shifan daxue chubanshe.

———. 1986. "Zhongyang xibei gongzuo weiyuanhui he shaoshu minzu gongzuo" [The Central Committee's Northwest Work Committee and its national minority work]. In *Huiyi yu yanjiu* [*Research and reminiscences*], vol. 2, 451–71. Beijing: Zhonggong dangshi ziliao chubanshe.

Li Yimin. 1936. "Huimin gongzuo zhong de jige wenti" [Several problems in our work among the Hui people]. In *MZWT*, 518–21.

Li Yushu. 1968. "Minguo chunian de waimenggu wenti" [Problem of Outer Mongolia during the early Republican Period]. In *Menggu yanjiu*, ed. Guang Lu, 42–50. Taipei: Zhongguo bianjiang shiyuwen xuehui chuban.

Li Ziyuan. 1995. *Zhongguo jinxiandai shaoshu minzu geming shiyao* [*Outline of the contemporary revolutionary history of the Chinese national minorities*]. Beijing: Zhongyang minzu daxue chubanshe.

Liang Qichao. 1901. Zhongguoshi xulun [An introductory essay of Chinese history]. In *YBSWJ*, vol. 6, 1–12.

———. 1903a. "Xin shixue" [New historiography]. In *YBSWJ*, vol. 9, 1–32.

———. 1903b. "Zhengzhi xuejia Bo-lun-zhi-li zhi xueshuo" [The theories of political scientist Bluntschli]. In *YBSWJ*, vol. 13, 67–89.

———. [1903c] 1957. *Xin dalu youji jielu* [Notes from a journey to the new continent]. Repr. Taipei: Zhonghua shuju.

———. 1907. "Lishi shang Zhongguo minzu zhi guancha" [A historical investigation of the Chinese minzu]. In *YBSHJ*, vol. 41, 1–34.

———. 1922. "Zhongguo lishi shang minzu zhi yanjiu" [Research on the role of minzu in Chinese history]. In *YBSHJ*, vol. 42, 1–34.

Lin Ganquan, and Ye Guisheng. 1985. "Yin Da." In *ZSP*, vol. 2, 1645–63.

Lin Hsiao-ting. 2002. "The 1934 Chinese mission to Tibet: A re-examintion." *Journal of the Royal Asiatic Society* 12.3: 327–41.

———. 2006. *Tibet and nationalist China's frontier: Intrigues and ethnopolitics, 1928–1949*. Vancouver: University of British Columbia Press.

Lin Huaming. 1996. "Hongjun changzheng yu minzu gongzuo" [Nationality work and the Red Army's Long March]. In *Changzheng dashidian*, vol. 2, ed. Changzheng dashidian bianweihui, 2046–51. Guiyang: Guizhou renminchu banshe.

Lin Huixiang. [1936] 1996. *Zhongguo minzushi* [*History of the Chinese minzu*]. 2 vols. Repr. Beijing: Shangwu yinshuguan.

Lin Yaohua. 1963. "Guanyu 'minzu' yici de shiyong he yiming de wenti" [On the use and translation of "minzu"]. *Lishi yanjiu* 2: 171–90.

Ling Chunsheng. 1938. "Jianshe xinan bianjiang de zhongyao" [Importance of developing the Southwest frontier]. *Xinan bianjiang* 2 (November): 121–26.

Lipman, Jonathan. 1997. *Familiar strangers: A history of muslims in northwest China*. Seattle: University of Washington Press.

———. 2002. "How many minzu in a nation? Modern travellers meet China's frontier peoples." *Inner Asia* 4: 113–30.

Liu Chun. 1950–51. "Minzu zhengce jianshou tiyao" [Summary of a lecture on nationality policy]. In *Minzu wenti wenji*, 74–93. Beijing: Minzu chubanshe.

———. 1988. "Kangri zhanzheng shiqi canjia minzu gongzuo de huiyi" [Reminiscence on my involvement in the nationality work during the period of resistance against Japan]. *Neimenggu dangshi ziliao* 1 (1988): 228–46.

———. 1996. *Minzu wenti wenji* [*Essays on the national question*]. Beijing: Minzu chubanshe.

Liu Dianjue, and Chen Fangzheng, comps. 1992. *Liji zhuzi suoyin* [A concordance to the *Liji*]. Hong Kong: Shangwu yinshuguan.

Liu Jun, and Zhu Yuan. 2006. "Railway to new riches." *China Daily*, North American ed., August 20. http://en.tibet.cn/news/tin/t20060822_142699.htm (accessed December 3, 2006).

Liu Li. 1999. "Who were the ancestors? The origins of Chinese ancestral culture and racial myths." *Antiquity* 73.281: 602–13.

Liu, Lydia. 1995. *Translingual practice: Literature, national culture, and translated modernity—China, 1900–1937*. Stanford, CA: Stanford University Press.

———. 2004. *The clash of empires: the invention of China in modern world making*. Cambridge, MA: Harvard University Press.

Liu Manqing. [1933] 1987. *Kangzang yaozheng* [*Mission to Tibet and Xikang*]. Repr. Taipei: Nantian shuju.

Liu, Melinda. 2006. "Tibet rides the rail." *Newsweek*, International ed., July 24. http://www.msnbc.msn.com/id/13879454/site/newsweek/ (accessed December 3, 2006).

Liu Qiqian. 1986. *Gu Jiegang xiansheng xueshu* [*Academic research of Mr. Gu Jiegang*]. Beijing: Zhonghua shuju.

Liu Xianxiao. 1965. "Chuanshan zhengzhi sixiang lunlue" [Introduction to the political thought of Wang Fuzhi]. In *Wang Chuanshan xueshu taolunji*, vol. 2, ed. Hunansheng zhexue shehui kexue xuehui lianhehui, 395–432. Beijing: Zhonghua shuju.

Liu Xiao. 1936. "Liu Xiao tongzhi dui menggu gongzuo de yijian" [The ideas of comrade Liu Xiao toward Mongolian work]. In *MZWT*, 511–13.

Liu Xiaoyuan. 2004. *Frontier passage: Ethnopolitics and the rise of Chinese communism, 1921–1945*. Washington, DC: Woodrow Wilson Center; Stanford, CA: Stanford University Press.

———. 2006. *Reins of liberation: An entangled history of Mongolian indepedence, Chinese territoriality, and great power hegemony, 1911–1950*. Washington, DC: Woodrow Wilson Center; Stanford, CA: Stanford University Press.

Liu Zhangda. 1926. "Lian'e zuiyan" [The crime of uniting with Russia]. *Xingshi zhoubao* 68 (June 6): 1–2.

Lodén, Torbjörn. 1996. "Nationalism transcending the state: Changing conceptions of Chinese identity." In *Asian forms of the nation*, ed. Stein Tønnesson and Hans Antlöv, 270–96. Richmond, Surrey: Curzon.

Lu Maode. 1926. "Ping Gu Jiegang *Gushibian*" [Critique of Gu Jiegang's *Gushibian*]. In *GSB*, vol. 2, 369–88.

Lu Minghui. 1980. *Menggu "zizhi yundong" shiwei* [*The complete story of the Mongolian "autonomous movement"*]. Beijing: Zhonghua shuju.
Lü Simian. [1934] 1987. *Zhongguo minzushi* [*History of the Chinese minzu*]. Repr. Shanghai: Dongfang chuban zhongxin.
Lü Zhenyu. [1940] 1961. *Shiqianqi Zhongguo shehui yanjiu* [*Studies on prehistoric Chinese society*]. Rev. ed. Repr. Beijing: Shenghuo dushu – xinzhi sanlian shudian.
———. 1941. *Jianming zhongguo tongshi* [*Concise general history of China*]. Hong Kong: Shenghuo shudian.
———. 1943. "Zhonghua minzu renzhong de youlai" [The origins of the Zhonghua minzu race]. *Jiefang ribao* (April 17): 4.
———. 1950. *Zhongguo minzu jianshi*. [*A concise history of the Chinese minzu*]. Rev. ed. Shanghai: Sanlian shudian.
Luo Lan. 1958. "Ping 'huihui minzu de lishi he xiankuang'" [Critique of "The current conditions and history of the Huihui minzu"]. *Xin jianshe* 12: 61–64.
Luo Zhufeng, comp. 1997. *Hanzu dacidian* [*Encyclopaedia of the Chinese language*]. 3 vols., miniaturized ed. Shanghai: Hanyu dacidian chubanshe.
Lustick, Ian. 2002. "Hegemony and the riddle of nationalism: the dialectics of nationalism and religion in the Middle East." *Logos* 1.3 (Summer): 18-44.
Ma Jinke, and Hong Jingling. 1994. *Zhongguo jindai shixue fazhan xulun* [*Introduction to the development of modern Chinese historiography*]. Beijing: Zhongguo renmin daxue chubanshe.
Ma Ruheng, and Ma Dazheng. 1994. *Qingdai de bianjiang zhengce* [*Qing Dynasty's frontier policy*]. Beijing: Zhongguo shehui kexue chubanshe.
Ma Ruheng, and Zhao Yuntian. 1991. "Qingdai bianjiang minzu zhengce jianlun" [Brief discussion of the Qing dynasty's frontier nationality policy]. *Qingshi yanjiu* 2: 1–14.
Ma Yi. 1939. "Miao-Yao jiaoyu zhi jiantao yu jianyi" [Review and proposal for Miao and Yao education]. *Xinan bianjiang* 7 (November): 604–13.
Mackerras, Colin. 1994. *China's minorities: Integration and modernization in the twentieth century*. London: Oxford University Press.
———. 1995. *China's minority cultures: Identities and integration since 1912*. New York: St. Martin's.
Maier, Charles. 2000. "Forum essay: Consigning the twentieth century to history: Alternative narratives for the modern era." *The American Historical Review* 105.3 (June): 807–31.
Mair, Victor. 1985. "Language and ideology in the written popularizations of the *Sacred Edict*." In *Popular culture in late imperial China*, ed. Johnson, Nathan, and Rawski, 325-59. Berkeley: University of California Press.
———. 2005. "The north(west)ern peoples and the recurrent origins of the 'Chinese' state." In *The teleology of the modern nation-state*, ed. Joshua Fogel, 46–84. Philadelphia: University of Pennsylvania Press.
Mao Zedong. 1925. "Zhongguo shehui ge jieji de fenxi" [Analysis of the various classes in Chinese society]. In *MZXJ*, 1, 3–11.
———. 1934. "Zhonghua suweiai gongheguo zhongyang shixing weiyuanhui yu remin weiyuanhui dierci quanguo suweiai daibiao dahui de baogao" [Report before the 2nd National Soviet Delegates Congress of the Zhonghua Soviet

Republic's Central Executive Committee and People's Committee]. In *MZWT*, 210–11.

———. 1935. "Guanyu muqian zhengzhi xingshi yu dang de renwu jueyi" [Resolution on the current political situation and the responsibility of the Party]. In *MZDJ*, vol. 5, 19–40.

———. 1938a. "Lun xin jieduan" [On a new stage]. In *MZDJ*, vol. 6, 163–240.

———. 1938b. "On a protracted war." In *SW*, vol. 2, 113–94.

———. 1938c. "The question of independence and initiative within the united front." In *SW*, vol. 2, 213–17.

———. 1938d. "Zhongguo gongchandang zai minzu zhanzheng zhong de diwei" [The position of the Chinese Communist Party within the national struggle]. In *MZWT*, 598–604.

———. 1939a. "Zhi He Ganzhi" [Letter to He Ganzhi]. In *MZWT*, 620.

———. 1939b. "Zhongguo geming he Zhongguo gongchandang" [The Chinese revolution and the Chinese Communist Party]. In *MZWT*, 625–32.

———. 1940. "Xinminzhuzhuyi lun" [On new democracy]. In *MZXJ*, vol. 2, 662–711.

———. 1941. "Gaizao women de xuexi" [Reforming our study]. In *MZXJ*, vol. 3, 795–803.

———. 1945. "Lun lianhe zhengfu" [On a coalition government]. In *MZXJ*, vol. 3, 1029–1100.

———. 1949. "On the people's democratic dictatorship." In *SW*, vol. 4, 411–24.

McCord, Edward. 1999. "Local militia and state power in Nationalist China." *Modern China* 25.2 (April): 115–41.

———. 1993. *The power of the gun: the emergence of modern Chinese warlordism.* Berkeley: University of California Press.

McGranahan, Carole. 2003. "Empire and the status of Tibet: British, Chinese and Tibetan negotiations, 1913–1934." In *The history of Tibet*, vol. 3, ed. Alex McKay, 267–95. London: RoutledgeCurzon.

McLane, Charles B. 1958. *Soviet policy and the Chinese Communists, 1931–1946.* New York: Columbia University Press.

Mehra, Parshotam. 1974. *The McMahon line and after: A study of the triangular contest on India's north-eastern frontier between Britain, China and Tibet, 1904–1947.* Delhi: Macmillan.

Mei Xinfu. [1934] 1970. *Xikang*. Repr. Taipei: Zhengzhong shuju.

"Menggu dahui bihui" [Closing ceremony of the Mongolian Conference]. 1930. In *ZMSS*, vol. 1, 754–58.

"Mengzang bianqu renyuan renyong tiaolie" [Regulations for the appointment of personnel in the Mongolian and Tibetan border regions]. 1937. In *ZMSD*, 5.1.5, 33–35.

"Mengzang huijiang ge difang changguan ji ge zongjiao lingdao renyuan laijing zhanguan shanglai banfa" [Regulations for the bestowing of rewards to senior officials and religious personage from Mongolia, Tibet and Xinjiang visiting the capital on an official visits]. 1935. In *ZMSD*, 5.1.5, 12.

"Mengzangju nicheng 'daiyu Xizang tiaoli dagang'" [The proposal of the Office of Mongolian and Tibetan Affairs regarding an "Outline of Regulations for the Treatment of Tibet"] 1913. In *ZMSS*, vol. 1, 49.

"Mengzang weiyuanhui guanyu menggu zizhi zhibiao zhiben yijuean" [CMTA's draft proposal for a temporary and permanent solution of the Mongolian autonomous movement]. 1933. In *ZMSD*, 5.1.5, 64.

"Mengzang xinjiang huibu laijing zhenjin renyuan zhaodai guize" [Regulations for receiving personnel on extended official visits to the capital from Mongolia, Tibet, and Xinjiang]. 1934. In *ZMSD*, 5.1.5, 4–9.

Millward, James. 1996. "New perspectives on Qing frontier." In *Remapping China: Fissures in historical terrain*, eds. Gail Hershatter, et al., 113–29. Stanford, CA: Stanford University Press.

———. 1998. *Beyond the pass: Economy, ethnicity, and empire in Qing Central Asia, 1759–1864*. Stanford, CA: Stanford University Press.

———. 2004. "Qing Inner Asian empire and the return of the Torghuts." In *New Qing imperial history: The making of Inner Asian empire at Qing Chengde*, ed. James Millward, et al., 91–105. London: RoutledgeCurzon.

Millward, James, and Ruth W. Dunnell. 2004. "Introduction." In *New Qing imperial history: The making of Inner Asian empire at Qing Chengde*, ed. James Millward, et al., 1–12. London: RoutledgeCurzon.

Millward, James, and Laura Newby. 2006. "The Qing and Islam on the western frontier." In *Empire at the margins*, ed. Pamela Kyle Crossley, Helen Siu, and Donald Sutton, 113–34. Berkeley: University of California Press.

"Minzu tongyixian de jiben yuance" [The fundamental principle of the national united front]. 1936. In *MZWT*, 525–27.

Minzu wenti yanjiushi, ed. 1941. "Huihui minzu wenti" [The Hui nationality question]. In *MZWT*, 861–933.

———. [1941?] 1993. *Menggu minzu wenti* [*The Mongol nationality question*]. Repr. Beijing: Minzu chubanshe.

Mitter, Rana. 1999. "Complicity, repression, and regionalism: Yan Baohang and centripetal nationalism, 1931–1949." *Modern China* 25.1 (January): 44–68.

———. 2000. *The Manchurian myth: Nationalism, resistance, and collaboration in modern China*. Berkeley: University of California Press.

Morris-Suzuki, Tessa. 1998. *Re-inventing Japan: Time, space, nation*. Armonk, NY: M. E. Sharpe.

Moseley, George. 1965. "China's fresh approach to the national minority question." *China Quarterly* 24 (December): 15–27.

Mullaney, Thomas. 2004. "Ethnic classification writ large: The 1954 Yunnan Province ethnic classification project and its foundations in Republican-era taxonomic thought." *China Information* 18.2 (July): 207–41.

"Neimeng renmin daibaio huiyi kaimu dianli kongqian shengda" [The magnificent opening ceremony of the Inner Mongolian People's Congress]. 1947. In *MZWT*, 1325–26.

"Neizhengbu deng guanyu menggu zizhi an huigao" [Ministry of Interior and others draft plan for Mongolian autonomy]. 1933. In *ZMSD*, 5.1.5, 63–64.

Ng-Quinn, Michael. 1993. "National identity in premodern China: Formation and role enactment." In *China's quest for national identity*, ed. Lowell Dittmer and Samuel S. Kim, 32–61. Ithaca, NY: Cornell University Press.

Ni Wang. 1933. "Ni-mu-e-te-suo-er baogao De Wang zai bailingmiao kaihui canjia renyuan shiqing shi mengzang weiyuanhui dian" [Mongolian Prince Ni's cable to CMTA about the true circumstances behind those who are participating in De Wang's Bailingmiao conference]. In *ZMSD*, 5.1.5, 95.

Ning Chia. 1993. "The Lifanyuan and the Inner Asian rituals in the early Qing (1644–1795)." *Late Imperial China* 14.1 (June): 60–92.

"Nuli shixian zhong zhengzhibu tichu de sida haozhao" [Work hard to realize the four great slogans of the General Political Department]. 1935. In *MZWT*, 267.

Onogawa Hidemi. 1981. "Zhang Binglin paiman sixiang" [Zhang Binglin's anti-Manchuist thought]. In *Jindai Zhongguo sixiang renwu lun: Minzuzhuyi*, ed. Li Guoqi, 207–70. Taipei: Shibao wenhua chuban shiye.

Onon, Urgunge, and Derrick Pritchitt. 1989. *Asia's first modern revolution*. New York: E. J. Brill.

Paine, S. C. M. 1996. *Imperial rivals: China, Russia, and their disputed frontier*. Armonk, NY: M. E. Sharpe.

Pan Chia-lin, and Irene B. Taeuber. 1952. "The expansion of the Chinese north and west." *Population Index* 18.2 (April): 85–108.

Pantsov, Alexander. 2000. *The Bolsheviks and the Chinese revolution, 1919–1927*. London: Curzon.

Pavlovsky, Michel. 1949. *Chinese-Russian relations*. New York: Philosophical Library.

Pei Wenzhong. 1934. "Preliminary report on the late-Palaeolithic cave of Choukoutien." *Bulletin of the Geological Society of China* 13: 327–58.

Pipes, Richard. 1993. *Russia under the Bolshevik regime*. New York: Alfred A. Knopf.

Poo Mu-chou. 2005. *Enemies of civilization: Attitudes toward foreigners in ancient Mesopotanmia, Egypt, and China*. Albany: State University of New York Press.

Purdue, Peter. 1998a. "Boundaries, maps and movement: Chinese, Russian, and Mongolian empires in early modern Central Eurasia." *International Historical Review* 20.2 (June): 263–86.

———. 1998b. "Comparing empires: Manchu colonialism." *International Historical Review* 20.2 (June): 255–61.

———. 2001. "Empire and nation in comparative perspective: Frontier administration in eighteenth-century China." *Journal of Early Modern History* 5.4 (November): 282–304.

———. 2005a. *China marches west: The Qing conquest of Central Eurasia*. Cambridge, MA: The Belknap Press.

———. 2005b. "Where do incorrect political ideas come from? Writing the history of the Qing empire and the Chinese nation." In *The teleology of the modern nation-state*, ed. Joshua Fogel, 174-99. Philadelphia: University of Pennsylvania Press.

Pusey, James Reeve. 1983. *China and Charles Darwin*. Cambridge, MA: Harvard University Press.

Pye, Lucian. 1990. "China: Erratic state, frustrated society." *Foreign Affairs* 69.4 (Fall): 56–75.

———. 1996. "How China's nationalism was Shanghaied." In *Chinese nationalism*, ed. Jonathan Unger, 86–111. Armonk, NY: M. E. Sharpe.

Qi Sihe. 1937. "Minzu yu zhongzu" [Nation and race]. *Yugong banyuekan* 7.12–13 (April): 25–34.

Qian Mu. [1939] 1989. *Guoshi dagang* [*An outline of our nation's history*]. Shanghai: Shanghai shudian.

"Qiangdu daduhe de xuanchuan gudong gongzuo" [Propaganda for arousing our work in crossing over the Dadu river]. 1935. In *MZWT*, 265–66.

Qu Qiubai. [1926] 1987. "Xiandai minzu wenti jiang'an" [Lecture outline on the contemporary national question]. In *Qu Qiubai wenji*, vol. 3, 493–95. Beijing: Renmin wenxue chubanshe.

Radchenko, Sergey. 2003. "The Soviets' best friend in Asia: the Mongolian dimension of the Sino-Soviet split." Working paper, Cold War International History Project no. 42, 1–30.

Rawski, Evelyn S. 1996. "Presidential address: Reenvisioning the Qing: the significance of the Qing Period in Chinese history." *The Journal of Asian Studies* 55.4 (November): 829–50.

———. 2004. "The Qing empire during the Qianlong reign." In *New Qing imperial history: The making of Inner Asian empire at Qing Chengde*, ed. James Millward, et al., 15–21. London: RoutledgeCurzon.

Reardon-Anderson, James. 2005. *Reluctant pioneers: The Chinese conquest of Manchuria, 1644–1937*. Stanford, CA: Stanford University Press.

Ren Yimin. 1986. *Sichuan jinxiandai renwuzhuan* [*Biographies of contemporary Sichuan personalities*]. 6 vols. Chengdu: Sichuansheng shehui kexueyuan chubanshe.

Rhoads, Edward. 2000. *Manchus & Han: Ethnic relations and political power in late Qing and early Republican China, 1861–1928*. Seattle: University of Washington Press.

Richards, John F. 2003. *The unending frontier: An environmental history of the early modern world*. Berkeley: University of California Press.

Richardson, Hugh. 1962. *Tibet and its history*. Oxford: Oxford University Press.

———. 1998. *High peaks, pure earth: Collected writings on Tibetan history and culture*. London: Serindia.

Rossabi, Morris. 1975. *China and Inner Asia: From 1368 to the present day*. London: Thames and Hudson.

———, ed. 1983. *China among equals: The middle kingdom and its neighbours, 10th–14th centuries*. Berkeley: University of California Press.

———. 1988. *Khubilai Khan: His life and times*. Berkeley: University of California Press.

———. 2004. *Governing China's multiethnic frontiers*. Seattle: University of Washington Press.

Rowe, William. 2001. *Saving the world: Chen Hongmou and elite consciousness in eighteenth-century China*. Stanford, CA: Stanford University Press.

Rui Yifu. 1938. "Xinan minzu yuwen jiaoyu chuyi" [My humble opinion on linguistic education among the Southwest minzu]. *Xinan bianjiang* 2 (November): 165–73.

———. [1942] 1972. "Zhonghua guozu jie" [Understanding the Zhonghua guozu]. In *Zhongguo minzu jiqi wenhua lunkao*, vol. 1, 1–10. Taipei: Yinwen yinshuguan.

———. [1944] 1972. "Zhonghua guozu de fenzhi ji qi fenbu" [Branches and distribution of the Zhonghua guozu]. In *Zhongguo minzu jiqi wenhua lunkao*, vol. 1, 11–31. Taipei: Yinwen yinshuguan.

Said, Edward. 1979. *Orientalism*. New York: Vintage Books.

Salisbury, Harrison. 1985. *The Long March: the untold story*. New York: McGraw-Hill.

Sautman, Barry. 1997. "Myths of descent, racial nationalism and ethnic minorities in the People's Republic of China." In *The construction of racial identities in China and Japan*, ed. Frank Dikötter, 75–95. Hong Kong: Hong Kong University Press.

———. 2001. "Peking Man and the politics of paleanthropological nationalism in China." *The Journal of Asian Studies* 60.1 (Feburary): 95–124.

Scalapino, Robert, and George Yu. 1985. *Modern China and its revolutionary process: Recurrent challenges to the traditional order, 1895–1920*. Berkeley: University of California Press.

Schein, Louisa. 1997. "Gender and internal Orientalism in China." *Modern China* 23.1 (Janurary): 69–98.

———. 2000. *Minority rules: The Miao and the feminine in China's cultural politics*. Durham, NC: Duke University Press.

Schiffrin, Harold Z. 1968. *Sun Yat-sen and the origins of the Chinese Revolution*. Berkeley: University of California Press.

Schmalzer, Sigrid. 2004. "The people's Peking Man: Popular paleoanthropology in twentieth-century China." PhD diss., University of California, San Diego.

Schneider, Axel. 2002. "Review of *Inventing China through history* by Q. Edward Wang." *China Journal* 47: 219–21.

Schneider, Laurence. 1971. *Ku Chieh-kang and China's new history: Nationalism and the quest for alternative traditions*. Berkeley: University of California Press.

Schwarcz, Vera. 1986. *The Chinese enlightenment: Intellectuals and the legacy of the May Fourth Movement of 1919*. Berkeley: California University Press.

Schwartz, Benjamin. 1964. *In search of wealth and power: Yen Fu and the West*. Cambridge, MA: Harvard University Press.

Serruys, Henry. 1987. "Remains of Mongol customs in China during the early Ming period." In *The Mongols and Ming China: Customs and history*, ed. Francoise Aubin. London: Variorum Reprints.

Shao Dan. 2002. "Ethnicity in empire and nation: Manchus, Manzhouguo, and Manchuria (1911–1952)." PhD diss., University of California, Santa Barbara.

Shao Yuanchong. 1930. Jianguo de liang zhong jichu [The two bases for building the country]. In *SYXW*, vol. 1, 211–18.

———. 1931. "Jiuguo yuwu yu fayang minzu jingsheng" [Saving the country from foreign aggression and fostering racial consciousness]. In *SYXW*, vol. 1, 233–36.

———. 1932. "Minzuzhuyi yu minzu shengcun" [Minzuzhuyi and minzu survival]. In *SYXW*, vol. 3, 23–32.

———. 1933a. "Minzu jianshe yu minzu shengcun" [Minzu reconstruction and minzu survival]. In *SYXW*, vol. 1, 365–69.

———. 1933b. "Minzu xing zhi hanyi yi fahui" [Giving play to and the significance of minzu character]. In *SYXW*, vol. 1, 376–83.

———. 1933c. "Qiaoshan huangdi lingkao" [Investigation of the Yellow Emperor's Qiaoshan tomb]. In *SYXW*, vol. 1, 369–76.

———. 1934a. "Minzu jianshe yu jiaoyu zhengce" [Education policy and minzu construction]. In *SYXW*, vol. 1, 388–92.

———. 1934b. "Minzu jiaoyu de yaodian" [The essentials of minzu education]. In *SYXW*, vol. 3, 217–22.

———. 1936. "Minzu wenhua de lilun yu shiji" [Theory and practice of minzu culture]. In *SYXW*, vol. 2, 421–27.

Shen Shun-Chiao. 1997. "Huangdi shenhua yu wan qing de guozu jiancheng" [The myth of the Yellow Emperor and the construction of Chinese nationhood in the late Qing]. *Taiwan shehui yanjiu jikan* 28: 1–70.

Shepherd, John Robert. 1993. *Statecraft and political economy on the Taiwan frontier 1600–1800*. Stanford, CA: Stanford University Press.

Shyu, Lawrence Nae-Lih. 1972. "The People's Political Council and China's wartime problems, 1937–1945". PhD diss., Columbia University.

Sichuan sheng kangding xian zhizuan weiyuanhui, comp. 1995. *Kangding xianzhi* [*Kangding county gazetteer*]. Chengdu: Sichuan cishu chubanshe.

Smith, Anthony D. 2000. *The nation in history: Historiographical debates about ethnicity and nationalism*. Hanover, NH: University Press of New England.

Snow, Edgar. 1968. *Red star over China*. First rev., enlarged ed. New York: Grove Weidenfeld.

So Wai-chor. 2003. "Nation, territory and frontier: Chiang Kai-shek's realism in action." In *Power and identity in the Chinese world order: Festschrift in honour of Professor Wang Gungwu*, ed. Billy K. L. So, et al., 65–119. Hong Kong: Hong Kong University Press.

Song Jiaoren. 1981. "Hunan shou menghui chengli dahui yanshuici" [Speech at the ceremony for the establishment of the Hunan Save Mongolia Society]. In *Song Jiaoren ji*, ed. and comp. Chen Xulu, 449–50. Beijing: Zhonghua shuju.

Spence, Jonathan. 1996. *God's Chinese son: The Taiping Heavenly Kingdom of Hong Xiuquan*. New York: W. W. Norton.

Sperling, Elliot. 2003. "The Chinese venture in K'am, 1904–1911, and the role of Chao Erh-Feng." In *The history of Tibet: The modern period: 1895–1959 the encounter with modernity*, vol. 3, ed. Alex McKay, 69–91. London: Routledge Curzon.

Stalin, Joseph. [1913] 1940. "Marxism and the national question." In *Marxism and the national and colonial questions*, 3–53. Moscow: Foreign Language Publishing House.

Stepan, Nancy Leys. 1991. *The hour of eugenics: Race, gender and nation in Latin America*. Ithaca, NY: Cornell University Press.

Stocking, George. 1968. *Race, culture, and evolution: Essays in the history of anthropology*. New York: Free Press.

Struve, Lynn, ed. 2004. *The Qing formation in world-historical time*. Cambridge, MA: Harvard University Press.

Sun Tzu. 1963. *The art of war*. Trans. Samuel Griffith. London: Oxford University Press.

Sun Yat-sen. 1894a. "Shang Li Hongzhang shu" [Memorial to Li Hongzhang]. In *SZSQJ*, vol. 1, 8–18.

———. 1894b. "Tanxiangshan xingzhonghui mengshu" [The oath of the Honolulu branch of the Revive China Society]. In *SZSQJ*, vol. 1, 20.

———. 1895. "Xianggang xingzhonghui zhangcheng" [The charter of the Hong Kong branch of the Revive China Society]. In *SZSQJ*, vol. 1, 21–24.

———. [1900] 1990. "Zhina xianshi ditu" [Map of Chinese territory]. In *Sun Zhongshan ji waiji*, ed. Chen Xulu and Hao Shengchao, 17–28. Shanghai: Renmin chubanshe.

———. 1905. "*Minbao* fakanci" [Forward to *Minbao*]. In *SZSQJ*, vol. 1, 288–89.

———. 1906a. "Zai dongjing *Minbao* chuanli zhounian qingqu dahui de yanjiang" [A speech at a ceremony in Tokyo to celebrate the ten anniversary of *Minbao*]. In *SZSQJ*, vol. 1, 323–31.

———. 1906b. "Zhongguo tongmenghui reming fanglüe" [Revolutionary manifesto of the Chinese Tongmenghui]. In *SZSQJ*, vol. 1, 296–318.

———. 1912a. "Changyi qianbi geming duikang sha-e yinlüe tongbao" [Telegram appealing for a monetary revolution to counter the invasion of Czarist Russia]. In *SZSQJ*, vol. 2, 544–49.

———. 1912b. "Guomindang xuanyan" [Manifesto of the Nationalist Party]. In *SZSQJ*, vol. 2, 396–99.

———. 1912c. "Linshi dazongtong xuanyanshu" [Proclamation of the provisional president]. In *SZSQJ*, vol. 2, 1–3.

———. 1917–19. "Jianguo fanglüe" [The international development of China]. In *SZSQJ*, vol. 6, 157–493.

———. 1919. "Sanminzhuyi" [Three Principles of the People]. In *SZSQJ*, vol. 5, 185–96.

———. 1921a. "Zai guilin dui dian-gan-ou jun de yanjiang" [Speech before the Yunnan-Jiangxi-Guangdong army at Guilin]. In *SZSQJ*, vol. 6, 9–40.

———. 1921b. "Zai Zhongguo guomindang benbu teshe zhu ou banshi chu de yanjiang" [Speech given at the special founding of a branch office of the Nationalist Party in Canton]. In *SZSQJ*, vol. 5, 472–81.

———. 1923. "Pi Deng Zeru deng de shangshu" [Letter criticizing of Deng Zeru and others]. In *SZSQJ*, vol. 8, 458–59.

———. 1924a. "Guomin zhengfu jianguo dagang" [National government's outline for national reconstruction]. In *SZSQJ*, vol. 9, 126–29.

———. 1924b. "Huanyan guomindang gesheng daibiao ji menggu daibai de yanshuo" [Speech at a welcoming feast for GMD representatives from each province and Outer Mongolia]. In *SZSQJ*, vol. 9, 104–7.

———. 1924c. "Sanminzhuyi" [Three Principles of the People]. In *SZSQJ*, vol. 9, 183–427.

———. 1924d. "Zhongguo guomindang diyici quanguo daibiao dahui xuanyan" [The manifesto of the GMD's First National Party Congress]. In *SZSQJ*, vol. 9, 114–25.

Sun Zihe. 1995. "Huang Musong ruzang shiwei" [The complete story of Huang Musong's mission to Tibet]. In *Xikang shishi yu renwu* [*People and events in Tibetan history*], 233–78. Taipei: Taiwan shangwu yinshuguan.

Suny, Ronald Grigor. 1993. *The revenge of the past: Nationalism, revolution, and the collapse of the Soviet Union.* Stanford, CA: Stanford University Press.

Sutton, Donald. 2006. "Ethnicity and the Miao frontier in the eighteenth century." In *Empire at the margins*, ed. Pamela Kyle Crossley, Helen Siu, and Donald Sutton, 190–228. Berkeley: University of California Press.

———. 2007. "Ritual, Cultural Standardization, and Orthopraxy in China." *Modern China* 33.1 (January): 3–21.

Tambiah, Stanley J. 1976. *World conqueror and world renouncer: A study of Buddhism and polity in Thailand against a historical background*. Cambridge: Cambridge University Press.

Tan Tiwu. 1934. *Neimeng zhi jinxi* [*Inner Mongolia past and present*]. Shanghai: Shangwu yinshuguan.

Tang, Peter. 1959. *Russian and Soviet policy in Manchuria and Outer Mongolia, 1911–1931*. Durham, NC: Duke University Press.

Tang Xiaobing. 1996. *Global space and the nationalist discourse of modernity: The historical thinking of Liang Qichao*. Stanford, CA: Stanford University Press.

Tao Yunkui. 1940. "Kaihua bianmin wenti" [The problem of civilizing the frontier peoples]. *Xinan bianjiang* 10 (July): 831–47.

Tay Lian Soo [Deng Liangshu]. 1987. "Lun Gu Jiegang zhi xueshu licheng jiqi gongxian" [Discussion of the course and contribution of Gu Jiegang's academic work]. In *Gu Jiegang xueshu nianpu jianbian*, 3–7. Beijing: Zhongguo youyi chubanshe.

Terrill, Ross. 2003. *The new Chinese empire: And what it means for the world*. Sydney: University of New South Wales Press.

Thierry, Francois. 1989. "Empire and minority in China." In *Minority peoples in the age of nation-states*, ed. Gérard Ghaliand, 76–99. Paris: Pluto.

Thongchai Winichakul. 1994. *Siam mapped: A history of the geo-body of a nation*. Honolulu: University of Hawaii Press.

Tian Tao, ed. 1999. *Qingchao tiaoyue quanji* [*Complete collection of Qing dynasty treaties*]. Haerbin: Heilongjiang renmin chubanshe.

Tibet Online. 1996-2007. "Chinese presence in Tibet: Population transfer." *Tibet online*. http://www.tibet.org/Activism/Rights/poptransfer.html (accessed December 3, 2006).

Tighe, Justin. 2005. *Constructing Suiyuan: The politics of northwestern territory and development in early twentieth century China*. Leiden: Brill.

Toops, Stanley. 2004. "Demographics and development in Xinjiang after 1949." Working papers, East-West Center, no. 1, May.

Townsend, James. 1996. "Chinese nationalism." In *Chinese nationalism*, ed Jonathan Unger, 1–30. Armonk, NY: M. E. Sharpe.

"A Treaty between all nine powers relating to principles and policies to be followed in matters concerning China." 1922. *American Journal of International Law* 16.2 (April): 64–68.

Tsou Jung [Zou Rong]. [1903] 1968. *The revolutionary army: A Chinese nationalist tract of 1903*. Trans. John Lust. The Hague: Mouton.

Tsu Jing. 2005. *Failure, nationalism, and literature: The making of modern Chinese identity, 1895–1937*. Stanford, CA: Stanford University Press.

Tu Wei-ming. 1976. "Hsiung Shih-li's quest for authentic existence." In *The Limits of change: Essays on conservative alternatives in Republican China*, ed. Charlotte Furth, 242–73. Cambridge, MA: Harvard University Press.

———, ed. 1994. *The living tree: The changing meaning of being Chinese today*. Stanford, CA: Stanford University Press.

Tuminez, Astrid. 2000. *Russian nationalism since 1856: Ideology and the making of foreign policy*. Lanham, MD: Rowman & Littlefield.

Turner, Frederick Jackson. [1893] 1962. *The frontier in American history*. New York: Holt, Rinehart, and Winston.

Tuttle, Gray. 2005. *Tibetan buddhists in the making of modern China*. New York: Columbia University Press.

Van Slyke, Lyman. 1967. *Enemies and friends: The united front in Chinese Communist history*. Stanford, CA: Stanford University Press.

Van Walt van Praag, Michael. 1987. *The status of Tibet: History, rights, and prospects in international law*. London: Wisdom.

"Waiwubu zhi geguo gongshi zhaoan" [Memoranda of the Ministry of Foreign Affairs to the diplomats of all countries] [1912] 1996. In *Zhonghua minguo waijiaoshike huibian*, ed. Chen Zhiqi, 7–8. Taipei: Bohaitang wenhua.

Wakeman, Frederic. 1985. *The great enterprise: The Manchu reconstruction of imperial order in seventeenth-century China*. Berkeley: University of California Press.

Waley-Cohen, Joanna. 2004. "The new Qing history." *Radical history review* 88 (Winter): 193–206.

Wang, David Der-wei. 1997. *Fin-de-siècle splendor: Repressed modernities of late Qing fiction, 1849–1911*. Stanford, CA: Stanford University Press.

Wang Fan-sen. 2000. *Fu Ssu-nien: A life in Chinese history and politics*. Cambridge: Cambridge University Press.

Wang Hui. 2006. "China plans five-year leap forward of railway development." *Sina English* [Online] http://english.sina.com/china/1/2006/1006/91082.html (date accessed June 4, 2007).

Wang Jianmin. 1997. *Zhongguo minzuxueshi: shangjun, 1903–1949*. [*The history of ethnology in China: part one, 1903–1949*.] Kunming: Yunnan jiaoyu chubanshe.

———. 2002. "Ethnonyms and nationalism in Xinjiang." In *Exploring nationalisms in China: Themes and conflicts*, ed. C. X. George Wei and Liu Xiaoyuan, 173–86. Westport: Greenwood Press.

Wang Jiaxiang. 1936. "Fandui riben diguozhuyi zhanling neimeng" [Oppose the Japanese imperialist occupation of Inner Mongolia]. In *MZWT*, 506–9.

Wang Jingwei. [1905] 1977. "Minzu de guomin" [A minzu of citizens]. In *Xinhai geming qianshinian jian shilunxuan*, vol. 2.1, comp. Zhang Xiang and Wang Renzhi, 82–114. Shanghai: Xinzhi sanlian shudian.

———. 1934a. "Wang Tiaoming guanyu chuli zhongyang yu xizang difang guanxi wenti fu Huang Musong dian" [Wang Jingwei's reply cable to Huang Musong about Sino-Tibetan relations]. In *ZMSD*, 5.1.5, 220–21.

———. 1934b. "Wang Tiaoming guanyu kaxia jiaobu qiebuke zuo zhengshi hanjian bing cusu gui shi gu Huang Musong midian" [Wang Jingwei's reply cable to Huang Musong stating that he must not send an official letter in negotiations with the Kashag and should quickly return to the capital]. In *ZMSD*, 5.1.5, 241.

———. 1934c. "Wang Tiaoming guanyu kaxia yutan kang-zang jiufen yi banzhan hui zang wenti duice shi fu Huang Musong dian" [Wang Jingwei's reply cable to Huang Musong about the policy concerning the Kashag's insistence on discussing the Tibet-Xikang border issue and the question of the Panchen Lama's return to Tibet]. In *ZMSD*, 5.1.5, 240.

———. 1934d. "Wang Tiaoming wei jiejue kang-zang jiewu xu yu huaifu zhongyang yu xizang guanxi bing xingshi zhi Huang Musong" [Wang Jingwei's cable to Huang Musong about solving the Xikang-Tibetan border issue, reviving Sino-Tibetan relations and other matters]. In *ZMSD*, 5.1.5, 226–27.

———. 1934e. "Wang Tiaoming wei jiejue zhongyang yu xikang guanxi duice shi fu Huang Musong dian" [Wang Jingwei's cable back to Huang Musong about the policy for solving Sino-Tibetan relations]. In *ZMSD*, 5.1.5, 226.

———. 1934f. "Wang Tiaoming yi xizang dangu yejing biaotai zhu dingqi huijing shi zhi Huang Musong dian" [Wang Jingwei's cable to Huang Musong about already informing the Tibetan authorities that he is returning to the capital within a set period]. In *ZMSD*, 5.1.5, 234.

Wang, Q. Edward. 1999. "History, space, and ethnicity: The Chinese worldview." *Journal of World History* 10.2: 285–305.

———. 2000. *Inventing China through history: The May Fourth approach to historiography*. Albany, NY: State University of New York Press.

Wang Xingrui. 1939. "Hainandao Liren laiyuan shishen" [Inquiry into the origins of the Li people of Hainan Island]. *Xinan bianjiang* 7 (October): 614–21.

Watson, James. 1993. "Rites or beliefs? The construction of a unified culture in late imperial China." In *China's quest for national identity*, ed. Lowell Dittmer and Samuel S. Kim, 80–103. Ithaca, NY: Cornell University Press.

Watson, James, and Evelyn Rawski, eds. 1988. *Death ritual in late imperial and modern China*. Berkeley: University of California Press.

Watts, Jonathan. 2006. "The railway across the roof of the world." *Guardian Unlimited* [Online], September 20. http://www.guardian.co.uk/china/story/0,7369,1573971,00.html (accessed December 3, 2006).

Wei Huilin. 1945. "Ruhe queli sanminzhuyi de bianjiang minzu zhengce" [How to establish Three Principles of the People's frontier minority policy]. *Bianzheng gonglun* 4.1 (January): 2–4.

Wei, Julie Lee, Ramon Myers, and Donald Gillin, eds. 1994. *Prescriptions for saving China: Selected writings of Sun Yat-sen*. Stanford, CA: Hoover Institute Press.

Wei Xiaotao. 1928. "Guomin zhengfu wenguan chuwei Wei Xiaotao yaoqiu chenming mengbian qingxing shi xingzhengyuan gonghan" [Public petition of national government civil official Wei Xiaotao to the Executive Yuan seeking clarification on the condition of the Mongolian frontier]. In *ZMSD*, 5.1.5, 36–39.

Wei Yuan. 1984. *Shengwuji* [*Record of military accomplishments*], 2 vols. Beijing: Zhonghua shuju.

Weidenreich, Franz. 1935. "The *Sinanthropus* population of Choukoutien (locality 1) with a preliminary report on new discoveries." *Bulletin of the Geographic Society of China* 14: 423–68.

———. 1936. "*Sinanthropus pekinensis* and its position in the line of human evolution." *Peking Natural History Bulletin* 10.4 (June): 1–56.

———. 1939. "On the earliest representative of modern mankind recovered on the soil of East Asia." *Peking Natural History Bulletin* 13: 161–74.

———. 1946. *Apes, giants and man*. Chicago: University of Chicago Press.

Weigh, Ken Shen. 1959. *Russian and Soviet policy in Manchuria and Outer Mongolia, 1911–1931*. Durham, NC: Duke University Press.

Weiner, Michael. 1997. "The invention of identity: race and nation in pre-war Japan." In *The construction of racial identities in China and Japan*, ed. Frank Dikötter, 96–117. Hong Kong: Hong Kong University Press.

Weng Wenhao. [1930] 1989. "Beijing yuanren xueshu shang de yiyi" [Academic significance of the *Sinanthropus pekinensis*]. In *Weng Wenhao xuanji*, ed. Pan Yuntang, comp. Huang Jiqing, 268–71. Beijing: Xinhua shudian.

White, Richard. 1991. *The middle ground: Indians, empires and republics in the Great Lakes Region, 1650–1815*. Cambridge: Cambridge University Press.

Whiting, Allen. 1953. *Soviet policies in China, 1917–1924*. Stanford, CA: Stanford University Press.

Wilson, Dick. 1971. *The Long March 1935: The epic of Chinese Communism's survival*. London: Hamish Hamilton.

Wong, R. Bin. 1997. *China transformed: Historical change and the limits of European experience*. Ithaca, NY: Cornell University Press.

———. 2000. "Two kinds of nation, what kind of state?" In *Nation work: Asian elites and national identities*, ed. Timothy Brook and Andre Schmid, 109–22. Ann Arbor: The University of Michigan Press.

———. 2006. "Citizen, state, and nation in China." In *State making in Asia*, ed. Richard Boyd and Tak-Wing Ngo, 91–105. London: Routledge.

Wong, R. Bin, Theodore Huters, and Pauline Yu. 1997. "Introduction: Shifting paradigms of political and social order." In *Culture & state in Chinese history: Conventions, accomadations and critiques*, ed. Theodore Huters, R. Bin Wong, and Pauline Yu, 1–28. Stanford, CA: Stanford University Press.

Wong Siu-lun. 1979. *Sociology and socialism in contemporary China*. London: Routledge & Kegan Paul.

Wong Young-tsu. 1989. *Search for modern nationalism: Zhang Binglin and revolutionary China, 1869–1936*. Hong Kong: Oxford University Press.

Wu Chin-ting. 1938. *Prehistoric pottery in China*. London: Kegan Paul, Trench, Trubner.

Wylie, Raymond. 1980. *The emergence of Maoism: Mao Tse-tung, Ch'en Po-ta, and the search for Chinese theory, 1935–1945*. Stanford, CA: Stanford University Press.

Xiang Da. 1979. *Tangdai chang'an yu xiyu wenming* [*Tang Dynasty Chang'an and central Asian civilization*]. Beijing: Sanlian shudian.

"*Xin Yaxiya* zhi shiming" [Mission of *New Asia*]. 1930. *Xin Yaxiaya* 1.1 (October): n.p.

Xikang tequ zhengwu weiyuanhui zhounian zhuankan [*Special one-year anniversary publication of the Xikang Special Region Administrative Committee*]. 1929. Kangding: Xikang tequ zhengwu weiyuanhui.

"Xingzhengyuan wei guanyu menggu zizhi wenti bugao" [Executive Yuan proclamation about the question of Mongolian autonomy]. 1933. In *ZMSD*, 5.1.5, 68–69.

Xiong Shili. [1939] 1984. "Zhonghua zhongzu tuiyuan" [A hypothesis on the origin of the Zhonghua race]. In *Zhongguo lishi jianghua*, 1–35. Taipei: Mingwen shuju.

"Xiuzheng mengzang weiyuanhui zushifa" [Revised Organizational law of the Commission on Mongolian and Tibetan Affairs]. 1932. In *ZMSD*, 5.1.5, 2–4.

Xu Youchun, comp. 1991. *Minguo renwu dacidian* [*Biographical dictionary of Republican China*]. Shijiazhuang: Hebei renmin chubanshe.

Yang Ce. 1997. *Shaoshu minzu yu kangri zhanzheng* [*The national minorities and the Sino-Japanese War*]. Beijing: Beijing chubanshe.

Yang Huiyun, comp. 1992. *Zhongguo huizu dacidian* [*Encyclopedia of Chinese Muslims*]. Shanghai: Shanghai cishu chubanshe.

Yang Lien-sheng. 1968. "Historical notes on the Chinese world order." In *The Chinese world order*, ed. John King Fairbank, 20–33. Cambridge, MA: Harvard University Press.

Yang Song. 1938. "Lun minzu" [On minzu]. In *MZWT*, 763–68.

Yano Jin'ichi. 1931. "Man-Mō-Zō wa Shina ryōdo ni arazu" [Manchuria, Tibet and Mongolia were not originally part of Chinese territory]. *Gaiko jiho* 35.412: 51–71.

Ye Guisheng, and Liu Maolin. "Lü Zhenyu." In *ZSP*, vol. 2, 1581–1603.

Ye Huosheng. 1984. "Wo suo liaojiao de Zhongguo lishi yanjiushi" [My understanding of the Chinese Historical Research Office]. In *Yan'an zhongyang yanjiuyuan huiyilu*, ed. Wen Qize, et al., 69–76. Changsha: Hunan renmin chubanshe.

Yin Da. [1940] 1989. "Zhonghua minzu jiqi wenhua zhi qiyuan" [The origins of the Zhonghua minzu and its culture]. In *Yin Da shixue lunzhu xuanji*, 301–18. Beijing: Renmin chubanshe.

Young, Ernest. 1977. *The Presidency of Yuan Shi-kai: Liberalism and dictatorship in early Republican China*. Ann Arbor: University of Michigan Press.

Yu Jianhua. 1944. *Zhonghua minzu shi* [*History of the Zhonghua minzu*]. Nanping: Guomin chubanshe.

Yu Xintun, 1981. "Sun Zhongshan yu riben guanxi yanjiu" [Research on Sun Yat-sen's relationship with Japan]. Beijing: Wenshi ziliao chubanshe.

Yu Ying-shih. 1967. *Trade and expansion in Han China: A study in the structure of sino-barbarian economic relations*. Berkeley: University of California Press.

Yu Zhengui. 1996. *Zhongguo lidai zhengquan yu yisilanjiao* [*Islam and China's successive regimes*]. Yincheng: Ningxia renmin chubanshe.

"Yuan dazongtong banfa chuanyu" [President Yuan Shikai's bestows an order encouraging the inter-marriage between the Han, Manchu, Mongol, Hui and Tibetan Peoples]. 1912. In *ZMSS*, vol. 1, 441.

"Yuan dazongtong ling gonghe zhengfu bushe lifan zhuanbu, meng, zang, huijiang, shiyi guibing neiwubu jieguan" [President Yuan Shikai orders the Republican Government not to re-establish a Special Bureau for Colonial Dependencies and returns direct administration over Mongolia, Tibet and Xinjiang to the Ministry of Internal Affairs]. 1912. In *ZMSS*, vol. 1, 441.

Zarrow, Peter. 2004. "Historical trauma: Anti-Manchuism and memories of atrocity in late Qing China." *History and Memory* 16.2 (Fall/Winter): 67–107.

———. 2006. "Liang Qichao and the conceptualization of 'race' in late Qing China." *Zhongyang yanjiuyuan jindaishi yanjiusuo jikan* 52 (June): 113–63.

Zeng Qi. 1925a. "Dao Sun Zhongshan xiansheng bing xu haineiwai geming tongzhi" [Mourning Mr. Sun Yat-sen and encouraging overseas and domestic revolutionary comrades]. *Xingshi zhoubao* 24 (March 21): 1–3.

———. 1925b. "Gongchandang yu fuidang" [The Communist Party and the Restoration Party]. *Xingshi zhoubao* 28 (April 18): 1.

Zhang Binglin. [1907] 1982. "*Shehui tonglun* shangdui" [A discussion of *Survey of Sociology*]. In *Zhang Taiyan quanji* [*Complete works of Zhang Binglin*], vol. 4, 322–37. Shanghai: Renmin chubanshe.

Zhang Ji. 1928. "Zhang Ji wei Enheemuer deng shengqing sheli mengqi zizhi weiyuanhui deng zhi Jiang Jieshi deng han" [Letter from Zhang Ji to Chiang Kai-shek and others about the request by Zhang Zhaoting and others for the establishment of an Autonomous Mongolian Banner Council]. In *ZMSD*, 5.1.5, 39–40.

Zhang Tingxiu. 1939. "Zailun Yi-Han tongyuan" [Another discussion of the common origins of the Yi and the Han]. *Xinan bianjiang* 6 (May): 501–9.

Zhang Wentian. 1938. "Guanyu kangri minzu tongyi zhanxian yu dang de zuzhi wenti" [On the problem of party organization and the anti-Japanese united front]. In *MZWT*, 605–6.

Zhang Xingtang. 1962. *Bianjiang zhengzhi* [*Frontier administration*]. Taipei: Mengzang weiyuanhui.

Zhang Xinwu. 1995. *Fu Zuoyi yisheng* [*The life of Fu Zuoyi*]. Beijing: Qunzhong chubanshe.

Zhang Xuguang. 1942. *Zhonghua minzu fazhan shigang* [*Historical outline of the development of the Zhonghua minzu*]. Guilin: Qiji xinan yinkeshi.

Zhang Yinglin. 1925. "Ping jinren duiyu Zhongguo gushi zhi taolun" [Critique of recent discussions of Chinese ancient history]. In *GSB*, vol. 2, 271–88.

Zhang Yong. 2002. "Cong shiba xingqi dao wuse qi: xinhai geming shiqi cong hanzu guojia dao wuzu gonghe guojia de jianguo moshi zhuanbian" [From the flag with eighteen stars to that with five colors: the change in the view of the state from a Han state to a multiethnic one during the 1911 revolution]. *Beijing daxue xuebao* 2: 106–14.

Zhang Zhuanxi. 1985. "Jian Bozan." In *ZSP*, vol. 2, 1528–61.

Zhao Gang. 2006. "Reinventing China: Imperial Qing ideology and the rise of Modern Chinese national indentity in the early twentieth century." *Modern China* 32.1 (January): 3–30.

Zhao Suisheng. 2004. *A nation-state by construction: Dynamics of modern Chinese nationalism*. Stanford, CA: Stanford University Press.

"Zhonggong Gui-Zhen bianqu dangwei guanyu xuanchuan fan Jiang tongyi zhanxian qishiwu tiao kouhao de zhibiao" [The directive of the Central Committee's Yunnan-Guizhou Border Area Party Committee concerning 75 anti-Chiang united front propaganda slogans]. 1948. In *MZWT*, 1333.

"Zhonggong zhongyang gei mengwei de xin" [Party Center letter to the Inner Mongolian Special Committee]. 1929. In *MZWT*, 100–7.

"Zhonggong zhongyang gei Yunnan shengwei de zhishixin" [Party Center directive to the Yunnan Provincial Committee]. 1929. In *MZWT*, 110.

"Zhonggong zhongyang guanyu menggu gongzuo de zhishixin" [Party Center directive on Mongolian work]. 1937. In *MZWT*, 545–47.

"Zhonggong zhongyang guanyu neimeng gongzuo de zhishixin" [Party Center directive on Inner Mongolian work]. 1936. In *MZWT*, 416–21.

"Zhonggong zhongyang guanyu shaoshu minzu duli zizhu de yuanze de zhishi" [Party Center directive on the principle of independence and self-rule among the minority nationals]. 1937. In *MZWT*, 579.

"Zhonggong zhongyang liujie wuzhong quanhui zhengzhi jueyi'an" [Draft political resolution of the 5th Plenum of the CCP's 6th Central Committee]. 1934. In *MZWT*, 205.

"Zhonggong zhongyang wei gongbu guogong hezuo xuanyan" [Declaration of the Party Center calling for a GMD-CCP united front]. 1937. In *MZWT*, 548–49.

Zhonggong zhongyang wenxian yanjiushi, ed. 1993. *Mao Zedong nianpu* [*Chronicles of Mao Zedong*], 3 vols. Beijing: Zhongyang wenxian chubanshe.

———. 1996. *Liu Shaoqi nianpu* [*Chronicles of Liu Shaoqi*], 2 vols. Beijing: Zhongyang wenxian chubanshe.

"Zhonggong zhongyang xibei gongzuo weiyuanhui guanyu huihui minzu wenti de tigang" [The policy outline of the Northwest Work Committee on the Hui nationality question]. 1940. In *MZWT*, 648–56.

"Zhonggong zhongyang xibei gongzuo weiyuanhui guanyu kangzhan zhong menggu minzu wenti tigang" [The policy outline of the Northwest Work Committee on the Mongolian nationality question during the War of Resistance]. 1940. In *MZWT*, 657–67.

"Zhongguo gongchandang diliuci quanguo daibiao dahui guanyu minzu wenti de jueyian" [CCP 6th National Party Congress' Draft Resolution on the National Question]. 1928. In *MZWT*, 87.

"Zhongguo gongchandang diliuci quanguo daibiao dahui tongguo de zhengzhi jueyian" [CCP 6th National Party Congress' Draft Political Resolution]. 1928. In *MZWT*, 86.

"Zhongguo gongchandang zhongyang weiyuanhui he Zhonghua suiweiai zhongyang zhengfu wei kangri jiuguo gao quanti tongbao shu" [The declaration of the CCP's Central Committee and the government of the Central Zhonghua Soviet to all compatriots about resisting the Japanese and saving the country]. 1935. In *MZWT*, 301–4.

"Zhongguo gong-nong hongjun erfangmian jun zhengzhibu guanyu er-liu juntuan changzheng de zhengzhi gongzuo zongjie baogao" [Outline report of the Political Department of the 2nd Route Chinese Worker-Peasant Red Army on the experiences of the 2nd and 6th battalions during the Long March]. 1936. In *MZWT*, 436–40.

"Zhongguo gong-nong hongjun zhengzhibu guanyu Miao-Yao minzu zhong gongzuo yuanze de zhishi" [Directive of the Political Department of the Chinese Worker-Peasant Red Army on work principles among the Miao and Yao nationalities]. 1934. In *MZWT*, 244–46.

"Zhongguo gong-nong hongjun zong zhengzhibu guanyu zhuyi zhengqu yimin de gongzuo" [Directive of the Central Political Department of the Chinese Worker-Peasant Red Army on paying attention to the work of winning over the Yi people]. 1935. In *MZWT*, 258.

"Zhongguo guomindang dierci quanguo daibiao dahui xuanyan" [Manifesto of the Guomindang's Second National Congress (Western Hills clique)]. 1926. In *ZGQZ*, vol. 1, 398–413.

"Zhongguo guomindang xuanyan xuanbu Zhongguo gongchandang zuizhuang" [Guomindang (Western Hills clique) manifesto announcing the indictment of the CCP]. 1927. In *ZGQZ*, vol. 1, 478–83.

Zhongguo lishi yanjiushi, ed. [1941] 1944. *Zhongguo tongshi jianbian* [*A concise general history of China*]. Repr. Shanghai: Xinzhi shudian.

"Zhonghua minguo linshi xianfa" [Provisional Constitution of the Republic of China]. 1912. In *ZMSS*, vol. 1, 326–45.

"Zhonghua suweiai gongheguo guojia genbenfa (xianfa) dagang caoan" [Draft Basic Law [Constitution] of the Zhonghua Soviet Republic]. 1930. In *MZWT*, 121–25.

"Zhonghua suweiai gongheguo xianfa dagang" [Constitutional Outline of the Zhonghua Soviet Republic]. 1931. In *MZWT*, 165–66.

"Zhonghua suweiai gongheguo xianfa dagang" [Constitutional Outline of the Zhonghua Soviet Republic]. 1934. In *MZWT*, 206–9.

"Zhonghua suweiai gongheguo zhongyang zhengfu, Zhongguo gongnong hongjun geming junshi weiyuanhui kangri jiguo xuanyan" [Manifesto of the Central Zhonghua Soviet Government and the Military Affairs Committee of the Chinese Worker-Peasant-Solider Red Army on resisting the Japanese and saving the country]. 1935. In *MZWT*, 320–21.

"Zhonghua suweiai zhongyang zhengfu dui Huizu renmin de xuanyan" [The declaration of the Central Government of the Zhonghua Soviet to the people of the Hui nationality]. 1936. In *MZWT*, 366–67.

Zhou Enlai. 1944. "Guanyu xianzheng yu tuanjie wenti" [On the question of constitutional government and unity]. In *MZWT*, 728–31.

———. 1949. "Guanyu remin Zhengxie de jige wenti" [Concerning several questions before the People's Political Consultative Conference]. In *MZWT*, 1266–67.

Zhou Kuntian. 1941. "Sanminzhuyi zhi bianzheng jianshe" [Three principles of the people's frontier construction]. *Bianzheng gonglun* 1.1 (August): 5–20.

Zhou Xiyin. 1996. "Hongjun Changzheng yu dang de minzu, tongxian he zongjiao zhengce" [The Red Army's Long March and the Party's nationality, united front and religion policy]. In *Changzheng dashidian*, vol. 2, ed. Changzheng dashidian bianweihui, 2040–46. Guiyang: Guizhou renminchu banshe.

Zhu Ruiyan, et al. 1985. "Fan Wenlan." In *ZSP*, vol. 2, 1473–1502.

Zhuo Wang. 1933. "Zhuo-te-ba-zha-pu deng wei buyuan zhuisui De Wang zizhi zhi Mengzang weiyuanhui dian" [Mongolian prince Zhuo and others' cable to CMTA expressing their unwillingness to follow De Wang's autonomous movement]. In *ZMSD*, 5.1.5, 96.

Zou Lu. 1930. *Zou Lu wencun* [*Preserved works of Zou Lu*], vol. 3. ed. Mei Ou. Beiping: Zhonghua shuju.

———. 1938. *Zhongguo Guomindang shigao* [*Draft history of the Guomindang*]. 2nd ed. Shanghai: Shangwu yinshuguan.

Zuo Zuohua. 1929. "Tunken qianshuo" [A cursory discussion of military colonization]. *Mengqi xunkan* 1.4 (May): 5–8.

Index

www.ingramcontent.com/pod-product-compliance
Lightning Source LLC
LaVergne TN
LVHW050305141224
799066LV00002B/72
* 9 7 8 1 4 0 3 9 7 4 7 9 2 *